TOP TEN THINGS

The Neuroscience On Sex Differences,
Music, Gaming and More

KIM BEVILL

BALBOA.PRESS
A DIVISION OF HAY HOUSE

Balboa Press books may be ordered through booksellers or by contacting:

Balboa Press
A Division of Hay House
1663 Liberty Drive
Bloomington, IN 47403
www.balboapress.com
844-682-1282

Print information available on the last page.

ISBN: 978-1-9822-6478-9 (sc)
ISBN: 978-1-9822-6480-2 (hc)
ISBN: 978-1-9822-6479-6 (e)

Library of Congress Control Number: 2021905034

Balboa Press rev. date: 05/28/2021

TABLE OF CONTENTS

Before you begin:

This book has the power to transform your life. Only you know why these 10 neurological ideas suggested by research have found their way to you. You are about to discover simple changes that will have a profound effect on your well-being, relationships, and career. Now is the time to do even a few things to become a better version of yourself, more kind, and more powerful. It is possible to use these 10 things to create energy that is contagious and brings innovation, health, and happiness that every brain deserves.

Begin now setting the stage for your journey by making sure you intentionally remove possible distractions and interruptions, avoid any clutter from your view and control wandering thoughts.

Maintain a calm "center" and focus on your breathing. If you have something on your mind or recurring thoughts, notice it, then reset your attention by returning to a calm state of being. Inhale then exhale thoughts and cleanse your mind with deliberate attention to the breath in and out.

Allow yourself to think of the life you've always imagined and wanted. You will find your way by reading the title of every chapter and notice which ones spark your interest. Each chapter represents thousands of hours researching, training and applying brain research over my career and I have no doubt made errors and mistakes that will embarrass me. Please forgive those imperfections.

I know this research and these strategies represent game-changing behaviors and protocol. The ideas in this book are based on neuroscientific and microbiological research and have the power to heal and improve every area of your life.

CHAPTER 1

SEX DIFFERENCES: THINGS YOU SHOULD AND WANT TO KNOW ABOUT MALES AND FEMALES

The first step is to know what they *are looking for in* a friend.

The day my mom called the doctor, what started as panic in her voice progressed into mild hyperventilation, "My son just drank a bottle of perfume! Wait, he just sprayed deodorant on his face. Hang on—" and then she dropped the phone. In those days, phones were attached to cords! She ran to catch my brother, but he ran through the opened front door. She screamed to my sister, "Vicki, get him! He's taken off his diaper again, and he's headed to the Mason's!" They were our neighbors three doors down and across the street. Mom returned to the phone in tears, "Is there something wrong with him?" The doctor asked if it was her first time at home with a 2-year-old boy.

Inexplicable stories are typical and always star: Boys, girls, and insanity. "Guess what my son (or daughter) did." Or "You'll never believe what my husband (or wife) told me!" With raised eyebrows and disbelief, we ask, "Does he have a brain?" or, "Is she crazy?" This gives way to genuine anger and concern for all sexes. The conversations end with friends offering heartfelt reassurances that they're all certifiable, they'll grow out of it, they've always known that person to be a complete jerk—followed by laughing, some screaming, and recognition that such frustrating behaviors will likely happen again. And again.

But sometimes, those differences aren't so funny. As adults, when stakes are high, even minor misunderstandings based on opposite sex differences may create conflicts that lead to broken relationships. A breakup isn't only sad but can take a toll on your emotional, physical, and financial well-being. Successful relationships are the holy grail of happiness and a good life for both men and women.

However, conflicts between the two sexes doesn't have to be a part of life. Neuroscience explains bewildering behaviors. Understanding sex differences help to escape awkward failures at school, work, and home. Relatively minor changes can galvanize or stimulate vulnerable relationships, improve your immune system, financial security, and creativity. A happy brain is more innovative and likely to think outside the box. The fact that you're reading about sex-based differences means you're one step closer to harmony (at home, in the workplace, and in school.)

The biggest obstacle to understanding the reality of men and women, or boys and girls, is that it is perhaps *the most controversial topic*. The fear of offending someone prevents the honest discourse necessary to address the differing neurobiological realities. Only by overcoming this taboo can we subvert maladaptive behaviors that result in divorce or failed careers and instead cultivate the best version of ourselves. It is important to say at this point the research is noticeably missing explicit gender affiliation; the subjects in the study identified themselves as male or female. Time on gender deserves more attention than this chapter.

The consequences of inequity can be dangerous in areas that may surprise you. Sex differences underly global general intelligence. Collective intelligence research consistently shows that the more heterogenous people in a group, the more innovative and improved the problem-solving performance.[1] Another collective intelligence study showed that groups of four or five people with more women performed 40 percent better. Female behavior that led to this effect was reading facial expressions that drove taking turns. Females deliberately watched faces to see when she shared too much information, or another person wanted to share. This is in stark contrast to the concept of dominating as a synonym to a trait of a leader.

> Training males to read faces increases their relationship skills, and training females to take risks increases the chances that women will enter or remain in male-dominated fields and increase intelligence needed to solve complex problems

But first, consider two questions about sex differences: Is society ready to admit that men and women are innately different? Does society have the courage to accept the implications?

Evidence shows that significant neural structures and specialized functions may explain the differences in cognitive abilities and behavior. What if failure to respect these differences is unethical or causes unnecessary inequities at home, work, and school? What if the behavior that seems bizarre is normal, not bad?

Sex Difference: Men and boys are looking to find someone to go do something.

Anyone who has spent time near boys and men has noticed their habits, noticed them moving, like they're in a constant state of "Let's go!" More than 1,000 male subjects surveyed answered the question, "What do you look for in a friend?"[2] They look for people who can accompany them in physical activities and to play or watch a game, go camping, climbing, hunting, golfing, biking.[3] For centuries, male activity ensured survival, and their specialized jobs, hunting for food and protecting themselves and others from danger, required constant action and attention to the surrounding activity. Finding companions increased their chances of success, and it still does. Companions are crucial to males, who define emotional closeness as, "Doing activities together."

In contrast, females define emotional closeness as, "Spending time together." Though they'll engage in activities, females don't consider that to be emotional closeness. They look for someone to talk with, to share with, and to spend time with. Girls lean in for chatting and whispering; women talk and make eye contact. "Striking difference" is how researchers explain women's choices in friends. Females reported feeling emotional closeness with people they share a secret with.[4] Males reported no interest in talking more and had even less interest in secrets. They even report "deliberately [avoiding] secrets for fear of prying."[5] Compare that with the 96 percent of married women who reported wanting to talk more with their husbands, but less than 8 percent of the husbands wanted to talk. They preferred to solve the problem, saying that would stop it from happening again.

A friend of mine told me the action-based needs for males explained a mystery about a trip her husband and nephew took. One week before the nephew's wedding, the two went on a six-day fishing trip, with an eight-hour drive each way. When they returned, she went out to greet him (she wanted to get the scoop on the upcoming wedding and the drama that comes with every wedding). "How was the trip? How is the wedding planning going?" She said he looked perplexed and took a few minutes to answer, "I guess it never came up." The wedding never came up! Compare the week before the wedding for a bride-to-be, not only would the wedding have been the only topic for the entire weekend, she would have never taken such a trip, but the groom-to-be went fishing before one of the most important events in his life.

Neuroscience may explain how innate differences in motivation result in puzzling behaviors. A male heading into the stressful part of planning a wedding doesn't say he wants to talk about his feelings about the event. During stressful times, he prefers to be alone, or at least to not talk about it. He's more likely to do something with a companion who will avoid prying into anything emotional or any drama. For women, it's the opposite. Her increased stress leads to more intimate friendship behaviors.[6] She'll hunt down a supportive friend to talk more than usual, and most often, the friend is another female. Researchers found that women under stress not only spend more time talking and making more visits, but her tendency to trust changes, too. Most females are more trustworthy following stressful events. Evolutionary psychologists suggest that trust helps women from damaging an essential relationship during tough times (especially with a male). Women protect their precious relationships during bad times to mitigate damage. The week before her wedding, the bride needs to talk, get reassurance and supportive words. Positive words increase our natural painkillers (endogenous opioids) in the brain's reward center. The groom needs to go out and do something, fishing.

Females tend to be more social than males and have superior social skills in all cultures. Even female infant macaque monkeys are more social than males and respond more empathetically to the emotions of their caretakers.[7] Human infants also respond empathetically to their caretaker's emotions. At 14 to 28 days old, females look at faces and make eye contact more than males. At only a few days old, females turn toward people and respond with upset, which are the antecedents of comforting behavior.[8] As females grow up, their play involves more supporting words—lots of words —and cooperation. Males look around the room more than at faces. During their lifetime, females spend more time talking, listening, and actively seeking out and socializing with others than males. Her survival depends on it. Universal longitudinal studies have shown that girls and women in 20 countries chose "people" as their interest (in daily activities, degrees, and professions), whereas males chose "things."[9]

I cannot tell you how many mothers have approached me, as a professional and a friend, with angst and shame to confess that their son was displaying learning disabilities. "He's not talking, yet!" I don't know how to explain without offending them that girls have a different verbal ability. Sex differences in language, interests, activities, decision-making, and risk-taking are powerful. Boys can be two or more years behind girls. Females exhibit greater social skills, empathy, "mind-reading," and verbal ability.[10]

This gap may result from girls' more sophisticated verbal abilities and social skills. Although tempted, comparing girls and boys is like comparing a car to a truck. They aren't the same, and the comparison sets up unnatural expectations. Something that tends to be noticed, "My daughter was talking by now, but my son isn't." Such comparison shapes attitudes about boys and girls, resulting in achievement and expectation gaps, and even leading to lifelong beliefs about intelligence and ability. Females are born with more neural connectivity to verbal and social skills, but the more males talk, the more neural connectivity they will have (and complex movement increases neural connectivity, too). Males encouraged or trained in behaviors that increase neural connectivity also increase verbal and social skills. Males outperform females in spatial reasoning, mental rotation, and analyzing systems.[11] Males are born with more connectivity within the brain hemispheres, which allows for greater eye-hand coordination and may be responsible for some superior abilities. But the more females engage in activities that build spatial reasoning capacities, such as open space exploration, Legos, puzzles, and video games, the better they are at such reasoning.[12]

The more we interact with and talk to people, the better we get at it, and it's a neural change!

Life provides an endless supply of juicy events to talk about and listen to, and that necessitates language. The more females use language, and the more complicated the situations in which they use it, the better they become at expressing their thoughts. Every conversation makes use of the corpus callosum, the part of the brain that integrates language with real life and emotion. It's made of nerve fibers that transfer and integrate information and underlie learning. The more females communicate, the more neural connections they have. If a woman's quality of life depends on her having a trusted support system, it is more important to successfully maintain her network, so effective communication increases chances for happiness. The corpus callosum is a structure made up of nerve fibers that transfer and integrate all information. Brain-mapping studies show the corpus callosum becomes larger with more sophisticated demands, it builds more neural networks that enhance connectivity. The more intricate the conversations, the more connectivity the language center with other cortical regions.[13]

The mystery of the opposite sex may be the result of genetic blueprints and environmental experiences but understanding how tendencies and preference affect behaviors, neurotransmitters, and hormones is a game-changer that helps to crack the code. Scientific studies show that the same thing can have opposite physiological effects on males and females. That allows a revolutionary insight. Sex hormones cause the same behavior to have a greater effect on one sex than on the other. Estrogen enhances the endogenous effects of social interaction[14] and may give females advantages in declarative memory and verbal fluency, at least until menopause, when the levels drop.[15] Meanwhile, testosterone reduces the number of words spoken (verbal fluency). Higher testosterone also correlates with important behaviors. To an extent, chemistry explains both the gap and the cross-cultural behaviors. Extensive studies show that sex is a determining factor in behavior: Men with less testosterone speak more words, and men with more testosterone engage in more violent or aggressive acts. The differences are indisputable and admitting this allows improved interaction.

- A University of Maryland study showed that 4- to 5-year-old females have 30 percent more FOXP2, a gene implicated in complex language development.
- Babies who utter more sounds receive more maternal attention. The average female uses language significantly earlier and has a larger, more sophisticated vocabulary and greater sentence complexity than boys of the same age.[16] Preferences for eye contact, *babies* looking at another's eyes, predict later social and communicative skills among macaque monkeys.[17]
- Females process emotions more accurately, remember details connected to people better, and show superior memory details related to people and superior scores higher in social ease. Females also have higher than average abilities in social cognition, according to computerized tests.[18]
- Talking increases dopamine in the left hemisphere in both sexes; this neurotransmitter lowers cortisol, increases trust and bonding, and improves cognitive function.[19]
- Prosocial behavior for both (talking, comforting, touching, hugging, and empathizing) increases activity in the brain's pleasure or reward center. These behaviors activate natural opioids, dopamine, oxytocin, and endorphins.[20] Estrogen enhances these effects.

Sharing good times and venting about upsetting ones requires using language like a tool, and the more the tool is used, the better we get at using it. Offering supportive words to help someone feel better (an appropriate response) is considered a female trait. Listening to someone who is upset while not offending them is one of the most therapeutic things humans do. Reassuring others is extremely important and requires social grace; it's not considered a male trait. The inability to support each other may lead to people, especially females thinking, "You don't care about me."

Using language is crucial to keeping and maintaining important relationships, and the ability to use it well is key in times of crisis. For many people, it's natural; for others, it requires lots of practice. The good news is that neuroscience suggests the more movement babies get, the better they process language. This seems to be a kind of natural or egalitarian "training." What if in the past, children with limited language skills lived a life so rich in complex movement that it stimulated growth in the neurons that underlie the ability to communicate. Science suggests that such movement improves our ability to talk about a bad mood or life stressor. These differences are especially clear when we compare brain maps of neural interconnectivity; the neural integration may indicate the function for neurons underlying good, not average, language, fast, not slow, learning, and good, not poor, social skills.

- Talking increases brainwave activity and increases dopamine in the left hemisphere from 20 to 100 percent. Dopamine fuels our executive system: Cognition: memory, decision-making, problem-solving, thinking—the good stuff we take for granted (Fuertinger, 2017)
- Real-time speech induces dopamine into the left hemisphere for language processing. It increases dopamine to the basal ganglia (a group of structures that are key to movement), receives information from the cortex, and then processes and sends back more. It "loops" and transfers to and from high-level processing: Emotion, language, and reasoning.[21]
- Most female conversations are face-to-face or on the phone, and females look for something they have in common to talk about, establishing commonalities, a love of saying "so do I." (Tannen, 2010). Research shows that text and email communication do not increase endogenous opioids.
- Male communication commonly involves comparisons during face-to-face interactions, such as "topping" one another on matters such as salaries and recreational activities. For males, phone conversations are for planning activities...conversations are brief and usually competitive. (Tannen, 2010)

A life of fun and harmony demands expert-level skill in complex language. The more challenging life is (getting along with others in school, engaging in new or challenging training, a difficult subject, developing an intimate relationship), the more that language use generates neural connections to transfer and integrate. The left hemisphere of the brain supplies words, the emotions connected or the meaning is processed and integrated with the right hemisphere. Conversation is usually loaded with negative emotions (in the right hemisphere) that must be integrated by the corpus callosum for processing (in the left hemisphere). This neural integration of words and emotions means that both sexes can explain feelings about a situation or why something happened, which is an extremely complex task. Like any other muscle, the more we use the corpus callosum, the larger and better it gets. The more complex the tasks we perform and the more frequently, the more we develop our neural network.

As we age, real-life experiences give more opportunities to interact, empathize, celebrate, or comfort. Females under stress seek to talk things over, while males, stress initially means he prefers solitude and avoiding talk, but like females, males eventually seek out support.[22] In times of extreme stress, during disasters, for instance, cortisol softens male traits and develop more prosocial behavior.[23] After something terrible happens, males are more likely to trust others, look for emotional support, talk about feelings, and seek explanations of what went wrong. Even though they tend to seek out females, in tough times, they will also confide in male companions. In times of war, soldiers develop deep emotional bonds, and their feelings of connection can last their entire lifetimes.[24] There is an interesting tendency for our left hemisphere to seek explanations for life events, especially the bad. It's a sort of obsession for our left hemisphere. After a catastrophe, like a natural disaster, people seek answers, even when there isn't a rational explanation.

Getting to the point of stress or anger is different for males and females. Remember, he says he deliberately avoids "anything emotional." For women, "How are you feeling?" is an easy opening to conversation. Both males and females want to interact with others, but males are more gregarious and engage in more complex activities with more friends. Females are friendlier, which research supports. It's universal.[25] Over her lifetime, a woman spends more time than a man does interacting with a small group of close friends.

Until their thirties, males tend to have much larger groups of friends but fewer one-on-one interactions, with fewer words. Most of their activities are competitive, goal-oriented, and action-packed, and such activities limit talking in general, especially about emotional upset. Respecting a male's tendency toward action and goals can make it easier to bridge to talking about feelings. Walking together increases the chances of a discussion but deliberately ask "what is happening." This is an action-based conversation; talking while shoulder to shoulder enhances the sharing in the interaction. Pairing movement with words allows for processing and asking about events helps his interaction because talking and walking stimulate dopamine in the left hemisphere (the language center), the structures in the basal ganglia (that loop motor action with cognition and emotion) allow him to articulate his emotions. The more he talks, the more dopamine he has in his left hemisphere. Talking increases his endogenous opioids. The more we talk, the better we get at it, and talking increases the size of the corpus callosum. Italian families talk at dinner every Sunday; social dinners on Sundays are a healthy ritual!

Increasing the size and stability of our support systems means more talk, laughter, and trust. Larger networks increase our access to critical help and resources for taking care of ourselves and our babies. More than anything else women do, our support system predicts our health, longevity, income, and self-reported happiness.[26] Talking and interacting are skills that help us live peacefully and happily with others. Saying things the right way helps us make and keep friends, build relationships, and offer support. The act of talking builds the neurons for functional connections that dictate intelligence.[27]

Interacting with other people increases the opioids in the reward centers of our brains—the same areas affected by drug use, depression, and anxiety. Without social interaction, we have less activation. Endogenous opioids, dopamine, endorphins, and oxytocin give us relief from pain, both social and physical, and reduce cortisol. Hugging, reassuring touches, and supportive words trigger activity in the reward center. Talking supportively and sharing experiences increases opioids, whether it's face to face or on the phone.[28] Most people report using text, email, and brief conversations, but they do not increase our opioids. Researchers found no positive neural response. Social interaction, especially laughter, increases neurotransmitters and makes opioid receptors more responsive to endogenous opioids.[29] One study using PET scans found that we don't even have to be hugging; just standing near a supportive person increases our relaxation and calmness.[30]

- Oxytocin, dopamine, and endorphins (endogenous opioids) increase with the size of one's social group and our physiological sensitivity to our own opioids. (Pearce et al., 2017)
- Oxytocin and endorphins improve our accuracy in reading facial expressions and empathy. Accuracy in identifying emotions increases the ability to know what the other is thinking, incredibly important for successful relationships. (Pearce et al., 2017)
- Synchronized activities (dancing, singing, laughing) increase group bonding. (Nummenmaa et al., 2016)
- Eating with others, especially dinner, results in higher rates of happiness, trust (during the meal), and "self-reported" satisfaction. (Dunbar, 2017)
- Frequency of family meals is correlated with greater bonding and better adolescent behavior. (Brown et al., 2016)

Differences in Behavior are Universal[31]	No. of Studies	No. of Countries
Females establish and maintain eye contact.	10	2
Females are more likely to have intimate friendships.	35	5
Females share more "secrets" with friends.	31	6
Males explore their environments more.	24	8
Males are more involved in directly competitive sports.	30	5
Males have more interest in athletic activities in general.	11	4
Males are prone to boredom.	11	4

Sex differences are the most pronounced during childhood and adolescence, but they last throughout adulthood. Researchers studied 8- to 22-year-old subjects (428 males and 521 females) and found compelling and consistent differences between the sexes.[32] Maybe the most important study on the human brain revealed the more educated subjects over 45 years old showed that smaller differences, meaning *experience*, affects innate structural and functional sex differences.[33]

- Male brains have greater volume and surface area (92 percent of males), which may result in differences in reasoning ability and superior visual, spatial, and numerical reasoning abilities. (Ritchie et al. 2018)
- There are more male high achievers and low achievers in *cognitive* ability than among females. (Ilescu et al., 2016)
- Males have more high and low achievers in *academic* performance than females. (Borkenau et al., 2013)
- Males have a greater variation than females in athletic performance. (Olds et al., 2006)
- Males have a greater variation in birth weight and adult weight. (Lehre et al., 2009a)
- Resting fMRIs show 54 percent of neural connections exhibit a sex difference. Males have more intra-hemispheric connectivity, especially connecting sensory and motor cortices, and better eye-hand coordination. (Ingalhalikar, 2013)
- Men are more likely than women to indicate interest in scientific, technical, and mechanical activities. Females are more likely to indicate interests in social and artistic activities. (Su et al., 2009)
- Females have greater verbally mediated memory and superior social cognition (Ingalhalikar, 2013) and more connectivity in the default-mode network-neurons active during social interaction. (Kocevar et al., 2019)

Sex Difference: Females use more words and more complex language early and throughout their lives.

Language is the tool females use to build their social networks. Conversations include words expressing feelings that require details to draw others in.

It's physiological. Smooth language use improves our chances of skillful interactions with romantic partners, bosses, colleagues, teachers, parents, children, and siblings. Accurate language can save a relationship, turn a work situation from strife to success, and produce innovative and novel solutions to problems. It is significant that one sex has more of a hormone that is correlated with verbal dexterity; more testosterone reduces the number of words one uses and results in less complex speech patterns.[34]

How to decrease divorce rates and workplace conflict:

My client, Mike, came home from work to find that his wife had invited the neighbors over for a happy hour. Mike opted out of the party and took a sandwich and beer to the basement, and his wife was furious. His choice wasn't made because he didn't care about her or the neighbors (if you consider his survival doesn't feel like it depends on his relationship with the neighbors). The evening's interactions with them would feature a good amount of talking. At the end of his day, Mike wanted to be alone and only knew unconsciously that he needed solitude to recharge. Maybe he used all his words or interacting for the day, and therefore chose to retreat to the basement.

Females may have more words left at the end of their day.

After an exhausting day, meeting, or trip, females look to talk to other females, usually the ones they were just with! Christiane Northrup, an OB/Gyn and the author of *Women's Bodies and Women's Minds*, asked more than a thousand men and women, "Who is the first person you call after a vacation?" Women most often called the person with whom they had traveled, and the average time of the call was 60 minutes. Men did not make any phone calls upon returning. Men use phones to arrange activities, and he averages less than three minutes. Spending less than three minutes on a call made women think the friend (male or female) was mad at them. Males look for more activities (what they define as emotional connections) and use their phones to arrange them.

How people use phones depends on sex: Women use them for real-time relationship interaction, and men use them as a tool. When both sexes understand "phone-use" (remember a male's neurological tendency toward activity rather than talking about feelings) helps to explain why he would choose to go to the basement. The prospect of social activities involving more words after a challenging day increases a tendency to withdraw or to use a smartphone. Phone companies polled males and found they use their devices for practical tasks, mainly related to work and responding or organizing. Females use them to talk and keep in touch with their friends.[35] Adolescent males spent more time playing games and using apps, and adolescent females spent more time talking with "valued people"— using their devices to build networks.

Talking doesn't equate with a dedication to a relationship, but the understanding of the importance of talking means is integral to relationships. Women's language abilities correlate with more talking and may contribute to improved language skills. The highly developed neural network in the female brain gives women more verbal memory, attention, and speed in communicating. Their neural networks have significantly more nodes (connections between neurons) and highly efficient neural processing, which may give women better verbal memory and attention.[36] Infrastructure connections, like bridges and roads, improve travel, more nodes connect neurons and provide enhanced centrality, an advantage in all neural processing.[37] Mentalizing means knowing what others are thinking without words.

- Females have more neural connections and functional connectivity between the amygdala and insula. Female subjects viewing angry faces have high neural activity. (Derntl et al., 2010)
- When the insula is active, the female subject had more empathy and accurate social understanding, which helps in identifying with the experiences of others. (Singer, 2009)
- Males under stress have disrupted communication between the amygdala and insula. (Mather et al., 2010; Taylor, 2007)
- Females under stress identify the emotions on a face more accurately than when she is not under stress; *men under stress are 59 percent less accurate at identifying an emotion.* (Mather et al., 2010)

Women use many details while men use few. Most men tend to "get to the point" and need others to do the same. Thus, the complexity of writing, especially if it involves references to emotions or feelings, may be the reason so many males hate writing. This is important because failure is different for males and females. If a male doesn't think he can succeed, he may shut down and lose long-term motivation: "I hate school." He may hate the questions he is asked in class and on tests: "How do you feel about this character?" or "Why did this character feel . . .?" Either of these questions requires writing about feelings, which can be more challenging for males (who reports avoiding discussing them).

Typical test questions are written in a way that leads males to think they're not good at writing or are stupid. Rewording a question to allow both males and females to answer it means respecting their differences. Males naturally perceive action and movement, and females process words and emotions earlier and easier. To get an answer from both includes asking, "What happened?" instead of "How would you feel?"

Could it come from the fact that the same thing fires up a man's right amygdala but fires up a woman's left amygdala? A ground-breaking study on memory showed that males and females looking at a picture responded in the opposite hemispheres. Larry Cahill, a neurobiologist at the University of California (UC) - Irvine, researched the neuroscience of memory and was shocked by the results. MRIs showed that males' right amygdala responded to an emotion-laden visual, while females' left amygdala responded.[38] The part of the brain that fires in response to the "gist" of a story is the right hemisphere, whereas the left-side language network processes "elements and details." These sex-based differences only emerged when researchers viewed fMRI results after instructing male and female subjects to view pictures and then submerge their arms in freezing water for three to five minutes to test the effects of norepinephrine on recall.

- Subjects viewed emotional pictures (accidents, graphic surgeries, snakes) and neutral (sidewalk, trash can, freeway overpass) and then sink their arm in the ice water.
- Two weeks later, the ice water subjects had more explicit, detailed recollection than those who put their arms in warm water.

- The same pictures resulted in activity in opposite hemispheres.
- The right hemisphere is active in males, while they are processing the "big picture," the gist of the action in a story, instead of the details. The left hemisphere is active in females when they are processing the details.
- Men do not traditionally recall details, but only the gist of a story. (Nielsen et al., 2011)
- Females taking oral contraception (that increases male hormones) had the same memory for the "big picture" as males and recalled significantly fewer details than other females.[39]

Getting a person's attention involves finding their innate preference before boredom appears. Storytelling engages our entire brain, male or female. A story includes rich, emotional details, and researchers have shown that this makes our brainwaves synchronize; it holds our attention. Neuroscientists at Princeton found using fMRIs that a real story engages the listener and creates empathy. In both males and females, the brain releases opioids in response to real and emotion-laden stories.[40] Humans can't help but listen and imagine what happened, and the more emotional details given, whether scary or funny or weird, the better. The more we listen, the better we get at listening, and this causes our brains to build neurons that allow for empathy and compassion.

School curriculums rarely have a juicy, real-life interest. Finding relevant, illustrative stories is crucial for a subject traditionally described as boring. I taught history, and I made sure to use "based on a true story" dramas that the students found so interesting they would say, "You made that up!" A preference for action means that what's interesting is a fast-paced feeling of "Let's get going." Streamline your directions and lectures and "get to the point." Details require males to have discipline and patience; teachers, spouses, salespeople, and doctors should plan accordingly.

Males and females use words (details) and language, such as in "Thank You" notes. The following note comes from a 17-year-old female in an international baccalaureate program:

Ms. Bevill,

First of all, thank you for writing me a letter of recommendation, I enjoyed both of your classes and am so glad that you are the teacher that is writing this for me. I also want to thank you for everything you have taught me. I have always been interested in psychology but it was your elective Psych class that convinced me to go into the field. I hope to eventually get my PhD in Psych and am looking forward to expanding the knowledge that you have given me. Not only did you spark my interest in psych but you also provided me with many needed tools and information for the future. Thanks to you now when I try to memorize something I break it down into chunks, following that handy 5-7 items idea has never failed me. That is just one of the many applicable side notes that I will never forget. You are an amazing teacher and one that I feel lucky to have had. I will miss you next year and I hope that we can stay in touch. Hopefully I will see you soon!

Thank you

Her words are emotional and explicitly describe feelings and our relationship (now and in the future). She uses many details to "support her answer." The same week her note arrived; I received an email from a 17-year-old boy in the same class. I've preserved the formatting of his note, which was the postscript to an email unrelated to school:

P.S. - I got a 6 for the psych test. Most corny line i've ever said: Thanks for your moral support. Yeah, i had to kill a couple of brain cells to say that.

On the IB test, a 6 is a high score; 7 is the highest possible, the equivalent of an A+. I ignored the errors (and the hours his teachers spent practicing capitalization) and went to an expert to find out whether "kill a couple of brain cells" was a thank you or insult. I asked Justin Matott, a popular children's author, and he didn't hesitate to answer. He said the young man wasn't just thanking me; he was gushing with emotion, so much that Justin felt embarrassed for him. I asked Justin about the survey in which males admitted to avoiding discussion of feelings, and he said he thought that was common knowledge.

Today, writing dominates assessments, grades, and test scores, and more males are dropping out or not continuing to higher education. Integrating emotions and using details to support an answer requires more time for neural integration, something the male brain develops later in their twenties. If educators allow parents and politicians to focus on test performance, this academic gap will remain because we are pushing for and assessing something the male brain is still working on. The twist is that test scores don't even indicate intelligence or future success, yet today we have education gaps resulting from our efforts to improve them. The push to increase scores has meant more time preparing for tests and reductions in P.E., specials, and recess, which improve males' academic success. In 2018, the American Psychology Association reported males are two to four years behind females as of 4th grade, and the gap increases with each grade.

Imagine for a moment that understanding biological differences could drastically narrow those gaps. Would you be willing to change just two things? That's what happened in one elementary school when the staff agreed to take training on neural differences. The two things were increased time involving movement and increased time making projects. The academic gap closed in one year, and males improved their literacy by two years, but females also increased their spatial reasoning, math, and (already high) literacy scores. Tailoring projects, curriculum, and daily activity accordingly could be magic.

What if parents, teachers, and bosses knew that male attention is drawn to exploration and extreme activities, whereas females are looking to find nice in people (not act nice necessarily) and to find things in common? Both character traits are invaluable in friends and for survival.

Male eyes are attracted to movement, perceive movement, and complex movements require and improve spatial abilities and increase testosterone levels (which are correlated with spatial reasoning and tracking moving objects). Testosterone also improves the ability to see embedded shapes (such as animals in the trees), which is valuable in a hunter-gatherer society.[41] Boys move, push, shove, and punch. They throw rocks, swing sticks, sometimes at each other, sometimes hit each other with sticks and even a backpack, and leap off and onto things. As I write this, I am looking out a window watching one construction worker push another down a muddy hill backwards. And these are two adults? How long would it take me to find women pushing each other over in rough-and-tumble play?

What's good for one sex is good for the other, but the same activity has a different benefit for each. Differences come from genetics, the environment, and understanding the impact of behavior on our neurotransmitters and hormones can enhance them. Some neurotransmitters, such as estrogen, increase the effects of oxytocin. They play a major role in determining behavior and can radically alter people's choices. Testosterone drives numerous behaviors, and extensive cross-cultural studies have shown it to be a major player in violence and aggression.[42]

Researchers arranged for preschool boys to visit an unfamiliar play area with new objects. When the boys entered the area, they covered the entire space exploring and inspecting objects, most of them making loud noises and moving during their creative play. After 20 minutes, the researchers sent a new boy into the area. Most of the others continued their activities indifferently or didn't seem to notice the child's arrival. Most of the boys were action directed.[43] None of them asked each other's names, but they played with or without the new boy. In many trials, they included him in their activities. The boys checked for his abilities in play; for instance, does he run fast, throw a football, block a kick, or have the strength to pick someone up?

Four-year-old females in the experiment "huddled" the middle of the area (70 percent of them, and many were noticeably upset). Less than 15 percent of the girls explored the outer areas or interacted with the unfamiliar objects. After 20 minutes, when a new girl entered, the majority approached her and began talking: "What's your name?" and "Why are you here?" Girls check for "niceness," maybe because kind and trustworthy friends are critical to them. Girls learn names, tell emotional stories, and share secrets soon after meeting. Girls play face to face and involve a lot of words but very little rough-and-tumble play. Their games are full of emotional talking and rarely include competition; instead, it was cooperative-like playing house, school, and dolls.

- Most females (including other primates) choose dolls, but not the females with high testosterone. Those ones choose mechanical toys more often, such as trains and cars.
- In CAH, a condition involving high androgen levels in females, the main hormone is testosterone. This is correlated with girls engaging in less verbal interaction, using fewer words, and showing less empathy and nurturing.[44]
- Males choose "masculine" toys, such as vehicles—tractors, fire trucks, helicopters—or building blocks, such as Legos, over dolls, kitchen items, and art materials. Females choose dolls, stuffed animals, and kitchen items.[45]
- Female subjects score high on "agreeableness" and report life goals that involve an interest in people: working with people or helping people. (Su et al., 2009)
- To remain in traditionally male-dominated fields of study (e.g., STEM), women must perceive real opportunities for emotional relationships, meaning, and purpose. Otherwise, they opt for a profession where they can "help others."

Studies show that boys prefer trucks, fire engines, and guns. Even in homes with gun bans, boys will use remote controls or even toast bitten into the shape of a gun. An MRI scan of a male brain viewing a weapon shows a significant response in the prefrontal cortex.

Sex Difference: Eye Contact. Women look at you when you're talking; men look around the room.

Women think eye contact means a person is paying attention. For females, eye contact is a lie detector in relationships. Survival required moms and aunts to supervise young children while performing multiple tasks—gathering and preparing food, tending babies—and community living provided support and regular social interaction. Living with others requires excellent social skills, and communication using our eyes and facial expressions is almost a language of its own. An expression can convey emotion, empathy, sympathy, and trust...eye contact is an essential skill.

Eye contact is a universal non-verbal cue for social interaction and communication.[46] To survive, males scanned their environment: Spotting prey and danger was a life-or-death job, and better vision improved one's odds. "Looking for something to do" as a matter of survival explains why males are oriented toward movement. It makes it even more important to show females, who think that eye contact means listening, that you care about them and what they are saying is important. If you don't look at a woman while she is talking, she can think that you're mad. When you talk, she looks at you exclusively. Males spend less time looking at faces and make less exclusive eye contact with others.[47] When two males face each other and make eye-contact, it suggests conflict, aggression, or a power struggle, even in animals.

The male's superior ability to spot embedded objects gives them a more effective visual system, a sort of "raptor vision," and helps in hunting because they can spot movement, whether prey or predator. Males have significantly more neurons connecting their visual and motor neurons than females. Longitudinal and cross-cultural studies have shown that males have better visuospatial and motor skills, whereas females' neural networks are more pronounced in areas of verbal interaction.[48] Unfortunately, the tendency toward movement does not improve males' chances of success in our culture, especially our often-traditional educational system, where the norm is sitting quietly for six or more hours a day.

In another time, the blue sky above and the ground below would hold clues for a hunter to find prey and *making exclusive eye contact* limits his awareness of the environment. Looking around is natural. To excel at hunting, males have more interconnected neurons in the eyes and hands, improving their coordination, and more interconnected neurons for visuospatial reasoning, improving their chances of survival.

- Males have within-hemisphere neural connections that enhance communication between perception and coordinated physical action (eye-hand coordination).
- Females have between-hemisphere connections and more neuronal networks in the DMN, the area that helps us intuitively understand others and think analytically, called "mentalizing."

Also, this explains a specialized neural network within hemispheres. In a study of more than 6,000 subjects, researchers found that females had better verbal abilities and males better spatial reasoning abilities.[49] The differences in spatial reasoning and math performance, especially at the highest levels, may underlie the male advantages due to neural wiring and higher testosterone levels. However, recent findings have shown that movement activities and competition allow for the development of the neurons that underlie spatial abilities. Having access to open space, putting together puzzles, using Legos, and playing video and computer games increase one's spatial reasoning and math performance. Integrating movement and training into the environment, a simple change, helps children develop spatial reasoning, which predicts math ability and the chances of pursuing a STEM career.[50] On the other hand, for females who participate in those activities, she has enhanced interhemispheric connectivity and increased performance in spatial reasoning.

Do boys have a superhero interest in what's happening, with their raptor vision? Although without the awareness of Jason Bourne, boys are aware of their environments and attracted to moving objects from the time they're born. Studies of nine-month-old babies, before "socialization," have shown that they will spend more time looking at a mobile than at a face.[51] Boys' actions and their preferences for rough-and-tumble or boisterous play are actually necessary for their healthy development. Testosterone improves visual perception and spatial rotation skills, and physical play, competition, and sports increase testosterone levels. Behaviors and beliefs directly affect spatial reasoning performance.

- Among young girls, time spent working on puzzles with their father predicts spatial reasoning. There is no such change in males scores. (Levine, 2011) Conversely, female teachers' math anxiety affects a girl's math achievement. (Beilock et al., 2010)
- In a comparison of males and females with similar math achievements, fewer females pursued STEM careers, and most eventually left the profession. (Ramirez et al., 2012)
- Girls who believe that their ability to do math is fixed and unchangeable have lower scores in math. (Burkley et al., 2010)
- A mother's stereotypical beliefs compromise girls' math performance. (Tomasetto et al., 2011)
- Parent's feelings of inadequacy in math also compromise their children's performance. (Maloney et al., 2015)

Sex Difference: Females recognize emotions more accurately than males.

Female brains require less activity to accurately identify emotions from facial expressions than male brains, which use more activity. Under extreme stress, women become more accurate.[52] By contrast, males are only 70 percent accurate at identifying sadness in females—barely above a D+. Under stress, men are even less accurate. What is more interesting, men are good at recognizing emotions in other men—90 percent accurate with sadness. Recognizing anger in another man could be a matter of life and death, as an angry man could mean a fight. An angry female is rarely a physical threat; she will use threatening words instead of violence.

Women's brains are wired for emotions in the way an engineer would design a motion detector. They have a sophisticated neural network with more neurons connecting the insula, temporal lobe, and frontal cortex (housed in her right hemisphere), which work to identify facial expressions (housed in her right hemisphere) the label, word, is formulated in the left hemisphere. Females maintain eye contact longer than males and have a superior social understanding and a greater sensitivity to emotional expressions.[53]

FMRIs show that the male amygdala has less interaction and connectivity between these areas active during reports of understanding emotional states. Under stress, females have increased functional connectivity in the frontal cortex and identify emotions more accurately, while males do so much less accurately. (Mather, 2010)

- Female monkeys exhibit greater social interest and skills than males at 10 to 28 days of age. They look at faces longer, maintain eye contact more, use more gestures, and stay closer to their human caretakers. (Simpson et al., 2016)

"How do you think you made the other person feel?" When I was a teacher, discipline meant talking to a student, explaining what happened in close detail, and then re-explaining in summary. But if I had considered the neural differences between male and female processing, I'd have known that a male needs you to "get to the point" and limit your words. Too many details and too much repetition loses his attention. My nature, as a female, is to explain in words and then summarize what I explained using more words. My tendency to tell him clashes with his biological disposition to figure it out.

If male neural integration suggests the big picture and not the details, and males tend toward action, one can avoid arguments by choosing a more concise language. The use of fewer words to get to the point could revolutionize cross-gender interactions. A tendency to "tell him" clashes with his biological predisposition to "figure it out."

Specific sex-based training suggests best practices for communicating with a male. Make direct eye contact, and use as few words as possible, such as, "Don't do that!" Talking while walking is even better. Then, move on. If they deliberately avoid discussing feelings, remember their innate attraction to movement to get better communication.

Sex Difference: When a man is upset or feels attacked, his fight-or-flight response is triggered.

Researchers had married couples read a "scripted argument," while measuring their heart rates and respiration. Both partners showed increased responses. After 15 minutes, the husband was instructed to leave the room, and once he left, his heart rate and respiration returned to baseline; meanwhile, the wife's blood pressure skyrocketed.[54]

Walking out of an argument is a highly emotional event for the female because relationships can be a matter of life and death (for her and her baby). Even a perceived threat to a relationship triggers her amygdala and cortisol.[55] This is an unconscious response to physical desertion, whether it's logical or illogical is irrelevant. For a female, exclusion by a friend triggers stress. Males have little physiological response to such exclusion, however, and even more interestingly, males are significantly less likely to exclude other males (he continues on his objective alone).[56] A man can go solo, hunt for his own food, and protect himself from threats. For him, his greatest stressor is the loss of a job, achievement, or respect. For him, survival doesn't require a network. While relationship trouble is upsetting and increases his responses in his sympathetic nervous system, it wasn't life-threatening and therefore may explain why relationship distress doesn't trigger his stress response like the female.

For males, the physiological stresses come from challenges to their achievements: Job loss, for instance, or the inability to provide for their family. Robert Sapolsky, neurologist and biologist found that challenges to men's authority brought fear, aggression, illness, depression, and even premature death. For men, prolonged subordination can lead to physical illness because it increases blood pressure and weakens the immune system for the duration. Confessing to stress or bad feelings puts one in a position of vulnerability (increasing stress hormones and blood pressure), so if a man is reticent to discuss his feelings, he needs time alone, and may need a period of time before he can share the stress and explain what happened.

A *Forbes* study showed that subordinates make more eye contact with their bosses than conversely. This indicates dominance and hierarchy:

- fMRIs have shown that the amygdala fires (processes glucose and oxygen) in both boys and girls when they view faces showing negative emotions.
- The amygdala of an adolescent female does not fire when she views an emotionally negative face. Instead, her prefrontal cortex is

active. This is the area active in speaking and high-level cognition (thinking, decision-making, creativity, self-reflection, self-control, and especially while writing).[57]

- The amygdala response of an adolescent male to seeing negative emotions (traditionally considered the fight-or-flight response) improves with age, as there is less amygdala activity and more prefrontal cortex activity.[58] With experience, he improves in labeling emotions, and the male corpus callosum increases in size.

Discussing emotions calms a woman's stress level but triggers a man's amygdala. Females call friends when they feel upset, but males want to be alone. For a teenage male, stress is inevitable, and his tendency to withdraw and stop talking is sure to catch the attention of a female. A teenage male's worst nightmare while under stress is his mother's attention. She'll hunt him down to offer help and support. She's committed to helping, which means talking, and he finds her relentless.

For one sex, the use of language to build and maintain friendships is therapy; for the other, negative emotions and discussions of feelings increases the activity in the fight-or-flight response. It's not shocking for males to confess to avoiding the topic: it increases their blood pressure and feelings of being attacked. Despite this, talking increases men's endogenous opioids (dopamine, oxytocin, endorphins), decreases stress, and increases bonding. Yet the verbal response would usually never indicate it; most males would say "I'm fine," or "Mom, stop."

So much research fails to control sex differences in their studies and often use only male subjects, humans or rats, and still generalize their findings to females. This is especially alarming for studies of female-dominant disorders. In one instance, researchers at an Ivy League college explicitly excluded women because "microstructural changes with the menstrual cycle" potentially mask the effects in the study. So, no female brains. For many studies, these differences can be a matter of life and death. Cahill conclusively showed that research findings are half-truths, if they're not broken down by gender.[59] Today, he campaigns for all responsible researchers to control for gender.

Sex Difference: The functioning of one brain structure increases intelligence.

More than 5,000 subjects allowed researchers to map the sex differences in their brain volume and surface area that are responsible for reasoning, memory, learning speed, and various social tendencies and interaction.[60] The well-intentioned saying that males and females have more in common than not may be deceptive. New technology has revealed the different specialized neural networks in males and females. The integration and volume of a male or female brain structure may suggest greater abilities. For example, better spatial reasoning.[61] Differences in structure and functional integration highlight the need to be informed of this science to address academic gaps, relationship behaviors, workplace interactions, professional interests, mental illness, aggression, and Alzheimer's disease.

Remember, considering the neurological differences requires an open mind and lots of courage. Although cognitive neural differences may suggest why most males have good spatial reasoning, that doesn't mean females can't excel in spatial reasoning or earn high scores in math. Recent studies have shown that sex differences are profound. The female brain has more neural connections between hemispheres and more neural bridges connecting social and language networks. Women's social, analytical, and intuitive skills are better. A female brain has greater neural connectivity in the default mode network (DMN), which is active when one "reads" what another is thinking. Mothers spend more time making eye contact with their male infants than with their female infants.[62] It's as if they know they must read the boy's emotions. The male brain has more neural connections for within-hemisphere processing, which could explain men's superior visual perception, eye-hand coordination, and spatial reasoning.[63]

Researchers are trying to develop a theory of intelligence for more than a hundred years. For the sake of argument, consider that their favorite theory has two parts. The first is the idea that intelligence comes from our brain's networks constantly changing and improving their integration (especially but not only the frontal and temporoparietal connections). The second is that a highly functioning DMN, the area active during social interaction, indicates intelligence. Simply put, the belief is that the neural foundation of intelligence is typified by flexibility and adaptability throughout the brain (which comes from learning and experience) and ***results in a thicker corpus callosum***. The more sophisticated our inter-hemisphere and intra-hemisphere connections, *the greater our fluid intelligence*. More practice with thinking, articulating one's feelings, reading, and recognizing emotions builds more neurons, and greater numbers of neurons improve hemispheric connectivity, as measured in size and function. Today, scientists believe the brain connectivity through the corpus callosum indicates superior general intelligence.[64] Structure integrates meaning:

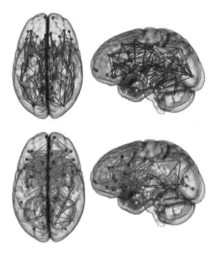

- Males have greater connectivity within a hemisphere (intra-hemisphere) neural circuitry that is active during visual, motor, and spatial reasoning. (Amft et al., 2015; Mars, 2012)
- Females have greater neural connectivity between hemispheres (inter-hemisphere) that is active during social interaction. DMN is the area that processes social cues and analysis. (Amft et al., 2015; Mars, 2012)
- Greater connectivity in the resting state is associated with higher intelligence scores. (Hearne et al., 2016)

Thicker the connections of the corpus callosum improve our ability of males and females to talk and write about and understand the intentions of others, a huge asset in life. Listening, learning, and demonstrating that we understand anything visual, emotional, spatial, or auditory or meaning in a relationship, industry, or school environment depends on efficient integration by this structure of the right and left hemispheres. I can't overemphasize the importance of this *integration* for communicating ideas, explaining behaviors, acting on innovation, and especially for its role in getting along with others.

Considering the importance of relationships, managing them is sort of a life-and-death task: Correctly identify facial expressions is essential. The ability to distinguish friend from foe, nice from angry, or hurt from fear can mean survival, if it is the face of a stranger or the preservation of relationships. Social skills are sacred. The ability to correctly identify facial expression resides in the right hemisphere, and the ability to select the right words to articulate our thoughts resides in the left. This hemispheric specialization plays an important role in relationship strife, physical aggression, or academic underachievement. Mike Gazzaniga, a brain scientist at Dartmouth College, reported being continually shocked at the crucial role this connection plays in our quality of life. Without it, our hemispheres act as two independent brains.

First, consider the true story of "Harry" to show the importance of this structure. Thirty years ago, Harry's doctors severed his corpus callosum to ease his daily seizures, and the implications may be the physiological basis of the disconnect from discussing feelings among males. Mike Gazzaniga, a cognitive neuroscientist at Dartmouth College, says he is continually "shocked" at the crucial role this connection plays in our quality of life. Without it, our hemispheres act as two independent brains. To demonstrate what the corpus callosum does, Henry was asked to look at the word "PHONE" while staring straight ahead to prevent his right eye from communicating with his left hemisphere (where his words reside). When asked what he saw, he said "nothing," but his right hand illustrated a phone. His right hand illustrated the phone again and again. Only after a minute or so did his left hemisphere deliver the words, "Oh, phone!" According to Gazzaniga, the left hemisphere seeks to explain, even when there are no logical explanations.

The corpus callosum allows us to understand the actions of others in social settings because a highly integrated neural network allows the left hemisphere to accurately match emotions to expressions to know what another is thinking. Females have greater neural connectivity in the corpus callosum.[65] The more time one spends completing complex tasks (verbally communicating feelings) and movements (playing an instrument or sport), the larger the corpus callosum becomes, and a larger corpus callosum correlates with a greater ability to communicate. The more males use any structure in the brain, the larger it becomes. Structures in the female brain don't get larger, no matter how much they're used.[66] Playing an instrument at any age improves function and cognition (refer to the Music Chapter.)

The structure isn't close to its mature size until around age 16 in females and 17 years in males.[67] Brain mapping studies of more than 5,200 adults show that after about 40 years old, the size of the male corpus callosum is comparable to the female.[68] This suggests a lifetime of complex demand builds the neural connectivity over time.

Despite this developmental difference, the academic focus on testing writing and reading demands performance from males and females years before one sex has the neural structure underlying the task. Instead, using hands on activities and projects to allow both sexes to learn and demonstrate learning engages both sexes, cultures, and diverse students.

- Functional MRIs show that boys who played the piano before seven years old have corpus callosum up to 25 percent larger than boys who practiced for less than an hour. Girls had no structural increase from practicing. (Schlaug, 1995) MRIs show that after a year of piano lessons, boys have a significantly larger corpus callosum compared to boys in the control group, but girls do not have any comparable increase. (Lee, Chen, & Schlaug, 2003)
- The function and structure of the corpus callosum (white matter made up of nerve fibers) change throughout development and aging, suggesting that nerve fibers grow more mature and organized (Tanaka-Arakawa et al., 2015)
- For women, connectivity becomes more sophisticated with experience but does not increase in volume. Scientists don't yet understand why the mass of a female's brain doesn't change.

- The corpus callosum (improves information integration: Thinking, articulating, writing), in the frontal cortex, is larger in females. (Tan et al., 2017, Cosgrove et al., 2007)

One structure in the brain correlates with intelligence. The corpus callosum—think of it as "broadband"—integrates our three-dimensional (3-D) world. The quality of our broadband dictates our success in learning. Without it, we cannot write or use words to demonstrate understanding. Writing essays and test questions requires us to use words to communicate sophisticated ideas, and this requires a high-functioning corpus callosum. Females integrate early. Regardless of her intelligence, a female brain doesn't show increased effort or burn more energy to accomplish tasks. A male brain processing an SAT problem exerts more energy. Men who scored more than 700 had more active temporal lobes than those who scored 540 and below. Gifted women had no additional activity in the temporal lobe.[69] MRI studies have shown that females have a larger corpus callosum when overall differences in brain size are controlled for (.03) and that young adult females have an even more difference in volume (.05). (Ardekani et al., 2013)

- The activity of white matter, (corpus callosum), is correlated with general intelligence. Diffusion tensor imaging (DTI) is a sensitive tool for measuring structural and functional activities in the brain's substructures. It shows the activity of white matter in the corpus callosum. (Hilger et al., 2017)
- The interconnectivity and functioning of the structure suggest that it indicates intelligence from childhood to adulthood. The most significant differences in size and function of the corpus callosum appear from birth to age 25. (Kocevar et al., 2019)
- More educated and experienced subjects show that increased function may affect the size of the male corpus callosum. Studies of 45- to 75-year-olds have shown little structural difference between males and females. (Richie et al., 2018)
- A higher-functioning corpus callosum is correlated with better verbal and performance abilities "independent of age and sex." (Karama et al., 2011)

- Males are born with a greater neural network that supports their enhanced visual-spatial skills and motor rotation. This pathway allows them to be better at visual tasks, such as rotating objects mentally. There are more males on the high end and low end of performance.
- The functioning of the corpus callosum is correlated with intelligence. (Jones et al., 2013)
- A high density of neurons in the corpus callosum is correlated with intelligence. (Kocevar et al., 2019)
- A larger volume in the corpus callosum is correlated with intelligence. (Clayden, 2012)
- High neural connectivity and cerebral activity is correlated with intelligence. (Basten et al., 2015)
- Connectivity of the corpus callosum in adolescence indicates intelligence. (Kim et al., 2016)
- A higher functioning corpus callosum is correlated with IQ and visuospatial abilities, which are the ability to identify visual and spatial relationships among objects. (Muetzel et al., 2015)

Failure to train on sex differences may limit intelligence for both sexes.

To illustrate this, imagine listening to a loud noise. In both females and males, loudness increases stress…increases norepinephrine, and increases testosterone. These neurotransmitters have the opposite effects in males and females. But first, consider the difference in hearing. As they age, males come to have a more limited range of hearing and don't hear as acutely as females but are more attracted to volume. A study published in *Forbes* magazine reported the effects of listening to a loud engine: the sound of a Lamborghini increased testosterone in the saliva of 60% of the male subjects and 100% of the females. Loudness attracts attention, which may explain car sales.

Hearing tests have shown that male babies' EEGs don't respond as much as females. Loudness affects females differently. Noise distracts and annoys them. In a male, loudness increases norepinephrine, which fuels attention and energy.[70] Kindergarten teachers have told me that they hear hours and hours of girls tattling on boys for being too loud. Loud noise increases norepinephrine levels, which energizes males but compromises female concentration. A study of premature babies in the ICU found that those who heard music left five days earlier than those who heard hospital sounds. However, girls left 9.5 days earlier, and boys did not leave any earlier. Researchers now show stress triggers risk-taking. Loudness increases risk-taking, and most males take more risks than the most risk-taking females.

Sex Difference: Risk management and risk-taking increase intelligence and money.

Did you know that your success in life is determined by your relationship to risk-taking? Not only is this shown by the data, but commonsense also says your ability to perform despite or because of a particular chemical determines your fame or failure. Hopefully, that's an overstatement because the idea is that our comfort working under pressure makes the difference to whether we run for home plate, follow a non-traditional major, or career path, invest in a new stock or security, or take any other real-life risk.

Controlled studies have suggested that one sex is more likely to get the right answer under stress, depending on the circumstances. Also, research has indicated who is more likely to invest in something that has no historical record. Whether it's a common matter like making an offer on a house or a big one like quitting a job, our sex predicts our choice. So, sex differences couldn't have higher stakes. From careers to relationships, sex determines our tendency to shy away or thrive under pressure. Neurological studies show that stress speeds up males and slows women's decisions, and males choose riskier options, while women choose more conservative ones.

To measure the effects of stress on decision making, researchers at UCLA asked subjects to dunk a hand in ice water for three minutes. The increased norepinephrine had a remarkable effect on the decisions they made in the risky setting. Females took significantly longer to decide and chose more conservative options.[71] Surprisingly, the increased stress had the opposite effect on males. They chose significantly faster and selected the riskiest options. This tendency makes males appear more decisive under pressure, which is often admired in the business world. Sound risk-taking must include the tendency to deliberate over an important decision.

Pressure also improves males' performance and calculation but impedes females. Neurologists asked subjects to add numbers and measured their accuracy. Both sexes performed equally, until they had to act under pressure. Increased norepinephrine made males told to "add faster" improve their accuracy. The stress increased the blood flow to the right prefrontal cortex.[72] However, the same increase in norepinephrine impaired the females' accuracy. Males got faster, and females slowed down. Training under pressure moderates this tendency.

Sex differences in neurons are found in every region of the nervous system. Short-term stress improves neural growth in the hippocampus, but after 21 days, it causes a 30 percent decrease in apical dendrites. Short-term stress in humans impairs the neural growth in a female hippocampus, but after 21 days in males, it has no significant effect.[73]

While pressure improves activity in the frontal cortex in males, stress triggers the emotion centers in females and reduces their speed and accuracy. In high-stake situations (performance, work, testing, interviews), females are reflective thinkers. They report thinking about a few of their answers and changing them: "Well, I can see how both could be true. I picked *a*, but *c* could be correct, too." Reconsidering answers reduces one's accuracy. When speed is a benefit, such as for standardized tests, multiple-choice questions, interviews, and stressful situations, for the most part, males have the edge. Slowing down to think over an answer or going back to reconsider and change an answer increases errors and often means running out of time. In the workplace, it makes one look indecisive. As reflective thinkers, females underperform under pressure and in timed situations despite whether they are high achievers, most females do poorly. For females to perform at their peak, they must train under pressure (sports is a natural form of training, as it involves practice under pressure). Knowing to prepare to perform with or without pressure is critical.

It's imperative to train high risk-takers (who are most frequently males) to understand the value of slowing down to consider the consequences. In addition to potentially saving their lives, it's also imperative to train those who are prone to avoiding risk, out of too much fear and caution. Failure to take risks can be as devastating as reconsidering choices. What seems like a harmless habit of taking a while to answer, or rethinking answers, may indicate an aversion to risk. It also means that females are less likely to pursue male-dominated fields (science and engineering), or to speak up in a male-dominated workplace. A relatively simple method can be used to train women to perform despite these tendencies. Women who practice performing under stress can improve their ability to perform in the presence of high cortisol levels. After the "Me Too" movement, it was essential to prepare males and females to handle stress. (Refer to In the Zone Chapter)

Risk-takers are instrumental to the survival of the human species. Thomas Crowley, a professor of psychiatry at the University of Colorado, points out that risk-taking behaviors were beneficial, such as warding off attackers or venturing into better territory. Risk-taking can benefit and further our cultural good, improve innovation, and be an asset in leadership. New careers, inventions, practices, and solutions involve risk. The desire to take risks can be a powerful motivating factor, too. Taking risks increases dopamine, which controls motivation, attention, and norepinephrine (energy).

- Stress has the opposite effect in males as females; it makes males take more risks.[74]
- Research suggests that under extreme stress, males seek female support (during moderate stress, males want to be alone); women seek same-gender friends for support and to increase their nurturing behaviors.[75]

Females are more likely to report that they dislike working under pressure and "negotiating." More than 40 percent of female subjects argued about the parameters of stress from a timed competition/assignment. One female stated, "We'll do a better job, if you allow us more time." Another answered, "You'll have better results, if you allow us to just finish the project." The problem is, it's impossible to avoid performing under pressure. Life happens under pressure, including romantic relationships, friendships, work, and decision making. The highest-paying jobs are in competitive- and incentive-based environments, and there are times that better performance requires more time.

The solution is to deliberately train under pressure for peak performance. University of Chicago researchers showed that practice under pressure allows women's brains to improve their ability to process under high levels of norepinephrine.[76] The more a woman performs math under norepinephrine, the higher her accuracy. But everyone should be trained to perform under pressure. For obvious reasons. it's risky for teachers or employers to say, "Females don't perform under pressure." This stereotype leads to underperformance ("choking") when an authority figure identifies a group as underperformers, whether it's people of color, women, or specific physical attributes. (Refer to In the Zone Chapter).

Competition motivates and energizes males, not females—if there's no winner, males don't see the point.

Performing under pressure is key throughout life. Stress can elevate males and females to performances they wouldn't have achieved otherwise and allowing practice in safe environments underlies this skill. People can do their work and have a clearly defined winner. Unless the leaking toilet, broken outlet, dirty laundry, or unfinished essay comes with a shot at setting a record for the fastest time, or even with full-body contact, there will be little motivation for males. Pressure and competition get otherwise unmotivated males to participate, interact, and even study, to win. In many areas of youth culture, competition has been removed, maybe to protect the majority from losing. But this prevents peak performance that comes from increased norepinephrine and surges of testosterone. In business, competition is still essential; success comes from an incentive to win. To prepare, activities in school need winners and losers; playing games isn't just fun, it teaches us how to behave after a win and, just as importantly, after losing.

When I taught high school, my students couldn't have cared less when I presented a review quiz game that I thought would be fun—that is, until I made teams of boys against girls. Then, the atmosphere changed. Without my direction, the boys began preparing, studying, and planning for the event. They became gladiators. When I asked a question, every boy's hand shot into the air before I could finish: "Me! Me! Call on me!" And not one girl raised her hand before the boys. Furthermore, the right and wrong responses to answers were shocking. If a boy got a question right, all the boys screamed and celebrated. If a boy gave a wrong answer, the same boys would scream, "You idiot! Shut up! You cost us a point." When a girl missed an answer, the other girls would scream, "Good try!" or "You'll get it next time!"

I walked to the girls' side of the room and asked, "Why don't you raise your hands before the boys?" After some silence, one girl leaned forward, as if speaking for the rest, and said, "I want to be sure I know the right answer." The girls' behavior when one of them got the wrong answer was the opposite of the boys. Even when the girls didn't know or like one another, they would provide comfort and support: "It's okay, nice try. It's all right." The girls continually lost this game, not because they didn't know the answers, but because the reward went to the first to respond. How much innovation is lost because incentives don't appeal to both sexes? Routine training as simple as a reminder to slow down to double-check to get the right answer, or consider a panel of males and females, verses another panel could increase chances of solving complex problems. Understanding the different motives of the sexes suggests that males and females working together could bring a full array of choices, assets, and liabilities.

Males are more likely to cite "bad luck" for stupid risks and to brag after successes. Another of my examples of boys taking risks is from the classic movie, *E.T.: The Extra-Terrestrial*. A young boy, Elliott, positively identifies the worst imaginable danger, an alien from another planet in his backyard. He races into the kitchen, screams about the danger to his mom, his brother, and his brother's friends: "It's out there. It's in the shed. It threw the ball at me. Nobody go out there." Every male in the room instantly runs outside. Some jump over the table to get to the danger faster. Boys' natural attraction to risk is especially pronounced when they're surrounded by other boys.

To measure the differences between males' and females' tendencies to take risks, experimenters asked subjects to toss a ring onto a peg from a distance. Each could choose to stand at 2, 4, or 10 feet. In isolation, most females stood at the 2- or 4-foot mark, and most males chose the 4- or 10-foot mark. In a follow-up, experimenters asked the subjects to choose again but now surrounded by same-sex observers. Females still chose 2 or 4 feet, but males who had selected 4 feet in isolation now chose the 10-foot mark. Males take greater risks when surrounded by other males; females do not.

Boys are much more likely than girls to sustain broken bones and head injuries or be killed in accidents. They overestimate their abilities, and controlled experiments have shown that males are motivated by the desire to impress when asked to take physical risks. Even when riding virtual bikes, boys were significantly more likely to turn in front of oncoming traffic, jump curbs, and ride up ramps. They reported being energized by the experience. In the same experiment, girls used the brake more than twice as often as bays and were more likely to report feeling afraid.

Even male macaque monkeys take more risks than females. At birth, macaques have a 1:1 male-to-female ratio, but in one study, this became 1:5 by adulthood.[77] The macaques' habitat had a highway running through it, and males would cross it, but females would not. It cost the males their lives. Males take more risks and unwise risks, whether alone or with others. They were more likely to cross the highway like the classic video game, "Frogger."

Identifying danger increases a male's chances of being attracted to it. Explicit warnings against drugs and alcohol identify a potential thrill. Drug Abuse Resistance Education (D.A.R.E.), a school program designed to stop students from using drugs, instead increases drug use in students who participate. Long-term studies have repeatedly shown that students who have completed D.A.R.E. are more likely to try drugs than those who did not. Providing a simple list of dangers while offering lots of opportunities for healthy risk-taking seems to be a better training practice.

Researchers at UCLA's Ahmanson-Lovelace Brain Mapping Center study the brains of the most extreme risk-takers to learn about their neurological pathway. Surges of dopamine and norepinephrine follow the same brain reward system as drugs. Recognizing this pathway will allow researchers to suggest risky activities and extreme sports that use the same pathway, as a sort of vaccination against substance abuse. Extreme sports and organized events that come with some safety regulations and protective gear increase the same neurotransmitters.

A friend of mine who loves to snowmobile told me that he and his "guy" friends look for meadows of fresh powder, then divide up and ride as fast as they can in different directions. When we took our daughters snowmobiling and found such a meadow, he was confused when the girls followed close behind. He wondered what was wrong. I told him that they were waiting for him to continue, so they could follow. He said, "I'd never do that. If I were with my friends, we'd all take off in different directions at warp speed." To clarify, he asked them on the drive home, "When we snowmobile, what do you want to do? Tear it up, or follow me?" They answered in unison, "Follow you."

Training people to calculate risk protects them from accidents and, most importantly, encourages non-risk-takers. Human behavior is contagious. People go where they see people who are like them. Males migrate toward males, females toward females, and everyone toward people of similar race and religion. If people are to take risks and go toward professions they're interested in, they must be willing to go where they are not in the majority.

Women make up 47 percent of the workforce, but only 25 percent of math and computer professionals and 14 percent of architects and engineers. Encouraging females to take more risks, for instance, through unconventional and faster methods of standardized testing, could lead them to pursue fields that they might not have entered otherwise, such as engineering, chemistry, and politics. Males can also be reassured and encouraged to choose traditionally female professions, such as health care, education, and social services. By training our society on sex differences, we improve the chances of keeping females in STEM careers once they enter them. Most females reported leaving these professions to pursue more "fulfilling" paths, where they can find meaningful relationships, but that means half of the profession's think tank is lost.

Sian Beilock, a researcher at the University of Chicago, had subjects solve addition problems under pressure. The time it took people to solve a problem depended on their gender. Males were more likely to take risks and solve equations using methods other than the ones taught in school, and they finished faster. (Males do NOT use conventional methods.)

When asked to compute 38 + 26, males used the following strategy:

1. Add 30 + 20 = 50 (faster calculation)
2. Add 8 + 6 = 14
3. Add 50 + 14

These steps are unconventional (risky) and faster (a bonus on timed tests). Females used the following strategy:

1. Add 8 + 6 = 14
2. Carry 10 over
3. Add the three numbers in the left-hand column, 3 + 2 + 1 = 6

This the conventional way to reaching the answer of 64, and the one most teachers provide. It is less risky but slower; a detriment on timed tests. Females followed the "rules" taught in school. Why are people trained on risk-taking? The tendency toward caution unintentionally keeps one sex from taking risks.

The way adults respond to boys and girls, even whether they like or dislike them, comes from innocent differences. When I chaperoned one of my daughter's middle school dances, I noticed that the girls all huddled together, some touching shoulders, and were dressed identically. The boys ran through the gym, often at breakneck speeds, darting between and around the all-female groups. Parents understand that rambunctious, perpetual action is normal boy behavior, but in a classroom, it makes teachers think males are loud, aggressive, or attention-seeking. In addition to being unimpressed with boys, this results in unconscious discrimination against them. We need training on the differences.

These differences can appear quite early, in subtle ways. A five-year-old male's answer to the question, "What did you draw?"

"It's a robot, and he shot somebody in front of a building, and it's on fire!"

Do testosterone and preference for movement manifest in artwork? In the book *Girls Draw Nouns and Boys Draw Verbs*, most girls drew houses, flowers, people, and pets, but most boys drew action scenes using few colors and few people. Here's a four-year-old male's answer:

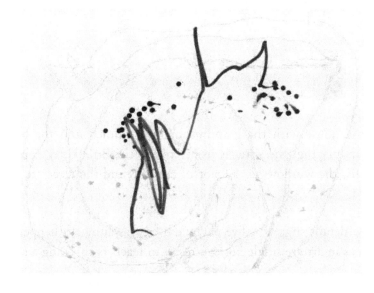

"It's a snake, and it's winding around and around and around, and it's hissing like this, *Hsssssssssssssssssss!*"

The preference for movement manifests in verbs and happenings. Here's a five-year-old female's answer:

"This is a house with the grandma making dinner, and the brother is upstairs playing, the sister is in her room, the little sister is playing with dolls, the window has a colorful curtain, and the trees are in the backyard."

All these details suggest a five-paragraph essay waiting to happen. The differences in art are subtle but can result in teachers thinking a student has a learning disability if they compare the work and verbal explanation and expect the results to be the same. Boys' answers seem underdeveloped and their thoughts violent (a robot on fire and shooting people) when they are simply interested in creating action and movement. Teachers refer twice as many boys as girls to special education (even though on average, boys' development is about two years behind that of females.) If we recognize that boys are different, are attracted to action, then we can't require them to read the same books as girls in the classroom. Ignoring biological differences means we can't understand why so many of them are bored and don't like the activity. Instead, nonfiction and adventures in which something is always happening can be more engaging. Illustrated stories, such as graphic novels and comic books (which are estimated to have 30 percent richer vocabularies than traditional books), attract readers looking for action and visual stimuli. Donalyn Miller, the author of *The Book Whisperer*, proposes the unthinkable: Allowing children to choose their own books.

People read what they love. A variety of interesting texts, both in print and online, will include adventure magazines, news sources, novels, and even manuals for video games to entice children into reading for pleasure. No more "class sets." If the selection doesn't engage everyone, we run the risk of people opting out of reading for pleasure. Naturally, some books are highly compelling and engage all readers, and it is important to inspire each other to read more. Success in the future will require reading skills.

- Choose reading materials that deliver action, adventure, and real-life stories that engage males and females.
- To find engaging material, think "10 most popular stories." I hit the jackpot by searching for "10 Best National Geographic Stories of the Year." The results were crowd-pleasing, like "Python Bursts After Eating Gator." Everyone hunched over computers to read. I couldn't shove them to their next classes after the bell rang—they insisted on reading the entire article.

Boys' brains require action and movement. For females, action and movement develop spatial reasoning skills. Mothers will tell you that movement is the main pastime of males. Rough-and-tumble play starts the moment they wake up and continues through to bedtime. The transition to school can be traumatic when kindergarten requires hours of quiet and stillness. Researchers have found that rough play engages the male brain and allows for natural development, and people who don't get enough are more likely to be diagnosed with attention deficits.[78]

Education must involve movement and action, sometimes loud, and always novel. That's why smart reading choices, alternative writing assignments, and action-filled books with oozing, dripping, slimy, and disgusting words keep boys' attention. These strategies also engage females and help them build spatial reasoning and computation skills. Never force a male to sit still to listen for more than 15 minutes. Get him up and let him move.

Competition increases testosterone. Higher testosterone is correlated with better spatial reasoning and math performance. Physical play, scuffling, fantasy play, monsters, and action heroes let students bring props to act out the most important parts of the curriculum. Once a male is involved in a concrete action or game, or in building a project, he writes using supporting details. Only writing for a real audience using real activities improves one's writing abilities.

Engaging males, especially in writing, may mean employing the unimaginable: Video games. James Paul Gee, author of *What Video Games*

Have to Teach Us About Learning and Literacy, opened a new avenue to anyone desperate to motivate children or husbands. Kids and adults are naturally engaged in video games. The game provides a path to engage a reluctant or uninterested male in reading, writing, and talking. Trade 30 minutes of reading something you love for five minutes of playing a video game. Do the laundry or take out the trash, and I'll leave you to enjoy your video game.

Tim Rylands, a teacher at Chew Magna in England, did just that. He played the non-violent game *Myst III: Exile* to teach narrative writing. He would pause and ask, "Where to go? Down to the ocean, or up to the observatory? Using specific details, explain your answer." His students used the supporting details that improved scores on standardized tests. Before this, his male students' literacy rate was only 67 percent at grade level. Afterward, 93 percent of the students, male and female, tested at grade level: Females at 87 percent, and males at 100 percent.

The type of writing didn't matter, whether narrative, expository, or persuasive; all could be used in relation to the setting of the game. Learning about characters, heroes, villains, strengths, and weaknesses; being asked to compare, contrast, and identify with characters, explain why—the applications of games to learning are limitless for both males and females. The students did not dread writing; they considered it fun. The action-based activity engaged the brain and provided concrete, tangible material for detailed descriptions. I'm not a fan of increasing video game use, but if children will play them anyway, they can be used as a bridge to healthy behaviors.

Playing with certain types of toys prepares females for a lifetime of spatial learning. To explain math abilities, the A- team at the University of Chicago investigated types of play and the effects on cognitive processing.[79] Research showed that girls who spent more time with puzzles scored higher in math by second grade. Giving females access to LEGOs, puzzles, video games, and open exploration allows them to perform at the same level as males. A higher socioeconomic background correlated with certain experiences provide spatial reasoning:

- MRIs show that females who play Tetris for 1.5 hours a week have improved visual processing and spatial reasoning after three months.
- After 10 hours of playing video games, sex differences in processing fade.

Teachers and parents with math anxieties pass along their limiting thoughts to their children, especially females.[80] Females are only behind males in math in countries where gender is a discriminating factor. After the SAT introduced a written section to its math test, females closed the gap with males. Although females do trail behind males in math achievement at the highest levels, this is true only in countries with gender discrimination. In Iceland, a country without gender discrepancies, females score in the top 1 percent at even the highest levels of math.

The factor behind differing math scores is environmental: Attitudes and experiences. There are no math gaps between boys and girls in low-income households. Only in upper- and middle-income households do boys score higher on spatial reasoning tests. Susan Levine, a psychologist at the University of Chicago, found that homes with high incomes have greater access to open space, which allows for putting together puzzles, using LEGOs, and playing video and computer games. Females with access to these kinds of experiences build their spatial reasoning skills. Integrating hands-on activities that encourage spatial reasoning and movement into daily life and classroom projects improves the neural networks that allow for STEM professions; not special programs and more homework

In the United States, politicians run for office on the promise to hold schools "accountable." One problem with this is testing, which is expensive and time-consuming. But the biggest cost is the fact that results don't correlate with life-long success, and poor performance simply makes the test takers (and their parents) feel stupid. Such self-doubt begins early and follows them through their lifetimes. Comparison comes naturally, but typical child development isn't easily measured; children follow different paces. Historically, males have "outperformed" females on standardized tests, but now schools are pressured to improve their scores by limiting things that used to allow both sexes to do well. Physical education, music, art, and recess have been cut. These trends are failing to respect the biological differences that allowed all children to succeed. Before 1992, boys were at grade level and outperformed females in standardized testing. Since then, boys have scored significantly lower in reading than girls on the National Assessment of Educational Progress (NAEP) at all grade levels.

However, the gap can be closed by implementing two things: Hands-on activities and movement.

1. Integrate regular movement into school (but understand why).
2. Provide hands-on projects that give boys concrete experiences to increase their use of details for effective writing. For females, making projects and engaging in movement develops spatial reasoning abilities.

Today, it's common in schools for five-year-olds to be trained to sit still, quietly, for long periods of time, to read and write for an hour at a time, and to be "test-ready." The irony is that reading and writing earlier may be the reason for the gap. In New Zealand, where the literacy rate is 100 percent, schools introduce reading at age seven or eight. In the United States, by age seven, non-proficient readers—mostly male— are labeled with individual education plans. Once given, these labels don't seem to go away.

Until the push toward standardized testing began, kindergarten focused on socialization and free play. This provided males with developmentally appropriate curriculums, which included fine motor skill development and socialization through interactive free play and natural physical activities. For females, the play and interaction allowed for hands-on activities and physical movement that improved their spatial reasoning. Specials (music, art, and physical education) stimulate growth in the neural circuitry underlying reading, writing, math, and social skills. Movements that improve balance, coordination, and interactive play are best for test-taking, especially in males.

When boys are put in one room and girls in another, they make record gains. A male language arts teacher took all the boys in the class off to add movement to their required literature studies. Their Measure of

Academic Progress (MAP) test that year showed unprecedented gains. When they entered in the fall, the boys should have tested at 224, but were at 219. After a year with this teacher who increased their movement and hands-on activities, the boys scored a shocking 227, two points above the expected 225. The district assessment director expected two-to-four points of growth and could not explain the spectacular eight-point gain.

To help girls with math, the male teacher worked daily to build personal relationships with each of them. If females engage naturally with relationships, connections, and talking, the teacher used that as a bridge to math concepts. At the beginning of the year, the girls' MAP scores averaged 226, instead of 229, where they should have been. But the following spring, they crushed their testing with an average of 232, a point higher than the expected 231, and a six-point gain overall, almost twice the national average. These results seemed to last, even after the girls moved on to a "non–gender trained" teacher the next year. Those females scored on average of 237, a full five points above the expected 232.

Paying attention to differences is priceless. What if the "old practice" of being required to show your work compromises male's math processing? Showing your work, like standardized tests require, could have compromised thinkers, including Bill Dreyer, the late California Institute of Technology (Caltech) biologist who won the Nobel Peace Prize for his theories about antibodies. He invented one of the first protein sequencing machines, which launched the human genome revolution. He said that he didn't move one step at a time; he moved many steps at a time. What if the push to take a test had stopped his thought process, extinguished his passion, and blocked his ability to do math and realize his potential? A return to recognizing differences, inspiring to learn, and finding time for moving will bring peak performance:

- Deliberately make eye contact to create a habit and guess what a person is thinking and feeling. This creates empathy and neural networks for good social skills.
- Talk about emotional topics and feelings. This is natural and engaging for females, but males experience stress as negative emotions trigger activity in the amygdala.

- When a man leaves an emotional environment (e.g., an argument), his physiology "recovers" to calm; for a woman, it escalates. Males avoid the emotional or overly personal; females are engaged by it.
- Encourage talking, ask what happened to bridge to sharing feelings. Moving while sharing (walking, or even driving) enhances articulation and limits eye contact for better neural integration.
- Talk or act out the important parts of a story. This gets a male's attention and allows for the use of details.
- For males, mental health and learning involve building and making projects.
- Teach people that a hard question can be reframed to get an answer more easily: "How did he feel when . . .?" can be reframed as, "What happened when . . .?" For instance, in an argument with an angry female or on a quiz or test at school.
- Males require and crave movement, happenings, and action: Projects, exploration, and opportunities to figure things out.
- Use movement, competition, and teams to help males in ordinary but necessary tasks, from good behavior and schoolwork to laundry and dinner dishes. Whoever cleans their room first, does the dishes fastest, sorts the laundry first, or without being told to wins bonus points.
- Reading materials and conversations must have action to engage males, especially in language arts. Relationships engage females, and these can be brought into math and science.
- Discuss some favorite movies and use these details (for writing or public speaking). Make eye contact training and deliberately read faces for emotions.
- Risk-taking improves the quality of one's life, finances, and relationships. Therefore, it should be trained. Teaching people how to calculate risk protects them from harm. For example, listing the pros and cons of financial, physical, and emotional consequences help to make better choices.

Stressed males make risky decisions quickly. Stressed females make less risky, more conservative decisions and take longer to make them. (Mather et al., 2011)

ENDNOTES

1   Aggarwal et al., (2019); Woolley et al., (2010).
2   Rhoades, S.(2004). *Taking sex differences seriously.* Encounter Books.
3   Roberts, S., Dunbar, R. (2015). Managing relationship decay: network, gender and contextual effects. Human Nature 26.
4   Ellis, L. (2011). Identifying and explaining apparent universal sex differences in cognition and behavior. Personality and Individual Differences.
5   Brizendine, L. (2006). *the female brain.* Broadway Books
6   von Dawans, et. al., (2019). Effects of acute stress on social behavior in women. *Psychoneuroendocrinology.*
7   Simpson et al., (2016). Experience-dependent sex differences in newborn macaques: Females are more social than males. *Scientific Reports.*
8   Taylor, S. (2006). Tend and befriend: Biobehavioral bases of affiliation under stress. *Current Directions in Psychological Science.*
9   Su et al., (2009). Men and things, women and people: A meta-analysis of sex differences in interests. *Psychological Bulletin*, 135(6), 859–884.
10   Christov-Moore et al. (2014). Empathy: Gender effects in brain and behavior. *Neurosci. Biobehav. Rev.*
11   Maeda, Y, Yoon S (2013). A meta-analysis on gender differences in mental rotation ability measured by the Purdue Spatial Visualization Tests: Visualization of rotations. *Ed Psychol Rev.*
     Gur et al., (2012). Age group and sex differences in performance on a computerized neurocognitive battery in children age 8-21. *Neuropsychology.*
12   Levine et al., (2005). Socioeconomic status modifies the sex difference in spatial reasoning skill. Psychological Science.
13   Tanaka-Arakawa et al., (2015). Developmental changes in the corpus callosum from infancy to early adulthood: A structural magnetic resonance imaging study. *PLos ONE.*
14   Dunbar et al., (2015). Managing relationship decay. *Hum Nat.*
15   Golz et al., (2019); Maitland et al., (2004). Selective sex differences in declarative memory. *Memory & Cognition.*
16   Burman et al., (2007). Sex differences in neural processing of language in children. *Neuropsychologica.*
17   Paukner et al., (2014). Neonatal imitation predicts how infants engage with faces. *Dev. Sci.*
18   Gur et al. (2012).
19   Fuertinger et al. (2017). Dopamine drives left-hemispheric lateralization of neural networks during human speech. *Journal of Comparative Neurology.*
20   Pearce et al. (2017). Variation in the b-endorphin, oxytocin, and dopamine receptor genes is associated with different dimensions of human sociality. *PNAS.*

21 Fuertinger et al. (2017).

22 Taylor (2006).

23 von Dawans et al. (2019). Effects of acute stress on social behavior in women. *Psychoneuroendocrinology.*

24 Kohn & Costa (2010).

25 Su et al. (2009); Ellis (2011).

26 Dunbar (2018). Social circles.

27 Kocevar et al. (2019). Brain structural connectivity correlates with fluid intelligence in children: A DTI graph analysis. *Intelligence.*

28 Pearce et al. (2017).

29 Caruano (2017). Social laughter as a neurochemical mechanism aimed at reinforcing social bonds: Integrating evidence from opioidergic activity and brain stimulation. *Journal of Neuroscience.*

30 Pearce et al. (2017).

31 Ellis (2011). Identifying and explaining apparent universal sex differences in cognition and behavior. *Personality and Individual Differences.*

32 Ingalhalikar et al. (2014). Sex differences in the structural connectome of the human brain. *Proc Natl Acad Sci.*

33 Ritchie et al. (2018). Sex differences in the adult human brain: Evidence from 5216 UB biobank participants. *Cerebral Cortex.*

34 Perez-Pouchoulen et al. (2016). Morphological and phagocytic profile of microglia in developing rat cerebellum. *eNeuro.*

35 Seong-Soo & Bo Kyung (2018). Smartphone use and smartphone addiction in middle school students in Korea: Prevalence, social networking service, and game use. *Health Psychology Open*; Rees & Noyes (2007).

36 Sun et al. (2015). Progressive gender differences of structural brain networks in healthy adults: a longitudinal, diffusion tensor imaging study. *PLos One*

37 Amft et al. (2015). Definition and characterization of an extended social-affective default network. *Brain Structure and Function.*

38 Cahill et al. (2004). Sex-related hemispheric lateralization of amygdala function in emotionally influenced memory: An fMRI investigation. Cold Spring Harbor Laboratory Press.

39 Cahill et al. (2011). Hormonal contraception usage is associated with an altered memory for an emotional event. *Neurobiol Learn Mem.*

40 Simony et al. (2016). Dynamic reconfiguration of the default mode network during narrative comprehension. Nature Communications.

41 Abramov, I., Gordon, J., Feldman, O. Chavarga, A. (2012) Sex & vision 1: Spatio-temporal resolution. *Biology of Sex Differences.*

42 Hoskin, Ellis, L (2021). Androgens and offending behavior. *Personality and Individual Differences.*

43 Dabbs et al. (2004). Heroes, rogues and lovers: Testosterone and behavior.

44   Engberg et al. (2016).
45   Ellis, L. (2011); Rhoades (2004), 29.
46   Paukner et al. (2014). Neonatal imitation predicts how infants engage with faces. *Dev. Sci.*
47   Ellis (2011); Dadds et al. (2014). Callous-unemotional traits in children and mechanisms of impaired eye contact during expressions of love: A treatment target? *Journal of Child Psychiatry.*
48   Biswal et al. (2010).
49   Ritchie et al. (2018). Sex differences in the adult human brain: Evidence from 5216 UB biobank participants. *Cerebral Cortex.*
50   Levine et al. (2018). Mental transformation skill in young children: The role of concrete and abstract motor Training. *Cognitive Science.*
51   Benenson, J., Tennyson, R., and Wrangham, R. (2011). Male more than female infants imitate propulsive motion. *Cognition.*
52   Mather et al. (2010). Sex differences in how stress affects brain activity during face viewing.
53   Connellan J., Baron-Cohen, S., Wheelright, J., Batki, A., Ahluwali, J., (2000). Sex differences in human neonatal social perception. Infant Behavior and Development.
54   Diamond et al. (2008). Every time you go away: Changes in affect, behavior, and physiology associated with travel-related separations from romantic partners. *Journal of Personality and Social Psychology.*
55   Stroud et al. (2002). Sex differences in stress responses: Social rejection versus achievement stress. *Biological Psychiatry.*
56   Berenson et al. (2013). Social exclusion: More important to human females than males. *PlosOne.*
57   Gee et al. (2013). A developmental shift from positive to negative connectivity in human amygdala-prefrontal circuitry. *JNeurosci.*
58   Killgore, W., Oki, M., Yurgelun-Todd, D. (2001). Sex-specific developmental changes in amygdala responses to affective faces. *Brain Imaging, 12.*
59   Cahill, L. (2012). A half-truth is a whole lie: On the necessity of investigating sex influences on the brain. *Endocrinology.*
60   Ritchie et al. (2018).
61   Hearne et al. (2016). Functional brain networks related to individual differences in human intelligence at rest. *Scientific Reports.*
62   Simpson et al. (2016). Experience-independent sex differences in newborn males.
63   Ingalhalikar et. al. (2014). Sex differences in the structural connectome of the human brain. *Proc Natl Acad Sci*
64   Kocevar et al. (2019) Brain structural connectivity correlates with fluid intelligence in children: A DTI graph analysis. *Intelligence 72.*

65   Ingalhalikar et al. (2014).

66   Lee, D., Chen, Y., Schlaug, G. (2003). Corpus callosum: Musicians and gender effects. Neuroreport.

67   Tanaka-Arakawa et al. (2015). Developmental changes in the corpus callosum from infancy to early adulthood: A structural magnetic resonance imaging study. *Plos ONE.*

68   Ritchie et al. (2018). Sex differences in the adult human brain: Evidence from 5216 UB biobank participants. *Cerebral Cortex.*

69   Haier et al., (2005). The neuroanatomy of general intelligence: sex matters. Neuroimage.

70   Banis et al. (2014). Acute stress modulates feedback processing in men and women: Differential effects on the feedback-related negativity and theta and beta power. *Plos One.*

71   Lighthall et al. (2011). *Gender differences in reward-related decision processing under stress.* Oxford University Press.

72   Wang, J., Rao, H., Wetmore, G., Furlan., P. (2005). Perfusion functional MRI reveals cerebral blood flow pattern under psychological stress. Proceedings of the National Academy of Sciences

73   McEwen & Milner (2017). Understanding the broad influence of sex hormones and sex differences in the brain. *J Neurosci Res.*

74   Banis et al. (2014). Acute stress modulates feedback processing in men and women: Differential effects on the feedback-related negativity and theta and beta power. *Plos One.*

75   von Dawans et al., (2019). Effects of acute stress on social behavior in women. Psychoneuroendocrinology.

76   Levine (2010).

77   Fedigan, L. and & Zohar, S. (1997). Sex differences in mortality of Japanese macaques: Twenty-one years of data from the Arashiyama West population. *American Journal of Physical Anthropology.*

78   Panksepp (2012). The Archaeology of Mind: Neuroevolutionary Origins of Human Emotion. New York: Norton.

79   Levine et al., (2005). Socioeconomic status modifies the sex difference in spatial reasoning skill. Psychological Science.

80   Gunderson et al., (2012). The role of parents and teachers in the development of gender-related math attitudes. Sex Roles.

CHAPTER 2

BRAIN ESSENTIALS FOR DNA AND TELOMERES: HOW WE DAMAGE IT AND HOW TO FIX IT

Would you treat each day in your life with kid gloves if science showed it dictates your behavior, your personality and your brain? Would you choose some behaviors over others if microbiologists and neuroscientists showed thoughts we think, sounds we hear and what we see immediately impact our cells and our neurons? Would you say yes if the positive and the negative in your day were laying the groundwork for what is to come in your week, month, or year. If you have ever asked, "What are the odds that would happen," you'll be fascinated by the evidence that suggests your life events predicted it. Consider one phenomenon that mortified sportscasters the first week back after Covid quarantine. The commentators marveled at how many injuries. A record number of NFL players injured so badly that they left the field...but it was no coincidence. The good and the bad in life correlate with ensuing illness, accident, or injury. What's worse, those events usually accelerate our biological age of our DNA. Any event changes our brain and drives our behavior. A stressful event for example can trigger out of character actions like impulsivity, a bad mood, binge eating or drinking, and other seemingly unrelated actions. While we cannot control what happens, we now know what behaviors can help us make it through the bad times and even repair the damage.

This is a user-friendly reference with simple principles for your brain including strategies to undo mistakes, enhance cognition, increase endogenous opioids, and regrow neural connections. Even a few behaviors can repair DNA damage. Once you understand you can manage life events, you can enhance DNA and return to learning, making memories, and build healthier neurons. The behaviors improve attention and motivation and reverse damage by triggering our own brain to make more telomerase. You will learn more than 30 ways to make more and begin undoing damage you are doing now.

Even one stressful life event within 5 years changes your DNA and increases your chance of accelerated aging by 47%! It is a nasty truth, the more marinating in stress neurotransmitters the more our telomeres shrink and increase the chance of your getting sick. One day of stress increases your chances of an accident. Researchers in Israel measured car accidents following a terrorist attacks and found that 3 days following attacks, the number of fatal accidents increased by 35%![1] What's worse, after an attack that killed more than 10 people, that number increased by 69%!

If it dictates your driving…where else is it controlling your life?

The Israel study shows how an upsetting event triggers stress (cortisol and norepinephrine) making it an unintended copilot. Considering we are unconscious of the effects; this may be the least of our worries. Hot-shot researchers discovered a stressor speeds biological aging by dissolving the telomeres that cap and protect our chromosomes. Stress shrinks those telomeres at a faster pace and accelerated aging speeds the arrival of whatever is awaiting us in old age. The process of aging means cells replicate, and those telomeres shrink while our chromosomes get shorter; perceived stress accelerates this. Experiencing life events like a world-wide, life-threatening pandemic is perceived as high stress. Even witnessing the stressful event on television, and discussing or toiling over the event, guarantees a high level of cortisol in our brain and body. The perception of negative or taxing events shrinks chromosomes and prematurely ages DNA. Shortened telomeres correlate with illnesses and changes to personality and difficult behaviors, even increases in impulsive decision-making, chances of obesity, type 2 diabetes, heart disease, Alzheimer's, Parkinson's, all cancers and mental illness.[2] What it means is whatever genetic tendencies you've inherited, they are far more likely to show up early, maybe even decades.[3] If your coming birthday will be forty-five your biological age could be fifty-five.

Forget dreading a birthday. Scientists have quantified how many years our reality of stress ages our DNA in 12 months. Biochemist Elizabeth Blackburn and Carol Greider discovered telomeres shrink faster with higher levels of cortisol. After swabbing the DNA of mothers of chronically ill children to measure telomere length (biological age) and then following up after a year, Blackburn and her researchers were shocked to find the moms' telomeres had aged 9 to 17 years.[4] Their research team showed what we do can lengthen telomeres by stimulating growth of the enzyme telomerase! The researchers found those who were stressed but met as a support group did not have shorter telomeres. Talking and interacting in weekly meetings increased endogenous opioids[5] that lowered stress and stimulated telomerase. The mothers' habit of sharing meaningful conversations and offering support to each other halted their telomeres from accelerated aging. The finding was a game-changer for anyone with a brain and, thankfully, inspired Blackburn to determine how to repair the damage. She and her team discovered an enzyme called telomerase, which lengthens telomeres. Due to their work, Blackburn and her team received the Nobel Prize in 2009! We can repair our telomeres. Knowing what to do and doing it are now essential steps!

If our thoughts and behaviors shorten chromosomes shouldn't they also repair them?

As we grow older, our chromosomes age, and their protective telomere caps naturally wear down. This is the important implication: if we live a hard and difficult life, we wear down those caps faster; as a result, diseases once considered part of old age start to affect us earlier. This research shows us what we do can manage our relationship to stress; we can increase endogenous opioids and lower cortisol which protect telomeres that protect our chromosomes. The average newborn's telomeres are 9.5 kb, and we age around 1,100 bp per year; eventually, telomeres shorten to their ultimate end, what we call natural causes. Chromosomes, inside the nucleus, are the structures made up of DNA, we received from our biological parents; these structures contain our genetic code with blueprints for how we behave, look, age, respond to life, and so on. Chromosomes replicate in response to life and shorten every time they replicate. This is natural aging!

Free radicals, inflammation, oxidative stress, and hormones accelerate the process and telomere wear.[6] Chronic stress is at the root of almost every DNA-dependent disease that used to manifest in later stages of life but is now more likely to manifest at much earlier ages.[7] In addition, as you would expect, events in our environment, especially stress-inducing events, trigger inflammation and oxidative stress, which shrinks the telomeres. Meta-analyses have shown mental illness, chronic life stress, early adversity, low financial status, and the death of a loved one increase inflammation and rapidly shrink telomeres.

It's not just the event: it's thinking about or talking about the negative experience. Those thoughts become chemical and increase damaging cortisol as though the stress is happening again. Having a tendency to worry ages us prematurely, and it happens fast. Take this to heart if you allow your life stresses to dominate your daily conversations or if you fixate on worries. Each time we worry or fret, we increase the chemicals that age us. What is essential is to make your priority for health is to tackle that tendency toward bad thoughts. A few hours of stress impact our cells immediately, and just a couple of months damages chromosomes. We can now mail in a blood sample to find out our biological age. Your tendency to perceive stress and worry is your marker; personality shrinks telomeres.[8]

Watching a scary event increases the chances of fatal car accidents.

If you habitually worry on any given day, consider the obvious differences between your day and that of a zebra. Stay with me here. A zebra wakes daily with a real chance of disaster! He should have constant worrying thoughts of what could happen at any moment. Stanford University neuroscientist and biologist Robert Sapolsky wrote *Why Zebras Don't Get Ulcers* to demonstrate the dangers of stress and the need for strategies to control it. His story is a perfect example! The zebra wakes enjoys some blades of grass, drinks from a stream, and walks with the herd. A zebra's daily existence is actually life and death, terrifying and deserving of the chronic stress chemicals norepinephrine and cortisol that accompany it, while the rest of us just have to think of something worrying to spike the same chemicals! Waking in the African savanna, a zebra dreads the day and worries constantly about what could happen. If the zebra is effected like the stressed mothers, the zebras telomeres would shorten the equivalent of 9 or more years in 12 months. However, the beauty of zebra thinking is not "Oh, dear. I'm afraid that a lion will be lurking nearby or near my offspring today." Considering how a zebra goes down (not a peaceful end), it makes sense to live in fear and worry. Sapolsky's point is that zebras live in the moment. Our job now is to mindfully train our attention to live in the present where we deliberately face each day without allowing thoughts of worry about being "ripped apart"! We never allow the thought of "Oh, dear. I'm afraid I am going to die a horrible death in front of the others." Instead, disciplining your attention to stay in the present and *away from a thought featuring a life stressor regrows telomeres.* Not this thought "What if today is the day my boss/teacher/parent is going to (figuratively) tear my throat out?" If this is you, you can stop the damage and the moment you focus on what's happening around you. Scientists found changing a thought to an event the present increases telomerase and repairs damage.[9]

Brain scans show 10–25% damage from loss of mass in the hippocampus after unfortunate life events. Things like chronic stress, high blood pressure, or drug and alcohol use decrease the size of healthy brain structures. This memory-maker has the most receptors for stress so is highly responsive to increased cortisol. That may explain how one event shows chromosomes accelerate their natural aging.[1]

Do you know how you respond to stress? Here is the essential idea to get from this reference book, the way we respond to life and stress if it is by eating food, refined food, drinking too much, spending or being around other people who do the same then we are getting old before we must... on a cellular level.

---

[1] For severe trauma, unrelenting memories, or debilitating anxieties, which have by far the fastest effect, nonmedical treatment is eye movement desensitization reprogramming (EMDR). EMDR allows a therapist to use a safe environment to help a client relive the event while undergoing eye movements and choosing a more peaceful way to remember, which dramatically decreases anxious responses and activity in the amygdala and lowers cortisol.ix

Unfortunately, the number of changes in your life during the last 5 years predicts your chances of serious illnesses, accidents, and sports injuries. More than 50 years of research shows the correlation between life changes and our health and wellness; the biggest stressors are the death of a close family member, divorce, financial crisis, major injury, and caretaking. One study polled 5,000 subjects to ask how many life changes (good and bad) in the previous few years.[10] One or two events predicted a more than 50% increase in chances of a serious illness *or accident* during the next 5 years. Football players with the highest number of life changes were significantly more likely to be injured. The way we deal with loss and change increases our cortisol; depletes our endogenous opioids; and makes us vulnerable to not only colds and flus but also the most serious diseases including autoimmune disorders, heart diseases, cancers, and the conditions lurking in our genes.[11] A stressful environment and our perception of it burns through the chemicals we need to protect our DNA; cortisol shrinks telomeres, so we age more rapidly and even hasten our demise.[12] Allowing our thinking to be about what has gone wrong (yesterday, a week ago, throughout life) or thinking of what could go wrong increases the risk for illness and addiction.[13] We know after only about 10 minutes, subjects looked for relief (support from others, usually for females, See the Sex Differences Chapter.)[14] In very little time, we self-medicate by behaving in activities that further hasten inflammation, oxidation, and aging: eating, smoking, drinking, and using drugs.

Any surge in cortisol spikes binge behavior

What we do to deal with life spikes our aging. I'll use my go to as an example. After a bad day, or in the face of a bad day I am more likely to open the pantry and select something I found at the store. The uncomfortable feeling from the anxious or stress-fueled thought guides me right to a chocolate chip cookie, or sometimes crackers with butter. My refined sugar as a strategy is problematic however, as following that initial joy (relief from thoughts) it then spikes insulin, my belly fat and accelerates aging of my telomeres. That eating increases inflammation; decreases my chances of making healthy food choices; (increases chances of type 2 diabetes, heart disease, and high cholesterol and so on). Researchers found this, one big sugary drink a day shrinks our telomeres significantly; only 8 ounces speed aging by 1.9 years, and 20 ounces add 4.6 years.x

Think for a moment if everyone knew why they made "weird" choices and if they could do even a few to repair it? Why do telomeres shrink too fast?

- Males' telomeres shrink faster than females' telomeres and may explain why so many diseases and prognosis differs on the basis of sex.[15]
- Mental illness increases low-grade inflammation and oxidative stress, which shrinks telomeres. Specifically, subjects with bipolar disorder have short telomeres at diagnosis and at late stage; short telomeres correlate with bipolar. Compared to unmedicated patients, medicated patients have limited shrinking after diagnosis.[16] Schizophrenia patients have shortened telomeres.[17] Untreated mood disorders shrink telomeres, and inflammation correlates with mental illness.[18]
- Depression and anxiety disorders shrink telomeres.[19]
- Heavy use of substances and alcohol shortens telomeres.[20]
- Actions that shrink telomeres include consuming refined sugar, fast food, and poor choices in drinks and not consuming enough dietary fiber, fruits, and vegetables.[21]
- Eating processed meats such as bacon, sausage, lunchmeat, and deli meat is oxidizing and decreases telomere length.[22]
- Large waist circumference, triglycerides, and cigarette smoking shrink telomeres.[23] Cigarette smoking also profoundly affects quality and length of life.[24]
- Obesity shortens telomeres.[25] Sedentary time accelerates telomere loss, and physical activity counters such loss.[26] Each additional hour of television viewing ages telomeres.[27]
- Heart diseases, autoimmune disorders, and infectious diseases shrink telomeres.[28]
- Chronic diseases and decreased kidney functions accelerate aging because of shortened telomeres.[29]
- Cancer correlates with inflammation and shortened telomeres.[30]
- Shortened telomeres increase the risk of developing breast cancer.[31]

- A stressful pregnancy shortens the telomeres of the fetus.[32] Stressful events in childhood predict shortened telomeres.[33]
- Children from adversity and adults who struggle to reduce impulsive decision-making have short telomeres.[34] Impulsive risk-taking increases with shortened telomeres.[35] Telomere length is inherited and correlates with attention disorders.[36]
- Pessimism (thoughts expecting less positive and more negative in the future) shortens telomeres.[37] Neuroticism (regular emotional distress, worry, rumination, and easily hurt feelings) correlates with shorter telomeres.[38]

You can undo the damage, but you need darkness!

It's impossible to prevent serious disease or slow early aging (of DNA) without melatonin. The first line of defense for telomeres, which control our biological aging, is respect for bat-cave darkness. There is no way to prevent premature aging if you don't get quality sleep—defined as time in total darkness and slow-wave sleep. Melatonin is the holy grail antioxidant for health and old age. Constant, low-level inflammation underlies mood disorders, anxieties, and chronic pain. If you only do one thing to protect your health, get 10 to 12 hours of total darkness a night so that your body can marinate in melatonin. This dream chemical is an anti-inflammatory and removes oxidative stress: the two factors that affect the brain and the body. All health and wellness depend upon controlling inflammation and oxidation. Melatonin is produced by the pineal gland and the retinas, which are highly susceptible to blue-light.[39] Even more melatonin, the youth antioxidant, is produced by the gastrointestinal tract and the skin.[40] Sunscreen and darkness are the fastest ways to increase melatonin levels for repair and healing.

"Light at night is a Group 2A Carcinogen."[41]

Darkness increases melatonin, and light lowers it. Working in artificial light during dark hours and sleeping without blackout conditions during light hours are practices that cause melatonin to drop. The chilling reality became clear years ago when a study of more than 10,000 shiftwork nurses showed extremely high rates of breast cancer.[42] Total darkness allows melatonin (from the pineal gland, retinas, gastrointestinal tract, skin, and lymphocytes) to protect tissues from inflammation and oxidative stress. Melatonin is even used as therapy for patients with pancreatic cancer. Tumor growth is inhibited by high melatonin.[43] A study showed that subjects with tumors who received blood drawn from volunteers at night had no tumor growth, while subjects with tumors who received blood drawn from volunteers during the day had regular tumor growth. That may be the factor underlying why an hour of sleep protects our health more than an hour of exercise does. The National Cancer Institute announced that to avoid cancer or even mitigate an existing diagnosis, people should sleep. The study found that cutting the last hour of sleep for a workout increased the chance of cancer more than 30%.

You can get started when you turn off lights after the sun goes down; turn your bedroom into a bat cave. Unplug night-lights. Move the television. Dim artificial lights. Without hesitation, train the kids not to panic in the dark. Even little ones need to learn that darkness is good for us and that turning off all lights before falling asleep is preferable. You can use glow-in-the-dark stars on the floor to light the way to the door.

Melatonin slows tumor growth, improves mitochondria, and aids in almost all cancer therapies.

- Melatonin (the study relied on supplements) significantly reduced tumor growth for pancreatic cancer, breast cancer, prostate cancer, and other cancers by lowering inflammation and oxidation levels.[44]
- Darkness and fasting increase melatonin production, even in times of high stress.[45]
- Looking into blue light (which is produced by devices such as cell phones, iPads, and computers)[46] radically lowers melatonin. Blue-light "glass" blocks the effects of light and allows melatonin production. To enter slow-wave sleep and get 8 hours (and 15 minutes; see the Memory chapter) of sleep, stop using cell phones and computers at least 2 hours before bed. Numerous studies have suggested 10 to 12 hours of melatonin are magic.

- Eight hours of sleep and don't believe anyone that say less than that is good enough! Our children and adolescents need even more sleep, as much as 9 to 11 hours (see the Memory chapter).

Just one night increases levels of tau, amyloid beta, chances of obesity, addiction, and cancer!

When we miss one night of high levels of melatonin, that bring quality sleep, the next day, the body has lower levels of leptin, a hormone produced by fat cells that signals being full or satisfied. One missed night means higher levels of ghrelin. Those two chemicals are implicated in the physiology of addiction.[47] High or low levels mean that we experience cravings and that we're more likely to eat or drink or use a substance. If you don't get a full 8 hours of sleep, you may crave the bad stuff—potato chips, cookies, soda, and other junk food—and these cravings seem to happen around 3:00 p.m. Melatonin counters cravings to eat, drink alcohol, smoke or vape, or use drugs.

> "I had a great night of sleep. I got about 45 minutes."
> —Buddy, *Elf*

No amount of no-doze, coffee, or energy shots can counter the effects of sleeplessness. It's not possible to control stress or mood or form memories without around 8 hours of sleep. Any bragging about needing only 5 hours of sleep is totally misplaced. Losing sleep increases blood pressure, heart rate, obesity, and type 2 diabetes. You will hear experts tout 7 hours of sleep, but they are wrong; the right amount of time is 8 hours and 15 minutes! The last 2 hours have the most time in stage 5 sleep, the activity in EEGs that mimic the activity of the previous day, a heightened level of neurotransmitters called acetylcholine improves memory. Subjects who slept only 6 hours showed *no new learning*. Without sleep, you will never maintain health, moods or store memories. Sleep apnea increases the chance of cancer, heart disease, and mortality.[48]

- Slow-wave sleep, most pronounced in stage 3 or N3, when the body is least responsive, lets the brain flush neurotoxins. Alzheimer's disease and Parkinson's disease manifest without quality sleep.

Recent studies showed that even a single night of disturbed sleep resulted in higher levels of amyloid and tau protein, which correlate with aging, in cerebral spinal fluid. Because of this breakthrough study, a lack of quality sleep is now considered an early indicator for a breakdown in optimal cognition and for neurodegenerative disorders.[49] Melatonin protects us from heart disease.[50]

- Melatonin controls insulin, diabetes,[51] and obesity and detoxes our brain and spinal fluid.
- Melatonin can counter the effects that a high-fat diet can have on heart disease.[52]

How does our neurochemistry work this magic? There's a tiny backstory.

Neurons produce neurotransmitters, store and maintain them, and decide to release them into synapses. Any emotion from happiness to sadness to fear means that our neurons have released the neurotransmitters that cause us to perceive such feelings. Neurons transmit the important messages in our highly interconnected neural system; provide quick or slow thinking; allow physical agility, such as keeping our balance, throwing a ball, hitting a target with a ball and so on. Once neurotransmitters enter the synapses and get to our receptors, life happens; neurotransmitters and receptors even allow us to perceive things that are funny, and then you can laugh with your friends or family or laughed at…like my family.) Healthy neurons have thick dendrites, so the faster your brain is, the more clever, creative, and innovative you are. The more synapses and interconnections you have, the better your cognition is regarding learning, memory, calculated risk-taking, and controlled social interaction. This is where things like intelligence come from. Marketers promise products that make us "smarter." Years ago, when I had even less common sense, I thought it was a good plan to join a moms' group. At the first meeting, one of the moms handed her baby a ridiculous black-and-white noisemaker and confidently sighed, "I wonder every day what's going to happen to the babies who can't afford these toys!" I rolled my eyes, threw up and never went back. I knew there had to be another way to be healthy and smart.

The studies started the smart craze when they showed a rat had thicker dendrites when raised in an "enriched" cage (with food and water, visualize

Picasso art on the walls, Mozart playing softly, state-of-the-art running wheel, and the such), a second cage considered "impoverished" (with food and water but no toys or ambiance). The enriched subjects had thick while the impoverished had thin dendrites. There was a third cage. Its independent factor driving thick dendrites didn't require equipment, was multiple rats! More cage-mates meant more dendrites and neural interconnectivity because the rats had to learn when to approach, avoid, and groom each other. Cuddle with this one. Dodge that one. He bites, takes food, stinks, and so on. These interactions increased intelligence. Having more peers to navigate makes an environment more complex. Without all the "right" toys, children surrounded by others learn social skills at a young age during play; they learn to share or sneak toys, to play with or get a sibling into trouble, to antagonize said sibling into a frenzy, and to make any long road trip miserable by playing "He's touching me!" Healthy subjects have social skills and get along with others! Every time a study is released by a neuroscientist, we trip all over ourselves and each other in our excitement to do that "new" thing for a better brain.

The brain requires regular blood flow, like the rest of our body, to fuel the cortex. The blood flow delivers the nutrients essential for intelligence, focus, learning and all other tasks we take for granted. Without the regular blood flow to deliver the neurotropic factors health and cognition are impaired or impossible. The less we move (standing or sitting), the lower the blood flow. The more neurons interact, and connect with each other the better our cognition, physical performance, stress moderation, control over emotion (worry, fear, happiness, sadness, disgust, and anger)!

The important neurochemicals:

- Cortisol is released when we perceive stress, it increases energy, attention, memory, physical performance. Chronically high levels suspend the immune system and accelerates aging. Cortisol even decreases calorie expenditure by almost half, increases binge behavior, and accentuates pain! High cortisol decreases caloric expenditure by 50%. Stress impairs memory and attention and increases depression and anxiety.

- Norepinephrine, a neurotransmitter, is considered a memory fixative. It increases attention and energy, or vigor. It improves survival and increases during a real or perceived threat, physical or emotional. Twelve minutes of stress trigger a search for relief, such as binge eating or drinking, drug use, or social comfort. Low levels of norepinephrine feel like low energy, such as struggling to get out of bed or to find motivation for a task, and make daily life require a seemingly excessive amount of effort. Medications can increase norepinephrine to calm depressive symptoms. High levels of norepinephrine are necessary for good mood, motivation, attention, self-esteem, and positive perception of how life is treating us. The weird thing is it takes more than a memory fixative to form a memory.

Thousands of years ago, our survival depended on not making a dangerous misstep. That may be why a stupid stunt is still followed by this memory fixative which is, "Note to self: don't do that again." If someone falls through the ice on a frozen pond, the freezing water triggers the neurotransmitter to store a fast memory "Stay off the ice!" When an emotion triggers the amygdala, the brain releases norepinephrine. In a landmark study, Larry Cahill designed an experiment to show norepinephrine as a memory fixative but found that subjects only recalled *meaningful* images (see the Memory chapter). Meaning comes from neurochemicals and can be therapeutic or devastating to human health.

Blood flow improves executive function, attention, and healing. After even a burst of a movement activity, we have an increase in blood flow in the frontal cortex. The increase spikes our neurochemistry, which is essential for learning, memory, and attention. By integrating a few minutes of movement after 10 to 20 minutes of being sedentary, such as sitting at a desk or on a sofa, we maintain energy levels throughout the day; movement is essential for attention and therefore all learning. The difference in mood, energy, and attitude is almost unbelievable! Any time a parent, teacher, or worker needs a boost to efficiency or wants to change a mood, a quick movement will work in an instant! A surge in brain-derived neurotropic factor (BDNF) can jump-start efficiency. Blood flow that comes with physical activity significantly enhances learning immediately following (see the Movement Chapter).

- BDNF, a protein in the brain, underlies all learning; without this protein, the brain experiences accelerated aging and cannot store memories. BDNF improves working memory and intelligence, increases our ability to process information, and even allows us to maintain a healthy body weight. The more complex our environment is, the more BDNF we produce. Listening to music, playing an instrument, and sprinting short distances are activities that increase natural production (see Music chapter). Listening increases painkillers.

- Endogenous opioids—dopamine, oxytocin, and endorphins—are natural painkillers that our brain naturally releases in times of need, including stress. In controlled studies, subjects told that they would have to give a speech began to look for support from strangers in only 12 minutes.[53] That means we can't tolerate stress for long before we engage in behaviors to mitigate the feeling; we have a very limited threshold for bad feelings and distress, such as exclusion, anxiety, and depression. Here is where we're likely to look to alcohol, drugs, cigarettes, and food to change our stress chemistry.

- Dopamine is the neurotransmitter that fuels executive function, allows us to pay attention, and is fundamental for memory. Vigorous movement stimulates dopamine production. Dopamine helps with impulsivity and fuels cognition, decision-making, planning, and creativity. As we age, we lose our dopamine producers and receptors; this happens faster in men than it does in women. Dopamine is key to the reward center of the brain, here drugs and alcohol work the area.

- Serotonin helps control mood, pain, social behaviors, appetite, sleep, memory, and self-discipline. The right level of serotonin allows for recall and appropriate social interaction and manages pain, both physical and emotional. Serotonin improves our ability to learn new information, recall what we've learned, and maintain the discipline to do what we need. However, serotonin is limited;

we exhaust it by the end of a challenging day. Fortunately, we restore levels after a good night of sleep. Numerous studies have shown that we replenish our limited serotonin supply overnight. When stress, pain, and challenges continue day after day, the recovery takes longer. Recovering from a life event or a trauma can mean a year of being short-tempered, living with more pain, being unable to recall even highly meaningful information, and experiencing sleep disruptions.

- Willpower, our self-discipline, is fueled by executive function and allows us to restrain ourselves and make our decisions. Each time you do something that requires willpower, a least favorable task, the blood flow increases, the prefrontal cortex grows more neural connections supported by chemicals, including serotonin.[54] After a challenging day "exercising discipline", plenty of research shows we have lower serotonin levels, but will end up increasing the "reserves". Chemicals, at the right levels, allow us to resist desires such as saying what we're thinking, so we now say yes, when we should say no. On a day someone hurts my feelings, makes me mad, or makes me wear grown-up clothes, I know I'm at risk for eating an entire bag of chips, drinking another glass of wine, and of course saying exactly what's on my mind!

- Low endogenous opioids mean irritably and feelings of isolation, depression, and pain; as a result, we crave substances and behaviors that increase those chemicals. Males and females seek out social interaction to relieve the discomfort. An anxiety state sends us toward a drug, a food, a drink, or anything else that increases our serotonin, oxytocin, and dopamine.[55] Carbohydrates, including fruits and vegetables, are antioxidants and become serotonin in our brains, but sugars and processed foods do the same. However, refined carbs—bread, chips, cookies, and candy—devastate the body and drop our natural levels of endogenous opioids. Sugar is a painkiller; a study showed that mice removed from their mother cried four times more than a mouse drinking a Coke did. Mice on naloxone, which interferes with feelings of reward, continued to cry.

Guess what counters life events and heals telomeres?

Choices and behaviors: Scientists found increasing antioxidants, anti-inflammatory agents, and certain activities lowers stress chemicals and increases telomerase production! Telomerase allows prematurely shortened telomeres to recover.[56] Researchers followed subjects with at least two major life stressors and found significant accelerated aging (on average 10 years) but the subjects who reported quality sleep, who reported eating fruits and vegetables daily, and who engage in *recreational physical activity* three times a week (for 42 minutes where heart rate and breathing increased and recovered intermittently). The researchers were shocked! Telomere length in women who had two major life stresses (such as loss of a loved one) but who slept, ate high antioxidants, and played for 42 minutes three times each week reported *no measurable aging after an entire year.*[57] It is possible to counter that dreaded life index stress number!

Eleven Things That Repair Telomeres and Stall Aging!

Your chromosomes can regrow telomeres! Increasing telomerase by controlling inflammation and oxidation is a miracle! High levels of antioxidants stimulate growth of the protein at the caps and lengthen our telomeres, thereby reversing accelerated aging,[58] lowering stress, and increasing endogenous opioids—the "feel-good" neurotransmitters. Endogenous cannabinoids, which your brain and body naturally produce, are chemicals that repair damage. Neurotransmitters like dopamine, oxytocin, endorphins, serotonin, GABA, glutamate, and more enhance the brain's ability to counter stress and enjoy optimal learning, memory, thinking, innovation and creativity. An increase in these neurochemicals counters stress and cognition and the accelerated cellular aging. Extensive research has shown the following behaviors and choices are effective at lowering stress and increasing growth for repair.

1. Movement: I'm usually proud if I get an hour of movement each day! But the reality is our bodies were meant to move during most of our waking hours. Doing so increases blood flow, circulation, energy, and attention. This act, maybe more than any other, lowers

cortisol levels, decreases feelings of depression and anxiety, and protects telomeres.[59] Physical activity improves processing speed, memory and executive function most with acute bouts of moderate to vigorous activity...with the most benefit after exercise[60]

a. Recreational physical activity-- with intermittent vigorous movement repairs and regrows telomeres. Play is an activity that naturally forces us into the present moment; it requires attention. For example, playing tennis pulls attention to the ball, the racket, the net, the other players, and the strategy. With lightning-fast speed one thinks and moves: where you should be and where you should go next. A study showed that 8.75 hours of recreational activity weekly provided more remission for colorectal cancer survivors than 3 extra hours of leisure time[61].

b. Play-- is an intensely enjoyable social activity. We engage in play naturally until around puberty. The reality of growing up means that we become the adults we hid from in order to play longer. Eventually, after taking on more and more of life's daily responsibilities, we don't even notice we don't play anymore. The minute we begin to play, our thoughts are in present time. The neurotransmitters are the opioids and cannabinoids involved in reward and motivation.[62]

c. Exercise! Even individuals in high-stress environments can improve telomere length in 6 months by engaging in 40 minutes of exercise 3 to 5 times each week.[63]

d. Dancing lowers stress and improves psycho-emotional health. Whether choreographed or improvised, publicly performed or privately performed, dancing increases subjects' ability to learn, pay attention, and improve motor coordination and visual spatial ability.[64] The social interaction involved (such as remembering the steps, listening to music, and following or leading) is therapeutic and enjoyable and stimulates the body's reward system. Such interaction brings about laughter and lighthearted fun! The University of London showed that dancing lowers stress; reduces physical and emotional tension; and improves mood, blood pressure, and joy. The highly engaging activity interrupts anxiety and decreases norepinephrine. The National Institutes for Aging demonstrated that dancing reduces the chance of Alzheimer's by 76%. The challenging act of dancing, especially ballroom dancing, is good for cognition: memory, stress, and mood!

2. Mindful training: According to Jon Kabat-Zin, everyone can benefit from "the awareness that emerges through paying attention on purpose, in the present moment, and nonjudgmentally to the unfolding of experience moment by moment." Training to deliberately choose to focus on the present makes an immediate difference in lowering inflammation and stress. Changing awareness to the in breath and the out breath for less than 15 minutes daily increases telomerase. Our language is usually full of negative or self-demeaning words; periods of silence are therapeutic![65]

> "Change the thought and the feeling must go!"
> —Louise Hay

   a. Meditation lowers stress hormones almost immediately, increases blood flow to the frontal cortex, and lengthens telomeres. Even "a brief daily meditation" reduces the damaging neurochemistry of depression, anxiety, and premature aging.[66] Regular meditation, even for 10 minutes each day over 6 weeks, increases gray matter and cognition, lowers blood pressure in a way that's comparable to medication, and works like marriage counseling does on couples. Neuroscientist and author Daniel Siegel studied more than 10,000 people who showed significant increases in neural plasticity and cognitive performance.[67] Multitasking is not efficient; in fact, multi-tasking can add up to 50% more time needed to complete a task.

   b. Meditative retreats-- are beneficial. Individuals who attend a retreat for at least a week downregulate the stress response and have better chances over time of improving immune function and lowering inflammation rates.[68]

c. Loving-kindness meditation-- means focusing attention on replacing negative self-beliefs with positive affirmations and on sending kind thoughts to others around you—both friends and enemies. Balancing our thoughts calms our negativity, and sending loving kindness (into the past, present, or future) releases recurring thoughts, lowers cortisol, and increases endogenous opioids.[69]

d. Kind acts and altruism training-- lower cortisol. Performing prosocial acts for others lowers inflammation, stress, blood pressure, and cholesterol.

e. Compassion meditation lowers stress and increases feelings of connection to others, even those who are unlike us; especially effective for intergroup bias.[70]

f. Controlled breathing-- increases blood oxygenation and decreases the level of cortisol in the synapses. In a recent study at a psychiatric hospital, one group practiced 30 minutes of controlled breathing for 6 days each week; another group took the antidepressant imipramine. At the end of the experiment, the antidepressant patients had a decrease of 73%, but the breathing group had a decrease of 67%.[71]

g. Do yoga--research has been conclusive on the effects of yoga; it reduces fasting glucose levels, blood pressure, inflammation, oxidation, and psychological stress. Yoga also improves quality of life for participants and lengthens telomeres.[72] The pursuit of downward dog is a powerful remedy for cortisol; the position calms the mind and burns stubborn belly fat. The 200 calories we burn in that hour is not enough to explain the beneficial effects on belly fat; subjects who practice yoga once a week for an hour will have 3 to 5 fewer pounds on the body. That's because yoga lowers cortisol, which protects the belly from storing fat.

h. *Choice*...Your perception of being in control improves your physical health and mood.[73] Twenty years ago, Lockheed Martin proposed a traditional or every-other-Friday workweek. Surprisingly, a year later, absenteeism had dropped in *both* groups. Consider offering children choices regarding important daily routines from bedtime to homework.

3. Music: Listening to music, playing an instrument, and singing are all activities that increase endogenous opioids and decrease cortisol and norepinephrine. As the frequency increases, so does our heart rate; music increases our endogenous opioids. Listening to some music increases learning and performance[74] (see Music chapter).

4. Foods and supplements: What you consume impacts aging and increase telomerase. Chewing anything improves attention, learning, and feelings of energy. Chewing gum reduces stress, thereby also increasing dopamine in our brains and enhances cognition. A study showed that gum chewers had 16% less cortisol hormone in saliva than non-chewers did.[75] The dopamine secreted from the act of chewing gum improves attention, memory stores, blood flow, oxygen levels, and energy.

   (The hypothalamus—the structure that regulates eating, drinking, internal body temperature, sexual activity, and even gambling—has an extremely high number of dopamine receptors.) Simply snacking, chewing, and drinking are activities that increase the chemical. Eating, especially protein and carbohydrates, increases test scores, positive attitudes, and reading speed comprehension.

   a. Fasting is a fountain of youth! Fasting –defined as fewer than 200 calories--increases function and repairs mitochondria, counters aging, decreases wrinkles and heals our skin faster (including acne, eczema, and psoriasis) and even wounds. Research has suggested that low caloric intake—600 calories--is also an effective way to lower inflammation, heart rate, blood pressure, and cholesterol.[76] Decreasing inflammation and detoxing our system allows our mitochondria to reset health, disease, and normal aging.[77] Some research showed even 2 days of fasting each month can reset mitochondria, improve autoimmune disorders, lower insulin, and counter type 2 diabetes.

b. Omega 3 is an antioxidant and anti-inflammatory that improves symptoms of ADD, depression, and asthma and even raises IQ. The substance helps us lose weight or maintain a healthy weight, increases telomerase, and lengthens telomeres. *The New England Journal of Medicine* showed that bipolar patients' mood swings were moderated with 2,500 to 5,000 mg of omega 3.[78]

c. Vitamin E, vitamin B12, and folate are antioxidants and anti-inflammatories that increase telomerase, which repairs and is associated with repairing telomeres to stop premature aging.[79]

d. Vitamin C reduces oxidative damage and inflammation to restore systemic health.[80] The beneficial effects on telomeres correlates with the associated improvements related to obesity, type 2 diabetes, blood pressure, cholesterol levels, eyesight, and aggressive cancers such as kidney cancers.[81] Kakadu plums, acerola cherries, rosehips, guavas, and yellow peppers have high levels of vitamin C and high antioxidant properties.[82] However, don't take supplements over 400 mg. Many studies have found that higher doses can increase the risk of heart attack.

e. Vitamin D reduces telomere attrition.[83]

f. Dark chocolate is good for you! Polyphenols in dark (85%) chocolate act as antioxidants and anti-inflammatories and are therapeutic, especially for athletes who have particularly high levels of oxidative stress due to muscular injury.[84]

g. Potatoes are high in vitamin C and help inflammation. Last year, researchers showed that regular consumption of sweet potatoes can reduce the appearance of wrinkles by 11%.[85]

5. Drinks

a. Water is vital. Drinking water dilutes cortisol, increases leukocyte production, lowers feelings of stress, and lessens anxiety-related behaviors.[86] Hydrated brains have improved cognitive flexibility and attention, while working memory in less hydrated brains has been shown to be reduced by 34%.[87]

b. Red wine: is a powerful antioxidant (polyphenols or resveratrol and flavonoids are the therapeutic chemicals in plants) and shown to "scavenge" free radicals.[88] More than 40 studies have shown that regular consumption correlates with heart and vascular health and reduces lethal cholesterol levels. Unfortunately, the studies researched the effects of consuming just 6 ounces at a time but enjoying red wine while surrounded by others offers two behaviors shown to lower stress.

c. Coffee is a significant antioxidant and anti-inflammatory that protects our telomeres.[89] One study showed three or more cups a day lowered the risk of developing Parkinson's disease (for those who drank the beverage throughout 19 years) and diabetes and increased mental sharpness and recall (for females not for males).

6. Nature: Viewing nature lowers cortisol and increases endogenous opioids. Looking at and listening to nature as opposed to urban landscapes correlates with positive moods and improves mental health.[90] However, sitting in a dry sauna lowers stress, relieves inflammation, and increases longevity.

7. Positive social behaviors: Looking at faces (especially the face of a romantic partner) reduces pain.[91] Eating dinner with others and emotional storytelling have similar effects.[92] Looking at electronics *significantly* decreases meaningful facial viewing and endogenous opioids.

a. Laughter: Fifteen minutes of laughter increase hope and endogenous opioids and decrease inflammation. Subjects who submerged a hand in ice endured 40% longer than those watching an educational video and 40% longer than those reading a magazine. Just anticipating laughter decreases stress by 50% and laughing for 30 minutes once a week increases serotonin and reduces cortisol and inflammation.[93]

b. Celebrations: Social traditions lower stress. The work to prepare them is exhausting, of course, but moments of gathering are therapeutic. Honoring birthdays, graduations, anniversaries, weddings, and special occasions increases human connections. Subjects in homeless shelters that held celebrations had greater "cohesion" than individuals in shelters that did not hold such events.[94]

c. Positive interactions: Getting good feedback about your skills, efforts, personality, abilities, or projects provides endogenous opioids. Barb Fredrickson suggested that three positives counter a negative; that means we need genuine, kind everyday events—positive words, feedback, help, and play.[95]

d. Massage: A massage of 10 to 15 minutes or more decreases cortisol in saliva, calms heart rate, reduces pain and suffering, improves mood, and boosts muscle repair after exertion or sports.[96] Orthopedic adjustments (chiropractic adjustments) decrease pain and increase endogenous cannabinoids.[97]

8. Setting and achieving goals: Listing or creating goals involves endogenous cannabinoids associated with long-term depression and mental health. Maintaining habits allows us to be highly effective and supports our self-discipline.[98] Switching habits to include new goals is also helpful. A novel environment allows for new routines and goals. For example, transferring to a new school can interrupt tendency toward "fighting"; the new routine can allow a person to achieve goals and lessen anger.

9. Writing--expressive writing of thoughts and feelings, both positive and negative, for 2 minutes 2 days in a row!

a. List and rate stresses. Write what's on your mind, in no particular order, and quantify those thoughts as most and least upsetting or stressful on a scale of 1 to 10. Quantifying abstract events that upset us pulls the stressors from the unconscious to the conscious so that we can deliberately process emotional events that drive aging or stress. Writing down as many examples of a stressor as possible was shown to lower anxiety scores in 3 months.[99]

b. Subjects who wrote about an emotional topic for 2 minutes each day over 2 days (4 minutes total) had significantly lessened pain reports in the follow-up.[100] Controls who wrote descriptions of their shoes over the same time had no change.

c. Use writing to manipulate your behavior. Self-talk creates behaviors! In a recent study, two groups of volunteers began exercise routines. The group instructed to write about their experiences, neither positively nor negatively, ended up exercising twice as long as the control did; the writing group also called their activities enjoyable.

d. Practice daily gratitude. At the end of a year, subjects who spent time every day writing down five things for which they were thankful reported feeling happier, having more fulfilling relationships, experiencing fewer illnesses, and spending more time working out. Forcing ourselves to perceive things to be grateful for and remembering to write them down guides the brain to look for positives and hold on to it long enough to record it.[101]

e. Download in writing. You can address fears surrounding an upcoming event. Subjects who spent up to 10 minutes privately writing out their concerns about an upcoming exam increased math scores 5–17%.[102] The fMRIs showed that thoughts (of fear or failure or consequences) activate the amygdala, which interferes with the structure and function necessary for performance, while those who downloaded had no interference from activity in the amygdala (they had already processed the thoughts). Athletes can use the strategy of downloading to increase high-stakes performance for competitions

10. Anticipating fun: This means noticing the good feeling that you get when you think of something fun! Looking forward to a Friday afternoon, an upcoming trip, Christmas morning, or a visit with friends or family makes the brain increase endogenous opioids.

Each time you think of the event, you decrease stress levels and promote recovery.[103]

a. The great feelings that you experience while enjoying the event (your trip, visit, or whatever) cause a flood of endogenous opioids.

11. Anything: Any activity, moment, or feeling that you decide is positive will decrease your cortisol. Expecting to feel better (or worse) means that placebos continue to perform almost equal to and sometimes better than pharmacological treatment. Our beliefs become chemical even down to helping the bald grow hair! A baldness study found that 85% of the subjects grew hair— including subjects in the control group! A whopping 42% of the men who thought that they were using the real treatment cream saw results. In another study, patients who underwent a sham knee surgery reported pain relief two years later. Imagine having a potion that lowers the cortisol that shrinks telomeres.[104] The more aggressive the placebo is, the more effective it is.

> "Your ability to feel discomforts bring
> with it the power to release them."
> —Australian Chakra Meditation

What Can Every Family, Employer, and Educator Do?

- Share a list of favorite strategies in every meeting, conference, back-to-school event, or public gatherings.
- Share and set the goals for healthy behaviors that maintain telomeres: sleep and darkness, food choices, recreational play, mindfulness, laughter, and more.
- Train yourself to fall asleep (and share the three ways with others; visit my website for recording or see the Memory chapter).
- Share with others at work and at home on telomeres and how our daily life directly affects them—for better or for worse. The sooner this is common knowledge, the healthier we can be.

- Pick a day! For long-term success, use your chosen day as a weekly opportunity to reset healthy routines that protect telomeres. My day is Monday!
- Institute regular trainings on the brain and mental health at work, school and home.
- Resist the tendency to dismiss stress relief as wasted time. Controlling cortisol and resetting telomeres are essential activities in education and in industry. Stress mitigating strategies increase productivity.
- Natural lighting, access to food and water, and mindful training increase learning and innovation.
- Employees, teachers and parents value health and long-term success, and will be receptive.
- Every gathering with more than 20 people (back-to-school night, conference night, public presentation: music concert, play, and sporting event is an opportunity to share methods for controlling stress and improving health and performance.)
- Create a mission statement to regularly remind yourself and your organization, educational or otherwise, that we as a nation value innovation and creativity, not computation or tests that tout an accurate measure.

What Everyone with a Brain Needs to Know

- Put your children to bed at a regular bedtime; they need 9 to 11 hours of sleep every night.
- Don't eat processed foods; the best foods are lean proteins, fruits, vegetables, nuts, and seeds.
- Get 60 minutes of movement and physical activity daily, preferably outdoors.
- Externalize negativity, bad days, and others' bad behavior.
- Teach mindful activities; focus solely on breathing in and out at least 10 minutes each day.
- All bedrooms should be totally dark like a bat cave, and all houses should be dim after sundown.

- Spend time without electronics after 8:30 p.m. Read as a group or a family or sit by the fire at night.
- Go for a 30-minute walk as a family. And don't forget to engage in play.
- Go for a 20-minute walk before work or school.
- Always have a bedtime routine, no matter how old you are.
- Begin each day by writing five things that you're grateful for

ENDNOTES

[1] Stecklov, G., & Goldstein, J. (2004). Terror attacks influence driving behavior in Israel. *PNAS.*

[2] Jafri et al. (2018). Major stressful life events and risk of developing lung cancer: A case-control study. *Clinical Medicine Insights: Oncology.*

[3] Blackburn et al. (2015). Human telomere biology: A contributory and interactive factor in aging, disease risks, and protection. *Science.*

[4] Blackburn et al. (2012). Too toxic to ignore. *Nature.* Originally released in Epel et al. (2004). Accelerated telomere shortening in response to life stress. *PNAS.*

[5] Fuertinger et al. (2017). Dopamine drives left-hemispheric lateralization of neural networks during human speech. *Journal of Comparative Neurology.*

[6] Squassina et al. (2019). Mood disorders, accelerated aging, and inflammation: Is the link hidden in telomeres? *Cells.*

[7] Puterman, E., Lin, J., Blackburn, E., & Epel. (2014). Determinants of telomere attrition over 1 year in healthy older women: Stress and health behaviors matter. *Molecular Psychiatry.*

[8] Lin et al. (2011). Telomeres and lifestyle factors: Roles in cellular aging. *Mutation Research.*

[9] Villami, Vogel, Weisbaum & Siegel. (2019). Cultivating well-being through three-pillars of mind-training: understanding how training the mind improves physiological and psychological well-being. OBM integrative and complementary medicine.

[10] Holmes, T., & Rahe, R. (1967). The social readjustment rating scale. *J Psychosomat Res.*

[11] Renzahold et al. (2013). Stressful life events and the onset of chronic diseases among Australian adults: Findings from a longitudinal survey. *Eur J Public Health.*

[12] Jafri et al. (2019). Major stressful life events and risk of developing lung cancer: A case-controlled study. *Clinical Medicine Insights: Oncology.*

[13] Fagundes et al. (2012). Basal cell carcinoma: Stressful life events and the tumor environment. *Arch Gen Psychiatry.*

[14] Von Dawans et al. (2019). Effects of acute stress on social behavior in women. *Psychoneuroendocrinology.*

[15] Barrett, E., & Richardson, D. (2011). Sex differences in telomeres and lifespan. *Aging Cell.*

[16] Huang et al. (2018). Leukocyte telomere length in patients with bipolar disorder: An updated meta-analysis and subgroup analysis by mood status. *Psychiatry Res.* Barbe-Tuana et al. (2016). Shortened telomere length in bipolar disorder: A comparison of the early and late states of disease. *Braz. J. Psychiatry.*

17 Polho et al. (2015). Leukocyte telomere length in patients with schizophrenia: A meta-analysis. *Schizophrenia Research.*

18 Mechawar et al. (2016). Neuropathology of mood disorders: Do we see the stigmata of inflammation? *Transl. Psychiatry.* Miller et al. (2016). The role of inflammation in depression: From evolutionary imperative to modern treatment target. *Nat. Rev. Immunol.*

19 Revesz et al. (2016). Depressive and anxiety disorders and short leukocyte telomere length: Mediating effects of metabolic-stress and lifestyle factors. *Psychol. Med.*

20 Squassina et al. (2019). Mood disorders, accelerated aging, and inflammation: Is the link hidden in telomeres? *Cells.*

21 Rafi et al. (2017). Dietary patterns, food groups, and telomere length: A systematic review of current studies. *Eur J Clin Nutr.*

22 Ligi, P. (2011). Diet, nutrition, and telomere length. *Journal of Nutritional Biochemistry.*

23 Revesz et al. (2016). Ibid.

24 Babizhayev et al. (2012). Smoking and health: Association between telomere length and factors impacting on human disease, quality of life and life span in a large population-based cohort under the effect of smoking duration. *Fundam. Clin. Pharmacol.*

25 Mundstock et al. (2015). Effect of obesity on telomere length: Systematic review and meta-analysis. *Obesity.*

26 Shadyab et al. (2017). Associations of accelerometer-measured and self-reported sedentary time with leukocyte telomere length in older women. *American Journal of Epidemiology.*

27 Loprinzi, P. (2015). Leisure-time screen-based sedentary time and leukocyte telomere length: Implications for a new leisure-time, screen-based sedentary based behavior mechanism. *Mayo Clinic Proceedings.*

28 Jose et al. (2017). Chronic inflammation in immune aging: Role of pattern recognition receptor crosstalk with the telomere complex? *Front. Imunnol.*

29 Bansal et al. (2012). Association between kidney function and telomere length: The heart and soul study. *Am. J. Nephrol.*

30 Fest et al. (2020). The systemic immune-inflammation index is associated with increased risk of incidence cancer: A population-based cohort study. Journal of Cancer. Shay et al., (2016)

31 Shen et al. (2009). Shortened telomeres: Oxidative damage, antioxidants and breast cancer. *Int. J. Cancer.*

32 Lin et al. (2018). In vitro proinflammatory gene expression predicts in vivo telomere shortening: A preliminary study. *Psychoneuroendocrinology.*

33 Osler et al. (2016). Stressful life events and leucocyte telomere length: Do lifestyle factors, somatic and mental health or low grade inflammation mediate

this relationship? Results from a cohort of Danish men born in 1953. *Brain Behav. Immun.*

[34] Yim et al. (2016). Delay discounting, genetic sensitivity and leukocyte telomere length. *Proc. Natl Acad. Sci.*

[35] Squassina et al. (2019). Mood disorders, accelerated aging, and inflammation: Is the link hidden in telomeres? *Cells.*

[36] De Souza et al. (2015). Telomere length is a highly inherited and associated with hyperactivity-impulsivity in children with attention deficit/hyperactivity disorder. *Front. Mol. Neurosci.*

[37] O'Donovan et al. (2009). Pessimism correlates with leukocyte telomere shortness and elevated interleukin-6 in post-menopausal women. *Brain, Behavior, and Immunity.*

[38] van Okenburg et al. (2014). *Does neuroticism make you old? Prospective associations between neuroticism and leukocyte telomere length.* Psychological Medicine.

[39] Prayag et al. (2018). Melatonin suppression is exquisitely sensitive to light and primarily driven by melanopsin in humans. *J. Pineal Res.*

[40] Acuna-Castroviego et al. (2014). Extra pineal melatonin: Sources, regulation, potential functions. *Cellular and Molecular Life Science.*

[41] Tan et al. (2015). Melatonin as a potent and inducible endogenous antioxidant: Synthesis and metabolism. *Molecules.*

[42] Blask et al. (2005). Melatonin depleted blood from premenopausal women exposed to light at night stimulates growth of human breast cancer xenografts in nude rates. *Cancer.*

[43] Tamtaji et al. (2018). Melatonin and pancreatic cancer: Current knowledge and future perspectives. *J. Cell Physiol.*

[44] Tamtaji et al. (2018). Melatonin and pancreatic cancer: Current knowledge and future perspectives. *J. Cell Physiol.*

[45] Byeon et al. (2014). Cellular localization and kinetics of the rice melatonin biosynthetic enzymes SNAT and ASMT. *J Pineal Res.*

[46] Tamtaji et al. (2018). Melatonin and pancreatic cancer: Current knowledge and future perspectives. *J. Cell Physiol.*

[47] Bach et al. (2019). Effects of leptin and ghrelin on neural cue-reactivity in alcohol addiction: Two streams merge to one river? *Psychoneuroendocrinology.*

[48] Carroll et al. (2019). Obstructive sleep apnea, nighttime arousals, and leukocyte telomere length: The multi-ethnic study of atherosclerosis. *Sleep.*

[49] Spinedi, E., & Cardinali, D. (2018). Neuroendocrine-metabolic dysfunction and sleep disturbances in neurodegenerative disorders: Focus on Alzheimer's disease and melatonin. *Neuroendocrinology.*

[50] Reiter et al. (2016). Melatonin as antioxidant: Under promises but over delivers. *Journal of Pineal Research.*

51   Raygan et al. (2019). Melatonin administration lowers biomarkers of oxidative stress and cardio-metabolic risk in type 2 diabetic patients with coronary heart disease: A randomized, double-blind, placebo-controlled trial. *Clin Nutr.*

52   Bose et al. (2019). Melatonin as a potential therapeutic molecule against myocardial damage caused by high fat diet (HFD). *Melatonin Res.*

53   Berger et al. (2016). Cortisol modulates men's affiliative responses to acute social stress. *Psychoneuroendocrinology.*

54   Baumeister et al. (2018). Self-control "in the wild": Experience sampling study of trait and state self-regulation. *Journal Self and Identity.*

55   Von Dawans et al. (2019). Effects of acute stress on social behavior in women. *Psychoneuroendocrinology.*

56   Chan, S. W., & Blackburn, E. H. (2002). New ways not to make ends meet: Telomerase, DNA damage proteins and heterochromatin. *Oncogene.*

57   Puterman, E., Lin., J., Blackburn, E., & Epel. (2014). Determinants of telomere attrition over 1 year in healthy older women: Stress and health behaviors matter. *Molecular Psychiatry.*

58   Blackburn et al. (2015). Human telomere biology: A contributory and interactive factor in aging, disease risks and protection. *Science.*

59   Caldwell Hooper et al. (2014). What keeps a body moving? The brain-derived neurotropic factor val66met polymorphism and intrinsic motivation to exercise in humans. *J. Behav Med.*

60   Abdelkarim, et. al., (2017). Relationships between motor and cognitive learning abilities among primary school-aged children. Alexandria Journal of Medicine.

61   Campbell et al. (2013). Associations of recreational physical activity and leisure time spent sitting for colorectal cancer survivor. *American Society of Clinical Oncology.*

62   Schiavi et al. (2019). Unidirectional opioid-cannabinoid cross-tolerance in the modulation of social play behavior in rats. *Psychopharmacology.*

63   Puterman & Epel et al. (2018). Aerobic exercise lengthens telomeres and reduces stress in family caregivers: A randomized controlled trial. *Psychoneuroendocrinology.*

64   Pessoa et al. (2019). Dance therapy in aging: A systematic review. *Journal of Physical Education and Sport.*

65   Schutte et al. (2014). A meta-analytic review of the effects of mindfulness meditation on telomerase activity. *Psychoneuroendocrinology.*

66   Boccardi, M., & Boccardi, V. (2019). Psychological wellbeing and healthy aging: Focus on telomeres. *Geriatrics.* Lavretsky, H., Epel, E., Siddarth, P., & Blackburn, E. et al. (2013). A pilot study of yogic meditation for family dementia caregivers with depressive symptoms: Effects on mental health, cognition and telomerase activity. *Int. J. Geriatr. Psychiatry.*

67   Villami, A., Vogel, Weisbaum, & Siegel. (2019). Cultivating well-being through three-pillars of mind-training: understanding how training the mind improves physiological and psychological well-being. *OBM integrative and complementary medicine.*

68   Conklin et al. (2018). Insight meditation and telomere biology: the effects of intensive retreat and the moderating role of personality. Brain, Behavior and Immunity.

69   Hoge et al. (2013). Loving-kindness meditation practice associated with longer telomeres in women. *Brain, Behavior, and Immunity.*

70   Weng et al. (2017). The impact of compassion meditation training on the brain and prosocial behavior. *The Oxford Handbook of Compassion Science.*

71   Markkanen, E. (2017). Not breathing is not an option: How to deal with oxidative DNA damage. *DNA Repair.*

72   Ughreja, R., & Ughreja R. (2019). Type 2 diabetes mellitus, physical activity yoga and telomere length: A literature review. *J. Insul. Resist.*

73   Ly et al. (2019). A reward-based framework of perceived control. *Frontiers in Neuroscience.*

74   Spivak et al. (2018). Influence of music therapy on telomere length: A brief review and a pilot study. *Biologija.*

75   Smith, A. (2010). The effects of chewing gum on cognitive function, mood and physiology stressed and non-stressed volunteers. *Nutr. Neurosci.*

76   Longho, V., & Mattson, M. (2014). Fasting mechanisms and clinical applications. *Cell Metab.*

77   Bragazzi et al. (2019). Fasting and its impact on skin anatomy, physiology, and physiopathology: A comprehensive review of the literature. *Nutrients.*

78   Tsoukalas et al. (2019). Association of nutraceutical supplements with longer telomere length. *International Journal of Molecular Medicine.*

79   Ibid. (2019).

80   Padayatty et al. (2016). Vitamin C: The known, and the unknown and Goldilocks. *Oral Diseases.* Furumoto et al. (1998). Age-dependent telomere shortening is slowed down by enrichment of intracellular vitamin C via suppression of oxidative stress. *Life Sci.*

81   Shenoy et al. (2019). Ascorbic acid–induced TET activation mitigates adverse hydroxymethylcytosine loss in renal cell carcinoma. *Journal of Clinical Investigation.*

82   Kumari et al. (2016). Effect of guava in blood glucose and lipid profile in healthy human subjects: A randomized controlled study. *Journal of Clinical and Diagnostic Research.*

83   Pusceddu et al. (2017). One-carbon metabolites and telomere length in prospective and randomized study of B- and or D-vitamin supplementation. *Eur. J Nutr.* 56.

84   Cavarretta et al. (2018). Dark chocolate intake positively modulates redox status and markers of muscular damage in elite football athletes: A randomized controlled study. *Oxid Med Cell Longev.*

85   Fruitas-Simoes et al. (2016). *Nutrients, foods, dietary patterns and telomere length: Update of epidemiological studies and randomized trials.*

86   Svendsen et al. (2014). Influence of hydration status on changes in plasma cortisol, leukocytes, and antigen-stimulated cytokine production by whole blood culture following prolonged exercise. *ISRN Nutrition.*

87   Khan, N., Westfall, D., Jones, A., Sinn, M., Bottin, J., Perrier, E., & Hillman, C. (2019). A 4-d water intake intervention increases hydration and cognitive flexibility among preadolescent children. *Journal of Nutrition.*

88   Tubaro, et al. (2019). A novel fluorimetric method to evaluate red wine antioxidant activity. *Periodica Polytechnica Chemical Engineering.*

89   Bakuradze et al. (2016). Coffee consumption rapidly reduces background DNA strand breaks in healthy humans: Results of a short-term repeated uptake intervention study. *Mol. Nutr. Food Res.*

90   Peng et al. (2019). Effects of the coastal environment on well-being. *Journal of Coastal Zone Management.*

91   Younger et al. (2010). Viewing pictures of a romantic partner reduces experimental pain involvement of neural reward system. *PLOS One.*

92   Dunbar et al. (2015). Managing relationship decay. *Hum. Nat.* Charles, S. J., Farias, M., & Dunbar, R. I. M. (2019). The aetiology of social deficits within mental health disorders: The role of the immune system and endogenous opioids. *PsyArXiv.*

93   Yoshikawa et al. (2018). Beneficial effect of laughter therapy on physiological and psychological function in elders. *Nursing Open.*

94   Leong et al. (2019). Birthday celebrations as a family homelessness intervention: A mixed-methods analysis. *Journal of Children and Poverty.*

95   Catalino, L., & Fredrickson, B. (2011). A Tuesday in the life of a flourisher: The role of positivity in optimal mental health. *Emotion.*

96   Zhong et al. (2019). Possible mechanisms of massage. *Biomedical Research.*

97   McPartland et al. (2005). Cannabimimetic effects of osteopathic manipulative treatment. *J Am Osteopath Assoc.* Rizkala et al. (2019). Does osteopathic manipulative treatment make a neuropsychological difference in adults with pain? *J Am Osteopath Assoc.*

98   Gremel et al. (2016). Endocannabinoid modulation of orbitostriatal circuits gates habit formation. *Neuron.*

99   Niles et al. (2015). Writing content predicts benefit from written expressive disclosure: Evidence for repeated exposure and self-affirmation. *Cognition and Emotion.*

100 Burton, C., & King, L. (2007). The effects of (very) brief writing on health: The 2-minute miracle. *British Journal of Health Psychology.*

101 McCullough, M., & Emmons, R. (2003). Counting blessings vs. burdens: An experimental investigation of gratitude and subjective well-being in daily life. *Journal of Personality and Social Psychology.*

102 Ramirez, G., & Beilock, S. (2011). *Writing about testing worries boosts exam performance in the classroom.*

103 Monfort et al. (2015). The impact of anticipating positive events on stress. *Journal of Experimental Psychology.*

104 Benedetti, F. (2013). Placebo and the new physiology between doctor-patient relationship. *Physiol. Rev.*

CHAPTER 3

FOOLPROOF YOUR MEMORY: THE SECRETS BEHIND A GREAT MEMORY AND QUALITY OF LIFE

If you play chess, it could mean you are smarter than you should be... fMRIs show the complex demands in the brain of an expert chess player (concentrates, memorizes, calculates) is different and shows superior cognition, brain mass and function as compared to others. A town in rural Mississippi, with only two stop signs and one elementary school, happened to have the highest ratio of chess champions in the United States. It started only a few years earlier, when a 6' 6" outsider perplexed the locals by introducing an after-school chess club. A little over a year later, after playing a couple of hours of chess per week, many of the children with below-average skills and grades improved their game and ultimately placed in the top 10 in a national contest...against chess-playing adults.[1] The same year that chess club began, those players improved their academic performance across the board— and, with that, the hope for their futures. Technology and neuroscientists help show the brain engaging in complex activities and how they train our attention and builds new neurons, all essential networks and function that allow the next level in the ability to think, innovate, and problem-solve.[2]

It's impossible to overstate the importance of intelligence for progress. The future we need depends upon peak performance for cutting-edge inventions and solutions we desperately need. This requires highly sophisticated neural networks for creativity, discipline and the skills to make it happen! We needed an intellectual boost after the massive upheaval following WWII, we needed a powerful alliance to keep world peace. The Cold War that followed forced leaders to fan innovative progress (science, technology, leadership, vision and more) as the mark of world-power to keep peace; and that demanded unparalleled ingenuity. Innovation and creativity require and is the result of highly sophisticated neural systems. When the Soviets launched Sputnik; leaders in the United States countered by demanding NASA engineers, scientists, and astronauts…to compete in a "space race". To "win" Congress approved unparalleled funding into education to build the intelligence in science and technology.

Attention, innovation, and problem-solving are intertwined…chess requires focus, sometimes for hours! Thinking about where to move next means staying focused on one thing while ignoring all else. Neurologist Richard Davidson explains, such a disciplined process builds neurons in the prefrontal cortex and increases gray matter. The ability to focus and ignore other stimulus requires discipline and practice. MRIs of subjects considered "life-long meditators" show atypically high levels of activity in the frontal cortex and a more mass when compared to non-meditators. The many hours practicing disciplined attention to the present (translates into considering a next move) builds a sophisticated neural network, is key for the highest levels of cognition.

1. Here is how it works: Memorizing trains the attention and increases neurons in the insula.
   ↓
2. Memorizing develops working memory (WM).
   ↓
3. Memorizing requires self-discipline and increases cortical mass.
   ↓
4. Increased working memory accounts for 50%-70% of intelligence.

You can only remember that to which you pay attention.

A 911 dispatcher (or an ER doctor, or an air traffic controller) can only send out emergency responders if they are able to pay attention to the incoming information from a caller. In our daily lives at work or in school, we all use our attention like a dispatcher. Then the dispatcher can take the next step to handle a situation; this is like our working memory. It's our working memory that holds information we are going to need and it's tempting to write it down or use a cellphone instead of remembering it (that's WM). Another example of your daily (WM) use: A few days ago, I bought my friend Anne a cup of coffee— "Venti, shaken, iced-tea, half-black, half-passion, no sweetener…" I panicked. I looked for my phone to write the details, the problem is the dependence on a phone excused me from using my working memory, the problem with that is neural circuits aren't paying attention in order to recall when I need it. Working memory is our ability to temporarily hold information, and it that information dictates upcoming behaviors: decision, choice, and more.[3] Working memory accounts for up to 50 to 70% of our general intelligence. General or fluid intelligence is the ability to solve a problem you have not yet seen…our future!

Your ability to attend to and recall more drives intelligence. In 2016, Randall Engle found that working memory *predicts* general intelligence.[4] In fact, this type of memory may account for up to 50-70% of abstract reasoning or fluid intelligence. This type of intelligence is about solving problems we have not yet seen, not the ability to score well on a test (crystalized intelligence). People with a high working memory ability do well at most types of learning largely because they can focus and concentrate. They have the greatest chance of achieving at the highest levels and performing well.

Practice using working memory to build your working memory!

Working memory has traditionally been considered hereditary and therefore relatively fixed. It's just that it's not true! Susanne Jaegii at the University of Michigan, Ann Arbor, showed that attention-training increases the number of items recalled by our working memory (that's intelligence). Subjects told to expect 7 to 15 items were instructed to remember the last four in order. After four weeks, the average increased their performance on a fluid intelligence test by six points.[5] She showed training attention (for recall) increases the number they remembered by 2, which means it's possible to improve working memory. Training a habit of paying attention (by asking for recall) improves intelligence, because a better working memory correlates with intelligence. The more subjects had to remember, the better their attention and working memory became (by improving their IQs and short-term memory).[6] The discovery is a radical departure from the idea that intelligence is relatively fixed. Working memory remembers a list of numbers:

7   3   8   1   6   2   8

What this means is that we can upgrade our brain; a better memory has neural integration with an improved function and more mass. Memorizing and relying on your memory not only builds WM but increases fluid intelligence.[7] Practice paying attention and ignoring distraction and practice using working memory improve intelligence! Training the brain to pay attention increases your brain's oxygen and dopamine production in the frontal cortex. This is a game-changer not only in education and industry, and for those with neurological disorders, Parkinson's, and attention deficits. Memorizing and paying attention grows more neurons in the prefrontal cortex and enhances the neurotransmitters and oxygen levels for sophisticated cognitive function. The more you use your working memory, the more neural connections you are developing; and the more you practice, the easier it gets...

The increase in dopamine and oxygen that comes with focused attention by Lars Backman at the Karolinska Institute shows more practice (like looking at the list above and recalling the last 4 in order), the more items recalled improves WM. After male subjects trained for 45 minutes a week for three weeks, their PET scans showed improved working memory, increased oxygen levels, and increased dopamine secretion in the frontal cortex...a potential cure for some attention deficits!

Training to pay attention is therapeutic for attention deficits!

Dopamine fuels the frontal cortex for important high-level cognition, especially academic and social skills. Low levels of dopamine limit your working memory (and often send people looking for help from tutors and doctors). Cognitive psychologist found the average person's working memory holds seven items plus or minus two, which means their experimental training increased their WM by a whopping 25%! That complex task of deliberate recall boosts dopamine production and oxygenation largely because it requires the brain to exert effort, it develops new neurons.

To memorize, you must focus and ignore other stimuli, and this builds the insula (the interior of the prefrontal cortex). Disciplined memorizing and ignoring distractions improve self-control. This simple finding, that memorizing improves attention, which improves working memory, turns over the idea that intelligence is fixed. A better WM allows our short-term memory to be better at transferring memories and to seamlessly integrate all new information, learning and memory…a better quality of life.

The 21st century is outsourcing your memory!

For centuries, daily life provided opportunities for attention and memory: remembering appointments, remembering a phone number, playing games, having face-to-face conversations, retelling stories, reading books—all without emails or phone memos as back-up. 21st-century technology is making those behaviors obsolete. If training the attention is necessary for memory, turning to technology to remember for us is compromising not just our ability to remember, but potentially our ability to innovate as well.

Memorization builds the neural network for problem-solving and innovation…which is intelligence! Building that network requires discipline—and the more you do what you don't want to, the better you are at it. Only discipline allows success in life, and it's built through small daily acts. The study that inspired this concept came at a 2008 MIT conference, neuroscientists presented the findings when one group of subjects were instructed to begin a workout routine *and* brush their teeth with their non-dominant hand. It turned out that the group maintained the workout routine for significantly longer than the other group of subjects, who were allowed to brush their teeth with their dominant hand. The non-dominant group displayed more activity in the insula. The effort increased mass and function in the insula.

Practice makes perfect…but if you don't practice anymore it you lose your discipline.

In our instant gratification culture, we can get it 7 days a week, 24 hours a day, buy-it now, with credit, and-ship-instantly world…we aren't patient because we don't have to practice waiting. Younger generations don't have experience with waiting, and no matter what your age, you don't have to be patient, a behavior that builds self-discipline. There was a time when children had to help with siblings, household chores, animals, and more. An increased disposable income resulted in fewer responsibilities around the home and less neurochemistry to support our health.

- waiting for a store to open, understanding closed on Sundays
- waiting in line (we go to another cashier, to another gas station when pumps are full)
- waiting for a letter, waiting for a person to be home for a phone call
- waiting for a television to warm up, computer to boot, printer to deliver
- waiting to find out the sex of an unborn baby

It was easier and faster for me to do my daughter's chores than spend time forcing her to do them. Despite my modest income, I justified paying for a cleaning service. I really blew it! Not only has she never cleaned a bathroom (which requires the most self-discipline for me), she went without the daily responsibilities that, as much as we don't like them, give us purpose and the satisfaction of completing them. Does the fact that we have a generation without chores to give the natural consequences work - reward and a culture where we no longer wait for *anything* result in a collective dip in feelings of self-worth, patience and self-control? Neurologically, discipline generalizes to the rest of our life. Any behavior that requires self-discipline builds self-discipline and the underlying neural network. Without this character trait there isn't a work ethic in school, the workplace, and interpersonal relationships! Training memory builds a network the brain needs in discipline. Memorizing builds attention while improving memory! In education, memorizing is a synonym to out of date teaching methods and scorned in favor of learning for "meaning".

Memorizing builds neural networks, and from that comes working memory, intelligence, and discipline.[8] This is not a mandate for requiring memorizing for a grade, it is the explanation for a missing piece, if you will, for training precious attention networks. Integrating games and daily activities that require ignoring distraction to focus to recall, build our ability to store deliberately store new memories!

- Working memory, attention control, and fluid intelligence are strongly interrelated constructs (Engle, 2016; Engle, 2002).
- Working memory is strongly related to attention control and intelligence (Kane et al., 2007).
- Improving working memory improves fluid intelligence (Au et al., 2015).
- The strong correlation between working memory and fluid intelligence is now considered a direct result of attention-demanding mental functions (Shipstead, 2016).
- Training attention through recall increases dopamine and oxygen in the frontal cortex. (Backman, 2011) Individuals diagnosed with attention deficits have low levels of dopamine and oxygen in the prefrontal cortex.

Memorizing is can now be a best practice for intelligence *and deep understanding*!

Despite the insults aimed at so-called "low level" processing, memorizing trains attention, increases neural mass in the frontal cortex, and forces the brain to "actively process" for future recall. On top of that, longitudinal studies show that mnemonic devices can result in long-term memories. This may be familiar "My Very Earnest Mother Just Served Us Nine Pickles" (sadly, pickles is no longer defined as a planet). Acronyms and acrostics work for recall: using the method requires attention and practice. Longitudinal studies show that the use of mnemonic strategies improves recall significantly and even increases cortical mass in the right frontal cortex. In a 2010 Norwegian study, at the end of 8 weeks, the group who used strategies to recall words showed the largest increase in the cortex, while the control group showed 8 weeks of cortical thinning consistent with aging. The strategy group remembered six more words than the control. The bigger the change in the brain, the greater the improvement in word recall.[9] The more we engage in word recall, the greater the change in the brain!

Google Brain: subjects informed they would not have access to the information in the upcoming task had 80% better recall of their content than the subject group who were not informed. The group not informed was the test group. They were able to retrace their steps online to the information but had little recall of the content…researchers call this "Google Brain".

> "A healthy memory is not the luck of the draw; it is the result of employing highly sophisticated methods to store memory. Great memories are not born, they are created."
> –Anonymous

The most 3 most sophisticated methods have now been verified with controlled studies. Purdue researcher Jeff Karpicke, randomly selected college students and polled them on their method of studying. Their most popular answer by far was re-reading material. To find out if this was really the most effective, they designed a controlled, double-blind experiment. They randomly divided 80 students into three groups (re-reading, free recall, and concept mapping) where each read a section of science text, then measured their inference and deep understanding. When he tested the subjects one week later, the results showed virtually no improvement for the "re-reading" group. However, the "free recall" group (instructed to read the text, recall as much as possible, and then recheck) showed the greatest retention. This required *actively* remembering what they had just read. The third group, instructed to create a concept map, outperformed the re-readers, but were far behind the "free recallers". Until this experiment, research suggested concept maps (a graphic representation of material) were the most effective tool for retrieval, organizing thoughts and constructing meaning. Before the experiments, the subjects were polled and overwhelmingly *expected* the concept map would be superior. It was not.

The new method showed free recallers scored about the same as the "mappers" (.78 vs. .81), but after a week, there was a 50% increase in free recall scores.[10] This "most effective" method shows active processing that requires deliberately recalling, (of what they'd just read) is the path to recall. For memory, for subjects to remember what they read, they didn't require *elaborate* study. Memorizing for recall requires active processing. A fail-proof lifelong memory requires deliberate attention and builds and sustains neural connection, which is quality of life. The solution for "google brain."

Simple tricks stop google brain and improve your recall!

The trick requires deliberate attention: placing content, deciding what to include, where to place, (spatial processing), considering how each interact and so on, forces processing and increases memory. The act of creating the "map" means you will illustrate with circles or squares, images or stick figures or any other images. The images that convey connections between ideas the mapper (artist) finds important ie: arrows, images, stars, numbers. Free recall underscores the importance of revising the methods of forming memories. Apps and programs that choose the images and arrows for integration remove the active processing, clicking an image-not-generated-by-the-individual skips the active processing required for memory. The simple trick is to use free recall to generate a map of the new content that includes images and other important information. Effortless memory and learning require deliberate attention and active processing which results (almost unconsciously) in a highly meaningful, brain-friendly "trick" (read, listen, watch then free recall onto a "mind map" using self-generated images, then recheck).

Mind Maps are the brainchild of Tony Buzan. His rules for mapping engage attention because they are natural for our brain. The steps force high-level thought processing and tricks like including personal connections, selecting a color that connects to, and drawing your own image…all require actively processing. This method is especially attractive for a reluctant learner, or complacent employee. Mind maps are so engaging that large corporations use it to enhance innovation and collaboration; huge mind maps allow departments a simple format for brainstorming growth, consider problem-solving, risk assessment and more. Choosing colors, designing the spatial layout, and figuring out associations with the familiar is naturally brain-friendly. It's an unconscious effort as the artist integrates meaningful details and enhances learning and improves innovation. As a result, it's memorable. The effort that the mapper exerts results in an 85% increased performance 30 days later. CITATION

- You pick the most important points.
- You pick a different color for each supporting idea.
- You pick and draw the illustrations.
- You place the concepts on the map.

At a neuroscience conference a New York College professor, Anthony D'Antoni shared how he had been inspired by frustrated Harvard law and medical students to test the value of mapping. Exhausted and overwhelmed marked the complaints he began a study by instructing half of the subjects to either create a Mind map or use self-selected notetaking. The half assigned to self-selected note taking and the other half, trained in Mind Mapping, chose important info from the lecture; both performed equally well immediately. A week later, the self-selected group scored below their baseline score by 30% of the original; mappers increased their connections and examples by 24%. In another study, at the end of a month, mappers recalled 85% as compared to self-selected none were instructed to study during that time. The act of creating the map forced the artist's brain to assign meaning, colors, and associations to new knowledge and increased their recall in a test of long-term retention.[11]

The 3 things necessary for recall, Small's three steps, are embedded in mapping and free recall

- LOOK at what you need to remember. Actively attend to the information. Slow down and take notice. Focus your attention deliberately.
- SNAP a visual memory (like you would a photo of a scene) so you have an image of what you want to remember and add details: unique, colorful, ridiculous, exaggerated.

- CONNECT by linking the mental snapshot to *anything you can associate with it* forces processing. Finding similarity or finding difference and even an abstract association forces the attention and processing and primes the brain for learning. (In the absence of background knowledge, this is a beginning.)

A magic way to improve memory: the peg word system...it's so effective it comes out of you as if by magic. The peg word system includes all the required steps that intrinsically force active processing: associating, visualizing, even moving. For the peg system, subjects write 20 new items (to learn or remember), then the processing comes in the second step of associating the number of the item to be remembered. For example if the first item is banana, then the number 1 is associated with a banana, if the second item is apple then the number 2 is associated with apple (associating the item or new content with something familiar begins the active processing and activates memory storage), the next step is to visualize it in a familiar context The third step is associating the item to a corresponding *movement The result is* deliberate attention, deliberate processing, rehearsing the items on the word (and setting it to a movement engages more of the brain)

For any educational or professional training, this is a godsend. For the unmotivated student or the challenged learner (under stress, self-conscious, tired, learning disability.) the process of "placing" a new item to be learned onto the peg word includes all the steps required for remembering... with minimal effort. Research shows that subjects who used this strategy significantly outperformed those who were learning "in context." Air traffic controllers learning a second language used the peg word system and outperformed the control group by 11%. The complete explanation is at the end of the chapter.

- Subjects who make an association and form a mental image score significantly higher than groups using traditional strategies for recall, especially females (Tabatabaei & Hejazi, 2011).
- Reflecting directly after a lesson increases recall by 18%; in a job-training program, employees who reflected on a day's training performed 23% better (Stefano & Gino, 2014).

- Memory for word-pairs increases by 200% when there is a larger space between initial retrieval and one week later. Recall is increased when there is single retrieval practice with a strategy, with break between the initial learning and final recall (Karpicke & Bauernschmidt, 2011).
- Practicing "retrieval" produces more learning than other effective encoding techniques (Karpicke & Blunt, 2011).

The Greatest Asset and Biggest Threat to Your Memory…is You.

You can force daily healthy habits and undo your own blocks to memory by changing a few behaviors! Memorizing trains attention and improves working memory. A good working memory results in intelligence (which we must have for a strong future of problem-solving and innovation anyway). Your beliefs about your memory inspire your behaviors to build a healthy memory or compromise it. If you think you have a good memory, you'll use it. If not, the lethal behaviors to memory begin with the words, "I have a bad memory; I have to write it down or I'll never remember it." As soon as you stop using memory, the neurons stop generating and connecting. The more you use your memory, the better it gets. It's like a muscle. Over time, you must use your neural networks to build your best memory.

Taking control back over your thought process requires discipline and the choice to pay attention to the present. We don't love this. It takes effort to stay present. Memorizing and mindfulness focus our attention in specific ways and forcing yourself to be in the present moment (anytime you meditate or use strategies) takes discipline. The more you do things you don't want to, the more discipline you have. Neuroscientists instructed subjects to use self-discipline when choosing between vegetables and brownies to see what area of the brain responded. MRIs showed the active area when we are asked to make a frugal purchase or choose healthy food over comfort food. Todd Hare, a neuroeconomist at University of Zurich, studies neural response during decision-making and found that subjects who resisted desirable had more activity in the insula in the prefrontal cortex…the area active during meditation.[12]

For thousands of years meditation has been considered a spiritual and religious practice. But western medicine and science now quantify what seems like magical benefits to individuals: improved attention and memory, learning, improved immune system, improved ability to control emotion, lower bad cholesterol and blood pressure, even repair troubled marriages! The more you practice paying attention, like the life-long meditators, the better you become at focusing on one thing. Daniel Siegel writes in *The Mindful Brain*, "The repeated firing of neurons in specific areas would result in markedly increased synaptic densities in those regions that were activated with mindful practice." The benefits pay off in dividends over time: present time focus decreases norepinephrine, increases serotonin, increases beta-endorphins, and calms our brain waves. The more we practice focusing on the present, the better our self-discipline becomes as well as our ability to pay attention, which improves working memory. Sara Lazar, a Harvard researcher, looks at the longitudinal effects of mindful practice and the hope for accelerated neural performance and asserts that many studies show that "meditation ameliorates psychiatric and stress-related symptoms."[13] The ability to keep our thoughts in the present builds the highest-quality neural network naturally. Training our thought process to remain in the present without allowing thoughts full of concern over the past or future keeps our chemistry a balance that allows our best version of ourselves. Happiness rates are higher for those who resist mind-wandering, and neuroscientists have found that as cortisol decreases our executive function can flourish.[14]

> "The true art of memory is the art of attention."
> –Samuel Johnson

If you've ever found yourself wandering around a room, struggling to figure out what you were looking for in the first place, you have thought you were losing your mind. Personally, I've had to walk all the way back to the room I left before I could remember what I was after! The instant I enter the room, the memory returns, and I spin around to go get what I needed. However, maddening this is, it's *not* a sure sign you are in the early stages of dementia. It is simply the reality of fractured focus. Imagine yourself in your life. You think of something you need to go after, but then what's your behavior? Once you set out to the task, where do you focus your attention? If you walk out of the room, pick something up to put away, answer a call, put the dog outside, and tidy a mess, you will lose your focus on your task. This isn't because of memory as much as your discipline to attend to your task…but you blame your memory instead of your bad habit of losing focus. Instead of blurting, "I have a bad memory," trust me and make sure you deliberately build your habits of memory! Set a trap so that you are forced to pay attention. You can even rehearse. Don't blame your memory! Instead, practice these habits: never use the words "I don't have a good memory" or "I forget everything."

Would you believe that researchers have put the "I can't remember why I'm in this room" phenomenon to a controlled study? If you are a multitasker in your daily life, you have experienced forgetting why you entered a room. Researchers at Notre Dame set out to explain why we cannot remember what we are doing from one room to the next. The answer is that passing a "divider" has an impact on our thought processes and our relationship to our environment. A doorjamb poses a break in our spatial experience and, with it, our thoughts. I do have an upside to the doorjamb phenomenon, though: if you are sad or in a distasteful mood, leave the room. The doorjamb fractures that focus on the bad feelings for some temporary relief.

1. Invoke my mother's rules:

   • Put your things where they belong so you don't lose them. (She said this in her sleep.)
   • Notes, numbers, appointments, and medication ALWAYS goes in the same place, NO MATTER WHAT. That way, they're always there, and will use no energy to remember where they are.
   • Use whatever organization system you want, but be consistent: always store your keys, cell phones, glasses, wallet, laptop, tablet, etc. in the same place.

2. Look, snap, and connect what you need to remember when you leave the room.

3. Say out loud what you are getting when you pass a natural break (a doorjamb), as it activates a second method to draw attention and active processing
4. Discipline yourself to use methods to force yourself to pay attention to your activities.

"Your dream takes passion and self-discipline"
—Lady GaGa

Having an undisciplined mind will bias your opinion of your memory! People who believe they have a poor memory have a smaller hippocampus two years later. Gary Small at UCLA studies adults with early onset dementia and has subjects rate their memory both subjectively and objectively. The subjective test showed that the subjects who believed they had a poor memory had a smaller hippocampus two years later. Subjects who thought they had a bad memory but scored well on the objective tests also had a decrease in the function of the hippocampus. Small found that, after two years, those who doubted their memory actually performed worse than those who believed they had a good memory, and the function of the hippocampus had declined. This was his *objective* test.

Look a list of 10 words (for 60 seconds) for recall: recalling less than eight after a 15-minute delay was a red flag for memory. His list...PLANK BANKER SAUCE UMBRELLA ABDOMEN

Small's *subjective* test was more involved; how they thought of their own memory with questions like how often do you forget names, faces, events, or directions? How often do you have to re-read? A low score showed a lack of confidence in memory, and that confidence drives memory. If you believe you have a poor memory, *you are less likely to rely on it*. Without use there are fewer cognitive challenges to provide the chemistry with blood flow and neurotransmitters necessary for attention and storage. Two years after the initial PET showed those with low confidence had a significantly smaller hippocampus. No matter the score, Small prescribes the act of practicing remembering in order to build it.

Would you believe your choices in your 20s may predict chances of Alzheimer's?

Intellectual curiosity (will you pursue higher education) and discipline (regular sleep may indicate neurological disorders later in life. So far, the choice that protects us from Alzheimer's for our lifetime…is to pursue a degree. Researchers at CASE Western Reserve University found the risk for Alzheimer's to be three times lower in people who had been active in their 40's and 50's compared to those who were not. These were the people who engaged in challenging activities such as reading, learning a language, playing an instrument, woodworking, doing jigsaw puzzles, painting, and playing board games. The most accurate indicator? The completion of a degree is a more reliable predictor than the inherited gene APOE-4 for contracting Alzheimer's. Any individual who seeks out and completes their degree may protect their cognitive health because they are more likely to have a lifetime of using more discipline than the rest of the population and the habit of engaging in complex cognition, especially memory. Discipline helps us to control chronic inflammation: managing stress, less refined food, obesity, coronary bypass surgery, and avoiding elective surgeries.[2]

An unlikely discovery by, David Snowdon, a gerontologist at the University of Kentucky, with more than 120 nuns uncovered one single difference in those who never displayed signs of Alzheimer's. The mystery was complicated by the fact that, despite the presence of posthumous neurofibrillary plaques, some of the nuns didn't show signs of the disease. An experimenter's dream provided controlled environment so they could find the factor: each lived in the same home, ate the same food, followed the same routine, and slept on the same schedule. They even wore the same clothes! Nuns had different duties! Some cooked, some gardened, some taught…the more challenging the job showed fewer symptoms of dementia (cognitive challenge builds healthier neurons). A few years after Snowdon published the book, someone in the convent found the box in

---

[2] Gary Small cautions against elective surgery because the effects are cumulative; blood flow is slowed, which lowers the amount of oxygen that the brain prefers. Coronary bypass is the most devastating, as the machines aren't as efficient as our hearts, and upwards of 50% of all patients leave with a cognitive deficit.

an attic full of his nuns' hand-written entrance essays on why they wanted to join the convent. Their ideas expressed in their essay predicted which would display symptoms. The more vivid the ideas in her autobiography, the more likely the nun was to undertake challenges and have a positive attitude that enhanced her longevity.[15] Sister Mary, one of the nuns who never got Alzheimer's, studied and learned throughout her lifetime *to get her degree at 41 years old* and had a positive attitude that doctors credited for her cognitive longevity. Those with idea after idea packed with details, even verbose and run-on sentences, showed the fewest dementia symptoms 60 or more years into the future. The youth who expressed joy and happiness lived up to 10 years longer...their perspective on life correlated with their health.

If you didn't write verbose ideas and had a poor perspective on life, don't think you're ruined! It's never too late—just begin now. From the moment you wake, while you are sleeping, you are engaging in behaviors that promote memory. From activities with people, to work, to learning, to play, what you do is improving your short-term memory. Over time, some or much of it will be transferred into long-term memory. Your daily experiences can come from what you pay attention to (sometimes we don't realize what we will remember). At any moment in time, your prefrontal cortex, working memory holds what is happening long enough to interact with "your life." The working memory doesn't hold much and it doesn't hold it for long, unless you *deliberately* focus on it and *use* a strategy.

Storing and retrieving memories whenlearning, performing at work, interacting with people, both ordinary and extraordinary events is dependent upon the hippocampus. The ability to store all new memories is the core of who we are. The famous patient H.M. underwent an experimental surgery where his surgeon removed his hippocampus; his brain never stored another memory in long term. As we age, this structure for new memories shrinks...after 60 years we lose about 1% of our hippocampal mass and .5% of our cortical mass.[16]

The best explanation of types of memory is an analogy I used from a 1984 family vacation to Vancouver. The transfer of daily life into our short term and eventually into long term is a working analogy to compare storing a memory to loading passengers onto a ferry travelling to another island. Our vacation as analogy is the locals told us to go for high tea on Victoria Island. The five of us set off to the ferry to head for the island to attend the tea, (two teenage girls, an 8-year-old naughty brother and bewildered parents). We gathered our things, lined up at the loading dock (analogy for WM), and loaded onto the ferry (like a hippocampus), prepared to travel to Victoria Island (long term memory) for high tea. Let me oversimplifies in effort to show how memory is stored. While the questions may seem ridiculous, you'll realize unconscious memory myths!

1. Is it possible to load infinite amounts of belongings onto a ferry for transport to the island?
2. Will the ferry arrive to the island instantly?
3. Is safe arrival with all belongings guaranteed?
4. Can a single missed maintenance check result in tragedy?

Answers show common misconceptions…

1. Of course the ferry has a limit on how much it can carry.
2. Of course memory doesn't happen instantly. (It took about 2½ hours to reach the island.)
3. Unfortunately arrival is not guaranteed. Things overboard, get lost, etc.
4. Obviously even one missed maintenance check could mean mechanical issues or worse.

Like the ferry, the hippocampus is responsible for eventually putting important parts of your daily life into long-term memory, like Victoria Island, the cortex stores our memories. The ferry, hippocampus retrieves and transfer from life into long-term storage. But, like the journey by ferry, the transfer will take time, up to 12 or 18 months (short-term) to long term. The smoother the waters, the faster the transport; that means the ore sleep, the less stress, and better nutrition improves the chances of storage.

This is extremely important for children, because to remember explicit requires additional resources and deliberate attention. Breaks from learning that type of content helps the hippocampus, (short-term memory) to process incoming information from our environment and WM. Limiting incoming content may help load the new information faster. Researchers at MIT have shown mice ran the maze significantly faster if they learn for 10 minutes followed by a 2minute break, compared to the mice who ran the maze for an uninterrupted hour. Important content delivered in 10 or even 15 minutes followed by a few minutes of a break, increases our learning and recall. Breaks allow more in less time.

How can it take a year or a year and a half for a memory to be stored long-term?

Much of our understanding of memory comes from patients with traumatic brain injuries. Memories lost from before the accident suggest how long it takes the hippocampus to transfer daily experience to the cortex (long term). After electroconvulsive therapy, some studies of patients lose memories from 18 months before the treatment (however, the ability to store memories improves for severely depressed subjects after). Any major stressor is a trauma and can prevent the hippocampus from storing new memories. Controlling stress and protecting sleep protects and aids the hippocampus in transferring events to long term. Less time to transfer increases our chances of storage; the longer a ferry is on open sea, the more vulnerable the cargo. Like a ferry in a storm, the hippocampus can be crippled by extreme emotions, stress, and fatigue. All brains require daily maintenance!

If you can't pay attention, your working memory can't load the information in the first place. That said, sometimes you remember things that you didn't deliberately process—i.e., stowaways on the ferry. It is possible to remember without consciously paying attention…but knowing how to ensure memory guarantees our quality of life! When you are "present" meaning, paying attention to the activity you are currently doing and not allowing your mind to wander, your working memory is at peak performance. The more you pay attention, the better your working memory. The better your working memory, the higher your fluid intelligence. That is, your ability to think, create, innovate, and problem-solve comes from deliberately training your attention.

Years ago, I heard my father say to this nice man who was thinking about buying my car, "I know she puts gas in it, and the light that says, 'Change oil' works." It sort of irritated me, how my sweet dad, willing to broker the sale of my beloved black Honda, knew I had no interest in what it meant to maintain a car. I guess it was true: I bought fuel and took it to have the oil changed. I don't know about maintaining a car, but I loved it and was keeping it even though I knew I was not going to learn the nitty-gritty. Maybe you can identify this with something like the workings of the brain: you know it is important and you love it, but learning about a synapse, a neurotransmitter, and an action potential is something you're not going to do. That's where I come in. I have taken the important points and put them into a format that you can absorb quickly, reference scientific studies, and use as a guide in making important choices that keep the brain in mint condition!

I know I'm supposed to eat right, control my stress, sleep, and exercise... but do I really know about the "fuel," the chemicals in my brain? Do you remember the commercial 'this is your brain on drugs'? In case you are like me with my car, this section is a simplified guide, hoping to explain neurotransmitters and their effects on health, memory our behavior (See Essentials Chapter.) When it comes to memory, certain chemistry, is essential to store a memory. Without it, you do not. Once the chemicals make sense, you'll put sleep, what you eat, controlling stress at the top of your priorities!

The simple fact is that increasing in blood flow naturally increases energy and improves attention. Imagine how many places we need this: work, household chores, school. Blood flow increases the levels of dopamine and norepinephrine, which are responsible for motivation. Simply put, increasing blood flow allows the optimal neurotransmitter levels, oxygenation, healing, learning, thinking and all executive function...think of it as the holy grail.

Neuroscientists have researched how the following neurotransmitters dictate behavior and cognition and have a profound impact on memory and learning.[17]

Dopamine:

- Fuels executive function and working memory.
- Fosters attention and problem-solving.
- Fuels reward system and motivation.
- Involved in movement and generated by movement.
- Allows decision-making.
- Promotes learning and memory.

Acetylcholine:

- Higher levels improve memory. (Our highest levels occur in the last two hours of sleep.)

When it is blocked, no new memories are made.

- Allows for cortical neuroplasticity and attention.
- Evokes the release of dopamine.

Serotonin:

- Improves moods; low levels correlate with depression.
- Provides feelings of well-being and alertness.
- Allows regular sleep (key for memory).
- Implicated in sleep, sexual function, and appetite.
- Helps to control stress and correlates with willpower.
- Plays a role in decision-making.
- Improves memory and decision-making.[18]

Norepinephrine:

- Helps to moderate mood and attentiveness.
- Acts as a memory fixative.
- Increases energy and spikes during stress.
- Improves perception of the world.

GABA:

- Allows feelings of calm.
- Improves balance and homeostasis.
- Counters excitatory chemical (glutamate) to improve learning and cognition.

Glutamate:

- Allows memories to be formed and stored.
- Provides long-term potentiation.
- Glutamate-receiving neurons are located in the hippocampus and cortex and are essential for learning.[19]

BDNF (Brain-Derived Neurotropic Factor):

- Promotes enhanced connections between neurons, which is like a fertilizer for learning and memory.
- Allows neurons to connect.

To form a memory, the chemistry is non-negotiable. Without norepinephrine, dopamine, acetylcholine, or other chemicals, there is no recall. Emotional events trigger the amygdala (the structure closest to the hippocampus) which triggers the hormonal and neurotransmitter response. The increase of norepinephrine, and dopamine increase the chances of storing a memory. James McGaugh, a memory expert at the University of California, Irvine explains that, without a response from the amygdala, "all memories would be stored with the same intensity." It's not a mystery, it's a reality that storage rests on a chemical surge. Researchers on memory and emotion show memory comes from "powerful passion,"[20] e.g., the surge of norepinephrine during a stressful or fearful situation. Memory is crucial for survival, and stress neurotransmitters are memory fixatives.

At first, the idea of norepinephrine as a fundamental piece in the mystery of memory sounded great, but this research quashed my excitement and instead made me sit upright with alarm. Larry Cahill, a neurobiologist at

U.C. Irvine, found that the effects of norepinephrine increased memory for meaningful stimuli, not neutral ones. In the experiment, he asked subjects to view a slideshow with emotional and neutral slides. Immediately following this, they placed their arms into a bucket of ice water for 3-5 minutes. After that time, the increase in norepinephrine, measured by their saliva levels, triggered the amygdala, the structure that responds to all emotional experiences to begin the communication that resulted in the surge. As expected, those with an arm in the freezing water remembered significantly more visuals two weeks later.

It's what he said next that I found upsetting: "The subjects increased recall for meaningful slides but not for neutral. Neutral was neutral." Wait! What? This means that, even with a memory "drug," neutral memories are NOT recalled! But if chemicals are all that matter, then the content should not! That revelation sent chills down my educator's spine, as it should for *any* instructor—because public school objectives, almost as a rule, have little emotional or what would seem on the surface to be meaningful curriculum! If we are to store a memory, we must perceive a meaningful experience (equivalent to having an arm in an ice bath) or there will be little recall. This means that the current curriculum will never work. If PET scans show the hippocampus only responds when the amygdala fired, it means we must have an emotional response to recall the visuals. The amygdala did not fire when viewing neutral visuals, and so the hippocampus did not respond. The amygdala triggers the hippocampus, saying, "Put this cargo on the ferry." This is important; store it.

Emotions are Chemicals... The Elixir of Memory

An emotional experience activates the amygdala to trigger the hypothalamus to release norepinephrine in response, most common is the fight or flight response. The activation begins a cascade of neurotransmitters when we feel disgust, happiness, sadness, acceptance, wonder, shame, joy, fear, etc. This is key for a memory; it's physical, and storage is impossible without blood flow to support it. These chemicals signal the ferry to load events for the island, they allow the hippocampus to get the signal to transfer to long-term. We remember better when it's followed by a negative or a positive emotional event because it triggers the physiology that enhances storage. James McGaugh, a neurobiologist at U.C. Irvine, has been researching memory enhancement since the 1960s. His work shows how neurobiological systems control our emotional arousal and are *closely* linked to memory. Emotions trigger stress hormones during the intense times of life and augment consolidation and long-term memory.[21] Even the chemistry following laughter increases memory; students who watched a comedy after a lecture had higher recall two weeks later.[22]

It's not surprising dramatic experiments involving shock, freezing, etc. improve memory, it doesn't seem like we have to go over the top to enhance our learning. There is plenty of research to show that even "mildly" emotional content triggers our chemicals for memory, unlike neutral information. We even remember mildly *emotional* words and emotional pictures increase recall for *procedural* skill.

Emotion improves the memory of all aspects of a story, not just the thematic center. For example, "Megan was doing poorly in school. She was about to lose her financial support from her parents."

vs.

"Megan was doing poorly in school. Her boyfriend dumped her on her birthday, and she contemplated the details of suicide."

And in another narrative with a date rape, subjects remembered significantly more accurate details of the story…because emotion increases attention and chemistry. Recall is significantly higher for the details of an emotional story, but the details were even more complete with the physiology that accompanies the emotion.[23]

• •

- Mildly emotional words have greater recall than neutral words (Kensinger et al., 2011).
- Emotional words increase recall and cognitive processing (Scott et al., 2012).

- Viewing emotional pictures enhances the memory for procedural skill (Steidl et al., 2011).
- Training with meaningful information followed by norepinephrine increases learning (Okuda et al., McGaugh, 2004)
- Post-training with mild stress enhances learning (McGaugh, 2012; Dornelles, 2007).

• •

Emotion following learning like watching a funny movie enhance recall (Nielson et al., 2012). Learning must be consequential. Any new policy, direction, or topic of study *must* be something that we perceive as important: beliefs, hobbies, interests, hopes, anything that we respond to physically or connect with *personally* (which is physically). The concept to be learned or skill, must be laced with something disgusting or horrifying or jubilant! Imagine how easy to augment even spelling words, vocabulary, and all training emotional learning!

Not "window" but "shattered window."

Not "hello" but "I refuse to say hello."

Not "forgot" but "I forgot to flush the toilet."

Any reading, text, or written information must have some emotional punch. People want to talk about what they just learned if it's emotional and meaningful. Justin Matott, a popular children's author (boys *love* his books), told me his books are "censored" in one of our local elementary libraries. The librarian told him she would never read one of his books to a group again. "They were so riled up, talking about the characters and how gross the story was... I just couldn't calm them down." I was impressed.

What she witnessed was the power of an emotionally charged story that changed the physiology of the listeners—the essential ingredient for memory and for an engaged reader! How many emotions we have depends on who you ask—but, whatever the emotion, it gives us better attention and memory. Emotions are cultural, contemporary, or even dependent upon the country;

some researchers identify 5, some 18, and some 23, but words for an emotion depending upon geography. Daniel Reisberg, author of "Emotion and Memory," dismisses the idea of a fixed number of emotions. For example, the Japanese have an emotion called "amae," which is the desire to be dependent (not a popular sentiment in our culture). Another example is the Tahitian culture has no word to convey sadness as an emotion, totally understandable. The German word "schadenfreude" is deriving pleasure from another's misfortune (which I believe is universal, but not openly confessed). New Zealand has an emotion to represent when someone wanders from their life after an outburst and disappears for a few days at a time, called "Wild Boar." The latter two emotions are my favorite. Regardless of the emotion, the vividness of the physiological response has a .71 correlation with an increase in accurate recall. Some emotions are more powerful than others:

Emotion	Recall Increase
Anger	.68
Happiness	.71
Sadness	.89
Fear	.90

This chemistry is memory fixative, even when it's not personal. Although a personal event is more emotional and vivid, recall is high for emotional events because it acts as fixative in the brain's chemistry. For the death of a parent vs. the death of a JFK, the accuracy in details were virtually identical (.661 vs. .641). Reisberg showed that students who were that told they had received a D (negative physiology) recalled significantly more details from a lecture than those who were told they'd gotten an A (peaceful physiology). While I'm not condoning falsely reporting a poor score to increase learning, but the McGaugh research reminds chemistry sets up recall. "Manipulating a mood" enhances learning! With any emotion, including novel stimuli our chance of attention and recall increases

Scene 1: A woman is driving her car to the store-- neutral and not recalled.

Scene 2: A woman was in a car accident on her way to the store--emotional and recalled.

Scene 3: A woman is riding on the hood of a car to the store--novel and recalled.

Novelty has similar effects as emotion on recall—increase recall but not as much detail.

Emotional allows attention and learning. Indiana Jones whip increases the chances for attention and recall (increases chance cargo will be loaded to the ferry). The physiology of emotion acts like Indiana Jones' whip to increase our chances of loading more complete details into our working memory and then hippocampus. That way, our daily life and experiences have the best chance of transfer to long-term memories.

What does a memory look like, and where is it stored?

Memory occurs as an adjustment or fine-tuning of the connection between the neurons. Each memory accesses a community of neurons when we need it, and the event changes their future communication. You see, the place where they connect is the physical property of memory, and the immense neural network is full of memories stored throughout the brain. Anything that you experience or learn is dependent upon neurons connecting with one another by sending and receiving messages in the form of a neurotransmitter. The neurotransmitters convey signals to and from neurons.

• •

Revise, rewire, rehab…a miserable memory!

If you decide the interpretation you prefer to remember, we know that every time you retrieve a memory, it is in a changeable state. Imagine what this means: every time you recall a memory, is it malleable? If the memory involved a painful or stressful emotion, you can now deliberately connect a desirable new detail to the memory…and potentially create remarkable changes, should you reinterpret the event. Karim Nader, a behavioral neuroscientist, conducted experiments to do just that. He first established an unpleasant memory for lab rats, a mild shock associated with a tone, then later recalled that same memory so that the rat connected it with the tone. After the memory consolidated, he played a tone to trigger the traumatic memory. Then, he paired the tone with a new *preferable* association, substituting a shock for a snack—and this alleviated symptoms connected to trauma, PTSD, and other fears![24] Nader's breakthrough research showed that the physiology of a memory is not static and changes when we recall.

Simply stated, if you remember a miserable memory and add a pleasant revision, your neurons involved in recalling the memory physically change. Formerly miserable memories potentially become palatable, improving your quality of life. How do we know that this works? Because, in the control where researchers did not trigger the bad memory and associate it with a new stimulus, there was no alteration in the original response to the bad memory; the memory remained bad. Because memory is dependent upon chemistry, the act of recall (thinking) prevents the memory from being stored in the same way. Maybe one day, this will even provide relief from heartbreak: Nader's work inspired the Jim Carey and Kate Winslet movie *Eternal Sunshine of a Spotless Mind*. The two went to therapy to remove the memory of their relationship so that they could forget the gut-wrenching heartbreak.

If you have a younger sibling, you already know how easy it was to get him or her into heaps of trouble. If you have children you watch regularly, it doesn't take long to see that what you did made them do the same thing…like little monkeys, or as if they were hypnotized. Mimicking a behavior— "monkey see, monkey do"—requires little independent thinking. This is how we survived through the centuries: Humankind learned and continues to learn to manage its environment, watching others hunt, starting a fire, wearing a fur, gathering food, planting seeds, and so on. What a simple methodology for learning! And it's one that we…well, have underutilized until now.

• •

In 1961, Albert Bandura showed that we learn quickly by observing when he designed the classic "Bobo doll" experiment to see what happened when children watched an aggressive television show. A third watched the version with a mallet-wielding adult, a third watched an adult without a mallet, and the rest didn't watch the show. After viewing the show, children were sent to play with a Bobo doll. Twice as many of the children who watched the adult hit the doll were aggressive.

Human behavior is influenced by what we watch on television, online media and movies. Obedience studies show people follow directions[25]. This makes it more important to know the message communicated in media. Watching others behaviors is extremely powerful., the Attorney General's Office released "overwhelming" findings that watching violence resulted in real violence. The idea that viewing influences behavior is not new, obviously, but if watching negative behavior increases negative behavior—shouldn't watching positive behavior do the same? The results of a meta-analysis are promising: A viewer is significantly more likely to replicate the viewed behavior depending on whether the message is positive or negative. The viewer is more likely to behave in a prosocial way after watching a positive message and is more likely to behave in a negative way after viewing aggressive content.[26] Watching altruistic behaviors had a significant impact because the content "involved explicit modeling of desired behaviors."

Memories and behavior come from watching video and movies with engaging soundtracks, and especially with text inserted into the image, (not below where sub-titles are usually placed)... recall increases by 80%. Because our visual cortex processes roughly 80% of all incoming information, it is not surprising that subjects process visual information 60,000 times faster than text. Learning by watching is what we do naturally, and the neural basis for learning by watching came from an accidental discovery by neuroscientist Marco Iacaboni. He found that macaques' motor neurons fired while they watched a researcher in the lab walk to open a door. Even though they were not moving, the neurons fired in *anticipation*. The monkeys responded as if this was happening to them personally. This explains why viewers become immersed in a movie, a television show, or celebrity gossip. The implications of those neurons watching another are promising for social skills and people lacking empathy from a "broken mirror-neuron" system.[27] Using television characters interacting helps to train individuals to appropriately respond in an interpersonal setting.

Physically acting it out forms a new memory.

Watching and learning takes a fraction of the time. Every lesson or training using "engaging" videos (whether from Hollywood, television, or online sources like YouTube) to teach the content speeds learning infinitely because it triggers emotion (the neurochemistry of attention and memory).

Watching a video speeds memory…but what if you *alter* an existing one?

The work by Nader certainly seems promising to help alleviate traumatic memories. But take for a minute the idea of planting a memory that was never there. This sinister idea is more than a plot for the next creepy film: it's a reality. Elizabeth Loftus is a psychologist at the University of Washington who studies false memories. In the last few decades, the validity of eye-witness accounts and recovered memories have been called into question because of her pioneering work on the reality of false memories. She found that, with a little suggestion, subjects can be prompted to recall experiences they never had. She surveyed groups of people who had recently visited Disney World and asked them to bring photos of their trip. She asked if they remembered taking a photo with Warner Brothers' Bugs Bunny. Her team then altered the vacation photos by adding Bugs Bunny. Subjects were again called in to look at the altered photos and asked to read a paragraph telling how many visitors to Disney World take photos with Bugs Bunny. The second time they were asked if they remembered taking a photo with Bugs, more than 30% of those in the study "recalled" it. Bugs Bunny is not at Disney World, and Loftus's suggestion led them to answer yes despite their real experiences. Because of her work, eye-witness testimony is no longer considered unequivocal and the power of suggestion is quantifiable.

Is it ethical to suggest what you want someone to believe?!

Experts know memories are highly susceptible to suggestion. The Loftus research, however, raises the question of character building, almost in the realm of indoctrinating. A visual hijack our belief system and acting it out forces a physical pathway for memory (reading from a script or imagining, this establishes the neural pathway). I know from working with teachers that people love acting out scripts and become so engaged, they don't want to stop. This surprising research means suggesting a new or different memory, associating with an existing memory, now automatically results in a "doctored" memory (physiologically). Pairing something new with the recalled memory uses the "power of suggestion." This means it's possible to alter or modify a past memory deliberately by adding alternative and manufactured details to soften the memory.

Psychologists use methods to help patients heal from trauma by suggesting a new version, or reading an alternative version of what happened, or viewing photos manipulated to have a different ending. Now this phenomenon allows us to create ideas that benefit employees, students and leaders. A deliberate memory can build beliefs of confidence, success, tenacity, self-discipline, likeability, or work ethic. Speaking as if the behavior we want is reality (by reading about it, or by role-play, or journaling as a goal, a public speech etc.), we are making a new memory. Saying allowed the behavior as if it is true forces the brain to establish a neural pathway. Manipulative use of recall? False memories lead a brain to consider a truth that furthers kind, efficient and positive improves our quality of life. Recalling a memory to deliberately pair it with a state of underperforming to one of growth!

Undermining self-limiting thoughts and fostering a positive memory to propose a more beneficial belief like each of the following ideas. Remember all the times you were successful in school? Or remember when we were impressed by your ability to pay attention and your accomplishments. Or even though things have been hard in the past, you focused on positive things in your life and worked through it. Or you always think of how capable you are. Or your teachers and instructors appreciate you in class. You always put in your best effort. Or you're calm under pressure, thinking through decisions and making good choices.

Suggest the memory that will support them in making healthy choices that encourage positive behaviors. Over 30 years ago, Louise Hay wrote

You Can Heal Your Life, a book written before neuroscience research was conducted. In this book, she stated that our thoughts created our reality. At the time, she was considered metaphysical, but today's neuroscientists have found the science to support her idea. So, you are what you think! The actions we take and the thoughts we think change our neurochemistry immediately. Robert Emmons researches the positive effect of writing five things we are grateful for and found that this improves chemistry *immediately.* Our thoughts are so powerful that just the anticipation of a positive event increases dopamine and significantly increases recall.[28]

5 Daily Habits for a Better Memory:

1. Sleep 8 hours and 15 minutes every night.
   Sleep researchers believe that the hippocampus, the structure that ferries our memories, is unloading the day's information into long-term memory. The cortex is active, potentially storing our day of learning permanently. Years ago, a researcher referred to this activity during sleep as the "ping-pong effect"—the explanation for the unloading from the hippocampus into the cerebral cortex in the last few hours of sleep (the sixth, seventh, and eighth hour of sleep). Your brain is listening to what you say, and you say what you think. But thoughts create your life. No longer say the words, "I can't fall asleep" or "I can never stay asleep." You now say only, "I fall asleep easily and stay asleep"

2. Control your stress.
   It's impossible to store memories if you cannot manage your stress... and it's impossible to control stress without sleep. This vicious cycle means that you must guard these two essentials in life, and it requires *great discipline* to manage.

3. Movement increases chemistry for memory.
   If you only do one thing to improve your memory...stand up! If you only do one thing to help attention and learning...integrate movement! All learning is dependent upon chemicals! Read the Movement Chapter.

- Gary Small, the memory expert, said, "If he could do only one thing, he'd pick walking three times a week." After six months, those who walk for 20 minutes three times a week have an increase in the brain-derived neurotrophic factor (BDNF), which allows neurogenesis, memory, and learning.
- Arthur Kramer, a researcher at the University of Illinois says to slow aging and boost cognition, walk three to four times a week.
- Only one 10-minute walk, changed fatigued (and grouchy) freshmen at a Texas university into reports of better energy, moods, and motivation.

The "10" habits with food for memory

Limit calories.

This is my least favorite nutritional change to improve memory, so I'm starting here. For decades, science has suggested that eating less food than we require is the healthiest for cognition and longevity. Reducing caloric intake by 20% a day from what your body craves is therapeutic. For me, that's 300 calories a day. New studies on fasting, however, may give us another alternative. Fasting increases BDNF and allows the mitochondria of the cells to improve their function and decrease inflammation

- Caloric restriction means eating fewer than 600 calories per day. Many studies find restricting for two days increases belly fat loss, energy, and insulin reception.
- Fasting means eating fewer than 200 calories per day. Fasting improves discipline, inflammation, the immune system, BDNF, type 2 diabetes, and obesity.
- Omega 3 Fish Oil
- Drink water and eat nuts: almonds, walnuts, and pistachios.
- Fruits and vegetables prevent cognitive impairment and could even prevent normal aging deficits.
- Nutrition modifies the dysfunction and improves our microglia, which enhances cognitive function and counters injury and neurodegenerative diseases.[29]

- Compounds found naturally in lutein, lycopene, polyphenols, and others act as therapy and positively impact microglia (Lozano et al., 2017).
- Lycopene decreases neuroinflammation and enhances cognitive performance (Sachdeva & Chopra, 2015).
- Lutein decreases neuroinflammation. In a study of 7,000 subjects, those with the highest levels of lycopene and lutein had a lower risk of developing Alzheimer's (Min & Min, 2014).
- Eating one cup of blueberries every day for 12 weeks increases memory by 25%.
- Frozen fruits and vegetables have even more antioxidants than fresh ones. Tufts University reports that the highest amount of nutrition is in frozen produce rather than fresh produce and recommends consuming 3,500mg of antioxidants daily (apx. five or more servings). Produce that's earmarked for freezing ripens with the highest amount of nutrients. (Fresh produce is picked early for shipping.)

Caffeine increases blood flow, which aids executive function and memory.

- A team of international researchers report that it prevents mood and memory impairments and may even selectively improve memory impairments after four weeks of increased consumption (Machado et al., 2017).
- Chronic caffeine consumption prevents memory decline (Cunha et al. 2010).
- More caffeine intake correlates with less cognitive decline or dementia (Santos et al., 2010).
Protecting microglia allows effective memory and concentration (Tufail et al., 2017).

The most effective way to build memory is use strategies to build recall!

The peg word system is the best, most powerful. Be clear, the issue of why to learn this, surfaced the day I learned it at the Cambridge conference. I learned it in just a few minutes, but I was surrounded by educators who dismissed it as a waste of time. I heard people around me asking, "Why would I put time into using that strategy when I could just write my grocery list?" In the years since I learned it, however, I've realized that the implications of this strategy are staggering. Once you know the permanent hooks, anything you need to remember can be "peg worded" and the brain is now primed for learning, and has a "to do" list. Learning each hook requires just three steps, and it is possible to learn them quickly. Given that our untrained working memory can hold about seven items (plus or minus two), this system with 20 items for a peg word more than doubles its capacity. This is the ultimate memorization practice, trains attention, training attention for recall increases dopamine production and oxygenation[30].

No matter what is placed on the hook, you will learn it! Visualizing, associating, and adding a movement force you to process the information, even if the connection is on a surface level. Think about it: anything placed on a peg word primes the attention so that the brain can *be ready to learn it!* Of course, this is essential for academic or professional learning, but it goes beyond that to *anything* you want your brain to do or think! You see, anything that goes on the list is forced into consciousness. In ensuring the ability to remember, it improves the chances of performing well in a high-stakes situation. "Hanging" any new information on the peg words increases the chances of completing a daily to-do list, accomplishing personal goals or plans for self-improvement.

My "self-improvement" peg word is like this: I find the positive in all things, I find five things to be grateful for daily, I edit my book daily, I save money regularly, I deposit in my savings account, I am efficient, I make dinner nightly, I get rid of things I haven't worn in a year, I ignore things that irritate me, I have an endless supply for my goals. Now I associate my peg word item to the behaviors I want to embrace...and I'M TELLING YOU, it is all now unconsciously on my to-do list. Hanging the peg word daily keeps it fresh.

If I had to pick only one strategy, I would choose the peg word system as the most effective for learning. Even though research shows that free recall and mind mapping are the two most powerful mnemonic devices, I would pick peg wording. This is because it allows for 20 "chunks" to be learned, managed, or stored. I use all three: free recall while creating and learning the pegboard, free recall of material to create a Mind Map, then returning to text to add to the map.

Don't expect anyone to want to learn how to use this strategy until its value and relevance are clear. The only reason it's impressive is that remembering 20 (not 10) items in order both frontward and backward after only a few minutes is a shocking and powerful display of working memory. Easily reciting 20 items in order by number and item is extraordinary. The side-effect is learning: putting information on the peg word improves your focus on that topic indefinitely. Forcing associations may not seem to be deep understanding, but it is a lasting foundation to learning. You will wow any audience watching your recall—but before you share your secret, make them explain how they would use it.

If you pick the peg word system...

1. Let another person choose a topic and write it where everyone can see. Have them list 20 items that relate to the topic they selected.
2. Challenge them to memorize the 20 to see how many they can remember (using their own strategy). Meanwhile, you will use the peg word system. This is only a few minutes.
3. Remove the list from view, then ask them to recite it as well as possible.
4. Once they count the number of items they got correct, stand where you cannot see the list (but they can) ...and recall each item IN ORDER. Wait for this, your brain will also recall the list in REVERSE! Ask them to have you prove it!
5. Ask them to say a number, then you'll recall the item.
6. Ask them to say an item, then you'll recall the number. IT WORKS! At this point, anyone witnessing will be ready to beg for your secret!

Don't show *anything* to anyone who asks how you have become so good at remembering something until they beg. Don't let them get away with needing it for a grocery list. We must consider how improving memory increases our ability to learn and think. Remember, no one takes this method seriously until they we realize a memorizing is more than a grocery list!

Tips to train how to use the peg word system:

- Stand for this so everyone makes the movement assigned to the permanent hook.
- While they're still standing, allow them to practice the five movements frontward and backward, then quiz them on the movements.
- Explain and demonstrate five at a time, then rehearse, continue with chunks of 5 until the 20th).
- The numbers and letters are associative, so you can recall them easier.

Hook	Item and Association	Movement
1.	Rhymes with sun.	Both arms make huge circle tracing the sun.
2.	Eyes (two on your face)	Use your first two fingers to motion toward your eyes, then away from your face.
3.	A triangle has three sides.	Use your hands to trace a big triangle.
4.	Four burners on a stove	Act as if touching each of the four burners.
5.	Fingers (into a toaster with five fingers)	Lower your fingers as if into a toaster.

(I'm positive this is NOT the official association for Hook 5, but I remember putting my hand into the toaster. I am sure it's a mistake, but I like it because it's potentially graphic…and anything emotional is easier to remember.) Stop after learning the first chunk of five. Learning in "chunks" is best. Always stand to demonstrate the move, and to review the association to the number. The rehearsal and practice improve retention.

Effort goes into learning the peg word only the first time, then all future usage is fast. Each hook is like a hook that attaches something (the item to be learned) to a pegboard.

6.	Rhymes with the old saying "pick-up sticks"	Bend down as if to pick up sticks off the floor.
7.	The soda 7-Up	Move hand to lips as if drinking from a bottle.
8.	An octopus has eight legs.	Hold palms together, then wiggle eight fingers.
9.	Rhymes with "line"	Act as if drawing a line exaggeratedly.
10.	Rhymes with "hen"	(This is stupid.) Place both hands under your armpits like Sister Mary Pat on *Saturday Night Live* when she is nervous.

*Stop to do the movements and practice all 10 frontward and backward.

11.	A picket fence looks like 11111111.	Place your pointer fingers together, then cross one hand over the next over and over as if they are forming a picket fence.
12.	Eggs are sold 12 at a time.	Exaggerate breaking a giant egg on someone's head.
13.	Black cat (an unlucky number)	Move your like petting an arched cat's back.
14.	February 14th is Valentine's Day	Position your fingers into the shape of a heart.
15.	Fifteen minutes of fame	Bend to a knee and outstretch arms as if to say, "Ta da, here I am on a stage with a spotlight on me"
16.	At 16, you can drive a car.	Hands as if on a steering wheel.

17.	*Seventeen* is a magazine.	Open your hands as if reading a magazine.
18.	At 18, we gain the right to vote.	Bend forward to make a checkmark in the air and exaggerate it.
19.	Unloading the dishwasher.	Lean down to pull out the rack.

I lost my notes and ironically couldn't remember the associations for 19 or 20, so I made them both up. When I couldn't think of anything, in a panic, I found myself unloading my dishwasher. As a result, this has no connection or association to anything logical, only that I was loading a dishwasher when I thought of it. I have since found the notes, but I prefer my stupid dishwasher example. There are so many things that load nicely into the dishwasher, and they are memory-friendly because of the bizarre novelty.

| 20. | A stop sign | Hold up an outstretched hand like a traffic cop. (I always think of Diana Ross and The Supremes singing "Stop! In the Name of Love.") |

Once you have the associations and the numbers, it's a "hook" on which you can "hang" anything you want to learn. This requires attention, processing, and practice, the three steps for learning. This mnemonic device allows for a huge amount of data to be loaded into the working memory. Given that you will practice hanging items on the hooks, it's an increase in memorizing, recall and rehearsal which increases working memory, shown to correlate with IQ.

Once you allow for the "list of hooks" to consolidate (giving it at least a day), show the learners how to associate and "hang" new items onto the newly established hooks. Like a peg board with permanent hooks, this is the template that allows the brain to learn 20 new items each time. But how do you "hang" new information onto the hooks? The answer is to think of *any* association between the number or item or movement that you can. There is NO need for an accurate or logical connection. The logical and "accurate" answer comes later; the association you initially make will allow your brain to learn the permanent 20 items. The associating and moving and visualizing primes the attention and fosters learning in the long-term. It also allows rehearsal and repetition, but the new content guarantees that your brain will pay attention. Risa Sperling, a researcher at Harvard University, has MRI data that shows that the hippocampus will stop responding if it has seen or is familiar with a stimulus. "It's as if the brain says, I already know that so I don't need to put energy into remembering it."[31] This research puts the age-old practice of rehearsal and repetition back into jeopardy. To rehearse new learning, there must be something new about it. Don't overthink it how to associate the novel item with a permanent hook...anything you put onto the peg; your brain will learn. Your brain is now on alert, and the process happens automatically. When to use for the peg word system...any time you need to learn.

- Force attention to a topic.
- Select 20 important concepts to learn (in a week of a class, semester, or training session).
- Vocabulary or a spelling list
- Math formulas
- Directions for a new task
- Memorizing information in a certain order
- Developing working memory
- Perceive the world you choose (the traits you want to cultivate).
- Anything requiring sequence learning
- Prepare for a speech.
- Prepare for a test. (My daughter peg-worded the important parts of the lesson on the steps leading to a revolution and scored 100%.)
- Plan an essay.
- Teach students to follow instructions.
- Improve your confidence in your memory and ability to perform.
- Prepare for a meeting or interview.
- List things to do for the day (increases efficiency and logical order).
- Retain auditory directions without access to phone/pen/computer.
- Anything you can think of that you need to learn, remember, or *believe.*

When I have many things to do (like running errands all over the city) and I'm overwhelmed...I peg word what I need to accomplish, and my executive function automatically puts it into a logical and much more efficient order. And remember how I keep a list of things I want to do better? The traits I wish I had been born with, the mother I wish I could be, the healthy dinners I wish I made regularly, the patience I don't have naturally. Peg wording the list keeps the ideas fresh in my mind, if I'm not using the system for another purpose.

These strategies will train your attention and build discipline while transporting whatever you choose into long-term storage. Thank goodness, my clients say they enjoy using these strategies. If creating Mind Maps, using free recall, and hanging a peg word is fun...that's a testament to how brain-friendly the strategies are. I'll never spend another minute using any other method. These three have the research behind them and are the best. Just make sure you habitually free recall anytime you are learning; it speeds preparation time and enhances the other two strategies.

Example for Personal Growth: "Personal Traits and Sports in Which I Want to Improve"

1. I am patient.
2. I am always prepared early.
3. I see the positive in everything.
4. I cook a healthy dinner most nights.
5. I engage in an hour of physical activity daily.
6. I don't say bad things about others.
7. I set and meet daily goals.
8. I save money regularly.
9. I get to bed early every night.
10. I eat lots of fruit and vegetables.
11. I keep my eye on the ball.
12. I stay low during play.
13. Slice is a good idea on a return.
14. My focus is on the game only.
15. I never allow words in my mind.
16. I visualize my next play.
17. Hit the ball harder.
18. I use my shoulder for power.
19. Hit crosscourt.
20. I focus on my breathing.

This is one of my personal peg word charts. When I work to associate, visualize, and set each of these to movement, I am training my brain to look for and make these things a part of my behavior. They will become automatic the more I practice, especially in my tennis game. For example, my peg word chart means I remind myself to focus on breathing and not words in my mind during a match, which improves my chances of getting in the zone.

"The existence of forgetting has never been proved. We only know that some things don't come to mind when we want them."

–Friedrich Nietzsch

ENDNOTES

[1] Alfonsi, S. (2017, March). *Chess instills dreams in kids from rural Mississippi.* 60 Minutes, CBS News. https://www.cbsnews.com/news/kids-fight-stereotypes-using-chess-in-rural-mississippi/

[2] Au, J., Sheehan, E., Tsai, N., Duncan, G., Buschkuehl, M., & Jaeggi, S. (2015). Improving fluid Intelligence with training on working memory: A meta-analysis. *Psychon Bull Review, 22*(2), 366-77.

[3] Fuster, J.M. (2015). *The Prefrontal Cortex* (5th Edition). Elsevier.

[4] Engle, R. (2016). Cognitive predictors of a common multitasking ability: Contributions from working memory, attention control, and fluid intelligence. *Journal of Experimental Psychology, 145,* 1473-1492.

[5] Jaeggi S. M., Buschkuehl, M., Jonides, J., & Perrig, W. J. (2008). Improving fluid intelligence with training on working memory. *Proceedings of the National Academy of Sciences of the United States of America 05/13, 105*(19), 6829-33.

[6] Kundu, B., Sutterer, D., Emrich, S., & Postle, B. (2013). Strengthened effective connectivity underlies transfer of working memory training to tests of short-term memory and attention. *Journal of Neuroscience, 33*(20), 8705-15.

[7] Au, J., Sheehan, E., Tsai, N., Duncan, G., Buschkuel, M., & Jaeggi, S. (2015). Improving fluid Intelligence with training on working memory: A meta-analysis. *Psychon Bull Review, 22*(2), 366-77.

[8] Kundu, B., Sutterer, D., Emrich, S., & Postle, B. (2013). Strengthened effective connectivity underlies transfer of working memory training to tests of short-term memory and attention. *Journal of Neuroscience, 33*(20), 8705-15.

[9] Fan, S. (2014, March). Can a mnemonic slow memory loss with age? *Scientific American.* https://blogs.scientificamerican.com/mind-guest-blog/can-a-mnemonic-slow-memory-loss-with-age/

[10] Karpicke, J. D., & Blunt, J. R. (2011). Retrieval practice produces more learning than elaborative studying with concept mapping. *Science,* 772-775.

[11] D'Antoni, A. V., Zipp, G. P., Olson, V. G., & Cahill, T. F. (2010). Does the mind map learning strategy facilitate information retrieval and critical thinking in medical students? *BMC Med Educ., 10,* 61.

[12] Makwana, A., Grön, G., Fehr, E., & Hare, T. A. (2015). A neural mechanism of strategic social choice under sanction-induced norm compliance. *eNeuro, 2*(3).

[13] Holzel, B., Lazar, S., & Gard, T., Schuman-Olivier, Z., Vago, D. R., & Ott, U. (2011). How does mindful meditation work? Proposing mechanisms of action from a conceptual and neurological perspective. *Perspectives on Psychological Science, 6*(6), 537-59.

[14] Siegel, D. (2007). *The Mindful Brain.* W. W. Norton & Company.

[15] Snowden et al. (2001).

16 Fjell, A., McEvoy, L., Holland, D., Dale, A. M., & Walhovd, K. B. (2014). What is normal in normal aging? Effects of aging, amyloid and Alzheimer's disease on the cerebral cortex and the hippocampus. *Progress in Neurobiology, 117*, 20-40.

17 Sukel, K. (Jan. 2012). *Neurotransmitters: A primer.* The Dana Foundation Website.

18 Sukel, K. (Jan. 2012). *Decision-making: Beyond dopamine.* The Dana Foundation Website.

19 Mukherjee, S., & Manahan-Vaughn, D. (2012). Role of metabotropic glutamate receptors in persistent forms of hippocampal plasticity and learning. *Neuropharmacology, 66,* 65-81.

20 Mueller, G., & Pilzecker, A. (1900). Experimentelle Beitrage zur Lehre vom Gedachrniss.

21 McGaugh, J. (2013). Making lasting memories: Remembering the significant. *Proceedings of the National Academy of Sciences of the United States of America, 6/18*, 110(2), 10402-7.

22 Nielson, K., & Arensten, T. (2012). Memory modulation in the classroom: Selective enhancement of college examination performance by arousal induced after lecture. *Neurobiology of Learning and Memory, 98*(1), 12-16.

23 Reisberg, D., & Hertel, P. (2001). *Memory and emotion.* Oxford University Press.

24 Nader, K., Schafe, G. E., & Le Doux, J. E. (2000). The labile nature of consolidation theory. *Nature Reviews. Neuroscience, 1*(3), 216-219.

25 Slater et al., (2006). A virtual reprise of the Stanley Milgram obedience experiments. Plos One.

26 Mares, M., & Woodard, E. (2005). Positive effects of television on children's social interactions: A meta-analysis. *Media Psychology, 7*(3), 301-322.

27 Iacaboni, M., & Dapretto, M. (2006). The mirror neuron system and the consequences of its dysfunction. *Nature Reviews. Neuroscience, 7*(12), 942-51.

28 Mather, M., & Schoeke, A. (2011). Positive outcomes enhance incidental learning for both younger and older adults. *Frontiers in Neuroscience, 21*(5), 129.

29 Pena-Altamira, E., Petralla, S. Massenzio F., Virgili, M., Bolognesi, M., & Monti, B. (2017). Nutritional and pharmacological strategies to regulate microglial polarization in cognitive aging and Alzheimer's disease. *Frontiers in Aging Neuroscience, 7*(9), 175.

30 Backman, et al., (2011). The effects of working memory training on striatal dopamine release. Science.

31 Alda, A. (2004). *Scientific American frontiers: Don't forget!* [Film]. Chedd-Angier/ CPTV.

CHAPTER 4

MOVING IS MAGICAL: THE 3 MOVES FOR INTELLIGENCE, PRODUCTIVITY AND HAPPINESS

If you are reading this, you are a direct descendant of a good mover! Only superb movements allowed them to escape predators and hunt and gather successfully. For me though, moving anywhere was the last thing I wanted to do when I weighed 50 extra pounds. At that time, I not only actively avoided anything exercise-like, I avoided anyone who suggested physical activity…my sister. She was always planning a "birthday" hike or walk, yuck. The curious thing, I still lost that 50 pounds, (kept it off, kept my sister), and I didn't lose it by exercising. Like everyone, I knew I should exercise, that it was good for me, but I still did not do it. Don't get me wrong here, I wish I knew then what I know now about certain physical activities. Cutting-edge science shows us that our unique movements have magical effects on the brain.

The moment we are born, our cells and our DNA interact with the environment and dictate our quality of life. Everyone's body is made up of cells, and our cells and DNA age every year. The older we get the "shorter" our DNA strand (read the Essentials chapter). What you may not know is our brain works magic when it produces an enzyme, called telomerase, which undoes life's damage at any age. Certain movements cause the release of those enzymes that rehabilitate our DNA, specifically, the cap at the end of our telomeres. That telomere cap slows aging and can heal damage from trauma and conditions previously considered irreversible. Imagine what it could mean that there are 3 types of physical activities that generate neural growth, emotional stability, better cognition, and productivity.

The instant muscles begin working our blood flow increases. Neurotransmitters increase blood flow, and those neurotransmitters drive memory, learning, and sophisticated thinking among many other incredible things. But neuroscience suggests those movements not only drive physical and emotional health but also innovation and intelligence. The activity builds our brain structures and engineers a sophisticated neural functionality. Ingenious studies show how it builds, rebuilds and rehabilitates neural function and increases gray matter. Depending on the type of movement, recreational play, exercise, or complex, it is therapeutic because physical activity causes structures in our neurons to secrete the enzyme that rehabilitates our DNA. The results from moving happen fast, and complex movement is even faster!

A simple idea of physical movement during the workday, classroom, and of course at home offers the possibility of a revolutionary change, fast and affordable. The foundation of the changes is to use *regular* bouts of movement to sustain our neurological equilibrium. Every single body needs oxygen badly for energy. Using our muscles oxygenates all cells, detoxes, fuels and more. The more we use a muscle the more we have oxygen, and more oxygen brings more blood flow, and more blood flow brings better cognitive function! Everyone knows movement is good, but not sitting is life and death. Sitting more than 3 hours in a day correlated with an increased chance of dying over the 9-year study for females and 6 hours proved deadly for males! Sitting is fatal... women sitting had a 35% increase in death, while men had an 18%. Time spent sitting increases chances of death from any cause in the longitudinal studies[1].

Males move more and sitting is different for males than females. Why do males store less belly fat and lose weight faster, why can she only sit 3 hours? This totally unfair advantage may be the fact that sex differences are greater than you think (read the Sex Differences chapter.) Perhaps because males have more muscle mass explains why they have a crucial need to move! Physical activity improves health and cognition for both sexes. However, for a male, he seems to require more physical activity for cognitive success; fitness accounts for up to 29% of academic achievement among males[2]. The extent to which he moves predicts his well-being. Males are more impacted by irregular sleep and have a greater chance of dying if he sits 6 hours a day.

- Physical activity improves processing speed, memory, and executive function most with acute bouts of moderate to vigorous activity... with the most benefit consistently following moving.[3]
- Regular movement activity (and sports-based activities) increases connections between colleagues, increase productivity and decrease illness.[4]
- More neural networks connect and increase successful integration of important information in our daily life allowing better learning, memory, comprehension, social interaction and especially attention to the task.[5]
- Movement underlies all health because it decreases inflammation and decreases diagnosis of all disease, including mental illness, chronic pain, coronary heart disease, type-2 diabetes, obesity, cancer, and arthritis.[6]
- Sitting more than 3 hours daily increases all mortality over the 9-year study, but the weakest immune system increased odds of surviving cancer with recreational activity.[7]

NOT all movements are equitable...the more complex the move, the more therapeutic! Some activities, like those requiring attention and balance and in the form of recreation as opposed to simple movement, offer even better benefits. The love of my life is tennis, so I was thrilled to find playing 3 times a week adds more than 9 years onto our lifespan. Playing that results in increased heart rate, need for oxygen and fun is magic; all this play creates a social network.[8] Researchers showed racquet sports topped the list, increasing heart rate and a need for sophisticated eye-hand coordination are golden for our neurons. In the last few years, the research on movement is Some therapy integrates moves which relieve symptoms of trauma (balance and coordination moves, and EMDR relies on eye movements). Some moves relieve chronic stress (yoga, walks, play). Some moves relieve symptoms of depression and anxiety (exercise and EMDR). Moves can even relieve impulsivity (buffers relationships) and they improve our moods (buffers relationships). More studies show following physical activity, subjects who identified themselves as difficult even had more social patience. Movement takes the edge off people with personalities of negativity, pessimism, and neurosis—and those with a consistent bad attitude. Guess what you must do as the physical indicators for all performance? For anyone who is looking for peak cognition throughout life, science points to the ability to balance, have endurance, and strength!

The 3 types of physical activity:

1. *Fitness related moves*
2. *Play related moves*
3. *Complex moves*

A revolutionary new practice of regularly moving could transform our feelings of what was a dreadful workplace, boring school, or homelife into a playful and positive one! Sedentary societies have higher rates of depression, divorce, addiction, underachievement, amotivation and illness. There was a time when you may have thought of exercise as a choice, now we know its movement and it is essential. Why this is? Daily routines had physical activities requiring *specialized movements*, extraordinarily complex cognition stimulates neuroplasticity. The more attention the move demands, the more you must maneuver physically to meet the objective, the better for the brain! The neurons that coordinate muscles for balancing (on a beam or on a log or to cross a river), are dependent upon the neurons we need to learn all new information. The ability to balance and coordinate predict learning and academic achievement, even lifelong intellectual ability. It's from physical activity that our brain develops the neural integration that is executive function: working memory, ability to pay attention, problem-solve, create, dream and much more.

- Moves establish essential cognitive "circuits" at birth, support lifelong executive function, even rebuild damaged neurons, protect from dementia and Alzheimer's, and help with intellectual disabilities.[9]
- Immediately after running between 1 and 3 miles there is an increase in BDNF by 186% and "unexpectedly fast" learning! Those who sat had no increase in performance. Subjects who "ran"

in the experiment, maintained an elevated level of BDNF weeks after the experiment, in fact, levels didn't return to baseline for 3 to 4 weeks, which means exercise enhances brain plasticity long after the exertion.[10]

- Exercise increases BDNF, the neurotropic factor responsible for all neurogenesis, new memories, and learning.[11] Movements that repair DNA also repair brain damage from stroke, trauma, mental illness, and neurodegenerative disease by stimulating new growth.
- More time is beneficial but vigorous is better with 45 to 60 minutes, *but as few as* 11 to 20 minutes spikes cognition.[12]
- Light bicycling increases performance on a vocabulary test *while* cycling, especially the lowest percentile. Those who cycled *before* the testing showed no improvement. Performance increased because of the increased blood flow while moving.[13]

You don't have to run; walking improves innovative thinking in 80% of those studied!

Humans have no choice but to move! Sitting for even an hour impairs mood and blood flow *and impairs learning and productivity*! No one can sit for more than 15 minutes without less blood flow. After 4 minutes of a movement your brain has a cognitive reset and in multiple studies, subjects reported feeling "less negative and less anxiety." Stanford researchers wanted to know if divergent thinking required an individual to be fit. Plenty of studies show physical fitness to support and protect cognition over a lifetime. They wanted to know what happens while we are walking as opposed to sitting. They asked more than 175 subjects to walk while thinking of a series of questions and were shocked to find an increase in innovation by an average of 60%! It wasn't practice either, only those who walked, indoors or outdoors, improved their answers. Creative divergent thinking differs *significantly* for subjects sitting, walking outside, and rolling outside in a wheelchair...walking outside opens the "free flow of ideas" and increases creativity by 81%.[14]

Those who walked then sat improved scores while those who only sat never showed improvement.

- "Friendly competing" in a game involving physical activity increased motivation because it increases activity in the reward center and increases dopamine. Movement acts as team building for employees, employers, parents and children, students, and teachers.
- Repairs damage to your DNA because movement decreases negative feelings and anxiety symptoms and counters the damage by "re-lengthening" telomeres. [15] Movement decreased the negativity for subjects who identified with personality traits considered pessimists.
- More than 800 subjects with symptoms of depression agreed to exercise and reduced symptoms significantly.[16]
- After intense physical activity (PA) subjects scored 20% better on a vocabulary test. Learning during activity increased the learning state significantly.[17]

Cycling = 3.7 years Running = 3.2 years Soccer = 5 years Badminton = 6.2 years

Tennis = lived 9.7 years longer than any other athlete

Complex movements are the most therapeutic, a Holy Grail for brain deficits!

The constant demand for the best strategy and constant demand for excellent eye-hand coordination result in better health and significantly longer life! Researchers followed 8,600 people over 25 years (Copenhagen City Heart Study), controlled for education, socioeconomics and age to find a particular recreational activity added years to their lifespan![18] Racquet sports top the list as the most beneficial movements because eye-hand coordination stimulates neural integration which correlates with intelligence, (see the Sex Differences chapter). Novelty of the moves critical for play boosts our dopamine and increases functional activity (especially in the reward center and frontal cortex). Not only that, but the social interaction woven into this type of activity further allows the brain to wire and rewire our neural function. In more than 15,000 subjects, they found a 47% decreased chance of dying over the course of the study. Subjects who were players had a 56% reduced chance of heart disease and stroke (swimmers 41% less, aerobics 36% less). All physical activity improves cognition and health, but certain types of moves have been shown to rehabilitate our DNA by undoing the effects of aging, protect us from depression and bring us feelings we call happy.[19]

We are at a critical time of mental and physical health and to consider the relatively radical policy of deliberately integrating movements is the least we can do. It immediately induces a "positivity" state, boosts efficiency immediately following, and the more vigorous the better. It is a guaranteed physiological reset for everyone with a brain! You will need it too if you spend 8 hours indoors, and if you spend 3 hours looking into a cellphone, then you are low on melatonin (researchers consider it the most powerful to control inflammation.) Antioxidants lower inflammation levels, the marker of health and wellness. Without blue light blocking glasses, artificial light obliterates melatonin levels and destroys the ability to sleep or stay asleep, which spikes inflammation. Total darkness increases melatonin to levels necessary for mental and physical health. Sleep issues are directly implicated in depression, anxiety, chronic pain, and tumor growth. Neurologists are alarmed at the effects of sleeplessness in the age of electronic devices, the light depletes melatonin for up to 5 hours following. But it is more than looking into the device, the hours looking at the screen has replaced the time we look at human faces. Looking at a face increases endogenous opioids we need for a good mood and healthy relationships. There is less opportunity for spontaneous human interaction with others, but if we now include physical activity, we can have more face-to-face interaction, and socializing increases the chemicals we need for learning, productivity, and moods.

Looking at it lowers melatonin and not *looking at faces* increases chances of addiction

Researchers showed bedtimes, physical activity and amount of screen time predict positive academic achievement. In fact, female sleep time and achievement is improved by as much as 40% if she is physically active or fit, yet males' academics can suffer by whopping 29%.[20]

- More time looking into a device (computer, games, tv, YouTube) predicts a later bedtime, poor fitness and a low GPA and more sedentary time (sitting). Sitting time with low screen time correlates low fitness but did predict grades (maybe from pro-academic behaviors.)
- Females had higher GPAs with or without fitness, if she is physically active, she has higher academic performance, but with activity is more likely to have a later bedtime.
- Males must have limited screen time, higher fitness for positive academic achievement and need physical activity as well! More screen predicted low activity, low fitness, later bedtimes, and poor academic performance.

Regularly integrating physical activity brings productivity and shoves us to the positive state!

I began integrating movements in my class, and now presentations, after I visited a P.E. class 20 years ago. Teaching high school at the time, I was shocked to see everyone involved—I saw motivation-magic! Immediately, I "stole" the idea and began researching the science behind it. The practice of instituting a few minutes of moving into trainings and conferences was unthinkable at that time. I wanted the increased energy I saw in that high school class but the response in my adult audiences shocked even me. Their moods and attitude for the rest of their time learning was unmistakable. Overwhelming evidence indicates movement accelerates cognition and learning.[21] Once you experience the before and after movement effect on the energy and moods…you will never go back to outdated practice called sitting.

- All physical activity, both acute and chronic, even a single bout, has a surprisingly good effect on memory of young to middle-aged adults. Even those with identified depression symptoms improved in memory performance.[22]
- All explicit learning, all learning that requires effort, must integrate movement for increases neural activity and the essential neurochemistry.[23]

- Physical activity in the workplace increases efficiency and innovation, mitigates stress and worry.[24]
- 15 minutes of a break significantly increases ability to pay attention (executive function: focus, working memory, innovation) following one hour of learning, yet moderate activity has the best effects.[25]
- A positivity state increases engagement, productivity, and innovation.[26]

A few minutes of moving even stops a grouch. Can it move a "hateful" culture toward kind?

I have watched the profound change even on the most unwilling participant: curmudgeons, unwilling colleagues, reluctant learners, teenagers. Even the grouchiest can't help but enhance their mood...after the few minutes of physical activity, they respond because of increased blood flow and the natural response to play (smiling, laughing, thinking in the present.) That is the closest guarantee for a reset especially to a positive mood as a person with a brain can get. That state correlates with increased innovation, problem-solving and enhanced productivity.[27] More than 300 studies of corporations and productivity found the correlation between increased wellbeing and happiness which translate into corporate profit and innovation.[28] Regular movement improves focus, decreases fatigue, and potentially resets a mind block, or impaired thinking, improves insight and enhances in-sync communication. As few as 20 minutes boosts physical health because it decreases inflammation, decreases depression symptoms and anxiety upon moving. Physical activity repairs DNA and slows aging.[29] (see the Essentials chapter)

Did its disappearance cause the epidemic of stress, anxiety, and sadness?

Terrifying findings from longitudinal studies point to systemic changes in schools as cause for the mental and physical health crisis for children born after 1990. At that time, the push to curriculum and a concept of rigor to take tests resulted in a 40% reduction in P.E. and as a result physical activity. The reviewers at the CDC cited, "The lack of leadership, support for leadership, teachers acquiescing to unrealistic new policies that favor curriculum over hands-on or physical movement have contributed to the current state of crisis." Conclusive evidence shows physical activity builds the neural network for academics, behavior, and health. Movement doesn't just trigger neural proliferation, the moment a body begins moving the increase in blood flow immediately improves thinking, decision-making, and attention.

- All physical movement is beneficial to executive function in youths; short bouts, sustained activity, physical fitness, especially for school-aged children. No research suggested school time devoted from academics for P.E. detracting from academic performance.[30]
- Children with more aerobic movement have better working memory: faster response times, more accurate executive functions, better inhibition.[31] Working memory accounts for even 50 to 70% of general intelligence (read the Memory chapter.)
- Until the early 1990s it was commonplace for assessment to include projects, making and creating and building with our hands (which increases our endogenous opioids and improves interpersonal connections.) Projects that involve real manipulatives, not a computer program, technology-based projects have merit but do not have long-term evidence of improving innovation.
- There are videogames that can improve cognition (read the Hollywood and PlayStation chapter). Dance Revolution increases activity and math and reading achievement.[32]
- More movement in a classroom increases math performance in primary, improves chances at fitness (and improves BMI), and improves cognition.[33]

Only organisms that move have a brain...

Harvard Psychiatrist and researcher, John Ratey retells the marine-life-drama of a sea squirt. He told us, as a tadpole, it swims in the ocean fully equipped with a brain and nerve chord to control its movements. Its mission as a youth is to identify an object like a ship, a rock, a pier, or dock to attach to permanently (me after work looking for a sofa). That story suddenly read like a Steven King novel, once the squirt stops moving, it begins digesting its own brain...because it is no longer moving! That's why I hated my 7th hour class! At the end of a day of sitting, they were digesting their own brains. If I could go back, I would have added 5 minutes, or even 3, of moving so they could have paid attention, learned and have been happy with a will to live!

- Sedentary people make more errors than active
- Even with 30 minutes of moderate activity before 5 hours of sitting provides no protection and fails to counter cardio decline.[34]
- Short bouts of regular physical activity as a part of daily living offers health benefits ...even brief episodes of vigorous activity.[35]
- Physical activity increases executive function, memory, processing speed in 18-50-year-olds.[36] Physical activity increases working memory by improving ability to pay attention in older healthy adults.[37]
- Light cycling increases blood flow and learning. Vigorous exercise also, cycling at 80% max heart rate increased BDNF, glutamate and GABA: essential to learning, memory, mood regulation and physical coordination.[38] Low GABA can trigger symptoms of depression and when exercise or a complex move increases levels, the symptoms subside. Those who cycled at 80% in the prior week had higher resting levels of the key neurotransmitters in following weeks.

How much time spent working out does not seem to protect like moving, the number of hours sitting predicts disaster! The good news is our brains do not have to digest itself, and it will not take 3 to 6 weeks (like an anti-depressant) to see, even a 10-minute walk changes our state. You may be surprised to find it's movement you're missing. Whether you lack motivation, have anger, have too much fat or for a moment have thought yourself a failure... pick a movement.

Even small amounts of physical activity improve health and bring noticeable changes to cognition (memory, decision-making, creativity), to health (even cardiovascular disease), and mood disorders (decreased depressive symptoms) and increased productivity and happiness.[39] A single bout of movement improves performance on cognitive tests and those effects endure *even after blood flow returns to normal levels.* UCLA biologist and neuroscientist, Larry Cahill's earliest research showed that the elevated levels of norepinephrine from movement enhanced recall for the task even if the movement happened within 72 hours of learning.

The 3 types of movement could heal your life!

Recreational physical activity or play, increase energy almost instantly, increase attention and limit distraction, increase short term memory and its transfer to long term. Play and recreation have a significantly greater impact on happiness...because it keeps us in "present time" with feel good neurotransmitters serotonin, dopamine, beta-endorphins! Activity induced blood flow increases well-being, life satisfaction and happiness rates (organized sports do not...the concern for performance and pleasing others counters the physical benefits).

- All people who spend more time in a recreational physical activity before and after a "health event" have lower mortality while more leisure time sitting is lethal. Those who spent 8.75 hours weekly in recreational activity lived longer (for 6 months to 2 years before diagnosis and had no increased risk of death). Those with close to 3.5 hours had the highest rates of death.[40]
- Physical activity of moderate intensity decreases chances of breast cancer diagnosis by 40% for active women, the equivalent of 3 hours of jogging or 24 hours of housework each week.[41]
- Children with fitness and more activity have superior cognitive performance and academic achievement.[42]
- Older adults who are physically active have 40% less chance of cognitive decline in their lifetime. Neuroimaging studies overwhelmingly show a larger hippocampus (records all new memories), white matter and the corpus callosum (larger correlates with higher intelligence, see Sex Differences chapter). Increases neural efficiency during challenging task and information processing.[43]
- For people recovering from a major life event (a death, financial disaster, divorce) only 42 minutes of a recreational physical activity 3 times a week protected their DNA from stress.[44]

The holy grail research is that certain *physical exertion repairs telomeres...*the neural basis of aging. Damage to DNA comes with aging and environmental and psychological stressors (read the Essentials chapter). Fitness is largely a genetic gift from our DNA, which is why some researchers find no academic benefit for subjects who increase their fitness, they already had the bonus it provided. The behaviors do to become fit, if we are not, stimulate neurogenesis and improve long term memory and cardiovascular health. Despite what you inherited, we all possess the ability to engage in behaviors more likely to increase our fitness, movement, play. Intense or moderate physical activity exponentially helps with intelligence and to speed learning. Acute, or single bout, movement provides a boost to cognition at every age but especially for anyone over 60 years old. The traditional work out with weights will increase muscle mass and gray matter. Exercising to get fit increases oxygenation (gold standard for healthy lungs and detoxification) and even adds more receptors during the stress of the workout for the stress chemicals you produce! Working out trains your receptors in your brain to remove stress neurotransmitters better, whether in or out of the workout. Exercise heals our mitochondria, increases heart rate and breathing. Activity increases neurotransmitters that activate the opioid system, dopamine, serotonin, and BDNF (brain-derived neurotropic factor) that allows for all cognition, social behavior and lifelong health.

- Activity increases ability to pay attention (cognitive function) even for inactive children.[45] Fitness is largely dictated by genetics, but physical activity compensates...those without fitness benefit from movement that brings the enhanced learning state
- After a year of "moderately intense" walking, subjects increased size of hippocampus by 2% as compared with yoga (and stretching controls who showed a 1.5% decline in gray matter. The movement groups (not control) increased spatial reasoning and accuracy in memory tests.[46]
- Higher aerobic fitness means the brain goes to peak learning state faster (P3 state...EEGs during an inhibitory task), made fewer errors, greater inhibition during Flanker test, better and faster "quality of information uptake."[47]

- It doesn't matter if you work or teach those who are not fit, moving them increases cognition!

There is HOPE, a type of movement brings big rewards!

Complex movement…unlocks your potential, the best version of yourself!

Without fitness complex movements exponentially increase cognition, balance, and stability. We have been running, chasing, kicking, tracking; all of which require our brain to process information from both hemispheres for "an integrated response". Challenging movement sends neural signals that must be integrated by both hemispheres (and it increases serotonin and endorphin levels, lowering stress and enhances recall) which forces functional integration. Following brain injury it is the low levels of dopamine that compromise cognition. While structures involved with dopamine are unchanged, the function of dopamine is compromised. Sophisticated movement that requires focus for a premeditated move improves function of dopamine quickly. A healthy, large corpus callosum provides for "quick" thinking, articulates speaking and communicating meaning to others, are the same neurons that manage and allow for accurate obstacle running or a complex martial art move. This constant cerebral intermingling allows us to integrate our 3D world. Movement builds neurons in the cerebellum, an area highly active during socializing. People on the spectrum have cerebellar deficits, movements may increase these neurons.[48]

The power of complex moving is quite simple. The left hemisphere activates during language (speaking, reading, writing) when primed with blood flow which enhances neural circuits during cognition. Subjects who squeezed a ball with their right hand as hard as possible for 90 seconds increased language processing significantly immediately following. The integration of the right-hand exertion demanded activity in the left hemisphere so the increase in recall was automatic. The 90 seconds of exertion had no such effect of increased processing or recall after squeezing with the left hand! Controls who squeezed nothing, had no increase in cognition.[49]

- Both hemispheres activating to integrate is extremely beneficial… like magic!

A *weak* electrical current (direct current stimulation) is a non-invasive technique shown to impact neural firing in the brain. Years of research shows a boost to skill acquisition, learning and neural plasticity. When researchers placed direct stimulation over the dominant motor hemisphere and the non-dominant…*both* hemisphere stimulation showed significant improvement in motor skill learning and motor recovery following stroke![50]

- Concussion recovery is enhanced by activities that increase blood flow.[51]
- Subjects who observed physical movement of others and instructed to imagine themselves doing the moves activated the same areas of the brain as dynamic movement.[52]
- Motor coordination, not agility, correlates with academic achievement and cognition in children.[53]

That makes it a choice…a step ahead of the competition, or 10 steps ahead?

Integrating builds the functional roadway of neural connections, they boost cognitive processing—from early development to older ages. Balancing a beam, balance while walking backward on a beam, catching a ball, require a focus of attention so the body can move accordingly. As the human brain "masters" the complex moves, cognitive delays and inappropriate behavior improves, even socially inappropriate behaviors. The improved functioning from neurons forced to integrate results in better cognition, academics (improved math skills and literacy) *and even working with others.* Neural pathways trained by complex moves are the same we use to pay attention and control impulses. Specialized movements require self-discipline and high repetition improves mastery. Anything you do that requires self-discipline builds neurons that activate with self-discipline. Training movements improves coordination and endurance build the willpower that is essential for success.

A well developed, highly utilized "neural highway" correlates with high intelligence, learning, even accuracy in articulating feelings and ideas[54]. Researchers show a larger corpus callosum correlates with higher general intelligence[55]. The complex movement-based activities (playing an instrument, a sport, play) result in a larger corpus callosum. Physical transformation happens fast. At the end of a year, mass in the right hippocampus increased 3.9%, left hippocampus by 1.8%.[56] Yet the changes began *within hours*.

- Coordination training increases spatial reasoning and increases mass in the hippocampus within 2 to 6 sessions (aerobic training took 6 months to show an increase in mass).[57]
- Balance and coordination activities improve young and older performance quickly (and taper at 6 months).
- Two years of amateur dancing significantly improves and protects cognitive abilities and posture, and balance and coordination.[58]
- Complex movement predicts academic achievement and intellectual ability throughout the lifespan and...
- Coordination training increases volume of the hippocampus in older adults. Motor fitness (not aerobic) is associated with hippocampal volume. Spatial reasoning increases as a result.[59]

Complex movement increases the size of the hippocampus and even improves spatial ability (find our way, complete puzzles, visually rotate objects, process math), while our language (write, speak, or comprehend intent and meaning of words and communication) is in the left. So given that feelings and emotions are processed in the right hemisphere, it means the corpus callosum must incorporate information from both sides to allow us to articulate or write using supporting details (emotional activate right side) when writing and speaking (language abilities in the left, read the Sex Differences chapter.) Increased complexity demands the integration of right and left so the brain grows new neurons and new connections to complete the action. The more difficulty, the more neurons fire together and result in growth—neurogenesis! Exercising with weights builds cognition, attention, but complex movements activate even more gray and white matter activity. Subjects told to imagine walking backward had the identical activation in the areas of the brain as during the walking exercise...with one exception, they also had more activation in the frontal cortex.[60] Balance, endurance, and strength are your secret "moves"!

- Three moves predict math skills, language skills: walking backward on a balance beam 6, 4 and 3.5 inches, running for 6 minutes and push-ups.
- Walking a beam forward and then backward increases function and balance...fast!
- Running for 6 minutes builds and demonstrates endurance
- Push-ups measure upper body strength (there are other activities for strength building)

Premeditating movement forces a deliberate focus on executing a move (so we can carry out the next step) and more neurons develop. A complex movement (juggling, hop to a mark, throwing a football to a receiver, sinking the basketball in the hoop) forces us into the present moment. There is no room for a loss of focus. We know from researcher Sarah Lazar at Harvard who studies the MRI scans of the brains of experienced meditators that the areas of their insula in the frontal cortex, the area involved in focused attention, is highly developed with significantly more neurons than a non-meditator. Regularly focusing attention to a task requires integration of information from the eyes, hands, feet, core muscles (requiring both sides of the spine) and ears is essential to life and are the same neural pathways involved in all cognitive activities. Complexity activates white matter and improves functional connectivity. Walking backward activates areas of the motor cortex, parietal cortex, and especially builds the cerebellum (an area key for our ability to act socially appropriate). The effects appear in only a handful of sessions.

Walking backward regenerates neurons lost to trauma, as does IMAGINING it!

Check your balance and that of your loved ones: have them walk a balance beam slowly, stand on one foot and scan the room from left to right, scan top to bottom. If you wobble? "Great, you have found an area in need of neural "repair". Often people seek therapy to train their children's visual integration in hopes of improving a problematic academic report. In many cases, this therapy results in higher fluency, even improvements in math computation. Eye-hand coordination correlates with reading and math, the ability to integrate the visual information with comprehension and computation!

- After mastery of complex/sophisticated/premeditated moves, parents and teachers report their child "suddenly" follows directions, or "follows through" with home responsibilities!
- With practice, specialized moves brought students 2 years behind in reading to grade level. An elementary school in England divided a group of 40 children with moderate to acute learning difficulties into 2 groups: one with whole language and some phonics instruction, the other group did the same only each lesson began with 10 minutes of tossing a bean bag from one hand to the other, while standing on a wobble board. After 6 weeks, those in the toss/catch group reached grade-level, the control group made no improvement.

Challenging moves force attention and that training means you can ignore distractions!

- Focus is required to catch, attention in the present is natural while balancing on a beam
- The activity requires attention to carry out premeditated move: an unstable surface, toss and catch an object on the unstable surface, now add the factor of closed eyes
- The eyes track an object and naturally train the brain to integrate information; this allows the eyes to read more words at a time, (called fluency) and improves comprehension
- Try this: tell a story while you are balancing. You cannot mistake that motor neurons are your cognitive neurons. Walking a beam impedes your cognitive ability to carry on a conversation.
- Training to ignore distraction builds neurons in the frontal cortex and brings peak performance: performance under pressure trains peak performance for athletes, for high-stakes performance at work, public performance, even in interpersonal relationships

Complex Activities...once you master, bring more difficulty! Close your eyes, imagine...

1. Stand on one foot: lift leg without weight, increase asymmetry (while they stand in line, to get their attention, to quiet for an activity)

2. Juggling: start with scarves or bean bags and make it more complex
3. Balance walking a beam: start with tape on a floor, then increase to a 6 inch-wide board, then 4.5 inch board then 3 inch. Each 8-foot beam requires 6 steps, then walk backward, then eyes-closed.
4. Walk a beam with balance and add a complex task (toss a ball/ bean bag then eyes closed)
5. Dance routine: simple to complex (search directions online: Square dance/Ballroom/ Line)
6. Use a balance ball and wobble board: stand and squat on the BOSU to challenge stability
7. Make marks on the ground with tape or chalk and hop to the mark, both feet, then one foot, then eyes-closed
8. Imagine the movement you want to master
9. Dance: Ballroom dancing is extremely complex and has the best effects on cognition.[61]
10. Classic trainings on complex moves: www.brainworkoutcenter. com by Paula Peron www.spacewalk.com by Frank Belgau

Organized sports are a 4th type of movement. The elements of play, complex movement and physical fitness in any given practice or game is guaranteed but the embedded pressure and expectation by coaches, parents and fans on performance seem to negate the emotional benefits. The role of a coach and spectators (parents for younger athletes) are a significant factor and the chances of negative feedback are high; scientific studies do not support organized as a consistent benefit to mental health. In fact, organized sports can contribute to anxiety and depressive symptoms.

Why does play and recreation have a significantly greater impact on happiness than organized sports? Play decreases stress and especially reduces the risk of depression in young adults.[62]

- "Present time" recreational activities lower stress and increases feelings of enjoyment because of the increased serotonin, dopamine, and beta-endorphins!
- Provides emotional stability: social interaction, sleep, nutrition, mitigate stress

- Personal control in the activity is the most therapeutic factor. When the individual has the power to be involved or not, they have low stress and feel at "ease"
- Individual control brings a sense of well-being (not controlled by coach or organizer)
- Outdoor activities allow the time in the sun that lowers melatonin levels and allow the right amount after dark for falling asleep quickly, getting into slow wave, and staying asleep.
- Cross-fit has the makings of the right moves but *must* be play and recreation and teams.

Our greatest hope is play!

The perfect moment for a game: catching or throwing at a target is just what we need for our brain. Despite anyone's disdain at the suggestion of movement, they will play anyway and after the break, recognize the increased energy and better mood...laughing, moving, interacting, increased endogenous opioids and are like an internal happy serum! Even the greatest skeptics will be shocked at the effect! A short 15 minutes of learning followed by activity or fun increases learning capacity! Researcher David McClelland found his MIT lab rats learned to run complex mazes faster than rats without breaks. The limited 10 minutes meant the rat consolidated new accelerated performance. It makes more sense, anyway, dividing incoming information into 15-minute chunks is brain-friendly. Chunking incoming information improves working memory and all information processing (see the Memory chapter). Movement increases blood flow and oxygenation that fuels[63] attention for 20 to 30 minutes and may even decrease the need for some to use medication for attention deficits.[64]

- Even 3 to 5 short physical activities (PA) for only 2 minutes have health and fitness benefits. Integrating regular PA to the school day or workday counts toward minimum daily movement and increases the chances for Americans to meet those guidelines,[65]
- Brief, high intensity "fun" activities set to music increase attention, decrease errors. Up to 10 minutes of an activity increases time on-task by up to 11%.[66] Their research found no reason to ask

students to come before school, or to extend the day…integrated throughout the day.

- Chances of sustaining movement increase by 50% when it is a group effort. Find another to walk with, you must surround yourself with people. Play catch, run relays, kick the can, line dance (a crowd pleaser, everyone secretly loves it but grown men do it solely because it is impolite not to…) throw a Frisbee, in pairs, in threes with small or large or any type of arrangement. Most important, remember the "games" you played as a kid and then notice what is considered "play" today and all around you. Modify any move to fun and bring it.
- Standing benefits v. sitting are clear, but "stand-desks" have a large cost, and limited effects on motivation, and add little or no team building that comes with interactive movement.
- Play Activities: kickball, ping-pong, corn hole, badminton, field-hockey increase group affiliation.
- Look for physical activities: Jump rope, walk/jog/run, plank, mountain climbers, squats, wall-sit

Never doubt the willingness to play, even if they are wearing a suit and tie…

Moving is the fastest path to energy, to counter stress and to bring feelings of happy. Playing increases endogenous opioids! Playing increases neural activity in the reward system: dopamine, serotonin, norepinephrine, oxytocin, beta endorphins and other chemicals that establish moods and learning. Unlike organized sports with the pressure of performing, coaching and managing parents, playing happens in a safe environment. Team building creates relationships and defuses "bully behaviors". People become "friends" with strangers quickly; playing together establishes a relationship and the team-like bond protects health and increases cooperation.[67]

You have absolute power…professionals, educators, parents, and everyone with a brain!

There is a reason why Google and Microsoft have the "Best Corporate Culture." If we are not guided into physical activity you will hear these words,

"I understand the research but I teach *content…I don't have time for games.*" Oh gosh yes, we do! The current sedentary culture has increased depression and increased rude behaviors and decreased feelings of joy and energy in our schools and our corporate institutions. Now it is essential to integrate movement to fuel beneficial outcomes. Within seconds of a game we laugh out loud, forget worries or fears, build relationships, and can quickly return to work and learning with renewed stamina, efficiency, and innovation.

"You don't have to stop for a movement break…they will take it without you!"

You must have courage, it's scary the first time you integrate some movement where there was none. A few years ago, I was invited to train 65 Superintendents at a State Conference about the beneficial effects of movement and respecting sex-differences. An hour into the training I was crippled with fear that they wouldn't approve of "movement" but I forced myself to stop my presentation, explicitly explain why the next 3 minutes would be to move (of all things, the most "aggressive" game…dodge the big fit ball!) Thankfully, within a few seconds of a game (while listening to a Led Zeppelin song), those sixty-something-year-olds were running and jumping to get away from that fit ball. Let me tell you that ballroom was loud with laughter, (even screaming), and motion and full of energy. At one point, I had to stop and lean back to duck a grandfather-looking-type dressed in suit and tie who had been running from chair cushion to chair cushion, who jumped in front of me from that chair ACROSS THE AISLE to another chair to avoid being "tagged." Hard laughing, running, and banding together to avoid the tag builds relationships; they were grabbing one another, protecting each other and themselves from my aim with the fit ball. About 10 minutes later, I called them back to their seats to continue training; so many commented how shocked they were by the game, by the new energy, focus and mood… and also surprised to be interested in continuing the session! My safety-first dodge ball game used a huge fit ball that never left the ground; if you were tagged (touched by ball) you do 3 pushups.

- Directed instruction on motor skills resulted in a successful intervention for underachieving students after a 9-year longitudinal study. Students without motor skill deficits reported highest performance in school while those with high motor skill deficit report lowest, and

- Longitudinal studies that followed students for 9 years showed subjects with daily P.E. for 45 minutes resulted in significant increase in motor skills. Males had significant academic success compared to males who had only 2 weekly P.E. sessions, there was no achievement gap for males and females in the 5 times for 45 minutes[68] and

- Motor deficits in 1st, 2nd and 3rd school years indicate attention and academic deficits

- Training balance and coordination improve attention and help academic and social skills[69]

- After 2 years of playing football those with good motor skills like balance and coordination had significantly higher IQ scores and "adaptive" behavior than children who did not play a sport.[70]

I can be hateful at the idea of a hard work out: running makes me think exhaustion, jumping rope makes me think shin splints, and lifting a weight makes my body shake. But that all changed after hearing Dr. Ratey at a conference when he announced even a *few minutes* of physical activity brings shocking results! After 5 minutes of jumping rope subjects could handle the symptoms related to depression, bipolar disorder, attention deficits, substance use withdrawal (specifically alcohol, tobacco) for another hour. They expected 20 minutes to do the trick, but the findings by far, surpassed their expectations...it happened at 10! I sat up straight at the 10-minute thing to say aloud "Yessssss!!!" For smokers trying to quit, it took only 5 minutes. People suffering from nasty withdrawal symptoms felt relief from their misery...they found 5 minutes on a treadmill allowed them to go for 50 minutes without symptoms!

Activity tempers the most painful symptoms a person can experience and now we have the research to show it improves our ability to learn, control ADD, deal with anxieties and moods, aging, and addiction. This at a time when legislators' decisions lead to cuts in P.E. and recess to spend more time preparing for standardized tests! Endless research refutes removing any recess or daily physical activity to improve performance. This isn't controversial, the findings are conclusive; physical activity and success and academics are intertwined. This couldn't be clearer... all of the "problems" we face in life, work and education improve when we're physically active. Not only will you feel better, you'll be able to think clearly and focus after one 10-minute walk!

- The U.S. is First in International Math Tests! Four physical educators in Naperville focused on getting students physically fit. When they began, more than 30% of their students were obese. They designed their Physical Education goal to physical activity daily for every student; within 3 years, their district reported a 3% obesity rate. They did 45 minutes of activity time before a reading group, while a second group read first then engaged in physical activity. The group who exercised first made *months* of advance over the other. In a time when international test score comparison is a rally cry to cut public education, Naperville High School students scored 1st on the TIMMS, that is the highest international Math score and 6th in Science!

- California and a large district in Kansas City followed almost a million children and their fitness and academic scores. Students with 5 days of 45 minutes of increased heart rates made significant gains in the academic courses but not equally! Fitness increased math scores the most and second highest increase in reading... not more homework or new costly programs or technical and expensive staff development.

Everyone needs to be moving, not sitting, or the brain is underperforming. What does that mean to a teacher, for business (office chairs and meetings) and parents managing "behavior"? Without movement we have boredom, anxiety attacks, and depression. Watch for the death stares on faces after motionless daily life! When a person 80 years old improves short term memory and problem solving, we can have hope. For mild memory problems, walking 2 hours a week outperformed the control who were educated about memory, and better than those who took medication by 50%.

Regular breaks mean a finish to the workday with dignity—after work we need the energy for family, recreation, responsibilities…OUR LIFE! Society can't afford the luxury of traditional sedentary behaviors because we owe it to ourselves and people around us every day to be "perky" …not just on weekends! At any given time, our daily life is so stressful that it impacts our quality of life: workplace pressures, financial strain, colleague strife, relationship problems, or social rejection make us feel overwhelmed and stress. Imagine how children feel who face stresses every day with little perception of control to manage what has become relentless pressure in a life without the daily movement and activity that protected us in years gone by. Interacting at school every day, withstanding social stress and working to live up to new academic expectations without the neurochemistry they need makes them vulnerable to the effects of mental illness and to substance use. It is even worse for those with special needs and intellectual disabilities, children from poverty, anyone learning English, and now for the student who does not write "proficiently". Anyone considered high risk needs regular games as it may be their time to participate without feeling inadequate and it forces the mood and energy to reset. Simply moving may counter underperformance, anxious feelings, or depression and allow a fresh return to work or learning. Moving allows anyone with a brain to perform, to process new information, to sit in a chair, or to be nice to the right people… especially those they prefer not to!

If we only do *one thing to make a difference*! Let's move it!

1. Lead with your research!
   Never bring movement of any kind to a non-traditional setting without explaining why! Always lead with your research or you will lose credibility. Neuroscience shows moving increases gray matter, white matter, attention, energy and self-control! No one will participate without it!

2. Physical activity is perpetual and at least hourly…
   Every learning and work environment must limit sitting to 20 minutes (especially children and adolescence). "Train" to return immediately following. (see the Navy Seal Training for explicit training for discipline). Modern schedules where long periods of sitting can be changed.

- Prevent pain: move regularly, hang on an inversion table (increases blood flow, helps pain immediately, and resets energy and cognition immediately following)

3. Notice changes in behavior: after one training, a principal hired to be a "disciplinarian", told the staff to integrate movement and games frequently. It took two months for the next student to be sent to a principal.

- Teachers in a lock down facility for males said they left a movement training laughing at how they had no doubt it would be chaos! Two months later they stood in front of me saying they owed me an apology. They accomplished much more and had better discipline and productivity. Most importantly, they said the greatest change was improved relationships, their students connected to them and to one another.

- Middle school teachers are funny, honest and intimidate me. One came to me saying, "You said get students out of their desks every 20 minutes. Well, I did, and they were jerks, and I yelled at them to sit back down." I sat down furious then stood up again, "No! I need to move as much as you do! We are going to do this again, you will play the game right and then get back to work for 20 minutes, then we will play again for a few minutes and you will get to work again! They did it and now I don't have to retire thanks to you. You gave me my profession and my life back." She casually turned away and continued walking—I then collapsed there with relief.

4. Integrate physical activity and movement with hands-on activities: Human development is promoted through play; high levels of thought processing, creativity, and innovation correlate with more playtime as a child and sophisticated movement with our hands and fingers (Brown, 2009) ALL LEARNING SHOULD INCLUDE PHYSICAL MOVEMENT AND HANDS ON

- Vigorous movement and play are essential activities for the long-term development of cognitive abilities and social development (Panksepp, 2012, Pelligrini, 2009)

5. Four to fifteen minutes of moving improves cognition during and after: Teachers reported class behavior to be significantly better after 15-minutes of recess as compared to students given no break (Barros, Silver & Stein, 2009)

- Ten minutes of class activity increases verbal and motor skills and time on task behavior—especially for special needs students (Mahar 2006, 2011)
- Students allowed to participate in recess are significantly more active and have a decreased incidence of diabetes and obesity (Babkes Sellino, Sinclair, Partridge & McClary King, 2010)

The fun of playing a game together hypnotizes into feelings of joy about the workday, school day, and especially time at home! You can't make this up, when I taught government, a senior boy said out loud, "I love Federalism"! He did not love Federalism, he loved the playtime laced into it, the physiology of play confused him to love the no fun stuff! In life we have things my Dad called the "no-fun" stuff. Using physical activity sweetens it, whether new rules, policies, testing or a bad day, 3 to 5 minutes of a vigorous movement, or "complex" move has a *significant* effect on energy and ability.

What if only a few minutes of playing, interacting with others like teammates and friends bring joy back to work and school? What if the side-effects are improved health (physical and mental), decreased health care costs, less fat, more muscle, better eye-hand coordination (increases visual integration and intelligence) increased productivity, happiness and result in kindness, and camaraderie?!

- Exercise dictates the size of the hippocampus (which stores new memories). Exercise creates stem cells, stimulates BDNF (brain derived neurotropic factor) and neural plasticity. Up to 40% of our spatial memory is attributed to this structure!!!

Train like Navy Seals so you can do what seems impossible

Let me tell you, anyone in a position of managing people needs to control attitudes!

Navy Seal team training is totally dependent upon calm under pressure. Seal training offers managers, teachers, and parents a concrete plan for training for best performance under pressure. In a horrifying underwater problem-solving task, seal instructors explained they would deliberately compromise breathing apparatus to allow Seals-in-training an opportunity to solve a nasty task while under water. Not surprisingly the task triggers panic. When the brain is worrying and anticipating something bad, our breathing changes unconsciously to roughly 10% our normal breath (that means oxygen deprivation if we are anticipating stress or fear attending an important class, giving a public speech, encountering a bully, negotiating with a superior, sport/theater/music performance), the low oxygenation can induce panic— Seals must master this physiology in life and death situations. However, less than 10% of them succeeded, so instructors turned to researchers at Drexel University. What they offered was a 4-step brain-friendly process to train Seals to avoid panic to be successful...even the instructors impressed when the success rate more than doubled to 25-35%. That training can take everyone with a brain to peak performance. First, deliberately exhale before and during to force efficient, oxygenated breathing. Second step is to set the goal! The goal is to fix the problem (untangle breathing apparatus, or successfully attend class, give the public speech, communicate well with a superior, play the best game/ perform in musical). Third is visualization. Imagine and see themselves staying calm in the water (while addressing the problem or stressful situation). The final step was to talk themselves through the situation. Seals used between 800 to 1200 words to reassure themselves during the stress. "I can do this; I will figure it out. Or words like they aren't really going to drown me, I will figure this out. I'll be fine."

The training interrupts anxiety, panic attacks, and the act of being a nervous wreck. The training is an effective method to bring "in the zone" performance. This training for Navy Seals is so powerful, and priced right that we owe it to ourselves to bring it to daily life in the event of a high anxiety moments. Exhale, set the goal (I will do my best on this test, I will face someone who frightens me), visualize what it looks like staying calm, and utilize self-talk... "I can make it through this, I'll be calm when I talk to that bully, I can do a good job on this test, etc...." Training before the situation allows you to find a center, calm, improved attention. The training is for peak performance (during a sport, fine arts performance, a test, an especially emotional situation, or if one day we need to repair the International Space Station). These simple steps allow managers, teachers, parents to get the collective attention of a group, effortlessly. One of my clients, a P.E. teacher, said this training has made her job a snap, as she can get many students who are moving around, talking and engaging with one another, in a huge open environment to stop on a dime to pay attention to her. When she announced "Exhale," there was immediate silence, all of them could hear her directions to "move to the next station."

Begin immediately integrating movement...

- Engage in after work and school programs ...40 minutes recreational activity 3 days a week
- Spend one to two hours outdoors every night after work and school and weekends
- Volunteer or participate in activities (walk-a-thon, family 5k, Physical Education classes, recess, afterschool movement programs)
- Collect and contribute ideas for games or fitness activities
- Sign an agreement to commit to a weekly agenda dedicated to more physical activity and healthy foods
- Everyone with a brain promises 20 minutes of movement before work/school
- Walk to work or to school and commit to weekend activities with physical activity
- Communicate with your child and teachers on the commitment to movement v. homework
- All meetings, all conferences include movement goals...to remind us it is essential

Strategies:

1. Daily routine with a walk around the grounds, at work or school.
2. Organize colleagues or friends to walk to work/school, to the store
3. Consider forming a "group" willing to play sports or get fit and build muscles.

4. Set a weekly agenda dedicated to adding healthy foods: less processed food, less fast food, less sugary drinks.
5. Stand up to traditional homework assignments and propose 30 minutes of continuous movement—outdoors for the best impact! Track progress and turn it into a contest!
6. Sign up for group/class/corporate groups to walk a 5k, or organize a walk around a holiday theme, fundraiser, social cause to raise awareness, etc.
7. Integrate a physical activity chart: place any movement into this chart

- Design to use for a day or week or a month of activities with one of the three types of moving

Movement Activity	No. Repetitions	5 Points	4 Points	3 Points	2 Points	1 Points
Jumping jacks or jump rope	30 times	Non -stop	Stopped once	Stopped twice	Stopped three times	Stopped four or more times
Toss to another or to a target	30 times					
Sit ups or push ups	50					
Mountain climbers	30					
Balance on one foot/ then other	30 seconds hold for 10 with eyes closed					
Walk a beam / then backward/ eyes closed	20 times					

- A single 20-minute episode of brisk walking improves executive function for fit and obese students immediately. It improves the brain's ability to manage a mistake, use less effort on a task, improve working memory, and improve attention to task (Hillman et.al., 2008, 2009)

- 40 minutes of exercise 3 days a week after school improved the ability of previously overweight, sedentary 7 to 11-year-olds to think critically, plan, and improve their social skills (Davis, 2011)
- In a district-wide study in Cambridge Massachusetts, physical fitness predicted success in higher math by 38% and successfully predicted English performance up to 24% (Chomitz, 2009)
- Children who took part in an after-school activity where they engaged in 40 minutes of movement activities (not cardiovascular training) increased their IQs by an average of 3.8 after 3 months (Davis 2010)
- Childhood obesity means their standardized tests are 8 to 10 points below fit children (Journal of Pediatrics, 2006)

"My students come into my class and immediately begin working on their charts. Their focus and attention are 100% from the time they walk in until they walk out." Make sure to work with your child's school toward integrating movement every 20 minutes. It is essential to sustain attention for all day learning. Make sure they know you understand the science.

- Back to School Nights, Conferences and Newsletters home feature research and data behind movement in school and the effects on cognition (innovation, creativity, and standardized test scores)

Integrate competition and cooperation and rewards for achieving goals

ENDNOTES

1   Van der Ploeg, H., et al. (2012). Sitting time and all-cause mortality risk in 222,497 Australian adults. Arch. Intern. Med.

2   Syvaoja, H., Hillman, C. et. al., (2018). The relation of physical activity, sedentary behaviors, and academic achievement is mediated by fitness and bedtime. Journal of Physical Activity and Health.

3   Abdelkarim, et. al., (2017). Relationships between motor and cognitive learning abilities among primary school-aged children. Alexandria Journal of Medicine.

4   Millet, G., Giulianotti, R. (2019). Sports and active living are medicine and education, happiness, performance, business, innovation, and culture...for a sustainable world. Frontiers in Sports and Active Living Journal.

5   Erickson, K., Hillman, C., Kramer, A. (2015). Physical activity, brain and cognition. Behavioral Sciences.

6   Hill, et al, (2015). Supporting public health priorities: recommendations for physical education and physical activity promotion in schools. Progress in Cardiovascular Diseases.

7   Campbell, et. al., (2013). Associations of recreational physical activity and leisure time spent sitting with colorectal cancer survival. Journal of Clinical Oncology.

8   Schnohr, et al., (2018). Various leisure-time physical activities associated with widely divergent life expectancies: The Copenhagen City Heart Study. Mayo Clinic Proceedings.

9   Erickson, K., Hillman, C., et. al., (2019). Physical activity, cognition, and brain outcomes: A review of the 2018 physical activity guidelines. American College of Sports Medicine.

10 Berchtold, N. Castello, N., Cotman, C. (2010). Exercise and time-dependent benefits to learning and memory. Neuroscience.

11 Verhoeven, et al., (2014). Cellular aging in depression: Permanent imprint or reversible process? An overview of the current evidence, mechanistic pathways, and targets for interventions. Prospects & Overviews. Bioessays.

12 Erickson, K., Hillman, C., et. al., (2019). Physical activity, cognition, and brain outcomes: A review of the 2018 physical activity guidelines. American College of Sports Medicine.

13 Schmidt-Kassow, et. al., (2013). Physical exercise during encoding improves vocabulary learning in young female adults: a neuroendocrinological study. PLOS ONE.

14 Oppezzo, M., Schwartz, D., (2014). Give your ideas some legs: the positive effect of walking on creative thinking. Journal of Experimental Psychology.

15 Verhoeven, et al., (2014). Cellular aging in depression: Permanent imprint or reversible process? An overview of the current evidence, mechanistic pathways, and targets for interventions. Prospects & Overviews. Bioessays.

16   Hallgren, et al., (2015) Physical exercise and internet-based cognitive-behavioral therapy in the treatment of depression: randomized controlled trial. The British Journal of Psychiatry.

17   Abdelkarim, et. al., (2017). Relationships between motor and cognitive learning abilities among primary school-aged children. Alexandria Journal of Medicine.

18   Oja, et al., (2017). Associations of specific types of sports and exercise with all-cause and cardiovascular-disease mortality: a cohort study of 80 306 British adults. J Sports Med.

19   O'Keefe, et al., (2018). Socially Interactive Exercise Improves Longevity: The Power of Playing with Friends. Journal of Yoga, Physical Therapy and Rehabilitation.

20   Syvaoja, H., Hillman, C. et. al., (2018). The relation of physical activity, sedentary behaviors, and academic achievement is mediated by fitness and bedtime. Journal of Physical Activity and Health.

21   Hill, et al, (2015). Supporting public health priorities: recommendations for physical education and physical activity promotion in schools. Progress in Cardiovascular Diseases.

22   Loprinzi, et. al., (2019). The effects of exercise on memory function among young to middle-aged adults: systematic review and recommendations for future research. Am J Health Promot.

23   Lambrick, D.; Stoner, L.; Grigg, R.; Faulkner, J. (2016) Effects of continuous and intermittent exercise on executive function in children aged 8–10 years. Psychophysiology

24   Tetrick, L, Winslow, C. (2015). Workplace stress management interventions and health promotion. Annual Review of Organizational Psychology and Organizational Behavior.

25   Janssen, et al (2014). A short physical activity break from cognitive tasks increases selective attention in primary school children aged 10-11. Mental and Physical Health.

26   Albrecht, et al., (2018). Organizational resources, organizational engagement climate, and employee engagement. Career Development International.

27   Fredrickson, B. L., & Branigan, C. (2003). Positive emotions broaden the scope of attention and thought-action repertoires. Cognition & Emotion

28   Krekel, et al. (2019). Employee wellbeing, productivity, and firm performance. Center for Economic Performance.

29   Puterman, et al (2018). Aerobic exercise lengthens telomeres and reduces stress in family caregivers: A randomized controlled trial. Psychoneuroendocrinology.

30   Donnelly, J., Hillman, C. Castelli, D., Etnier, J., Lee, S., Tomporowski, P., Lambourne, K., & Szabo-Reed, A., (2016). Physical activity, fitness, cognitive function, and academic achievement in children: A systematic review. Medicine and Science in Sports and Exercise.

31 Scudder, M., Lambourne, K., Drollette, E., Herrmann, S., Washburn, R., Donnelly, J., Hillman, C. (2014). Aerobic capacity and cognitive control in elementary school-age children. Medicine & Science in Sports & Science Exercise.

32 Hayes E, Silberman L. (2007). Incorporating video games into physical education. J Phys Educ Recr Dance [serial on the Internet].

33 Have, et. al., (2016). Rationale and design of a randomized controlled trial examining the effect of classroom-based physical activity on math achievement. BMC Public Health.

34 Younger et al. (2012). Acute moderate exercise does not attenuate cardiometabolic function associated with a bout of prolonged sitting. Journal of Sport Sciences.

35 Stamatakis, et al, (2019). Short and sporadic bouts in the 2018 US physical activity guidelines: is high-intensity incidental physical activity the new HIIT? Br J Sports Med.

36 De Greef, et al (2018). Effects of physical activity on cognitive function in apparently healthy young to middle-aged adults: a systematic review. J Sci Med Sport.

37 Chang et al (2013). Physical activity and working memory in healthy older adults: an ERP study. Psychophysiology.

38 Maddock, et., al. (2016). Acute modulation of cortical glutamate and GABA content by physical activity. Journal of Neuroscience.

39 Millet, G., Giulianotti, R. (2019). Sports and active living are medicine, and education, happiness, performance, business, innovation, and culture...for a sustainable world. Front. Sports Act. Living

40 Campbell, et. al., (2013). Associations of recreational physical activity and leisure time spent sitting with colorectal cancer survival. Journal of Clinical Oncology.

41 Kobayashi, et al (2013). Moderate-to-vigorous intensity physical activity across the life course and risk of pre- and post-menopausal breast cancer. Breast Cancer Res Treat.

42 Syvaoja, H., Hillman, C. et. al., (2018). The relation of physical activity, sedentary behaviors, and academic achievement is mediated by fitness and bedtime. Journal of Physical Activity and Health.

43 Erickson, K., Hillman, C., Kramer, A. (2015). Physical activity, brain and cognition. Behavioral Sciences.

44 Blackburn et al (2015). Human telomere biology: A contributory and interactive factor in aging, disease risks, and protection. Science.

45 Davis, C., Tkacz, J., Tomporowski, P., Bustamante, E. (2015). Independent associations of organized physical activity and weight status with children's cognitive functioning: A matched-pairs design. Pediatric Exercise Science.

46 Erickson, et al., (2011). Physical activity predicts gray matter volume in late adulthood: the cardiovascular health study. Neurology.

47   Raine, et al (2018). Large-scale reanalysis of childhood fitness and inhibitory control. Journal of Cognitive Enhancement.

48   Wang, et al., (2014). The cerebellum, sensitive periods, and autism. Neuron.

49   Propper, et. al., (2013). Getting a grip on memory: unilateral hand clenching alters episodic recall. PLOS One.

50   Vines, et al., (2008). Dual-hemisphere tDCS facilitates greater improvements for healthy subjects' non-dominant hand compared to uni-hemisphere stimulation. BMC Neuroscience.

51   Prangley, et al., (2017). Improvements in balance control in individuals with PCS detected following vestibulsr training: A case study. Gait and Posture.

52   Taube, et al., (2015). Brain activity during observation and motor imagery of different balance tasks: An fMRI study.

53   Fernandez, et al, (2016). Motor Coordination Correlates with Academic Achievement and Cognitive Function in Children. Front. Psychol.

54   Kocevar, et al., (2019). Brain structural connectivity correlates with fluid intelligence in children: A DTI

55   Hearne, et al., (2016). Functional brain networks related to individual differences in human intelligence at rest. Scientific Reports.

56   Niemann, C., Godde, B., Voelcker-Rehage, C. (2014). Not only cardiovascular, but also coordinative exercise increases hippocampal volume in older adults. Front Aging Neurosci.

57   Kocevar, et al., (2019). Brain structural connectivity correlates with fluid intelligence in children: A DTI

58   Kattenstroth, et al (2011). Balance, sensorimotor, and cognitive performance in long-year expert senior ballroom dancers. Journal of Ageing Research.

59   Niemann, et. al., (2014) Ibid.

60   Godde, et. al., (2010). More automation and less cognitive control of imagined walking movements in high versus low-fit older adults. Frontiers in Aging Neuroscience.

61   Lakes et al., (2016). Dancer perceptions of cognitive, social, emotional and physical benefits of modern styles of partnered dance. Complementary Therapy in Medicine.

62   Memmen et. al., (2013). Physical activity and the prevention of depression in young adults: A prospective study. Am J Prev Med.

63   Inagaki, et al (2019). Imaging local brain activity of multiple freely moving mice sharing the same environment. Scientific Reports.

64   Ratey, J. The Revolutionary New Science of Exercise and the Brain. Little Brown

65   Stamatakis, et al., (2019). Short and sporadic bouts in the 2018 US physical activity guidelines: is high intensity incidental physical activity the new HIIT? Br J Sports Med.

[66] Mura, et al., (2015). Effects of school-based physical activity interventions on cognition and academic achievement: a systematic review. CNS and Neurological Disorders-Drug Targets.

[67] Rice, E. L., Adair, K. C., Tepper, S. J., & Fredrickson, B. L. (2019). Perceived social integration predicts future physical activity through positive affect and spontaneous thoughts. Emotion.

[68] Ericsson, I., Karlsson, M. (2012). Motor skills and school performance in children with daily physical education in school – a 9-year intervention study. Scand J Med Sci Sports

[69] Budde et al., (2008). Acute coordinative exercise improves attentional performance in adolescents. Neurosci. Lett.

[70] Calik, et al, (2017). Examining the impact of intelligence quotients on balance and coordination in adolescents with intellectual disability. International Journal of Sport and Health Science.

CHAPTER 5

WORK WITH YOUR
HANDS: IT INCREASES
INNOVATION, CREATIVITY,
AND MENTAL HEALTH

What if using your hands protects us from depression, divorce and increases intelligence?

We never seem to be out of problems, and one thing is sure, most people look to place blame! The high rates of problems: at work or problems of no work, school is terrible, family and friends are terrible, feelings of worry or hopeless thoughts. There may be a surprising way out. Hear me out on this, what if loads of problems have a common denominator? That would be good because there may be one solution. What if something as primal use of our hands is the reason we are creative, have good *moods*, increase intelligence, and feel happiness? What if the highly adaptive, multi-faceted ability to use our hands to navigate our daily life, also provides the neural wiring and *neurochemistry* for a huge range of benefits from daily doses of patience and health to intelligence and spatial reasoning?

For thousands of years, we have problem-solved, used physical prowess, and "MacGyvered" with available objects before we could buy them, figuring it out could have meant life-or-death. We had to make our own solutions and products to survive—and certainly to progress. The need for engineering a solution forces us to use our environment, and for our hands to work with our brain. This interaction triggers the neurochemistry and function underlying intelligence and innovation. Problems from like staying safe, having shelter, having food required intelligent ideas and use of our resources aided by skilled hands to make it happen.

Like the most valuable player in a championship, human hands were the *most valuable tool*. They allowed us to hunt, gather, create or make, and eat or cook food (a labor and time intensive task even one hundred years ago); hands problem-solved for survival. Now the evidence points to using them as a key to intelligence. Daily demands and challenging tasks stimulate significantly more neural networks, and over many thousands of years of using them resulting in the brain becoming more creative and intelligent (which may explain exponential innovation and technological breakthroughs.) Frank Wilson, a neuroscientist, worked with injured patients and found that immobilizing a hand decreased neural connectivity. Without a need for sophisticated and complex use of hands, the neural interaction decreases! Hand use increases the mass of the frontal cortex; the intricate neural demands require sophisticated functionality in the brain! After only a few days of immobilization, the corresponding regions of the brain decrease in activity.

The instant we begin using our fingers, the profound effect is increased activation and growth of neurons, especially in the left hemisphere (read Sex Differences chapter). Nobel laureate neuroscientists Eric Kandel and Michael Marzenich measured the effects of "digital manipulation" in the brain of an owl monkey. They taped his fingers together, immobilizing two for an hour each day for three months to record changes in neural connections. When they compared the neural differences between the moving vs. immobilized state, the substantial increase in the size of the cortical mass of the moving fingers was shocking. Moving and interacting with our environment activates our sensory and motor systems; fMRIs show that activation in this region increases dopamine and predicts *understanding*!

Interacting and physical vs. *online and virtual*? Sensorimotor activation speeds learning and meaning.

- Learning in absence of concrete and embodied hands-on experience adds *significant* cognitive load. (Pouw et al. 2014)
- Interactive protects working memory depletion during math (Vallee-Tourangeau et al., 2016)

- Teaching practices that include even a brief physical experience were critical to understanding science concepts like angular momentum. increasing the number of college-level science, technology, engineering, and math graduates by 33% (Kontra et al., 2015).
- Subjects with "embodied cognition" (vs. online or virtual instruction) have greater activation in the sensory and motor systems and superior acquisition for relevant information, learning, and reasoning.

Physics subjects with hands-on *and* virtual showed significant activation and had higher recall than virtual without embodied, hands-on interaction (Johnson-Glenberg et al., 2016).

- Authentic natural environments bring significant neurobiological benefits to cognition, behavior, emotions and health and healing. Natural increases alpha brainwaves and calm (Lambert et al., 2016)
- The activity in the brain of professional dancers who have performed the specialized move, is significantly more active during watching a video of the dance than those of novice dancers (Burzynzka et al., 2017).
- Professional hockey players understand a complex hockey move and activate the motor system to a significantly greater degree than fans with only viewing experience (Beilock et al, 2008).

Physical and interactive is key to engagement. Hands-on is non-negotiable!

Managing and surviving an environment means that we use our hands and integrate 100% of our physical world. More than 80% of all incoming information is visual. Memory is constructed from experience and knowledge. Visual memory results in a whopping increase in long-term memory...by 83%! In a landmark 1973 study, researchers showed a massive increase in human recall for concrete images of objects as opposed to abstract ones. We process real life quickly and effortlessly because our neurons activate significantly more than when passively watching, especially in males, the increase in attention and resulting neural integration is significant during exploration (read Sex Differences chapter.) Real experience is synonymous with motivation and drives passion, increases endogenous opioids to calm anxiety and depression symptoms. When it comes to the brain, learning is natural with experience, and allows less effort for understanding. Research at MIT by Konkle found memory for what we see, visual data, is even more profound than previous studies indicated.

- The brain has a massive capacity for recall of objects, as they naturally capture the attention.
- Visual long-term memory is extremely high, even when viewing thousands of visual representations of items.
- Our brains even perceive hand gestures and can problem-solve with them better than when using words or actions. Researchers found that using hands to gesture provided better understanding and coordination of speech for meaning (Trofatter et al., 2015).

Your brain must feel accomplishment after *exerting effort*...or your brain can't feel rewarded!

Feeling rewards, the increase in 'feel good' neurotransmitters support healthy brain function and our moods. The nucleus accumbens acts as our brain's monitoring system; it integrates our emotion and motor functioning and is our reward center. Pleasure, motivation, energy and desire to invest effort are dependent upon the neurochemistry modulated by the nucleus accumbens. Neuroscientist Kelly Lambert had decades of experience researching the fascinating behaviors of the human brain until her mother's death. Her loss drove her research the half of those taking antidepressants who don't have relief. For the brain to feel satisfaction, the motor system must exert effort to activate our effort-driven rewards circuit. Even our skin conductance tests showed without exerting effort, we no parasympathetic response. Working with our hands activates the nucleus accumbens, key for processing what feels like rewarding. Physical effort that results in a "product" is something to show for our existence which brings satisfaction *neurally*. That physical effort is satisfying to the brain and is a feeling of, "it matters I was here today." We have estimates of depression at more than ten times than in prior generations. The CDC reported suicide rates have increased 35% between 1999 and 2018.

Our cortex is shaped by life experiences, but we must exert *effort* to feel the rewards of being alive.

- Depression is "an underactive seeking urge" (Mayberg, 2017).
- Stimulating/training/enacting the primitive behavior of "seeking" naturally sets a positive mood, which stops negativity and relieves pain (Pankseep, 2012).
- Imagine this ancient practice, creating objects solves an incredible variety of our social problems. Only half of surveyed employees' report job satisfaction!

Your 'nucleus accumbens' analyses if it is pleasurable. Is it meaningful? Is it rewarding? Is it worth lots of effort?

The prefrontal cortex activates instantly upon thinking of a solution that requires using our hands and increases blood flow and essential neurotransmitters. The effort is motivating, increases neurotransmitters and activates our emotion and motor system; the frontal cortex is anticipating, planning, and problem-solving. Lambert placed mice into different environments; half were given food *unconditionally*, while the other half had to forage—digging, scratching, and *clawing* for their food. The clawing-for-food mice had stable moods and satisfaction levels. "It's easier to just do it for them!" I never thought to ask her to claw for her breakfast.

- Researchers found cortical reorganization (decreased EEGs in the frontal cortex) and increased activity with the central and parietal region when the right index finger was immobilized for 48 hours. Complex hand movement stimulates interaction between the frontal cortex and stimulates cortical function; after immobilization, the brain adjusts its functional interactivity (Fortuna et al., 2013).

- Immobilization changes the frontal central and parietal functions and decreases coherence in implicit memory.
- Working on a task increases activity with cortical circuits. There is a disrupted connection of brain functioning after immobilization, especially in planning, sensory integration, and motor acts.

Using our hands increases intelligence, creativity, and motivation...

The more skilled the work with hands, the higher the intelligence; Wilson found that surgeons, musicians, rock climbers, and jugglers had the fastest task-learning times. When he worked with immobilized high skilled patients like musicians or wood workers the decreased neural integration happened with jaw-dropping speed. Using our hands may have taken thousands of years for evolutionary improvement of neural progress, but the decrease in activation took only 2 days. The more humans use their hands to solve complex problems, the more activation. The more we use our hands, the more our brains build neural connections and functional integration brings more intelligence. Did the great minds who put man on the moon have that innovation and creativity because they spent more time playing as children?

Cal Tech Jet Propulsion Lab, a hub of innovative, cutting-edge science and technology, may offer insight to a surprising source of intelligence. Neuroscientist Stuart Brown wrote *Play*, a book that suggests the more our children play with their hands the better our chances of nurturing intelligence, including future hot-shot scientists and engineers. The best and the brightest came from necessity in the 1960's when innovation offered our best chance for world peace. They had to do things that had never been done!

Is the best innovation behind us? Brown's book suggested the fear of the "old" scientists and engineers entering retirement. At first the attitude toward the incoming recruits valued policies like recruiting from Ivy League schools and demanding the highest grades. But then, those incoming minds had one brilliant theory after another that suffered glitches and failures. The directors scratched their heads and called the retirees to ask them personal questions! The best and the brightest minds of the technological sixties did not have the highest grades, nor were they all Ivy League. That Dream Team had hours of experience playing as children. The more time spend using their hands, the more innovation and creativity. They did not have on and off buttons, they found something to do. Their curiosity even took them to disassemble toasters, hand mixers, radios, and televisions. David Kelly, CEO of global design and innovation company, IDEO, said he disassembled his mother's piano, which sat in pieces for years. Electronics would have been easier for his mom. More access to electronics does not increase literacy; more electronics correlates with depression.

> "It is a part of the human drive to explore
> and interact with the world."
>
> – John Ratey

Hands-on projects and real-life experiences may guarantee the attention and motivation for *anyone* with a brain. Participating in life happens because real experience builds precious background knowledge, naturally. Real experiences whether free-play or carefully planned can pave ideological perspective, sensitivity, and beliefs. Our scientists and engineers and mathematicians who put the first Man on the Moon did not attend a STEM school. They spent time outside for hours, played make-believe and made things, they fixed and assembled, and most played an instrument (music instruction was commonplace in public schools at that time).

Workplaces, homes, school *can use their hands…* even a simple concrete product?

Isn't it delicious to consider that engaging our fingers in a complex trial-and-error tasks generates *motivation?* Finding a way to make things that come from finding problems to solve include us as a part of a community and solving problems that matter provides a drive (anything that gets us off the couch is a result of the nucleus accumbens). If a concrete project improves your motivation or feeling of happiness then let's find one and start with small. Think of planting seeds or making a thing like a shelf/box/

fence or anything, then take a photo of it because at the end of a day there is a photo to show for it. The magic of completing a project, is a healthy neurochemistry. Without behaviors that stimulate these endogenous opioids, a low level increases the chance of turning to a substance to take up the slack.

Animals who are in physical or emotional pain shy away from play, which increases endogenous opioids. More play reduces pain and increase social attachment. The more complex the task, the better! Physical activity and challenges allow the brain to recover from stress while building healthy brain cells. Complex thoughts and actions that require trial and error for learning forces what Harvard researchers call "cross-talk," where both hemispheres must integrate information for executive planning (also called a cross lateral movement). Rote or simple moves do not (see the Movement Chapter). The moment our brains begin the process of problem-solving and designing, we're given a task that stimulates chemicals to heal, improve our cognition and even find strength we didn't know we had.

Starting now everyone can be a part of the solution by supporting public education and protecting instructional time and funding for hands-on instruction, music, art, and P.E. because these experiences increase neuroplasticity. Thinking and using our hands for a purpose and failing and trying again are a natural part of life and need a safe setting. The ability to get it wrong and rethink it, allows us to get it right so to pursue an idea for an eventual breakthrough (without a meltdown and endgame thinking). This type of learning is incredibly important to control stress and improve resilience underlying mental health. The expectations in school by teachers and parents are consistently in the top one or two stressors children cite; and it persists into college age and then beyond. The high expectations for personal success have increased steadily in the U.S.

- The suicide rates for men have increased 28% and for women increased 55%, in the United States and is steadily increasing (Hedegaard, 2020).
- Rates increased 42% between 2001-2016 (Stone et al., 2016).

Prioritizing making and playing provide a paradigm shift can alleviate pain and elevate our potential in other surprising ways. The outdated idea that attention deficits doom someone to a lifetime of limited abilities and medication can now become an idea of beginning with vigorous play, with loads of movement. Jaak Panskepp found that beginning the day with 20 minutes of play or movement meant a day of increased attention and productivity. In *Anthropology of the Mind*, his book is about just this; the skyrocketing diagnoses of attention deficits have an inverse relationship to the amount of time kids play. The symptoms, including adults, decline with hard play. The research on play and moving, especially Lambert's research showing using our hands for extremely meaningful measures— generates energy and supports mental health. Play is a path to creativity as the brain secretes dopamine and results in motivation. Dopamine fuels our executive function and ability to ignore distraction, decrease impulsivity and learning, and memory. Vigorous activity and risk-taking increases dopamine, norepinephrine, BDNF (essential for neurogenesis), and serotonin.

Using our hands and our fingers for complex tasks improves mood immediately.

Making projects hijacks your brain into being present. Researchers at UCLA show us that present-time processing allows us to recover from stress levels during a negative thought process, and simultaneously increases serotonin which helps attention, learning, and moods. The increased norepinephrine and cortisol subside, while serotonin reduces impulsivity (and ADD symptoms) and promotes social interaction; moving and laughing increase our endogenous opioids! Making and creating interrupts stress, lowers cortisol, and creates a playful atmosphere. Parents know that a game or project that their child won't leave is golden; teachers also know what a great accomplishment when no one wants to leave class.

Flow is why we have feelings of satisfaction and that is mental health.

When you were a little kid, did you ever get so involved in your play that you forgot to eat or even go to the bathroom...for hours? And even when called repeatedly to go home, you almost couldn't stop? This state (where time disappears and feeling immersed) is when creativity and ideas flow. Mihaly Csikszentmihalyi is one of the main founding researchers of Positive Psychology. His life's work is dedicated to the magic of creativity and the increased life-satisfaction associated with more time experiencing "flow". When we are engaged in, and creating a project where our skills match the task we spark creativity and are highly motivated. David Elkind at Tufts University researches motivation, saying, "Love, work and play are three inborn drives that power human thought and action throughout the life cycle. Play is our need to adapt the world to ourselves and create new learning experiences." To "fire" up imaginations, we have to have some hands-on activities that result in a state of flow, play, and motivation.

> "The best moments in our lives are not the passive, receptive, relaxing times . . . The best moments usually occur if a person's body or mind is stretched to its limits in a voluntary effort to accomplish something difficult and worthwhile" (Csikszentmihalyi, 1990)

Play is our experience of hands-on and embodied interaction. For little humans, play is their motive, and a natural learning experience. Maria Montessori's vision of hands-on play continues to produce students who outperform those in the traditional settings. The Montessori model respects natural learning with trial and error, testing hypotheses, and fostering insights. Frequent movement, interaction and play are key for neural development. Longitudinal studies show these children are more resilient, successful in academics and report good attitudes toward learning. Making meaningful products or projects in the workplace, school and home that bring flow allow trial and error bring the brain-based satisfaction to our reward circuits. Projects mean working with others, problem-solving, cooperation, and integrating, even competition, to create and progress toward our best selves. The brain provides the chemistry for this sort of performance, norepinephrine boosts attention and energy especially for males. If you are going to motivate males then there must be a winner... or they won't see the point (see the Sex Differences chapter).

Just pretending is powerful change in the brain. Acting out a scenario 'as-if' it is real, like actors in a play, is a real-life activity that physically results in neural responses. Imagining and engaging in as-if experiences increase recall significantly (see the Memory chapter). Elizabeth Loftus is the expert on our malleable memory and researches how our brain with minimal suggestion forms a "new" memory. If we are to use the idea of acting out what we want to be, what behavior we want to encourage, or anything we hope to learn, it could be the most simple and cost-effective step we can take this minute. Regularly as-if experiences and purposely imagining the goal become chemical, change our neural function and our behaviors. Now your workplace, or school, or, most important, home can drive positive actions. Imagine what it looks like and we are a step closer to what seemed impossible. Imagine what it looks like and feels like to be patient in the face of frustration, to respect calm in the face of tension, to have a solution at hand, to be able to understand, to learn, to be successful and more.

Real is always best practice, and it is always the right plan

The fact that real-world, hands-on activity provides for a healthy brain and intrinsic motivation isn't a shocking revelation. John Ratey, an expert in Neuropsychiatry, calls touch the "most powerful and intimate form of communication, that can move us, allow us to love or hate across gender, age, culture." Without touch, humans suffer, one reason is touch increases endogenous opioids. The long-term studies on Romanian orphans show profound deficits in their social and emotional development, with heart-breaking barriers to bonding with caretakers and life-long health issues. On the other hand, babies who are held frequently have the lowest stress and low rates of heart disease with healthy body weights over their lifetime.

More movement and less stress are especially important for adolescents; their need to move and interact with the physical environment begs for field experiences. The hormonal explosion requires and results in sporadic and sometimes bizarre behaviors while they have an intrinsic need for engagement, entertainment, and movement. Not more technical and online and screen time, but face to face and eye-hand coordination activity.

Different experiences improve our performance. In two different trials, golfers were instructed to practice the *same* 80-yard chip 100 times. A second group instructed to practice chipping from different distances: 30 shots from 80 yards, 30 from 110 yards, and 30 from 100 yards (totaling 10 fewer practice shots). Guess which group showed more improvement? Those who practiced at different locations—fewer shots with a variety of experiences increased performance!

Online and virtual? "That's crazy."

Steve Jobs believed in face to face and said, "Creativity comes from spontaneous meetings, from random discussions. You run into someone, you ask what they're doing, you say 'Wow' and soon you're cooking up all sorts of ideas." In He found genius and instigated creative interaction; he condensed Apple with Pixar and three buildings became one. All paths led to an atrium where interaction allowed useful random conversation. John Lasseter said the theory worked from day one, "I kept running into people I hadn't seen for months. I've never seen a building that promoted collaboration and creativity as well as this." The low-performing employees interacted with one or two colleagues at most, while the highest performing ones interacted with four to nine different people on a single project! While we have to respect the spread of disease, our collective intelligence is the magic behind innovation and health!

Necessity is the mother of invention. Coffee drinking in the lounge, now through plexiglass or a mask, gave us the "Swiffer". Engineers saw someone spill coffee grounds all over the floor, when that broom pushed the grounds instead of cleaning...the table emptied! The history of innovative giants come from solving problems. More than a hundred years of great happened not because thinking of a great ideas; instead, they looked for great *problems*.

Now is the time for some radically useful solutions! In a recent article, *Wired* magazine's Mark McClusky identified the innovation trend as one to *perfect* current technology, not to produce profoundly new. The world is grappling with colossal problems like managing a pandemic and circulating a vaccine to all people (even those without modern technology), modifying global social unrest, record poverty and equitable inequality, addressing climate change, and tackling incurable disease. The time has come to shelve operation increase storage capacity for a Jobs-like, laser-focus on an out-of-the-box, clever idea for solutions. This is the time to use our hands and make and create every day!

New in real-life for our hands and thinking?????

We need new because it is interesting. The brain craves interesting and novelty...90% of the time. Even animals are attracted to new. It allows us an edge in life; we are highly aware of something that is out of the ordinary we notice quickly and unconsciously assess whether it is a threat: do I befriend it, will it attack me, will we keep a distance? We can use this method to get attention to promote extraordinary thinking and learning! All real-world experiences are replete with colors, shapes, sounds, smells that engage our senses and attention and odd or distinct features provide that unconscious interest for engagement.

Dr. Seuss craved novel and his genius make-believe breathed life into children's literature at that time especially awful. He dreamed playful rhymes and rhythms, crazy colors, and loads of novel creatures to it along with the occasional alternate universe... It hijacks the brain. Using what we know is *intrinsic* motivation at little cost. Our brains devour visual information effortlessly, so harnessing this energy fuels motivation. Visual and physical engagement means that our hands are forced to put effort into a task, such as to illustrate an idea or thought. Representing a concept without words is a complex task, especially to share meaning using the fingers. Fourteen-year-olds in a language arts class were instructed to illustrate vs. select an image, the illustrators significantly outperformed the control by 15% and up to 50%. Why? Because working with our hands engages our attention to produce a product. David Hayes and William Henk showed our intrinsic preference for the real world: Subjects who learned about written prose tested one month later showed that "illustrators" (stick figures with lines or sophisticated with shading) performed 48%-55% better on recall, while the control scored only 13%.

Building and exploring improves spatial reasoning, especially for females (see Sex Differences Chapter).

It's not easy to turn off the electronic device to go outdoors to play, playing hard is worth the effort. It's not easy to fix, or repair, or Do It Yourself, but designing, creating and building (anything you need) is challenging and worth starting. It's not easy to learn to play a musical instrument or find a group or class or choir to sing, but it's worth what it does to the brain. The side-effect of these behaviors maintains our neurochemistry and provides intelligence, the side-effects of using our hands protect us from depression, divorce, obesity and more. We will NEVER improve our collective health inspire innovative professions until we reorganize; but we need help of all educators! Forget a quest for improved test scores, schools must be allowed to integrate play, hands-on, music and the rest of the brain-friendly strategies central to innovation and creativity! Our kids today require assistance to be motivated to learn, we have no choice, we need them to become a part of our braintrust so we have to stop the 50% drop out rates (in some areas of this country).

Common real experiences can stop hate, foster kindness that results in 100% making it!

The true story of a Language Arts teacher disarming her class to create bonds and friendship that took them to graduation. She taught at risk freshmen from a high-crime area near Los Angeles; the class was packed with children from opposing cultures, different languages, and even rival gangs...but this heart-warming story has a happy ending. They all contributed their real-life experience to make up a book turned major motion picture, "Freedom Writer's Diary." They used real experiences and learned about other people and learned about people who lived in another time. The teacher, Erin Gruwell, worked extra jobs (even found a benefactor to help her pay for it) to fund trips where children could experience real life to learn. Carefully selected trips and speakers engaged them naturally while breaking down invisible barriers between the classmates: Museum of Tolerance, *Schindler's List*, and even a trip to Anne Frank's attic in Amsterdam. Live and face to face is easier for the brain to process, remember, and understand. The live experience provided a level playing field so everyone had background knowledge. They journaled about their live experiences immediately after, which not only allowed them to practice and improve writing, but also allowed for a powerful form of self-help, that allowed healing from hardships in their lives. Within months, the barriers disappeared, and kindness increased exponentially. Four years of this type of learning atmosphere, and teacher, resulted in 100% of the children graduating from high school. They broke down differences and build relationships and respected one another. Positive relationship interaction increases feel good chemicals like endorphins, oxytocin, dopamine, serotonin and more. Looking at a face, listening to a story, venting to another, talking about something meaningful increase endogenous opioids (see Essentials chapter).

The U.S. no longer leads the world in innovation. The American Association of Science Advancement reports that the US ranks 60th in the world in its proportion of college graduates receiving natural science and engineering degrees. Carl Weimer, a recipient of a Nobel Peace Prize, dug deeper into the "60% phenomenon". Why did most of the engineering and science freshman drop out? They answered they were afraid to be wrong when they were looking for the right answer, he blamed teachers. I disagree; our communities say things like, "hold teachers accountable" but for what? Shame on us for doing what we are told! Teachers can stop teaching useless curriculum. Parents send their children because they trust the teacher will teach and act on their expertise. Any teacher who does they are told instead of what they know is excellent is in the wrong profession. Of course your job is challenging beyond comprehension; you straddle your building expectations (principal, district, parent) with lessons that will inspire and shape your student's life. You're willing to invest in your work and even put your own family second. You can balance and keep your job and your dignity and your health.

Standardized tests instead of P.E. classes, music programs, art and hands-on. Time for preparing instead!

The danger in education is that the last 20 years pushing test performance meant more emphasis on reading and writing but not more innovation or trial and error. Anyone with poor grades in literacy believes if they do not read and write well, they were not intelligent. Students were leaving education to get away from the reading and writing and the low-level performers left the fastest. The crisis with this is the loss of a braintrust. What genius brain quits pursuing education because of a belief that reading and writing is fixed? The ability to write is natural after a hands-on activity! Cary Moskovitz and David Kellogg hunted down the answer to effective writing in a science inquiry lab. It happens in the context of actually "doing" science. We must have concrete steps for intuitive writing:

1. Writing must be in a form *actually used by scientists.*
2. Writers must have something *meaningful* to say.
3. The writing had to be presented to a *real audience.*

The ability to problem-solve and build in response is key for health and wellness throughout our lives; meanwhile reading and writing happen at different rates (many people do not write well until late in college and sometimes never). Using our hands results in innovative and creative students. Our focus has to be toward skills that bring neuroplasticity as opposed to something like reading and writing. Those skills are the supporting skill to concepts that really matter. For example, Bill Dreyer received average grades in high school but went on to win a Nobel Peace prize for his work on DNA repeating sequences. Agatha Christie was illiterate until her early 20s, later contributing over seventy books to society. Say no to the belief that performance on literacy tests, or showing our work somehow translates into future success. The only thing that seems to predict lifelong learning and curiosity is excitement for life, reading for enjoyment and ability to mitigate our relationship to stress. Making things could be perfect to bridge the gap for reluctant learners. Projects as focus now guide reading for and writing for a purpose can spark passion.

Field trips are better for motivation and social interaction than the fanciest 'meet and greet'.

No one who has ever planned, executed, attended, chaperoned, or survived a field trip has quickly volunteered for another! I am no exception. I have done these trips and been exhausted, not to mention freaked out, by whatever unexpected weirdness came up. But as much as I'd love to comply with the new district rules abolishing field trips—I can't! They may be the most applicable, brain-friendly, common-sense way to show our students why we need to be educated.

Field trips are the means to demonstrate how the real world relies on math, the written and spoken words, and every other skill we are teaching. Visiting a television and news station, police department, a courtroom, hospital, or accounting firm, we have to get into the culture where it is happening. Witnessing and interacting is the importance of the skills we need. Touring universities or businesses and finding the scientists or labs and showing them lawyers and judges and using the written word and speech is brain friendly. Regular visits to museums for every citizen allow artists and musicians to inspire ideas integral to our culture, social cohesion and future innovation.

One day, I was picking up my daughter early from school, with my back to this conversation, I heard a young boy reading his mother the riot act: "Mom! I told you, NEVER take me out of school on a Microsociety day!" I turned around to see the boy protesting leaving school early! I realized right then that this was the model for learning. Microsociety was real-make-believe! His presence mattered for something. His teammates needed him to perform his duties...classes worked together to make products or provide services.

> "Too much emphasis is on teaching conclusions rather than letting the students experience the fire in your gut."
> – John Staver, Purdue University

I hope so! George Richmond taught high-risk students, and they learned their content and skills because they needed to know them. He created a world where they reported every day to a "micro-society" that was fully equipped with a local government run by kids as well as a post office, a news station, businesses, and hospitals, all staffed with employees: accountants, cashiers, designers, bankers, postal workers. Each business and government facility needed to advertise and trade, which demanded all the skills essential for the workplace at that time. Reading and writing are the foundation of being a fully contributing community member who is both a worker and consumer, whether in a market, a courtroom, or a newsroom. They learned their computations because they HAD to buy, sell, borrow, and pay taxes. They needed geometry to create a floor plan or jewelry, and they needed algebra or statistics for financial reports. Social studies were taught through the embedded citizenship and governing and conflict negotiation. The necessity for persuasion or influence and causes and effect are crystal clear. Science and the need for systematic discovery inspires experiments; manufacturers need these products. Healthcare as necessity, green-minded planning and recycling become realities and not theories. Here, they learn because they need the information and seek guidance to ask the questions they need answered. Consider what this means for potential training and educating!

While working on projects the brain is engaged and forgets time and fear of failure; learning and mental health is a natural side-effect. Working with our hands daily is an experience that increases innovation, creation. The worry of failure is different here, making things teaches us that everyone makes mistakes (no punishment or lower grade). We must find real problems to solve…wait for them to demand to learn! Con them into wanting the answer…

Identify a problem. It must be personal. I asked Gloria Steinem what motivates people to action. It was after a speaking engagement, and I stalked her that night. She walked toward me (wearing black leather pants and looking drop-dead gorgeous), I told her that my students believed women are treated equally today. Her nonchalant reply was, "I'm not surprised. Not until they feel it personally like in sports, extracurricular clubs, locker room, social expectations, and consequences will they care." Then she continued walking past me with her guards.

To hook them? If you want to engage, then find a passion that creates a product or a vision. They must generate the problems, this is engaging. They generate topics and the leader throws out less important to narrow to 10 choices, then narrow that list and on. Conclusive educational studies have repeatedly shown that student-centered learning results in the highest rates of engagement and effective teacher-student relationships. Jeffrey Cornelius-White researches student-centered learning and how it increases our academic achievement, especially among English-language learners. Steve Jobs hosted an employee retreat once a year, he asked what ten things the company should visualize for the coming year. He said no to the stupid stuff, and then told them to pick 3. Thinking, visualizing, choosing all engages the brain and builds passion.

Use what fires you up, it's contagious

One teacher whose students couldn't wait to get to her class every day used her favorite movie to provide the content for all of the skills she was teaching. Another teacher taught at the middle school that fed into my high school. Year after year, I'd have a student who told me about how they'd learned history as it related to his favorite rock band! His students came to me loving to learn about history and remembered impressive details, even if they weren't fans. One teacher in Boulder, Colorado threw out her curriculum one year when she realized that her students who had limited English were failing to show success. She taught the rest of her year through showtunes, and 96% of her ELL students showed improvement on standardized tests.

They have to experience problems or inequality firsthand.

How can we do this? Consume the media: Pour through news and current topics, movies (for themes and social situations), newspapers, magazines, popular internet searches, and books; do surveys (asking what students believe to be the biggest issues they face, what Americans believe to be the biggest issues they face, what the future's biggest issues might be); assign students surveys to take to their families (what do you do, or what happens daily that you would change if you could?) and neighbors (what issues is this area, community, or state facing?); send students to survey a particular area to scope out problems/policies or practices that are causing problems.

1. Use simulations and role play: pretend to be in the real situation and imagine what it would be like if it happened to them. Use blindfolds; play the appropriate sounds; use objects.

   - I transformed my classroom into a "sweatshop" to teach students about industrialization. I dimmed the lights, turned off the air, forbade them from communicating (to build a language barrier), gave some opaque instructions (to simulate a lack of education and literacy), assigned positions (from managerial to manual labor), and assigned credit to each position to simulate pay inequity. Five stations had to work together to create a product (gloves) that would pass an inspection for extra credit. They loved the activity despite the "harsh" conditions and returned to class the next day for debriefing. The students were genuinely angry about the conditions, the power hierarchy, the problematic communication, the lack of control, and all of the other complaints that workers have in this workplace. Simulations create passion and understanding.
   - Another version: Greeting Card Company. My sister created a business in her classroom where students asked for donations and materials to write, decorate, and produce Greeting Cards for all occasions. They sold them at Back-to-School night, conferences, plays, and concerts to raise money for supplies in their classroom. No one missed a day!

2. Field trips allow us to witness life in action.
3. Invite guest speakers...dream big. Ask the PERFECT person for your group to hear. Many speakers have the funds to travel to you. Erin Gruwell brought in speakers from around the world. One of my clients brought in Paul Rusesabagina, the hero from *Hotel Rwanda*.
4. Inspire through your passion. Moods are contagious, and you'll inspire with your favorite things...

   - *Show Tunes.* In desperation, an ELL teacher took her unmotivated students on a field trip to see a musical. When they returned, she noticed that they enjoyed the show and wanted to talk about their experiences. She quickly found curriculum in the song lyrics, and musical score into their mandated curriculum—for the rest of the year. The students were highly engaged, and more than 90% showed improvement for the first time on standardized tests.

- *Titanic.* The movie inspired many people to learn the history surrounding the ill-fated ship. One of my clients returned to her elementary school classroom and harnessed her students' interest for this event. They learned all of their content using the story of the Titanic. They decorated their room using measurements from the ship to recreate as much as they could to scale, and their readings, writings, science, and math were all applied using the sinking of the Titanic as the real-life event. The students made record growth on their test scores, and they were highly engaged!
- *The Beatles.* Year after year, I would have students who would break into applause and tell me how they had a teacher in middle school who taught every single history unit through the history of the Beatles! Every topic was in relation to where they were and what countries they traveled to. The uninteresting topics—politics, economics, social movements, and beliefs and values—now came to life with the energy and real happenings of the Beatles laced in!
- *Earthquakes or Acts of God.* Science has been left out of many classrooms. This is an easy way to re-integrate the topic. A few years ago, a teacher introduced her students to a website with data on all seismic activity around the world. Fascinated with real-time data and earthquake-watching, they arrived in class highly motivated to follow the activity. The data provided math lessons, geography, culture, reading for a purpose, and writing with meaningful details!

5. Do projects every day. *Make something.* Each day, the human brain needs to build something.

- *Create a book/project* using Dr. Seuss books as a template.
- *Publish* a magazine—electronic or print.
- *Sculpt* an object related to a concept or topic.
- *Manipulate* something (pick something you can use over and over: Legos, constructs, Lincoln logs, Tinker toys, straws, or any

item purchased in bulk) to represent an object relevant to the skill or topic being taught. (Using real-world objects leads to an 82% recall rate.)

6. Present all work to a real audience (families, companies; include writing, projects, research, etc.).
7. Brainstorm and produce an all-encompassing event or project (as a team, company, class, or family).
8. Design a "Patch" or "Special Event" Card. NASA has designed a patch for every mission to outer space. What factors would your class select for your badge to commemorate your year together?
9. Have "achievement" belts: Martial arts classes assign a white belt to each student. Adding colored tape to the belt will keep track of their progress. Every business, classroom, and family member need a belt with colored tape (figuratively) to show an important behavior or achievement.

Hammers and nails engage every teenager, adult, and unmotivated brain!

What solutions can a hammer inspire? All citizens of industrial countries support public schools in order to improve opportunities for all, which in turn supports the safety of our entire country. Economic opportunity decreases crime rates. "I don't have kids in school anymore! I shouldn't pay for it in taxes, it's not fair." Access to quality education, publicly funded, provides access to learning, no matter what your social class. This increases the chance that all can enjoy the benefits; when someone else's child learns skills, how to behave responsibly, how to interact, and the fundamentals of literacy, we improve our collective quality of life. Everyone deserves to leave their home, be in public, and not fear attacks, purse snatching, mugging, robbery. Our public schools provide the best plan for fighting crime and reducing the size of our prison system. Our tax contribution to schools is key to our future. U.S. dropout rates have increased to 25% and 50% in some inner cities in the last 25 years, not coincidentally at the time for a push toward increasing standardized testing and cutting hands-on activities and specials. More than 70% of all prison inmates have no high school diploma. The institutionalization costs are more than $30 billion a year.

That means that classrooms are essential for engaging the brain—the most important place to excite, entice, and inspire action. In a system where no one works together on a project or produces a product, there is a high risk of unmotivated students and a culture that stifles innovation. That's exactly what is happening in schools across the nation; few students are embracing school with passion. Every single time I work with educators, after an hour or so of training on the brain, a teacher with sadness or anger – maybe both – will ask how these things will work when they have students who just don't care. Truly great educators are reporting alarming rates of students who are totally apathetic and show no interest in learning. The Gates Foundation conducted one of the largest studies on drop-out rates and found one of the leading answers to be a lack of meaning and a lack of feeling connected to someone.

Begin a project/season/semester with seeds and water and watch what happens over time. Use the growing plants to compare literal and hypothetical changes and build *social connections* (on any topic: photosynthesis, measurement, *responsibility*). One day, as my students arrived, I provided seeds, soil, cups, and water. There were no explicit directions. They picked seeds, planted them, and watered them, but the rule was that no one watered anyone else's seeds. I never mentioned the seeds again even when they asked me, and I really don't know why. What began to happen was a lesson to me on the topic of intrinsic motivation to remind me of the importance of brain-friendly activities.

They actually arrived early to class to check on their seedlings, and within two days, some saw growth! The chatting began: whose was growing, whose wasn't, how much water they'd all used, and so on. A week or so later, we had a three-day weekend, and they asked if I'd come in to water their baby-like sprouts. "Never!" I said while I celebrated that I had found something they cared about. One of my students even sent a younger sibling to water theirs on a sick day—and sent a sitter!!!!

The motivation to water the seeds reminded me that very simple things are the best tools. Engagement was HIGH, and all it took was a few packets of seeds. When I said goodbye to them at the end of the year, I talked about the seeds as an analogy for their efforts resulting in something magic. I said something like this: Seeds are magic: They begin in a kernel, but with water and sunlight, they become a plant as if by magic. What we don't see is the minerals in the air and soil and other supporting factors. These seeds are all of us, who make good choices, like coming to school, working to learn, working with others... And one day, a little miracle will happen.

In the name of fueling innovation and good relationships, and a love of learning...we have to protect our mental health and protect academic success. Measuring our children's performance is a bogus idea, it's not possible to measure human potential with a test. They are humans developing at different rates, with so many factors we can't possibly quantify them. Diane Ravich reports to congress on the history of education and testing but shared that our nation has never produced world-renowned test performance.

Hands-on activities allow us to set goals and get immediate feedback in real time.

- Hands-on activities require and are more effective with cooperative learning.
- Hands-on activities lend themselves naturally to writing/summarizing/public speaking about the project with a real audience who has a genuine need to know.
- Making things with our hands builds the neural circuits that promote innovation, mental health, and happiness.

Additional ideas:

- Resist buying new. Repair stuff, if you can use your hands. It's good for the brain and *merciful on the environment.*
- Repurpose and recycle items to avoid adding to a landfill. You will think outside of the box.
- Value and engage in play every day (also children who play have higher linguistic scores and reading scores). Play outside games: hide and seek, sardines, kick the can, king of the hill... Be creative.
- DON'T buy. Encourage problem solving and low-cost solutions for electronics and toys alike.

- Support "constructive" and "deconstructive" play. Unplanned time means leisure time and boredom. Here is where it's easiest to encourage them to take apart household items (that are ready for recycling or a garage sale) and put them back together like David Kelley, the founder of IDEO.

- Do your work with your child at your side. Discipline and values are passed on when parents demand help. Make sure to assign responsibilities (both easy work and the challenging), work in the garage, cleaning, organizing, etc. Everyone learns to cook, to paint, or to build a shed—without completing a task there is No Feeling of Accomplishment, and those provide neurotransmitters key to mental health (without them we are at risk for substance use.)

- Don't shield yourself or your kids from work (it doesn't give them a better life or help them). Working and using our hands builds the effort-driven neural circuitry key to mental health.

- Value stories: listening to a story and making eye contact increases the endogenous opioids that protect health. The gold standard in raising a child (academic and social success) is time with the parent, and sharing stories builds relationships...key to mental health.

Employees and Educators: Train parents on the research behind a hands-on curriculum and its connection to innovation, creativity, and the STEM professions. Encourage nontraditional thinking and educate on the importance of problem-solving and its role in innovation.

- Turn off electronic devices as often as possible. When you're with another person, make it a goal to never look at your phone. Opt for activities and physical experiences, especially outdoors. Technology integration does NOT enhance lifelong learning or STEM pursuits. Electronics decrease literacy rates and mental health.

- Actively observe your world: Notice what doesn't work, things you think should be changed, people you want to help.

Connections to others, hands-on projects, and problem solving can bring about what we never imagined possible and build the neural network that supports our best version of ourselves

REFERENCES

Beilock et al., (2008). Sports experience changes the neural processing of action language. PNAS.

Burzynska et al., (2017). The dancing brain: Structural and functional signatures of expert dance training. Frontiers

Brown, S. (2008). *Play: How it shapes the brain, opens the imagination, and invigorates the soul.* The Penguin Group: New York.

Fortuna et al. (2013). Cortical reorganization after hand immobilization: The beta qEEG spectral coherence evidence. *PLOS One.*

Hedegaard et al., (2020). Increase in Suicide Mortality in the United States, 1999–2018. Centers for Disease Control. National Health Statistics: https://www.cdc.gov/nchs/products/index.htm

Johnson, A. (2012). Incubator of Innovations. *Science.*

Kandel, E. (2000). *Principles of neuroscience.* citeseerx.ist.psu.edu/viewdoc/download?doi=10.1.1.470.551&rep=rep1&type=pdf

Kaufman, A. B., Butt, A. E., Kaufman, J. C., & Colbert-White, E. N. (2011). Towards a neurobiological model of creativity in animals. *Journal of Comparative Psychology.*

Kelley, D., & Kelley, T. (2012). Reclaim your creative confidence. *Harvard Business Review.*

Konkle, T. (2010). Conceptual distinctiveness supports detailed visual long-term memory for real-world objects. *Journal of Experimental Psychology.*

Kontra, C., Lyons, D., Fischer, S., & Beilock, S. (2015). Physical experience enhances science learning. *Psychological Science.*

Fries-Gaither et al. (2011). Penguins and polar bears integrates science and literacy. *Sciencemag.org.*

Harvard Mental Health. (2010). *Cultivating a "winner's brain."*

Isaacson, W. (2011). Steve Jobs: A biography by Walter Isaacson. Simon & Schuster.

Johnson-Glenberg et al. (2016). Effects of embodied learning and digital platform on the retention of hysics content: centripetal force. Front. Psychol.

Lambert, K., Hyer, M., Bardi, M., Rzucidlo, A., Scott, S., Terhune-Cotter, B., Hazelgrove, A., Silva, I., & Kinsley, C. (2016). Natural-enriched environments lead to enhanced environmental engagement and altered neurobiological resilience. *Neuroscience.*

Lambert, K. (2010). *Lifting Depression: A neuroscientist's hands-on approach to activating your brain's healing power.* Basic Books: New York.

Lambert et al., (2016). Natural-enriched environments lead to enhanced environmental engagement and altered neurobiological resilience. Neuroscience.

Lempinen, E. (Editor). Can a new vision bring new life to biology class? *AAA News & Notes.* Sciencemag.org.

Merzenich et al. (2014). Brain plasticity-based therapeutics. *Frontiers in Human Neuroscience.*

Pankseep, J. (2012). The Archaeology of Mind. Courier Westford Pub.

Pouw et al., (2014). An embedded and embodied cognition review of instructional manipulatives. Educ. Psychol. Review.

Stone et al., (2018). Vital Signs: Trends in State Suicide Rates — United States, 1999–2016 and Circumstances Contributing to Suicide — 27 States, 2015. Morbidity and Weekly Mortality Report: CDC

Trofatter et al. (2015). Gesturing has a larger impact on problem-solving than action, even when action is accompanied by words. *Language, Cognition and Neuroscience.*

Vallée-Tourangeau et al., (2016). Interactivity mitigates the impact of working memory depletion on mental arithmetic performance. Cogn. Research

Wilson, F. (1999). Hand: How its use Shapes the Brain, Language, and Human Culture. Pantheon.

CHAPTER 6

RELATIONSHIPS PREDICT
SUCCESS: SURE TIPS
FOR MENTAL HEALTH
AND LONGEVITY

"She needs to learn when it's time to work and not
to play, and to stop "Mothering others"
...wrote my Kindergarten Teacher on a first report card.

When my family moved to Colorado from California, I was a complete wreck: I missed my friends, I missed my house, I dressed in ponchos and I froze every time I left the house. That all changed the day I was assigned a seat next to Karen Stelman! Every word she said made me laugh. Within a few days I couldn't wait to get to school to sit by her. It was like the clouds of sad parted and I felt happy again.

One of the most wonderful things in the world is being with a best friend

The neuroscience explaining why you love to laugh and be with your favorite people is impressive. Though studies on laughter are in the infant stages, we know laughter is integral to all relationships and is nothing less than magic. In one study with more than 1,000 subjects, researchers instructed each to select the "speakers" they would choose as a friend. Subjects overwhelmingly chose speakers who laughed as opposed to those who did not[1]. It's a main ingredient we look for as *likeability* gives us a clue that a laughing person is a safe person; it's the universal invitation to be my friend. Here is why you need to know this, the better the ability to maintain a group, the happier and healthier you will be over your lifetime! That feeling of joy is now explained by years of science. Research gives that data that predicts whether we will be successful, you see, it's²scripted by our ability to have friends.

Why do you like them? The laughing! People like people who laugh!

In 1938, Scientists at Harvard University began one of the most compelling studies in history and revealed the secret factor for a long and happy life. That search followed two groups of men: 268 who attended Harvard, including some fascinating Americans like President John F. Kennedy and Editor Ben Bradlee (the Pentagon Papers and Watergate), and a second group of 456 boys (16-year-olds) from the poorest areas of inner-city Boston, many who lived without hot or even running water. What were those factors that resulted in happiness and health over a lifetime? Every few years they collected data, and as of now, the original subjects are in their 90s and researchers follow over 1,000 of their children. The 80 years of data, the longest study in history, show quality of relationships dictates our quality of life.

Not socioeconomics, not race, not genes predict success or quality. The predicting factor is how much joy he found in his relationships. Good relationships were good, strife and turmoil were bad for health. The more socially connected to family, friends, and communities the better wellbeing. Any who felt isolated and or felt "lonelier than he wanted to be" aged significantly faster and had poorer health by middle age. Meanwhile, those who felt they were living in warm and loving relationships were more protected than those with more money or fame or achievement. Not cholesterol levels but relationships predicted health at 50 years-old and self-reported happiness in their relationships correlated with physical health.³ Love and kindness with those around us protected their neurons and DNA...especially into their 80s!

The more friends you have the longer you live...

Relationships don't just predict health either; they increase intelligence, quality of life, and how fast we age. Heads of state build good relationships to keep peace and negotiate for our best interests, as do leaders of corporations. Members of families build and maintain good relationships with each other for sanity, happiness and connection over a lifetime. Those people surrounding us influence our daily feelings of joy, moods, and ultimately, happiness. An even more interesting finding predicts our behavior and resulting character traits among other things that would surprise you; they showed actions of the people within our physical space influence our behaviors more than you could imagine. Nicholas Christakis and James Fowler followed a classic longitudinal study with years of data to show that your likelihood of smoking, eating too much, being in a happy mood, come from the person you are closest. Proximity influences more than you would expect; the data showed our emotions like joy and happiness travel through your group. You do what your friends, your friend's friend, and those friend's friends are doing!

They used the Framingham study which began following WWII, because military doctors returned from Europe with the realization that other cultures did not have high rates of cardiovascular mortality. They wanted to identify the factor that increased American's chances of heart attack. The 70-year study showed behaviors spread through social networks like a contagious disease. They found we "share" obesity, smoking, loneliness, happiness and many other things we don't think of as a communicable. Depending upon the type of relationship we are more likely to match the behavior. A spouse or close friend increases the chance of obesity and increases the chance of quitting smoking but not a neighbor or acquaintance. For a sibling, loneliness doesn't spread; however, loneliness spreads to a friend.

Another surprise was behaviors and moods don't always spread to the opposite sex. For whatever reason, females are less susceptible to a male in a bad mood. Males do not "catch" female moods. The most irritating finding was the one-way communication of a teenager mood to the parent's mood. It gets worse, a parent's good mood has no effect on the teen's mood.

Moods are so contagious we are more likely to feel lonely if someone close to us feels lonely…ironic. The next-door neighbor is contagious, but one living farther down the street is not. BUT a sibling doesn't affect our loneliness-perhaps according to Christakis and Fowler, we know we are born into it and are separate from their fate. But if they live next door-we succumb to feeling lonely.

They found proximity and frequency spreads emotion...

A next-door neighbor has the *greatest* impact	35%
A friend within a mile	25%
A sibling within a mile	14%
A spouse	8%

> "How happy we are in our relationships...
> dictates our physical and mental health."
> –Robert Waldinger

Maintaining relationships drives and feeds our neural pathways and eventually creates a healthy network for the biology (especially for females) that can mitigate stress. Even a slight social rejection increases her stress and increases cardiovascular response, increases her inflammation and can lead to profound health consequences. After a perceived rejection that response intensifies and can predispose her to a life of more illness, premature aging and a shorter lifespan.[4] Males are harmed by rejection stress also, but for him, his physiology is not as devastated as hers. One of many important differences in the sexes.

The inequality of the sexes shows up in difficult conversations! Research at UCLA showed the most significant physical stress to women is a perceived threat to a relationship. During a conversation about a controversial topic between partners, males and females both have an increased level of stress, but when he was instructed to leave the room, his cardiovascular system recovered quickly, her stress spiked. That means anytime a female is in an uncomfortable discussion she is unconsciously (or consciously) managing a surge of stress; work, school, or home strife compromises health and with it her ability to think (see Sex Differences chapter.) Those who stay married have less than half the chance of dying early as compared to those who remained single or divorced.[5] The 80 years of data of these people showed relationships and connections to others resulted in a longer and happier life. The researchers followed 1,500 people and compared death rates. Married men outlived divorced and men who remarried.

- Married couples who report a caring and low conflict relationship share health indicators.[6]
- Happy relationships increase the health and immune system, while devastating can decrease health factors.[7]
- The more people we surround ourselves the better our levels of pain, depression and fatigue. Loneliness increases our perceived levels of health symptoms.[8]

The thrill of being in love is pure joy. No one wants the agony of breaking up!

So why are divorce rates so high in our country? Madly in love is an exquisite moment in time where no one is offended, no one gets mad over a misunderstanding and no one wants to end the evening early. There is a time frame where trust is solid as a rock and there is no fear of a breakup. Yet so often those who are the most in love, then break up (over something inconsequential), then get back together, then break up and it's the end. Even when both know it is the wrong relationship, they will fight for it. The last attempt is to try everything or a last, desperate attempt at repairing with counselors, with active listening, improved communication, and a focus on date nights. However, despite this the divorce rate is roughly half. Somewhere around 25% of those who go for professional help report a happy marriage a year later. Until the research by Sue Johnson, marriage psychologist, there was little hope for success once there was relationship trouble. After a year of her training, relationships in trouble showed more than a 75% success rate. Emotion Focused Therapy, designed by Johnson, respects that we are not rational, we are emotional and what seems like an inconsequential offense is a big deal to one person...solution? Convince them you understand how awful it was for them and that it will never happen again!

> "Our study has shown that the people who fared the best were the people who leaned into relationships, with family, with friends, with community."
> –Robert Waldinger

Because relationships are not logical...they are not necessarily fixed with a systematic, logical solution. Love and attraction aren't usually rational! She found relationships are only in real jeopardy when one or both doubt the other. The repair comes when each feels safe and secure with their partner. When two people initially fall in love the feeling of security is guaranteed. Trouble arises when one partner feels the other doesn't love them anymore—not necessarily a conscious idea. Johnson's research shows repairing the relationship requires repair to trust. In order to accomplish, one must acknowledge the fear of loss of emotional security and receive a genuine apology so healing in the relationship becomes possible.

Naturally, I am guilty of the thing we can never do...use examples. It seems so logical to make the case about the issue. Like most females I know, and everyone in education, I train myself to use vibrant and specific examples to make my point (aka winning the argument). That sets up a defensive interaction that quickly moves into making demands which are most often not met. Johnson's data shows this cycle of withdrawing support and affection ultimately veers away from healthy discussion and the relationship dissolves!

Those who choose to stay single have two times the chance of dying early!

Considering we take on the behaviors of our group; healthy ties with our friends can lower death rates and rates of disease, even accidents. Lisa Berkman at Harvard University showed people with the least connections have 2 1/2 times the chances of dying over 9 years![9] Our friends are a bit like a prescription. Daniel Siegel is a neuroscientist who followed women who joined a support group after a cancer diagnosis. The data showed the breast cancer patients in support group had twice the survival rate as those who chose not to go to the group. Those who connected with others had "increased feelings of strength and power and reduced feelings of vulnerability." More friends who we connect with increases our longevity as does a support group.[10]

Once we know how important interacting with others, how much it changes chemistry, and how monumental the effects on our biology, we are more apt to prioritize and engage in deliberate behavior (policies, activities, routines and such) meant to build trust. Not only that, commitment to relationships improves productivity not just recidivism and will create an optimal learning setting. By building relationships and starting in our home, we build trust and harmony and intelligence and that's why everyone with a brain has to learn to manage their behaviors and to get along with others.

> "There isn't time, so brief is life, for bickerings,
> apologies, heartburnings, callings to
> account. There is only time for loving, and
> but an instant, so to speak, for that."
>
> –Mark Twain

Even small stressors change our physiology and stall the immune system. Even a scrape will take 2 or 3 extra days to heal. A UCLA study showed couples asked to argue about a minor conflict while wearing heart and EEG monitors to show the immediate changes to heart rate and brainwaves. Remember how that effects his cardiovascular system? It increases activity in the amygdala (fight or flight, emotion center). That's why the male instructed to leave the "arranged argument," had lowered blood pressure and returned to his baseline quickly. But you see, hers did not; hers SKYROCKETED. Her feeling of loss isn't necessarily rational. She has to deliberately calm herself down: breathe to the count of ten, self-talk to herself "he's not leaving this relationship, he is taking a break." The more practice she has thinking and performing under an increased level of stress, the better her performance becomes (see In the Zone chapter). Engaging in conversation about what to do to calm down, how to dispel feelings of loss and other physiological response can protect her from disease. When she lowers her stress levels after a conflict, her immune system can rebound.

A Stanford study found long-term happiness to be significantly higher in a home with a female who says she deliberately orchestrates interactions in the family. I hate when everyone is mad because I am so stressed. Feeling the "burden to manage emotions" allowed significant benefits to the family as a whole; surprisingly, the data showed little impact where the father cooled quickly.[11] Deliberately lowering her stress level after an upsetting event improves her chances of a long-term marriage significantly.

The real reason marriages and relationships fail? A fear that you don't love me anymore!

Almost all girls, even as she grows up, respond to negative emotion and move to intervene to help when someone feels bad. Considering women depend upon others and trusted relationships for her survival (historically) and the wellbeing of her baby...evolutionary biologists suggest that threat is a life and death concern to her. For the most part, many studies show women overwhelmingly feel a responsibility to manage or solve conflict in the home.[12] Yet despite her efforts to manage conflict, the data on lifespan for married males consistently suggests half of all families will go through a divorce. It's a behavior that researchers can identify in a 15-minute discussion; responding with anger results in cardiovascular issues, and stonewalling (refusing to discuss) predicts musculoskeletal issues. Tight muscles that result from not speaking or discussing crush nerves over time and lead to chronic pain.[13] So, what if preparation ahead of the argument, before the negative emotion, before resentment can protect people from ending relationships? Fewer surgeries, less cardiovascular illness and higher intelligence come with less conflict!

We cannot survive alone. Historically, we have depended on others for help with the necessities: hunt and prepare food, build shelter, allow for better protection. Thousands of years ago it was essential to be a part of a group; males needed help...carrying food to the group, females needed help...when taking care of a baby! Even a "bad" relationship improves our chances, there's another person to call 911 in the event of a health emergency. We connect consciously and unconsciously... especially when people laugh a lot.

The more relationships, good or bad, decreases your chance of dying in the next 9 years!

What would happen over time if you didn't have anyone to talk to on a bad day? Subjects answered questions involving "who would you call" on a survey. Those who had fewer than 5 people outside their home had three times the chance of dying by the end of the 9-year study. That data from Berkman at Harvard University, showed too few friends is *more* lethal than obesity, alcohol, poverty, smoking, and overall poor health. Those who said yes to being connected to someone they could lean on had the best health.

1. My friends can get me through anything
2. There are groups for whom I would make great sacrifice.
3. I feel a strong commitment to my family

If you have someone to lean on, you'll grow a larger brain! In a landmark study, Elizabeth Gould, the neuroscientist who discovered neuroplasticity, studied groups of rodents: the control remained sedentary, rodents ran a treadmill alone, and rodents ran with other rodents. For 12 days they measured new growth of neurons in the brain. The alone group in isolation had no increased gray matter. It seemed the isolation stopped their brain from recovering from the stress with exercise. The group of runners on the other hand had lower levels of stress because their after-running togetherness lowered their cortisol and allowed them to grow new neurons. The isolated rats had begun with the same amount of gray matter as the sedentary rodents and there was no change for either group. The healthy behavior only increased gray matter when they returned to hang around with the others after their physical exertion.

People with more than 6 social ties outside the home lived longer lives than those with four!

The Journal of American Science published another study with 276 volunteers who agreed to be infected with a cold virus. Researchers swabbed volunteers' *nostrils* with snot from people with a common cold. After the grizzly visit to the lab for some snot, researchers waited to collect information on which subjects contracted the virus. Those with more than 6 friends were less susceptible to a cold and even if they did get the virus, had 30% less snot and were less infectious.

It looks like quantity over quality for friends; those with 6 ties did four times better than those who had fewer...unfortunately, as we age our network decreases. Larger and smaller depends on life choices of course, but people with a college degree have 2 times the network as those who don't finish high school. Peter Marsden, a Harvard researcher, writes about social trends in the United States in the last 40 years; we have significantly fewer connections, which leaves us at a greater risk for loneliness. UCLA researchers have been tracking loneliness rates for over 40 years. While it seems like an abstract mood to measure, study and predict, it's highly reliable. The survey is available online and if you're curious, the number will quantify lonely or connected. The research has quantitative validity and you'll find the number of a lonely or connected nurse or teacher or employee for pinpoint diagnosis of lonely symptoms.

Feeling lonely activates the amygdala (fight or flight) which increases cortisol and norepinephrine. This constant state of high alert puts them at risk for blocked arteries as well as impairing cognitive performance.[14] Depression and loneliness cause the body to have increased inflammation and our genes shrink and are even less responsive 6 months after a depression passes.[15]

Loneliness shortens lifespan, increases infections, increases heart disease and depression. Even the perception that we are lonely makes us vulnerable to the physical ailments. That is, a lonely person is more likely to view their social interactions more negatively and form worse impressions of people— and they even pay more attention to negative cues and spend more time discussing that negative. That is why the amygdala is overly active and triggers stress. Social rejection and the concern of loss of a relationship increases chronic inflammation; especially for females.[16]

Our genes influence our friendship "character". In one study that included more than 1100 same-sex twins, researchers compared social networks of fraternal and identical twins. It turns out our tendency to connect with friends is genetic and *could account for up to 37% of our behaviors with friends*. Our parents' passion for friends is passed to us, our parent's tendency to have friends who know one another is passed to us, or to be the center of attention, it's written in our genetic code.[17] What if simple acts of befriending another not only improves your life, but improves the chances your child will make more friends and be healthier and more successful as a result?

What to do? Just 10 minutes counters loneliness and even dementia!

Engage in 10 minutes of "friendly chatting" to get to know another person. Researchers instructed subjects to get to know each other and found significantly improved working memory (correlates with intelligence), self-monitoring (allows us to calm down), and the ability to ignore internal and external distractions.[18] This improvement to executive functioning happens instantaneously, even better than improvements following completing crossword puzzles. Social graces mattered! There was no improvement in the group instructed to "compete" or to deliberately match or outperform during the conversation (one-upping.) We are attracted to others who are similar, cooperate, and allow us to share our ideas...that is when we want to be their friend.

- Interacting with people increases endogenous opioids, dopamine, serotonin, endorphins, increases neurotropic factors (helps build new neurons), lowers cortisol
- We are attracted to those who are similar and synchronize...we befriend those who are like us or have something in common, even who do what we do.
- Approaching increases feelings of closeness and likeability
- People who laugh are significantly more likeable
- Groups of people "share moods"

Good relationships predict success at work, a stable home-life, and strong academics!

Unlike a reverse-911 call, real social networks are complicated, efficient and extremely powerful. Considering we have been dependent upon others for survival it makes sense that more people increase our chances. Not unlike when royal families arranged marriages to avoid war, secure trade, and matters of life and death. We are personally dependent upon relationships for our quality of life: from buying chocolate and coffee, to military bases, to managing oil, to eating, vacationing, parenting, and marriage!

Your brain knows what someone else's brain is thinking...

Marco Iacaboni, an Italian Neuroscientist, discovered monkeys *know* what another is thinking as if it is happening to them. The neurons that allow the monkey to anticipate and understand another's motive, intentions, and feelings effortlessly allow for empathy and compassion. As a result, we know the brain has mirror neurons...they function in a way to tell us what others are thinking simply by watching...these neural circuits allow us to be even better at getting along with others; it promotes socialization. These very neurons also speed the acquisition of knowledge, we learn by watching others. The result is effortlessly empathizing and even synchronizing and interacting with one another; and it's unconscious. Behaviors and movement between "connected" people are sort of choreographed: one leans forward, the other leans forward, crossing or uncrossing legs (at the same time), a gesture or hand movement, drinking from a glass, these mimicking movements make us more attractive to a potential friend and even mate.

In fact, researchers found when subjects who were dating matched movements of the other, they were significantly more likely to pursue a second date. Researchers at University of Brittany found business negotiators who copied gestures and mannerisms had a higher success rate, closed more deals, sold more products and have higher ratings on customer satisfaction surveys. This neural system may explain our social interaction. People on the autism spectrum have trouble with interpersonal relationships. They have trouble reading another's intention, emotion and what we call inuendo. Temple Grandin said she was an adult when she was shocked to find people communicate information with their eyes. Without a well-adapted mirror neuron function, we do not synchronize. Yawning is contagious; you watch someone yawn and your empathizing neurons encourage you to yawn; people on the spectrum do not yawn because they see someone else yawn.

What did you say and how did you say it? We match in every conversation... and its unconscious.

Anytime people are having conversation, the individual who perceives the other as having more power or influence matches their vocal pattern. We match the vocal cadence of the person we are speaking to, or they match or mimic. These vocal inflections between speakers reveal our perceived social hierarchy. This is like a "dance" in interpersonal conversations where the "subjective" mimics the patterns of the one perceived as superior. This helps chances of survival or benefits if the other is powerful. Researchers measured the matching years ago when Larry King hosted a "talk show" that featured guests of all ranking: political, celebrity, leaders and other personalities. They found that Larry King was matched by people commonly considered in "lower social stature" and he matched personalities considered superior (Former President George Bush, Former President Bill Clinton, Yasser Arafat). These are fun: he matched Liz Taylor, he matched Barbra Streisand, he did NOT match Dan Quayle (former Vice President) and *did NOT match Bill Cosby.*[19]

Matching behavior and mirror neurons allow for social communication and social networking that allows an individual to be much more intelligent than in isolation. We share meanings we couldn't get if we understood only our own minds. These neural networks allow us to "read" one another, be smarter with one another and maybe even share our moods and emotions. We share health behaviors, voting habits, eating tendencies, exercise routines, organ donation status--we are even more likely to do something if a friend of friend does it! Understanding the look on your friend's face could change lives!

What is the number one factor that improves group intelligence? It's not a robot!

A very clever experiment found the smart factor. It sits on a quite simple truth, the only thing smarter than a smart person is more persons. I'll get back to why the "look on your face" matters. Keith Sawyer researches groups of people and the effects of brainstorming and collaborating on their collective intelligence. When he presented at the neuroscience conference, he showed the game he designed in the early 80's and said it was typical of an early game; he was the sole designer. More designers bring higher level sophistication and drive innovation...he referenced his teenage daughter's favorite game. It did NOT have one designer, there were over 200 designers! Individual intelligence grows with collaboration.

The first gamers and the games they designed were very basic in those days. Back then was something like "pong" …scrolling upward and downward we played "ping-pong." Today, games are extremely complicated (requiring manual dexterity to operate an avatar, reading clues on the screen, watching for an upcoming problem to solve, figuring out and using intuition to move to the next level and much more I don't comprehend). Today's video and computer games are so sophisticated precisely because there are hundreds of people working as programmers (designers, producers, artists, and more)! Better games come from more individuals; we have more intelligence together than we do individually. A high performing group of individuals creates its own momentum which creates and innovates and improves. Working as a team feeds each other's momentum.[20] The factor was not one intelligent member…it's a group. Robots are programmed to learn, as of yet, they do not increase collective intelligence in the presence of more programmed artificial intelligence (AI).

Intelligence comes from spotting the look on their face!

The group who paid attention to emotion by realizing the look on the team member's face increased intelligence *by 40%*! Researchers asked over 650 subjects to work together to solve problems for novel tasks: a new computer game, shopping, negotiating, puzzle-solving and brainstorming. The smartest groups stopped talking when *it looked like a group member wanted to say something*. The person speaking recognized the look on someone's face and stopped talking to allow that person to share. As of this writing, artificial intelligence does not.

The groups where each shared more built on one another's contribution for improved solutions. In groups where one person dominated, intelligence showed no increase. When that collaboration is muted by a domineering team member; a solution could be lost! Why did some groups allow sharing while others dominated? Members with emotional sensitivity. A speaker who recognized a look on their face (I have something to say) had a collective increase of a whopping 40%. The groups with more females had the highest rates of emotion sensitivity.[21] Today, there are Fortune 500 companies who explicitly train employees and project team members to monitor the looks on faces, to identify emotion in order to enhance their sharing and further the group's task. Make no mistake, it was NOT more people that increased intelligence, it's was equality of participation. The experimenters were shocked that more females naturally allowed more turn-taking.[22] Training on our natural tendencies can help to prepare males for negotiating relationships. Areas of our society unknowingly push the idea of leadership and power as "taking charge" and "being assertive in a group" and give limited results if not resentment.

Behavior spreads through online social networks…three friends away!

We even do what our friends do online. When a "friend" downloads an application on Facebook we all do. Not only did the chances of a friend downloading increase significantly, but so did the friend of the friend who downloaded, and then again…three degrees of separation. The contagious behaviors don't stop at our real-life behaviors but virtual as well.[23] In light of online behavioral behavior, it's more important because of deliberate autonomous computer programs ("bots") designed to manipulate voter behavior by spreading propaganda designed to interfere in our elections. People were more likely to comply with the "bot" message and also more likely to copy their online-friend's behavior. Here the reality of relationships and the power of doing-what-our-friends-do is now dire in a democratic society. After the 2016 election, organizations had exponential power with their fake online identities when they spread propaganda to defeat the unsympathetic candidate (false information spreads four times faster than factual). The social strife and political turmoil in our communities means people in our country struggle to choose kindness. Human behavior is contagious, online and offline, so we can bring healthy changes to our daily life.

- Social influence has profound impact on human behavior; online social media is powerful in the questions regarding behavior, technology and how much to share. (Graf-Vlachy et al 2018)

- Spending time with more individuals in a group results in an increase to cognitive intelligence; it's important to know behaviors of other individuals to increase chances of survival. Even birds in the wild tend to spend time with one bird, usually a mate. In captivity birds spend time with more than one mate and have superior cognition (Hobson et al 2014)
- Turn-taking and number of women in a group increase "group intelligence" (Woolley, Aggarwal, Malone, 2015)

If there's one thing we know from quarantine, we will choose to be together regardless the risk!

Our experience with quarantine and the ensuing disgust with isolation shows how interconnected we are. People love being together and we desperately need each other or we feel as if we are losing our minds. There is another lesson we learned about our part of our economy. Each person buys and spends which helps each of us in a community. We have to be together to visit, and to keep money in circulation or we go into psychological and economic depression. Human beings are essential. Getting along with each other is essential. Many studies show doubling your real-life social network results in the positive equivalent of increasing income by 50%, (*there is no known increase when online "friends" increase*).[24]

What does a robot and artificial intelligence have to do with your mental health and your personal quality of health? Who doesn't want to save money or to get your products faster? It's tempting to choose artificial intelligence to get what we want faster. Who doesn't love faster or cheaper, and who likes to wait? That's a reality giant tech companies can capitalize on! Companies who chose productivity and cut costs by choosing to automate have fewer humans and inadvertently limit the human interaction that is brain friendly. The "soft skills" that allow us to operate at our peak are now priceless because employees with social skills drive improvements, see how to specialize or devise more productive ways to further goals. Naturally improving, innovating, and pioneering for specialized advance is a human hallmark.[25]

Humans are insightful and drive innovation; their experience inspires transformation and progress. People have always created the culture that gives us genius ideas, growth and productivity. We have to deliberately build a trusting and innovative culture with employees who have the social skills to continuously increase collective intelligence and a constantly evolving landscape of growth. The choice to automate and use robotics masquerades does not. It may lower expenses, but a human workforce is a choice that saves in less obvious areas and enhances all industries in the long term. Looking into a human face increases endogenous opioids, reward and pain killing neurochemicals, while looking at automation does not. The more we look at faces and share meaningful stories, the better people get at communicating and empathizing with others.

- Talking increases dopamine in the left hemisphere; those neurotransmitters lower cortisol, increase trust and bonding, and improve cognitive function.[26]
- Prosocial behavior (talking, comforting, touching, hugging, empathy) increases activity in the brain's pleasure center...our reward center. These behaviors activate our natural opioids, dopamine, oxytocin and endorphins.[27] Estrogen enhances the effects.
- Females are more accurate in emotion processing, superior in memory details connected to people, and superior scores in social "ease." Females have "higher than average" ability in social cognition in computerized tests.[28]

Deliberately training social skills is integral for increasing general intelligence by 40%!

The question of how to improve our intelligence holds the future of our innovation. Consider a study of the effects of training students to identify emotions and the effect on social interaction. They found labeling an emotion increased academic success regardless of accuracy. More than 200,000 students in the study increased in academic scores by an average of 11% to 17%.[29]

Explicitly training to deliberately pick a word (label) for the emotion on a face defuses confrontation and may help calm bullying behaviors. Activity in the amygdala stopped for a subject told to think of a word to describe their emotion while reading an upsetting story. During an fMRI, reading the emotional material increased activity and the consumption of glucose and oxygen. Once the subjects said a word to describe what they felt (control group did not label) the activation in the amygdala stopped. The control group did not say a word to describe and the activity didn't switch from the amygdala to the frontal cortex. Regardless of accuracy, the minute they selected a word the activation went to the cerebral cortex--our highest level of thinking and processing.

How many emotions can you list? How many emotions do you see daily at work or in your home or in your community? The researchers were shocked to find most 3rd grade children listed only 3 emotions: happy, sad and mad. Some unfortunate people don't have natural social skills so training them is non-negotiable! *Simply choosing a word* neutralized the emotion that activated the fight or flight or emotional response that comes from negative stimulus; the teachers reported significantly fewer negative interactions and better relationships after the training. Instructional training happened one day a week where they introduced a word for an emotion on a person's face (photo, fictional or non-fiction story, video clip or other), and instructed them to pick a word for the face or for the person in the story. Regularly considering another's emotion or their own emotion by generating a word to label it stopped activation in the amygdala and allows processing at the highest levels of cognition, decision-making, thinking and more. Decreasing conflicts, lowering amygdala reactivity (common for someone with anxieties), decreases anxieties, increases academic success, prosocial interaction and improves connections in a group of people.

5 steps of "training" to shift from the amygdala to frontal cortex:

1. Self-Awareness: be aware of own feelings, interests, strengths, and values (picking any word)
2. Self-Management: use your own awareness of emotions to calm stress, control impulses, think through challenges, express

emotions appropriately, set and monitor goals (productivity or academics)

3. Social-Awareness: empathy for others, deliberately use a word to label what they may be feeling
4. Relationship Skills: cooperation, resolve conflict, consider their perspective and what thinking
5. Responsible decision-making: ethical, safe, social-norms, respect for others, well-being of one's work or school or neighborhood or larger community

Which skill provides more benefit in life: academic skills or social skills? By now, you may have noticed there are charming people who get the raise, the promotion, the breaks, as they seem to get away with *everything*. Social skills training on maintaining relationships, more than curriculum, are in high demand by employers as well.

Sitting next to someone happy enhances mood, creativity, productivity and improves decision-making. Happiness increases cognition and team performance. In fact, Christakus included a study where researchers followed a cricket team. Each player recorded moods during the game over the five days. A positive mood report increased the entire team's performance; that is, teams with the most players who reported the happiest moods...were the teams with improved performance. The outcome of the game had no impact. If we are drawn to people who are happy and positive, that means they are like saltlick for us! Training how to interact for positive and training that we can look for laughter and joy brings happiness, and happiness depends upon the happiness of those around us! It's a whirlpool.

Since we are always preparing ourselves, colleagues, children, for a world that does not yet exist, be sure to include preparing good social behavior! The one skill that will never go away is building and maintaining connections with others...success demands it. We are not doomed to poor friendships like we are doomed to losing our hair, but we are in trouble if we tear one another down. Access to this type of education has never been more important!

Hillary Rodham Clinton is right "It takes a village" for the rest of our lives!

The studies show the ability to build a good relationship actually predicts academics with more reliability than at risk factors predict failure. In fact, the studies are so compelling, relationship building should serve as the go-to intervention for all low achievement. The important relationship is parent children which dictates student to teacher! When a student has a positive connection with a teacher, they have a significantly increased chance of academic success.

How do we know they are connected? Ask these 3 questions…

1. Are people treated fairly at school?
2. Are you close to people at school?
3. Do you feel a part of the school?

Students who go to school together have similar proximity to a next-door neighbor. They now have a chance at increasing happiness by 35%. What if we train them to be happy, look for happy, pretend to be happy, and explain why! The key to success is to get along with others; that means we have to train them to find what makes them happy, and actively work toward happiness, every day.

Evidence shows us connecting results in success…

Positive relationships naturally bring relevance that engages and encourages thinking. Students in learner-centered classrooms outperform all other educational strategies in academics. The evidence shows increased participation, improved critical-thinking, increased math achievement, lower dropout rates, motivation, increased IQ, higher grades. Jeffrey Cornelius-White found learner-centered classrooms result in significantly higher numbers of quality relationships. Learner-centered happens when the teacher integrates the student's interests to teach curriculum and projects which naturally improve relationships. The intrinsic motivation makes learning in that environment effortless and enhances discourse. Students in these classrooms report significantly more social connections and have very low rates of disruptive behavior and fewer absences.

Teachers spend more time with certain students...oh no! You would be wrong if you think the amount of time a teacher spends with a student means it's a positive relationship. Studies indicated teachers spent more time with males, but it turns out time interacting is NOT an indicator of a positive relationship-- it's indicative of a bad one. Basically 2 words indicate the connection: conflict and closeness. Kathleen Rudasill, researcher at University of Lincoln-Nebraska found conflict is simply disharmony, "I always seem to be struggling with..." Whereas closeness is warmth and open communication. "I share an affectionate, warm feeling with..." Conflict or closeness predicted academic achievement or failure.

Educational trends have forced public education into valuing the trek to increase test scores which has had so far tragic effects. State departments push policies that drain the meaningful curriculum to make room for test-preparation. For a truly excellent school system, state legislators have to require State departments to force public educators to build a solid relationship with every student. So many leaders and administrators believe the evidence-based instructional strategies ensure success. Harvard researchers found higher quality relationships between teacher and student encourages participation and engagement[30]. The more a child participates and is engaged the higher their academic performance...at every level. The quality of the relationship predicted academic success and outperformed instructional strategy. A good relationship helps to neutralize threats to academic success: problems with mom, bad behavior at school, cultural and linguistically diverse, low cognitive ability, problematic or harsh or neglectful parenting, males in general have disproportionate academic struggles.

After a child begins elementary school, they spend more wake-time with their teacher than a parent. The teacher is a significant support system to even the best parent. For a child who does not have a stable parent it seems that a relationship in the classroom makes up for it. The better relationship between a student and teacher the less bad behavior. I ran into a student I had in class 13 years ago last night while Christmas shopping. She described herself as quite a handful in high school, not the typical teenager; instead, a cocaine runner who felt no need for school. I remember her very different. I could have said quiet, well-mannered and respectful of education. She laughed and said no, it was a respect for one of my fellow social studies colleagues that kept her in school and behaving well every day. She said 3 of her teachers believed in her and she said as a result…did what she needed to graduate.

Connected students means long-term academic achievement and behavioral achievement. Connected students have the lowest rates of depression, highest self-esteem and were most comfortable with their families. The most encouraging finding is those children who are the most positive about education have the lowest rates of drugs and alcohol with the lowest rates of stress and the highest GPA. There are other relationships that are a major support for academic success. The relationships we take for granted are key for teacher student; the more connected a parent to teacher the more the student is likely to bond with the teacher.

> "They are fundamental to our emotional fulfillment, behavioral adjustment, and cognitive function. Disruption or absence of stable social relationships blasts our minds and biology like no other event." Dr. Levin Goldman 2009

Where to Connect?

Everywhere you look you have an option at connection: who cuts your hair, who works at your bookstore, take something to a neighbor, go through an old address book, search for classes and "clubs" where things you like are happening (political, movie, food-based, books, museums etc.)

> Go find happy people! "The closer proximity and frequency mean greater chance of being happy!"
> Nikolas Christakis

Relationship training changes behaviors of bullies and the bullied!

How do we know programs change human behavior? Even the most stubborn, ugly social behavior called bullying can change by 20%. Bully-Proofing reduces incidents by up to two times that of the control. Even simple goals: remind children (and adults) to avoid negative situations, build positive relationships, make good decisions, avoid anti-social behavior.

Relationships are key because people who are bullied are often different from others, and can find it hard to make friends, or are lonely. The added stress of bullying means even more suffering emotionally and physically. Although some people are just bullied, we need to actively work to train all students to build and sustain relationships as if their lives depend upon.

Everyday networks evolve from the natural tendency of each person to seek out and make many (or few) friends, to have a large or small family, or to work in a personable or anonymous workplace. Deliberately creating relationships with friends and neighbors, to stay connected to the extended family and build relationships in the workplace for a safe and supportive network of people brings innovation, health and efficiency! Systematically establishing healthy interaction results in improved cognition and health. This touchy-feely concept traditionally considered a soft-skill, and the opposite of rigorous, is the foundation of all business interactions, all politics, lowers the divorce rate, and even reduces accidents.

- In 300 top UK businesses, surveys showed decision-makers, 80% of all hiring criteria fall into the "soft skills" category (Pareto Law, 2017)
- Harvard Research shows labor markets are increasingly favoring social skills, they facilitate cooperation and experience greater relative growth; the "female advantage may be the driving factor in narrowing the gender gap since the 1980s." (Deming, 2015)
- Swedish study shows the propensity toward relationships may drive females who are successful in completing engineering programs. A cluster-study showed the graduates were inspired by "doing good for the society, people and environment in their future careers." (Engstrom, 2018)
- Personality traits, character skills, socio-emotional skills, predict future academic and social skills more accurately than achievement tests (Kautz, Heckman et al 2015)
- Intervention and direct instruction of "soft skills" have beneficial long-term success (Algan 2014)

- Human development and skill development significantly impact social mobility (Heckman 2014)
- Deliberate social skill development fosters positive character traits (Heckman 2014b)
- Strong interpersonal skills reduce the costs of coordination and improve cultural globalization in the digital age (Tett, 2017)
- The U.S. has a particularly strong emphasis on interpersonal skills, a need for high order abilities like fluency of ideas, active learning and originality (Bakhshi et al 2017)
- Health and longevity are dictated by the number of our relationships with others (Fowler & Christakus, 2009)

> "Leave all the afternoon for exercise and recreation, which are as necessary as reading. I will rather say more necessary because health is worth more than learning."
> –Thomas Jefferson

Relationships give us a long and healthy quality of life…all over the world

There are four regions in the world with an inordinately high concentration of people who live to be 100 years old. Daniel Beutner wrote, The Blue Zone, about the common practices of those who live to be one hundred years old. Each behave in ways (that spreads to others) shown to be healthy. First and foremost, they have to feel needed. They commonly report feeling the desire to contribute to a greater good. The most protective environment is in the middle of their family where children need them (most industrial countries higher daycare). When the centenarian shares household relationships and responsibilities there are significantly fewer who seek out an assisted care facility. Living with family embeds them into social networks and social interaction with family and neighbors daily! He found they had these in common:

1. Report a strong sense of purpose, are needed, and want to contribute to a great good
2. Live with their children and grandchildren, visit their neighbors often

3. Do physical work daily, have a healthy BMI, exercise regularly, walk 5 miles a week
4. Spend time with like-minded people, have a sense of humor and laugh with friends
5. Volunteer time to a favorite cause; gardening regularly lowers stress & improves flexibility
6. Social and financial support: the culture in the Japanese area included financial and social support and a positive attitude that bad times are in the past

If you only do one thing? Pick one of the following behaviors to make a habit!

How to begin to make great changes? Pick the things easiest to implement first! Only do one or two or three things at any given time. For the best results, have someone who agrees to do those things with you! Studies continually show us we have a better chance of continuing a behavior, creating a habit, in the middle of others. Behavior is contagious.

First…I advise you DON'T EXERCISE. Instead, embed movement to your daily life! Physical activity is the most effective way to permanently integrate movement into your life. When additional steps are a regular part of life, we have the best chance of keeping it (read the Three Types of Movement chapter.) Walking to the mailbox, a friend's house, the library, the park, from the parking lot to the store, school, work, church embeds behaviors. It's pretty easy to stop a gym or added workout regime.

Second…They ate fewer calories using a daily routine to reduce calories without using *any* self-discipline (sometimes by more than 20%). Brian Wansink designs studies quantifying human behaviors based upon the environment. His controlled studies show the size of a package dictates our consumption behaviors; how much we eat, how much we drink, how much product we use! He found a large package meant subjects ate 23% more than those with a small package. One subject group offered ½ pound of M & M's ate 71 candies, while the subjects offered a pound of M & M's ate 137 candies…almost 2 times the amount. Offering half the size results in almost a 50% savings with no effort at controlling intake of a high sugary, high fat snack! We purchase in large quantity to save money at the checkout, but the caloric and economic savings only trickles down to when you downsize at home into a smaller container.

A recent study showed the incidence in Type 2 Diabetes and increase in attempts at suicide may be attributed to the massive increase of sugar. The popular sugary drink intake correlates with an increase in depression around the world. Wansink's studies shown an illusion that unconsciously influences our pouring habits: we see a tall class as being longer than horizontal. That means we pour more into a short squat glass than into a tall glass, our perception doesn't seem to account for the additional space in the shorter glass. As a result, subjects drink 25-30% more from a short and wide glass. Despite training, even professionals pour less into a tall thin and more into the short squat. Why do you care? You can increase consumption for water and decrease sugary intake by 20% to 30% without any effort!

If we use and consume significantly less quantities from small bottles or containers, be careful at wholesale where all products are in bulk. A simple behavior of transferring from a big container into small could make a sizeable difference.

Third...Very little processed meat: no lunch meat, bacon or prepared meats (or food)

Fourth...A glass or two of red wine each day.

Fifth...Create a sanctuary to "downshift" and relieves stress.

Sixth...Belong to something! Develop a spiritual side. For example, people who attended meetings once a month (where there are people) had the same health benefit as moderate physical activity. Researchers followed 3,617 people for over 7 years and found the health benefit to be the same.

Seventh...Make family a priority, they don't have to share DNA but they have to be close. The MacArthur study followed 1189 elders between 70 and 79 years old for 7 years and found those who live with their children had less disease, ate healthier, had lower stress, fewer accidents and had the highest cognitive and social skills.

Eighth…Surround yourself with people who think like you! When you are with those who share your values, perspectives and otherwise, you share common behaviors connected to health and other goals. Make a daily habit to be with people 30 minutes of being "present" with them, not multi-tasking or thinking of other things to do, or that you should be doing. The best step toward a healthy relationship is to NEVER look at your phone (not a text, email, social media, game)

"Do you have any idea who you wanted to become?" Never doubt that you can pursue it. Your job is to notice when the universe delivers a clue. You'll know when you feel energy. Where do you like to pay attention? When you notice what gets your blood boiling, you'll know where to look for your purpose and the greater good you can do!" What if you are destined to do something amazing? Become a Nelson Mandela! Move toward becoming your own version of Bill Gates or LeBron or Stephen King, Tom Hanks, Steve Jobs, Alexandria Ocasio-Cortez or Oprah Winfrey? Most important, what do you want your relationships to look like?

I never wanted to be a teacher, never wanted to learn history, but *because* my history teacher in high school was the best storyteller I've ever known that one of my degrees is history. In those days, my clue was the intellectual curiosity for ancient topics (possibly considered useless), "Is that really how Cleopatra died? Did they really bury the Pharaoh's mistresses with him? The Guillotine was efficient and price-effective…this is the stuff Mr. Ward said that stuck in my head! The anxiety of not knowing one of these essential questions drove me to get a major in History. There is no way Mr. Ward knew he had that power; that teacher-student relationship changed my life! It was years before I realized that is where all success originates…people.

> "Anyone person's change in behavior can bring
> the change." Nicholas Christakis

- Get started now...say good morning and good night
- Write thank you notes
- Find something entertaining to do...a common ground
- Replace screen time with face-to-face time
- Choose to take long walks
- Go find music together
- Learn to dance
- Never repeat what you are told...it breaks trust (of the person you share it with)
- The courage to tell what you're really thinking (I don't like that... try this)
- Make them laugh and find them funny
- Ask them questions about thoughts, dreams, and laugh often
- Balance your friend's concern by saying "maybe you don't need to worry about that because..."
- Go find what makes you laugh (movies, clubs, hobbies, amusement park, groups of people)
- Reach out to a family member you haven't spoken to for some reason
- Make sure you listen to whatever upsets your loved one as if it's life and death
- Reassure your loved one that anything you did that hurt them; you won't do it again (don't argue)

Find more friends

- Start a group that meets regularly (movies, cookies, a common cause, a current events chat, etc.)
- Forgive anyone who needs it
- Go to family gatherings and host regular family gatherings or monthly extended family dinner
- Go where others engage in activity (sport, theater, woodwork, sewing, escape room, top golf)
- Never decline an invitation, always make eye-contact and smile.

Strategies for a happy romantic relationship:

1. Respect the need for nurturing and safety
2. Be cognizant of a recurring argument...whomever brings it up over and over is sharing an event that they cannot process. Stop and explain the hurt. Apologize profusely and explain how it will never happen again...regardless of how trivial it may seem.
3. No "rumination" ... reliving negative stories (reinforces neurological pathway for negative)
4. Respect time for self and applaud accomplishments.
5. Ensure time with her girlfriends, and him with his guy friends).
6. Regular activities to build or make things with your hands (together and or separately).
7. Acknowledge the need to nurture...bossing isn't always intended as criticism. Over time, bossing can erode closeness and create resentment.
8. People need to tell "stories" (sometimes called "gossip" if it holds a misleading fact or a lie).
9. Plan ahead when sharing about your relationship, will you share this with your family or friends?
10. Find a common interest...learn to dance...it's essential for a happy marriage!

Strategies to build Relationships between children and students

- Show and tell about contents in a "Me Bag" where they bring personal items: photos (self, favorite person, family, favorite thing to do) bring the favorite item in house, favorite food, favorite smell, song that gives them chills, favorite movie and book--anything important.
- Talk to each other in an attempt to get to know each other for 10 min
- Train 5 steps for social and emotional skills
- Play games (one on one and teams)
- Engage in physical activity (games or fitness)

- Explain the fine art of listening and how to stop "ONE-UPPING" another
- Accept help (great way to bring people to you, and make them feel valued)

Strategies for Employers, for Teachers:

1. Write a thank you note every week, month, for personal thank you or to community member
2. Ask them to bring a photo of personal life relating to emotions: happiness, disgust, anger, progress, loneliness, funny, cooperation, playful, empathy, letter of alphabet, a color, embarrassment, a problem, fear, creative, interests, strengths, values, weaknesses.
3. Tell a meaningful story about any personal topic, because sharing connects people.
4. Take group photos daily, weekly, and post or play slideshow
5. Laugh constantly, make eye contact
6. Plan to eat dinner together: in a public place, restaurant, or home
7. Present and display "work": projects, what you read or wrote, accomplishments of any kind.
8. Person-Centered objective: allow them (employees/students/children) to share interest for future learning and training
9. Ask for and maintain EXCELLENT social skills: don't ignore small acts of rudeness or mean talk or inappropriate language
10. Attend an outside event to connect, invite family and friends

For Parents and Grandparents:

- Talk to child daily about something at school (ask a direct question or you will get "I don't know")
- Read to your child: pick interesting, move toward a book where each night the family reads a page or a chapter (builds reading fluency and family cohesiveness...correlates with academic success)
- Regularly discuss what to and what not to do for making and maintaining friendships
- Go to your child's teacher to build communication (in elementary school, middle and high school). Teachers need to know you

are aware of school requirements and interactions. A gesture to communicate you are open is golden: send a note, a mug, go to conferences and back to school night regularly.

- Briefly communicate the most important traits or behavior the teacher needs to know about your child. The 10 Do's and Don'ts when teaching your child (ppt to help your child: photos, your child's strengths and fears, etc....)
- Encourage your child to try extra-curricular activities
- Communicate your commitment to a good night of sleep, real food (not processed), daily reading
- Research behind homework (nightly traditional is not supported with evidence)

Additional Research:

- Loneliness correlates with poor executive function, and results in diminished cognitive performance on test. Social isolation increases the risk of death as much as cigarette consumption and more than inactivity or obesity. Loneliness shortens life span, increases infections, increases heart disease and depression (Greg Miller, 2011)
- Touch has a significant effect on moods and feelings of connection; only 15 seconds increases a flood of serotonin, oxytocin and endorphins.
- Touch, laughter, and extreme physical activity increase our Nerve Growth Factor, which stimulates nerve growth.
- Quality of relationship between teacher and student dictates academic achievement (O'Conner & McCartney 2006)
- 10 minutes of "friendly chat" where people are instructed to get to know one another increased cognitive performance as much as working a crossword puzzle. Chatting to get to know another improved working memory (which correlates with IQ and high stakes performance), self-monitoring, ability to suppress internal and external distractions (Oscar Ybarra, 2010)
- Relationship building should serve as intervention for all low achievement (Birch & Ladd 97, Furrer & Skinner 2003, Pianta 1999, 1997, 2004.)

- O'Connor, E., Dearing, E., & Collins, B. (2011). Teacher-child relationship trajectories: Predictors of behavior problem trajectories and mediators of child and family factors. American Educational Research Journal, 48 (1), 120-162.
- O'Connor, E., (2010). Teacher-child relationships as dynamic systems. Journal of School Psychology, 48 (3), 187-218.
- Good relationships between students are good for health and academic success. Azmita, Hartup and Newcomb showed actions and behaviors related to exploring topics increased significantly. They have more dynamic conversation and remember more about the conversations and learning tasks.
- Students who perceive teacher support have improved decision-making, self-efficacy and vocational choices (Metheny, McWhirter & O'Neil 2008)
- Friends provide one another with cognitive and social foundations that generalize into improved learning and improved social interaction (Hartup 1996)
- People with fewer than 2 connections have more illness (Peter Marsden 2006)
- At-Risk Factor of bad behavior in the classroom is counteracted with a positive relationship with a teacher (Gregory & Ripsky, 2008)
- Black American and Latino students perform better as a result of a positive relationship with a teacher (Ewing & Taylor 2009, McLoyd, 2009; Nzinga-Johnson, 2009; Burchinal, 2002)
- Poor, authoritative, and neglectful parenting are risk-factors negated by a positive relationship with a teacher (Dearing, Dreider & Weiss 2008; Flanigan 2007; O'Connor and McCarthy 2007; Buhs, 2006)
- Relationship with a teacher increases performance for males as shown by standardized tests (Rudasill, 2011; Justice 2008; Hamre & Pianta, 1999)
- Training students to identify emotions and training on self-awareness in social-emotional relationships increased academics by 11-17%, (Joseph Durlak, 2008, Casel.org)

ENDNOTES

[1]   Provine, R. (2012). Curious Behavior: Yawning, Laughing, Hiccupping, and Beyond. Belknap Press of Harvard University Press. Provine, R. (2001). Laughter: A Scientific Investigation. Penguin Books.

[2]   Laakasuo, Dunbar et al, (2020). That feeling of joy is now explained by years of science. Success and healthy is scripted by friends. Frontiers in Psychology.

[3]   Mineo, L. (2017). Harvard study almost 80 years ago has proved embracing community and improving relationships is helping us live longer. Harvard Gazette

Waldinger, R. (2015). Study of Adult Development. TED Talk

[4]   Slavich, et al (2010) Neural sensitivity to social rejection is associated with inflammatory responses to social stress. PNAS vol 107

[5]   Friedman, H. S., & Martin, L. R. (2011). *The longevity project: Surprising discoveries for health and long life from the landmark eight-decade study.* Hudson Street Press/Penguin Group USA.

[6]   Shrout, M. R., & Kiecolt-Glaser, J. K. (2020). Individual, relational, and developmental–contextual pathways linking marriage to health. American Psychologist

[7]   Kiecolt-Glaser, J. (2018). Marriage, divorce and the immune system. American Psychologist.

[8]   Jaremka, et al, (2014). Pain, depression and fatigue: Loneliness as a longitudinal risk factor. Health Psychology.

[9]   Umberson et al., (2010). Social Relationships and Health: A Flashpoint for Health Policy. J Health Soc Behave.

[10] Siegler et al., (2013). More friends who we connect with increases our longevity but so does a support group made up of people with a similar plight! Annals of Behavior Medicine.

[11] ibid.

[12] Bloch, L., Haase, C. M., & Levenson, R. W. (2013). Emotion regulation predicts marital satisfaction: More than a wives' tale. Emotion, pp. 130 –144.

[13] Haase et al, (2016). Interpersonal emotional behaviors and physical health: a 20-year longitudinal study of long-term married couples. American Psychological Association.

[14] Miller et al, (2010) Why loneliness is hazardous to your health. Science vol 331 pp 138-140

[15] Miller, Greg., Cole, Steven. (2012) Childhood adversity increases risk of chronic inflammation and depression. Biological Psychiatry.

[16] Erlich et al (2015) Trajectories of relationship stress and inflammatory processes in adolescence. Development and Psychopathology.

[17] Miller, G. (2010). The seductive allure of epigenetics. Science Journal.

18   Ybarra, Oscar et al. (2010). Being unpredictable: friend or foe matters. Social Psychological and Personality Science.

19   Gregory, S., and Webster, S. (1996). A nonverbal signal in voices of interview partners effectively predicts communication accommodation and social status perceptions. Journal of Personality and Social Psychology.

20   Gostick, A., Elton, C. (2010). The Orange Revolution: how one great team can transform an entire organization. Free Press: New York.

21   Woolley et al., (2010). Collective intelligence and group performance. Science

22   Woolley et al., (2015). Collective intelligence in teams and organizations. Current Directions in Psychological Science.

23   Onnela, J., Reed-Tsochas, F. (2010). Spontaneous emergence of social influence in online systems. PNAS vol. 107

24   Helliwell, J., Huang, H. (2013). Comparing the happiness effects of real and on-line friends. PlosOne

25   Deming, D. (2017). The growing importance of social skills in the labor market. National Bureau of Economic Research

26   Fuertinger et al (2017). Dopamine drives left-hemispheric lateralization of neural networks during human speech. Journal of Comparative Neurology.

27   Pearce et. al (2017). Variation in the b-endorphin, oxytocin, and dopamine receptor genes is associated with different dimensions of human sociality. PNAS

28   Gur, et al (2012). Age group and sex differences in performance on a computerized neurocognitive battery in children age 8-21. Neuropsychology.

29   Durlak et al. (2011). The impact of enhancing students' social and emotional learning: a meta-analysis of school-based universal interventions. Child Development

30   McCarthy, K., and O'Conner, E., (2007).

CHAPTER 7

MUSIC AND THE BRAIN: LISTENING IMPROVES MOOD, HEALTH, KINDNESS AND INTELLIGENCE

When I was six, my parents bought the soundtrack to the hit movie *American Graffiti*. Until my older sister threatened to kill me if I put the needle back at the beginning one more time (that was repeat when I was a kid), I listened to "At the Hop" by Flash Cadillac and the Continental Kids 75 times. I couldn't get enough of that song, and I had to listen to it over and over. I danced like crazy and sang along to every word. It was 145 seconds of pure energy; that is, until she walked into the room to scream "don't play that song one more time!"

Listening to and making music not only excites and electrifies us, it develops neural pathways (like constructing rails of interconnected tracks for a railroad network) that enhance neural success. These pathways involve the neurons we need for life, thought, and all our behavior. Our neural networks are created by our experiences, and music is an example of a sophisticated challenge that improves the networks for language, memory, and learning. Music training builds networks much like the railways for delivering and receiving information in speech, conceptualize and process math, reading comprehension, spatial reasoning, map skills, and improved social interaction. Over a lifetime, this training results in neuronal growth in musicians. Research shows that they have larger structures and more mass in the brain, and more sophisticated interconnectivity; perhaps as a result, musicians are less likely to develop dementia and tend to have better hearing than non-musicians. It seems that the complexity of the training produces superior brain functionality. But even if you're not a musician, there is now research showing many benefits that come with listening.

Music is so powerful even an audience's neural pathways are enhanced as if by magic.

When I say this is what we know about your brain on music, the audience can't hold in their excitement: "What sort of music should I play?" "Doesn't music improve test scores?" "Can you listen to music instead of drugs when having a baby?" What music do you play for work?" "To sleep?" "To read?" When I began researching the effects of music decades ago, there were already years and years of experiments showing the correlation between musical performance and cognitive performance, enough to suggest that we should have music playing, at least in the background, in offices, schools, and homes every day, as of yet, we don't.

Research on playing an instrument, singing in a choir, and listening has grown immensely, and it is compelling because of the enormous body of evidence; but now the causal nature of the findings suggests we act to integrate ASAP. Music directly stimulates and reinforces neural growth, facilitates cognition, provides the neurotransmitters for moods and for neuroplasticity, and even regrows damaged neural tissue and improves intellectual deficits.

Which music does this? Depending on pace, rhythm, and volume, each genre has a different impact, so the answer depends on the effects you're after! The most therapeutic kinds of music seem to be baroque, classical or non-repetitive (usually slow with less than 60 beats per minute), and *your preference*, but it depends on the effect you are looking for.

Playing a musical instrument and singing in a choir stimulates neural growth in the language centers in the brain as well as the entire brain, increases energy, and improves mood, health and even increases our spatial reasoning. We have always known music is good, but we no longer have to consider it common sense, the therapeutic nature of music is now supported by empirical evidence.

There's no question we love music. We crave it, listen to it constantly, spend lots of money on it, and even develop crushes on musicians. This is because music is directly connected to the reward centers in the frontal cortex. Neurobiological studies show the quantitative effects of listening and playing on increasing neurotransmitters and hormones that affect us like pharmaceuticals, meaning it can be therapeutic! Just thinking of a song you love changes your neurochemistry—and that satisfying feeling when you press play—is a healthy high. Now we know it builds a path to maximum cognition!

You don't know it, but you respond to all sounds, even those you aren't aware of. Every sound you hear affects your brain and body. A clanging bell, a blood-curdling scream, a roaring jet engine, a growling dog, a crying baby, even leaves blowing in the wind are processed by your ears and brain and affect your autonomic nervous system. It's all about the bass, tempo, pitch, key, and rhythm: the elements of music force the brain to increase or decrease blood flow, pulse, blood pressure, even respiration. Listening to music affects one's immune system, energy levels, pain tolerance, and memory. It inspires movement, sets a mood, and grabs your attention.

Neurological studies can explain some of those incredible effects; once you understand, we can custom use it like a priceless tool! Great composers craft music that evokes emotion and exerts power over an audience; they design it to create precise responses and can even dictate its interpretation and meaning. Nina Kraus, a neuroscientist and "sound trailblazer," researches the role of listening to music, playing music and speaking another language in developing neural networks in the brain. She found that the ability to perceive relevant sounds in the environment gives you such an advantage in life that the ability itself predicts success (in academics, in the workplace, in social interactions). My favorite thing she does in her lab is play music, and using sensors to record our brainwaves, and then play back the soundwave—they are the same sound! What you hear is following an electrical response, our brainwaves, that when played back through a speaker sound like what you listened to.

Everyone's brainwaves match the sounds we are listening to. Entraining is unconscious synchronization of our EEGs where they match the sounds we hear. When I think of all the god-knows-what-all-sounds I have heard in my lifetime, a discovery that my brainwaves match each sound is a potential way to collectively improve health and wellness. Even an unwitting "listener" responds to sound and the EEG shows it. If you can't imagine what these EEGs or brainwaves look like, checkout *Meet the Parents*. The Dad, Robert DeNiro, interrogates Ben Stiller, sticks electrodes on his head, to detect a lie. I'm not sure how accurate it is for lie detecting, but this measures brainwaves. Depending on the time of day and our activities we are involved in, our frequency will be faster or slower. It's influenced by what we hear!

Playing an instrument, listening to music, listening to language, singing require we hear ourselves in order to adapt to our environment. Your EEGs are matching and synchronizing with all sounds: voices talking, drums beating, music playing, everything! The ability to hear the important sounds in our world, increase the mass of our neural network in the brain. The more we listen, the more we need the sound in the environment, the more complex means the more neurons your brain grows to hear them.

Think of the power you have if you know which sounds to listen to!

Background music improves accuracy and healing. Almost thirty years ago, researchers at the University of Washington found listening to light classical music increased accuracy and improved subjects' performance while copy-editing a manuscript, by a whopping 21%. Another study showed that hospital patients in need of wound care who were allowed to choose from fifty songs just before and after laceration repair had significant reduction in pain.[1] Still another showed patients listening to music during a colonoscopy required significantly less sedation than the control.[2] Slow easy-listening music calms the sympathetic nervous system and stimulates the parasympathetic nervous system.

- Music affects nervous systems, brain waves entrain with beats, and your heart and brain synchronize.
- The sympathetic nervous system is activated by epinephrine and norepinephrine (fight or flight) in response to perceived stress; its response is to increase the heart rate, constrict the blood vessels, cause rapid, shallow breathing, and constrict the pupils.

- The parasympathetic nervous system maintains a slow heart rate, dilates the blood vessels and pupils, increase the digestive juices, and relax the muscles in the gastrointestinal tract (colonoscopies check for an abnormality).

When ears integrate sound, it stimulates the nervous system, increases endorphins and serotonin (and affects cognition). The beat of music affects the pulse, blood pressure, and brainwaves.[3] This means different paces and volumes have different effects. Listening affects our hearts, lungs, and brains, whether we're engaging in conversation or priming ourselves to face danger. The autonomic nervous system allows us to take action when we need to. Faster music increases dopamine, norepinephrine, and even growth hormones, and it can motivate, invigorate, and energize us. The Rolling Stones are my choice in the afternoon to counter my fatigue. Think of a favorite and fast beat song to recharge before a meeting or a class in the last hours of the day, and certainly for exercise. While it is not my preference, the research suggests that listening to slow music improves our endurance during exercise and returns the heartrate to its baseline faster, a sign of fitness.

That means listening to develop neurons in the brain, strength and performance

Listening to music and singing brings deeper, slower breaths that increase oxygenation and lower stress. A fast beat increases energy, focus, and attention—but don't play fast music while reading or writing. Slow is best for reading, writing, or transitioning or for calming down. The effect on the muscles is measurable: greater blood flow increases strength and endurance.

Blood also delivers neurotransmitters that improve executive function which improves all sorts of performance. Soft music with fewer beats increases blood flow, which may be why listening to it improves pain thresholds, moods, and stress. This may underpin its therapeutic benefits. When music slows our pulse, the parasympathetic nervous system is stimulated and allows the heart and lungs to recover faster, for instance following the strenuous workout. Even subjects identified as non-exercisers who listened to their favorite music recovered significantly faster after vigorous cycling[4]: in one study, non-exercising males cycled while listening to heavy metal and again while listening to slow baroque music, while having their heart rate variability measured. Even though the subjects reported no interest in heavy metal or baroque music, their heart rates returned to normal significantly faster when they were listening to Pachelbel's Canon in D Major than to heavy metal. Interestingly, listening to heavy metal music for five minutes increased activation of the sympathetic system, which increased blood pressure, and slowed the parasympathetic nervous system.[5]

The brain, heart, and respiration synchronize with the beat and "hijack" the central nervous system to relax or energize, and to heal. This speeds baseline recovery and offers healing and therapy for trauma from workouts, stress or anything else. This means listening to slow should follow a stressful event such as a crisis or a vigorous workout, or for cardiac patients using the treadmill stress test of cardiac function. Listening to one's favorite slow music right after the test is a fast, pleasant tool for accelerated recovery...a measure of fitness.

BDNF is a neural growth factor known to increase neural plasticity, protect new neurons, and maintain neurons. As complex activity increases, this growth factor increases. This is a Miracle Grow for your brain. An increase in BDNF accelerates learning and forms new memories and new learning throughout our life. The more we have the better we are at sophisticated, complex movement.

- Improves working memory and information processing, prevents lasting weight change, and improves nausea (Noble et al. 2011).
- Suppresses the appetite and increases weight loss (Wang et al. 2007, 2010). Prevents weight gain (Lapchak et al. 1992). Improves glucose metabolization (Yamanaka et al. 2008). Improves energy consumption and increases metabolic rate (Wang et al. 2010).

Listening to music increases BDNF and after two weeks of a more complex or enriched environment where learning something new like a language or playing an instrument, amounts increase significantly. Surprisingly complex movements increase it more than exercise. Four weeks of running increased slightly, while a complex activity increased it significantly. It seems to be the challenge because research shows meditation increases BDNF; a highly complex and challenging activity (stress impairs BDNF).

Considering what listening does for accuracy and heartrate, I often think of the times I've demanded silence in my classroom and at home. I could have used the right music to improve whatever we were doing. I never thought I might be preventing the best and most accurate performance.

We don't live in silence. Listening is what we do naturally during waking hours and sleep. The average person in the U.S. processes more than 30,000 sounds every day, and the nervous system attends to its surroundings continually. Of course, there are times when we need just silence, like during sleep and certain types of conversation (I never have music in the background during my talks). But listening is a 24-hour, 7-days-a-week scanning system.

We listen unconsciously. Researcher Lars Jarup found that for people living near airports, loud has disturbing health effects.[6] Five thousand people living near six major airports were found to have higher blood pressure than people living farther away. The proximity of their autonomic nervous systems caused the unconscious sympathetic nervous system to increase blood pressure anytime residents could hear landings and takeoffs. Birds have higher stress levels near industrial noise too.

People in comas also respond to sound. Epileptic patients have fewer seizures when Mozart is playing in the hospital room.[7] Listening to K448 drops seizures by half after 2 weeks. And listening improves doctors' performances. Fast music pumps up the heart rate and pulse, while slow music calms the autonomic nervous system. The frequency of the beat accelerates healing; fast increases strength, slow increases endurance, and slow allows us to recover from a stressor faster. Music improved their performance because it activates our physiological pathways and calms physical responses.[8] When they were listening to a concerto, plastic surgeons' pulses matched the beat of the music,[9] and they worked faster and better.

Experienced plastic surgeons and resident plastic surgeons were instructed to listen to their preferred music while suturing. A panel of surgeons then compared the time to completion and the quality of work and found that those who listened to music of their choice outperformed the work with regular background noise. Those with music stitched the wound (of a pig) significantly faster and with superior quality (assessed by an independent panel of plastic surgeons) than those not listening to music.[10] This leads to a prettier tuck, repair, or lift, and less time under anesthesia reduces complications and hospital costs. All doctors finished faster but new surgeons finished 7% faster while experienced surgeons even 10% faster. Why does listening to music improve the work of experienced surgeons more than the new surgeons?

There is more to consider when broken down by gender. The female surgeons spent 12% less time working, while males spent 6% less time. Is it the music women chose? The evidence suggests music with a slow beat is therapeutic, reduces stress, and increases blood flow and alertness. Are women more likely to choose such genres or do they hear music differently? One study by Da Silva et al in 2014, omitted subjects from the study because listening to heavy metal spiked the activity in women's sympathetic nervous systems but not men's.

Music in the operating room overall may improve work, reduce complications, and save costs as long as staff can hear well enough. By some estimates, the savings after only a year may be $100,000.[11] Hearing it helps the patient too. Only 30 minutes of music eased anxiety for patients on a ventilator. Their *physiology* changed significantly as compared to the patients without.[12]

Listening following heart transplants? They didn't ask whether they liked opera music; mice just recovering from the surgery lived longer. Mice listening to Verdi's *La Traviata* lived 26 days; those listening to all Mozart lived 20 days. The mice that listened to music with fewer beats, such as New Age,

Enya's *Paint the Stars*, lived only 11 days. Mice without music, mice with only tone frequencies, and deaf mice lived just 7 days. Certain music provided brain (hearing) support that resulted in mice living three times as long. That pace of the opera set the pace for the heart, and since our EEGs synchronize with sounds of the environment it provided a type of *aural pacemaker*.

Music calms the specialized immune response that normally triggers rejection.[13] That must be another reason why listening to piano music immediately upon waking in the ICU helps patients recover from heart surgery: patients whose hospital staff played five hours of piano and left five hours earlier than patients who didn't listen to the piano music.[14] But even for patients listening to their chosen music post operatively had higher oxygen saturation and less reported pain after open heart surgery.[15] Open heart surgery is considered one of the most painful post op recoveries.

Music improves cognition after surgery. Not just classical music: scientists asked 26 subjects to perform cognitive tasks for an hour a day while listening to five different types of music, and they found that electronic dance music was the most beneficial. When subjects listened to EDM, they were the most efficient and accurate. Listening to music for four hours after knee and hip surgery also significantly increased patients' cognitive scores. The group without music did not match their scores until day three.[16] Surgery requires the anesthesiologist to manage pain and slow blood flow for the duration, so the brain is deprived of oxygen. Listening improves blood flow in the frontal cortex and accelerates healing.

Listening to slow music lowers anxiety. A study published in *Psychosomatic Medicine* reported that 40 elderly people waiting for cataract surgery listened to music through headphones and maintained their pre-surgery blood pressure, while another group without headphones had elevated blood pressure. No conscious effort was needed for them to remain calm. But music with the right beat has the ability to calm brains from beta waves to alpha waves and to improve endurance and strength.

Music improves efficiency in the workforce. Sixty years ago, Musak, the provider of elevator and airport music, was already claiming that background music "you can hear but don't listen to" increases efficiency. They claim that AT&T and DuPont cut training time in half with background music, and that Equitable Life Insurance increased its output by 17% after only six weeks. Mississippi Power and Light also reported that the efficiency of "key punch operators" increased by 18.6% after nine months of listening to background music.

Music in the background can be a major part of creating a productive spatial environment. In consideration of psychological and physical needs in the workplace or schools we must plan and design areas that encourage "groupthink", enhance productivity, all while containing the spread of disease. Recent trends in office design open work areas without dividers, the idea was based on studies suggesting interaction fuels collaboration and innovation. While research shows collaboration does increase collective intelligence or "groupthink", open-plan designs compromise efficiency and increase absenteeism. Those partitions dividing colleagues may have protected their ability to stay on task and stay healthy. Significant evidence suggests that instead of the anticipated benefits, data now suggests open office workers need more sick time, more time to complete projects and have lower job satisfaction. In the open setting, not only does it increase the spread of disease, the brain unconsciously pays attention to visual and sound events in our 3-D world we see around us. The increased sick days comes from distracted and interrupted by what we see and hear as it spikes stress level and our immunity and innovation, read Essentials chapter.

Playing soft music is a cost-effective way to mask variable-aural-distractions of public institutions. School districts have invested precious resources in "open" buildings, and the additional strain on attention requires extra effort in concentration.[17] If slow music provides health and productivity, it's a cheap fix and allows process reengineering without workforce reduction.

Listening to certain types of music increases strength, pace, and coordination.

Subjects walked farther when listening to music and reported a better mood. Fast music increases the neurotransmitters involved in motivation.[18]

Of course, listening to music is fabulous, so pairing it with any activity no doubt improves our attitude—for me, music makes grading projects and cleaning tolerable. Some of the findings are paradoxical. You would expect fast music to increase strength and endurance, but music with a slow 90 bpm increases strength while walking, running, or dancing. Researchers at Colorado State University found that cross-country cyclists who listened to instrumental music increased their distances by 25%. Fast and lively music makes us stronger. Researchers at York St. John University asked people to hold a weight while listening to either motivational music, rhythmic music, or no music. The motivational music group held their weights significantly longer than either of the others, and the rhythmic group held their weight longer than the no-music group. The subjects also reported that the livelier the music was, the more vigorous they felt.

After work, after lunch, or anytime your energy is lagging...

Get music when walking is the last thing you want to do. If you can get your headphones on, music with a fast beat will increase the length of time you walk. College-aged women, walked on treadmills significantly longer when listening to music, especially fast music. Groups listening to music thought they had exerted the same effort, but had actually gone 20% longer, and the fast-music group walked longer still.[19]

It's not just walking. Researchers found listening increases endurance in weightlifting by as much as 15%—lifting a dumbbell is easier with Aerosmith! A sample of male athletes aged 22 to 30 years listening to different variations of music (fast or slow, loud, slow and loud, fast and soft, slow and soft) had more strength during loud and fast music. They even had significantly more hand-grip strength than men listening to the same music at a lower volume.[20] In another study, older men listening a fast beat lifted weights 10% heavier than those in silence. What happens to the electrical activity in the brain is interesting. Music downregulated waves in the frontal central and parietal regions during exercise, distracting them from the exertion and improving their performance and their perception of the workout.[21] If you're human, you've cursed the pain of a workout and the people who don't currently work out may love to know—using music, or the *right* music is key!

What if it took five minutes—would you listen? The original "Mozart effect" has been heavily criticized because numerous attempts to replicate failed. However, it marked the beginning of the quest to measure the effects of listening to Mozart. The original study by Gordon Shaw and Francine Rauscher was an attempt to determine the effects of passively listening to Mozart on the spatial-reasoning section of the Stanford-Binet IQ test: ne group listened to white noise, another relaxing music, a third to classical Mozart. They found 36 graduate psych students scored 8-9 points higher on spatial-reasoning portion of the IQ test after listening for 10 minutes and found enhanced processing that lasted about 10 minutes.[22]

Today, the Mozart effect has been replicated: they were right all along. Since the original study, eight more studies showed listening to the first movement of Mozart's K. 448 improved mental imagery and temporal ordering.[23] The researchers were looking for changes in the ability to mentally rotate objects, a measure of spatial reasoning. Another study found superior spatial reasoning in 38 non-musicians after they listened to K. 448. Even after ruling out the effects of mood and arousal, listening improved reasoning. Listening to that 4 minutes of Mozart enhanced attention for the purposes of processing environmental information without increasing mood or arousal.

Why is this Mozart sonata more therapeutic than Beethoven? It's possible that it's more intricate or complex to process information coming from two pianos and four hands. The two hemispheres of the brain are integrating information from both, unconsciously, which demands sophisticated neural function. That integration builds and trains our neurons for improved function and high-level reasoning.

Just listening improves mental imagery, spatial reasoning, and working memory.

Working memory is the ability to focus on information at hand, for instance, when you take an order at Starbucks, you use your working memory to relay the special drink requests. Without the ability to focus on incoming information to use it right away, we would be lost and frustrated. More studies of light classical music have shown listening improves mood, arousal, and vocabulary. However, the catch is choosing between focusing on the task and focusing on the music in the environment: in reality what this means is learning or performing novel or cognitive functions that require computation (arithmetic, multiplication, reading comprehension) silence beats background music.[24]

Listening before and after a surgery improves both stress and recovery, and all cognitive tasks. After heart surgery, patients often lose cognitive processing because of the reduced oxygenation. But those who listened to Vivaldi's *Four Seasons* for 30 minutes just once a week *doubled their vocabulary words and increased their verbal fluency*, according to researchers.[25] It doesn't have to be common for patients, especially older people, to have trouble with memory following a major surgery. Surgery limits incoming oxygen and can have significant effects on short-term memory for months afterward. Another study of elderly patients found that those who listened to Vivaldi's "Spring" for 30 minutes after a major surgery improved their social interaction, working memory, and cognitive performance over the next few weeks. Listening had a positive effect on their cognition, arousal, attention, and mood.[26] In another study, people listening to Mozart increased their spatial reasoning, and subjects who found the music "emotional" also increased their autobiographical memories.[27] Cardiac patients who listened to Vivaldi for 30 minutes while exercising also more than doubled their verbal fluency and improved their self-reported mood and energy.

Musicians have superior verbal recall and visual recall.

Sixty 60 Chinese women who had been musicians for more than two years were invited to participate in an auditory recall trial. Their verbal recall was consistently 16% higher than that of non-musicians. However, their visual recall was identical to that of non-musicians. Playing an instrument develops neural circuitry related to auditory processing that enhances memory.[28]

Listening improves verbal fluency—being quick on our feet, answering questions, articulating ideas, formulating clever thoughts. Loss of verbal fluency is the main indicator for dementia. Processing sound for verbal dexterity begins in the auditory cortex of the left hemisphere. FMRI scans show that Brodmann's area activates when we respond to hearing relevant information. For a "novice" listening to music, the response time is about two seconds, but as the listener gains experience, the response comes faster until it's immediate. It's like a TV show I watched as a kid: *Name that Tune*. Contestants gambled that they could name a song or artist within a certain number of notes. Whoever named it with the fewest notes won.

Magic starts in the brain when you hear a sound, integrate the information (voices, notes, music), process it, and voice your answer. Let's say you're listening to the first few notes…say bars of a song: "On a dark desert highway. . ." The hippocampus "searches" the cortex to find "classic rock," "The Eagles" (but neurons still fire even if you can't think of the group's name), and eventually "Hotel California." The process is often accompanied by moving, singing, or humming, at least for me. Then you connect it to a life experience, and the emotional response is almost instant.

The right music can ignite a response in pretty much everyone with a brain. Deep inside the temporal lobe is the emotion center, the amygdala, which activates in response to emotional stimuli, and the hippocampus, our memory maker. Music cues up memories full of emotions whether you like it or not. At any time—during a commercial that ruins a great song by playing it to sell a product, when you're in a mall, a restaurant, or a doctor's office with background music, you're in the middle of whatever, and here comes a song can come on that hits you with a *boom* and brings up a memory, great or sad. You know why? Emotions, music and memory are indelibly associated. Minor keys, typically considered moody and sad, activate larger neural areas than major keys. They are processed differently, in the right striatum, and fMRI scans show that the same rewards are activated as when a subject is tasting beer. Major keys, typically considered bright and happy, activate the left middle temporal gyrus, which may be why music improves cognition; that's the area of information processing.[29] The left middle temporal gyrus interacts with the prefrontal cortex and is involved in social anxiety and semantic processing; strokes in this area interfere with speech comprehension and word recognition.[30] Major keys activate and increase the neurons involved in cognitive processing, and they may rebuild neural networks damaged by injury or stroke.

Music training builds neural networks essential for learning and memory.

Every time you play an instrument or sing, you use and therefore build neurons. These are the same pathways you use for speaking, learning language, recognizing words, and improving your lifelong memory. Repeated use and training require consistent firing in these networks and will result in greater mass and integration in brain structures. Increased functioning in the hippocampus, the amygdala, the reward centers, and the cortex are associated with the most sophisticated mental demands and long-term memory.[31] Longitudinal studies show playing brings incredibly beneficial changes. Six-year-olds (who have highly plastic networks) with musical training versus those without had significantly more cortical thickness in the left and right posterior superior temporal gyrus after two years (in Wernicke's region, which controls comprehension, language, and social cognition). The researchers also found higher connectivity in the corpus callosum. Among school-age children, only those with music training showed significant structural or functional changes,[32] meaning training, practice, and learning to play caused the increase in size.

- Significant changes can happen in as little as fifteen months in developing brains[33]
- The functionality and structures we develop by playing music and singing improve our short-term, long-term, and working memory. The overlap results in superior attention, learning, and cognition[34]
- The musician's brain is larger, and highly integrated, and unconsciously analyzes
- The human brain predicts what's coming next but not if it is a repeated beat[35]

Musicians listen from the moment they pick up an instrument or sing a note, and fMRI scans show their brains don't just listen, it analyzes. While listening to a concerto, they have more brain activity than non-musicians. Musicians also have greater blood oxygenation in the right prefrontal cortex, parietal cortex, and insula during working memory tasks than a non-musician.[36] The structural differences caused by music training lead to more neuronal activation in the hippocampus and the frontal and temporal cortices and better short-term auditory learning. In a study at McMaster University, Larry Roberts found musicians used less energy to play simple piano tunes than non-musicians; their neurons could "hear" and analyze music better.

Maps of the musician's brain show their structures are larger: the motor cortex and auditory and visuospatial regions.[37] The complexity of playing an instrument results in male musicians having 5%- to 15%-thicker cortical matter than non-musicians. Years of processing highly complex sounds and hand-finger integration might cause this. The corpus callosum, an axonal bundle that integrates information (articulate emotions, written and verbal communication) can be as much as 15% larger in male musicians (the researchers did not study female musicians).[38]

These changes don't take years. Takako Fujioka compared neural growth in children with and without training and found indisputable evidence that those who play violin for just one year have "striking changes in the left hemisphere." Even if you're not six, you should start playing an instrument. At any age, playing an instrument increases blood flow, oxygenation, and neural activity and brings plasticity immediately. However, an earlier onset means more precise play and learning-related neuroplasticity.[39] Recent studies have shown that the younger a child learns to play an instrument, the better their cortical processing throughout their lifetime.[40] Playing an instrument also boosts cognition at any age, even in people with mild dementia, and improves hearing by stimulating the growth of new neurons.[41] Musicians have significantly lower rates of dementia and better hearing than the general population.

Music boosts IQ, pain tolerance and immunity

The effects of listening to music are both neurological and pharmacological. Listening increases BDNF, serotonin, endorphins, dopamine, acetylcholine, and norepinephrine and lowers cortisol. And Stanford's Avram Goldstein showed the neurochemistry of music by giving medical students naloxone to effectively block the effects of enjoying music. Not only did the subjects report that they didn't enjoy the music; the naloxone interfered with benefits from the placebo as well.

Nine months of weekly choir training and piano instruction resulted in children increasing their IQ scores by an average of 3 points over children who received drama instruction or no instruction at all. Greg Schellenberg at University of Toronto, Mississauga, measured changes in Wexler Intelligence test scores for 132 six-year-olds. Over the study period, the children gained 4 points on average, which was expected for their age and school attendance in school, but children receiving singing or piano instruction scored almost 3 points higher than that, that's a 7-point gain.[42]

Singing in a choir increases immunoglobulin, a measure of immune response, accelerates healing, and improves mood. Although stress surges by 350% during a live performance, the low-stress rehearsal improves singers health and reported moods. Singing in or listening to a choir has a positive effect on immunoglobulin.[43] Singing is a complex task and can rehabilitate people with brain damage who can no longer understand or formulate language. Singing requires the brain hemispheres to integrate, increases blood flow, and generates new neural growth in areas damaged by stroke or head trauma.[44] One researcher found that "integrated choral" music for institutionalized seniors led to reported increased quality of life, and greater engagement with others, and improved depression symptoms.[45]

Listening to just fifteen minutes of music reduced cortisol by 25% and increased interleukin, lymphocyte stimulation, and cellular protection against AIDS, cancer, and other diseases. Reduced stress allows the immune system to fight microbial threats better. Listening to music affects heart rate, energy, and strength. Michigan State conducted a music study in which subjects listened to New Age music (David Lantz, Eric Tingsan, and Nancy Rumbel), mild jazz (Kenny G), or classical music (Mozart) or Ravel (Impressionist) and were given saliva swabs to test for reductions in stress chemicals. Listening to music impacts heart rate and energy and strength.

Listening to each for just twenty minutes reduced stress and improved pain tolerance, and our immune system. Researchers had 36 subjects listen and experience a 25% decrease in levels of cortisol and a corresponding drop in interleukin levels, which are markers for inflammation and health.[46] The control group read a magazine had no decrease in stress markers.

When more than 25% of Americans take medication to moderate depression symptoms, it is critical that we all know listening to fifty minutes of music every day improves symptoms. Listening therapy helps with depression, Ann Maratos works with patients allowed to choose traditional, Latino, slow or instrumental and they show significant improvement, the same improvement as with psychotherapy, after six weeks and often earlier.[47]

Listening relieves depression even for elderly in assisted living facilities… even when they argue

Older people often suffer from higher rates of depression than the rest of society and listening to music significantly reduced their symptoms.[48] Listening also helps people with severe mental illness reduce their symptoms.[49] No matter their age or gender, people in institutional settings experienced relief from mental illness after sixteen weeks of listening to music.[50] Depression symptoms improved after people listened to music even twice a week for ten weeks.

German researchers designed a study in which elderly people either participated in a recreational singing group (even though more than a few were irritated they had to sing) or received interactive group therapy with no singing. Those who sang for thirty minutes over three weeks had significantly better improvements in their depression symptoms than the other group.[51] As little as thirty minutes improved depression symptoms, while there were no improvements for those who did not listen to music.[52] Another study showed that thirty minutes of Western, Indian, Chinese, and Malaysian music led to fewer anxiety symptoms and greater relaxation after two months.[53]

- Active musical therapy for elderly people (listening to their favorite music for one hour a week) enhanced recovery, positive feelings, social abilities, speech, and comprehension (Damiano et al. 2015)

- It improved agitated behavior in people with dementia (Lin et al. 2011).
- Active engagement in music-making and dancing elevated endorphin release and improved pain thresholds (Dunbar et al. 2012).
- Elderly people who worked out and listened to music had relief from mild and moderate depression after three months (Verrusio et al. 2014)
- Women recovering from alcoholism had reduced anxiety after 45 minutes of music therapy (Gardstrom 2013)

Groundbreaking work showed the role of music and language as a dual neural system and made the colossal revelation that the two share pathways. Music training develops the neural pathway that underlies the language that is essential for academic success. A Patel's research showed that auditory information is integrated into a single stream. As a result, music training improves the neural encoding and comprehension of speech and comprehension. Early musical training (like early bilingual education) improves the ability to understand patterns corresponding in otherwise identical sentences in an unknown language. The ability to understand variations in pitch, amplitude, and intensity is key to successful communication (prosody is every move, gesture we use to communicate meaning). Using the right intonation is essential for communicating and instrumental to the acquisition of language. Music training allows for better understanding of intonation, so that strings of words can be meaningful. This is the key to successful social interaction and academics.

Decades of neuroscience shows the neural circuitry and music for enhanced high order cognition. Incredible studies by A Patel research on the relationship between music and enhanced neural tracking and language (music and language neurons overlap) offer some of the most promising avenues to spontaneous learning, enhanced memory and accelerated learning. Cognitive processing and music are rule based and according to Patel, "have limited elements with an infinite number of combinations that require the most sophisticated high-level thinking." Sound has a rhythm and melody and activate Broca's area. Sound training improves the neural encoding of speech.[54] Listening to and playing music is an easy way to prepare the brain for language and for highly complex cognition. This suggests that cognitive resources are transferred from one domain to the other because they are common neural circuits.[55]

Musicians have a superior auditory working memory--critical for learning and intelligence.

Nina Kraus, a neuroscientist and "sound trailblazer," identified the importance of making music and listening to sounds. Listening for the music in the environment trains the brain to *pick important* information out of it which grows more sophisticated neurons. More neurons allow us to hear the most important information in our daily life. I was shocked when she pointed out the obvious implication of music for everyone with a brain. The ability to listen to the relevant sounds in a sea of what otherwise would be noise, is key to lifelong success. Most of us take for granted that we should listen to a teacher instead of the background noise in a classroom, listen to the boss instead of the sounds in the office like a phone or computer or colleagues talking, or listening to a friend talking instead of any other sound. We naturally filter out irrelevant sounds like an overhead light or fan or a passing car or group of strangers talking. Kraus quantifies the effects of sound and music on the brain and our responses (unconscious) to sound. The faster the brain's response to a sound, frequency following response (FFR), the faster we learn. The faster response is typical of a healthier brain; young people respond quickly, as do musicians and second language speakers.

Listening to notes to match the melody trains the brain for "effortful" listening, just like language acquisition does. A musician's brain routinely searches for the right sound in the environment, and as a result musicians' neural networks are sophisticated. The neural pathways used for processing language are more developed in musicians and improve all their language skills.[56]

Every time we hear, we process sounds, which causes brainwaves that look like soundwaves. EEG scans shows the physical results of neurons communicating electronically. The healthier the brain, and the faster the FFO and the more neural connections; a faster response is correlated with learning and intelligence. Musicians have faster responses to sounds and display the same healthy neural responses as young people do. Playing an instrument (like learning a new language) enhances sound processing and the neural representation of pitch and timing in sounds of speech.[57]

Learning a second language grows neurons like playing an instrument.

When I began playing the clarinet in fifth grade, my main method was listening so I could mimic what I heard, I was no protégé. Listening to the environment to see if I matched and to see if I played the right notes forced my brain to listen for a particular sound, which requires more neurons. Those neurons created pathways also used as language pathways. Musicians process language significantly faster than non-musicians. Learning a language means listening for the right sound. This requires neurons to fire and bind together to create neurons and more connections, the same we use for learning and memory. Over time, a regular practice of listening for meaning and for speaking in response, learning another language builds additional networks, like a musician. Both have an overall increase in general reading achievement.[58]

Musicians have higher standardized test scores than non-musicians. UCLA researcher James Catterall led an analysis for the U.S. Department of Education called NELLS88. This ten-year longitudinal study followed 25,000 students who had been involved in music programs. Across the board, the students scored higher on standardized tests and reading proficiency. Musicians have better cognition, hearing, and self-reported life satisfaction than non-musicians. This sizeable study shows that playing an instrument establishes neural networks, improves cognition and creativity, and improves math reasoning.

After two years of playing an instrument, lagging students close the gap

According to Nina Kraus, children from poverty or whose mothers had little education hear roughly 30 million fewer words by the age of five. With less exposure to vocabulary sounds, their brains do not have experience selecting important sounds (instead, there is more neural noise), and their attention to important stimuli is inferior. Language differentiation is even shaped prenatally. But Kraus's research showed two years of playing an instrument can close the performance gap in language levels when test scores matched the national average.[59]

- Jennifer Prescott showed students who had only two years of instruction scored up to 57 points higher on the verbal section of the SAT and 41 higher on the math section. Scores increased for all students, regardless of socio-economic background.
- In study of second graders, a group who received piano instruction and practice with a math video game outperformed a group who received extra English lessons and the same video game.; the third group received no special lessons but also played the game. Four months later, the students who played piano scored between 14% and 41% higher on a test of ratios than the other two groups.
- Positive affect, a good mood and happiness improves all learning.[60] Music can grant the positive state for learning, working, interacting and primes the brain for enhanced cognition, and brainwaves entrain with the beat.

Music training improves hearing

Playing a musical instrument improves cognition and hearing, no matter one's age.[61] A study published in the *Journal of Neuroscience* in 2015 showed older adults who start playing an instrument process more sounds with less neural proliferation than younger adults but have stronger functional connections between multiple auditory areas in the brain. Playing an instrument significantly improves the brain's ability to process sounds, especially in noisy environments. Kraus's studies show basic auditory training improves behavioral performance and changes the firing of auditory neurons: the more a person hears and experiences through hearing, the more neurons and the neurons seem to learn better.

Health and longevity are related to hearing. I ordered a saxophone for my dad instead of a hearing aid. In one study, subjects showed a significant increase in gray matter in their frontal cortex after only three weeks of being trained to detect small changes in pitch. The sophisticated neural connections required to play an instrument, coordinate fast and slow movements, and use both the right and left hand require and create a masterful network of neurons. Elizabeth Spelke of Harvard Medical School studies the neurostructural and cognitive changes related to playing musical instruments. In one experiment, brain scans showed people who started playing an instrument for an hour a week and continued for fifteen months had significant changes to many neural networks, in particular increases to the size of the corpus callosum. Those subjects had physical changes in brain structures and improved math reasoning, geometry, and map-reading skills.[62] That means that dropping music programs from public schools could significantly affect performance in spatial reasoning and mathematics. Spatial reasoning is the ability to mentally rotate images of abstract physical objects. It is an indicator of IQ.

- Playing an instrument results in a 34% increase in spatial reasoning at the end of a 2-year experiment. (Viadero 2008)
- Musicians pay attention while integrating their movements, manage timing, and other complexities, which affects their cognitive abilities. A team of sound researchers found enhanced inhibitory control correlated with consistent drumming (Slater et al. 2018).[63]

Playing music can also mean 135% more gray matter in the cortex

Learning to play an instrument builds the networks used by chess players, mathematicians, scientists, engineers and potentially all creative and innovative people. Gottfried Schlaug, a neurologist and the head of the Harvard School of Music, has been studying the effects of musical training for more than twenty years and has found striking differences in the musician's brain. Musicians can have up to 135% more gray matter in the auditory cortex. The corpus callosum is also sometimes 15% larger. Practice increases the neural connections in the corpus callosum, which allows for interhemispheric communication, and more sophisticated demands like reading music and playing instruments develop an intricate network that allows for more effective use of language, words and use. The left hemisphere can now communicate with the right hemisphere, allowing for more sophisticated speech, writing, and rich articulation of thoughts and feelings.

You don't have to play the instrument to get the effects.

Pascual-Leone of Harvard instructed musicians and non-musicians in a simple five-finger piano exercise, which the subjects agreed to practice two hours a day (impressive) for five days. As expected, there was increase in the neural territory the brain devoted to playing, as shown by the transcranial-magnetic-stimulation. The subjects were then instructed to *think-only* about playing the piano. The motor cortex still responded, and they also increased the neural growth just as when they physically rehearsed the sequence. That might explain how video games affect the brain and inspire us to play musical instruments.

To make up for the music programs that have been cut from daily curriculums across the U.S., Tod Machover, a professor and composer at MIT, wanted to get music to as many children as possible. He decided to create video games to simulate musical training. He designed *Brain Opera*, the *Toy Symphony*, *Hyperinstruments*, and *Hyperscore* to engage people in singing and playing instruments. The most influential game was *Guitar Hero*. My favorite time I've ever played was when my 75-year-old mother played, watching the screen and trying to play the drums (I laughed till I wiped tears.) Never doubt the power of a video game to influence behavior. Since the game's release, the number of people enrolled in guitar lessons in the U.S. has tripled.

Plato once said, "I would teach children music, physics, and philosophy; but most importantly music, for in the patterns of music and the arts are the keys of learning." Oliver Sacks, a neuroscientist and the author of *Musicophilia*, credits music with allowing the limitless embedding of words in a uniquely human medium. Songs with lyrics have allowed centuries of cultures information to be passed on without written language and to pay attention for the purpose of learning information. Deliberate attention in order to play an instrument (to the instructor, to the music, to placing the fingers, etc.) trains the musician to ignore distractions. Paying attention to one stimulus increases our memory, and working memory correlates with IQ. Musicians are disciplined, which may help to explain why so many have excellent academic performance and grades. At one time, the majority of music majors who applied to medical school were admitted—by contrast with only 44% of biochemistry majors.[64]

After only one month of musical training, 90% of the students in one study showed improved attention and language skills.[65] Half of the subjects studied visual arts, and the other half learned rhythm, pitch, melody, voice, and basic musical concepts. After one hour a day, changes in their neural networks increased their brain volume, and the subjects improved in geometry, spatial reasoning and map skills.[66] The changes were egalitarian, too: spatial differences based on gender *disappear* after women learn to play instruments.[67] Music and speech affect EEGs and are the fastest way to evoke emotion.

The first time I heard "Eruption" by Eddie Van Halen, I got goosebumps. This also started my lifelong crush, which might explain why I paid $200 for a concert ticket when I was old enough to know better. When the rhythm increases, my heart rate goes with it. That's why I can't listen to "Kashmir" by Led Zeppelin when I'm driving—the gas pedal follows the song's pace. On the other hand, I don't have that response to Stevie Nicks, her music makes my skin crawl, and I reflexively change the radio station. Some songs are just too sad, and some artists just grate on me for some reason. Music is emotional.

When I listen to the songs of my youth (especially Def Leppard), I can feel my energy rising. "Take My Breath Away" by Berlin brings back memories of my high school sweetheart, and I had to listen to opera after a heartbreak. I listen to Van Morrison's "Into the Mystic" as a reward for completing a particularly hard job, as it makes me feel pure joy. When I listen to Beethoven's "Moonlight Sonata," I stop speaking, breathing, or moving and just soak it in.

Sounds invoke emotions—for example, the infamous music in Jaws warns the audience that something very dangerous is coming, the music announces an unseen villain. *The Exorcist, Silence of the Lambs*, and *A Nightmare on Elm Street* all have scores designed to evoke emotions. Some themes are designed to motivate and energize, like *Raiders of the Lost Ark* or *Star Wars*. *Forrest Gump* lines up songs that make the listener feel connected to the story. Take a page from composers and use music to enhance the mood or the atmosphere in your own life, or to effortlessly connect people for a shared moment. People who attended Woodstock in 1969 can attest to how the music, coupled with the shared desire for peace, resulted in unity for thousands of strangers that weekend.

Soundtracks have great power; they delight, energize, sadden, and thrill by hijacking our attention.

Broadway musicals and soundtracks are magic. Some run for decades, holding audiences rapt with emotion. The music of Andrew Lloyd Webber allowed *The Phantom of the Opera* to fill theaters for more than 24 years, and *Cats* for more than 28. Music is emotional, and it hijacks our chemistry and attention to feed our reward systems. Soundtracks make the movie, producing intense feelings like joy and fear. The scene in *The Big Chill* where the friends dance to the Temptations' "Ain't Too Proud to Beg" brings me joy and energy; I dance myself every time I see it. The opening credits to *Rocky* make me jump up and celebrate because composer Bill Conti put together notes that inspire me and fill me with energy—once, my sister and I did sit-ups to exhaustion while playing this theme. As for the scariest soundtrack, in a moment of poor parenting I once told my daughter she should watch *Jaws*. Why I thought this was a good plan I have no idea, but the moment I started the movie, the joke was on me— she hit the mute button. It's was a whole different movie that way; my daughter brags that she wasn't scared for a second. But when I saw that movie as a kid, I lived a mile from a river, and I never swam or even took a bath again without a fear of sharks. John Williams shared his thoughts when composing, "I used notes to tell where the shark was and how fast it was approaching. The notes get faster, shorter, and closer together so the audience can feel the shark coming faster and faster become anxious.

Steven Spielberg told Williams he didn't have a shark, in fact, it wasn't finished until the last few scenes. In effect, Williams composed a score that allowed the audience to experience the fear of a great white!

Considering the physical effects of music may offer a method to moderate our moods; take for example depression symptoms. In months with less sunlight, even a few minutes of music improves mild depression is a promising treatment, and for some people it works even faster than that. In one study, patients agreed to listen to music for 50 minutes a day instead of having a weekly appointment with a psychotherapist. Those who listened to Bach or Mozart had a significant reduction in depressive symptoms after four weeks. Only half of those who attended the psychotherapy sessions reported improvements in symptoms.[68] Many studies have found that listening to music improves mood, affects the heart rate, and significantly improves the most difficult symptoms of depression.[69]

Music changes physiology, so it's quick to change attitude and mood. Only fifty minutes every day could change the physiology of depression. Patients allowed to choose traditional, Latino, slow or instrumental showed significant improvement, the same improvement as with psychotherapy, after six weeks (for many even earlier).[70] Your favorite music lowers your anxiety, relaxes you, and improves effective medical treatment.[71] People aged 55 to 64 and given the choice of listening to Western, Chinese, Indian, or Malay music (all at 60–80 bpm) significantly reduced their depression symptoms after six weeks.[72] Even a single thirty-minute session improved symptoms significantly; no one in the non-music group had any such change.

It's no longer common sense that music counters depression, it's now quantitative; meta-analyses show that music patients consistently experience improved depression symptoms.[73] In one trial, subjects were instructed to select ten favorite songs every day that made them feel happy. Over six weeks, the majority of them reported significant improvement. The instruction directed their thoughts from potential rumination on negative thoughts to directing them to think of and select ten favorite songs. The direction to think of favorite songs which improved their beneficial neurotransmitters and lessened depressive symptoms. Listening also meant they lived longer. A longitudinal study by Swedish researchers involving more than 15,000 subjects showed that attendance at cultural events involving concerts or choir singing was associated with both health and longevity.[74]

Nostalgic music inspires people and increases strength and youthful feelings

Years ago, Harvard psychologist Ellen Langer recruited a number of 70- to 80-year-old men to spend a week at a monastery that had been revamped to look like 1959, with the appropriate decor, tv shows, songs on the radio, and magazines. One group was told to reminisce about that time of their life, and the other was instructed to pretend it was 1959. Both groups were put through cognitive and physical tests at the end of the week, and the men who were instructed to pretend it was 1959 showed significant improvements in memory, strength, vision, flexibility, and even intelligence.

The songs of our youth have a therapeutic punch. All music has an effect on our nervous system, whether fast or slow, it improves our performance. But fast music can impair our ability to concentrate on mental tasks and to recover from stressors. But the superpowered songs are those that were popular when we were eighteen to twenty-two. The oldies trigger the most powerful physical responses. Even anticipating listening to a great song increases dopamine and alerts the dopamine receptors to expect something wonderful soon. PET imaging shows dopamine reaches a peak while we're listening to music, which improves executive functions.[75] Even after a disappointing concert, dopamine receptors can continue anticipating for a couple of days.

Songs support Alzheimer's patients who walked into the training room remembered to begin their physical therapy when their favorite music played in the background—hits from their late teens and early twenties. Oliver Sacks described how Alzheimer's patients at Beth Abraham Hospital had improved recall and symptoms when they listened to music that evoked an emotional response. One of my favorite clients used to faithfully visit her uncle in an Alzheimer's facility even after he didn't know her anymore, but one day she brought her mother's piano music, and was shocked at his response. He sat by her and visited as if before the disease, it only lasted twenty minutes, but listening to the familiar music increased his dopamine so that he was cognizant.

Any songs support Parkinson's patients, they don't need an emotional connection to music to reap its therapeutic benefits. Listening to any music increases dopamine, which allows them to move with less physical stutter and relieves the compromised cognitive performance. I once visited a friend's mother who has Parkinson's on a day when she couldn't stand up. I turned the TV to a music station, and within 45 minutes she could stand unassisted.

For stroke patients, familiar and positive songs can be therapeutic. At the stroke rehabilitation center in one Texas research hospital, therapists are integrating emotionally powerful songs into treatment of people profoundly affected by stroke. They are finding the familiar and the positive increase brain activation and functional connectivity, improving speech, mobility, and quality of life. One patient, Kathy from Louisiana, suffered a stroke that left her all but speechless and wheelchair bound. Her musician husband played Johnny Cash's "I Walk the Line," and when she sang along and even finished the lyrics without the music playing, they credit Johnny for her full recovery.

Listening to the right music accelerates learning...so bring it to the workplace, homelife, and school!

The 1970s had a free spirit and a sound of its own. George Lazanov put his passion to empirical study of music and the question of does it accelerate learning, he showed it sped learning a second language. Oslander and Schroeder showed that students learning French acquired vocabulary faster while listening to baroque music—but only slow baroque music. Why? Slow baroque lowers heart rate, respiration and entrains the brain, our autonomic nervous system. Lower stress levels mean lower levels of cortisol, and lower cortisol allows us to do everything better (heal, sleep, learn, solve problems, etc.).

Listening to "non-predictive" music enhances calm, reading, falling and staying asleep.

Many types of music affect the heartbeat and blood oxygenation or brings physiological relaxation but some types of slow music may be therapeutic, even magical. The non-predictive references the style of the composer who never repeats the melody and doesn't follow the pattern our brain expects and as a result, lowers cortisol, lowers blood pressure, improves blood flow. Trained musicians naturally predict music. I had no idea what this meant until one after another, my clients (musicians, conductors, music teachers) came to tell me they always predict, but after listening to the non-predictive they stop. For one Conductor, she made a point to tell me she had been afraid during flying her entire life, *really* afraid. That is until she put in headphones with the right music, non-predictive.

What's a predictable song? Your brain listens to the melody and naturally anticipates the next notes, like in the Mozart classic we know as "Twinkle, Twinkle, Little Star." If you want to add, "How I wonder what you are," you are predicting. Musicians are aware of predicting where the music is going. Many musicians have come to me over the years to explain how they predict music, saying things like "I always pay attention to music, but when I listened to Steven Halpern's music (the only musician I know who sends out his music for independent testing). I didn't know where it was going and stopped." When there's no pattern, the brain relaxes and improves its thinking, reading, writing, and even sleeping abilities. One of my clients who is a non-predictiveness skeptic is also a musician who conducts orchestras. She had a fear of flying that made her miserable for a long time, and she told me that listening to non-predictive musing put her at peace during takeoff for the first time ever.

- When I was still teaching had my students listen to non-predictive music by composer Steven Halpern. Bobby said it was the first time he had read a chapter "straight through without stopping".

He said ordinarily by the end of a sentence he would get up to wander to another room, often to antagonize his sister, return for few more sentences, set fire to the carpet, and so forth. (He really did set fire to the carpet—I verified with his parents at conferences.) I was so happy when he told me that when he put the Halpern song on repeat, his attention deficits stopped. With that music playing, he read a chapter without stopping "for the first time in his life".

- My friend's child had devastating tantrums from the time he was very little. I witnessed one where she took him to the car to calm down. Tears ran down his blotchy red cheeks just like tears ran down my friend's face. She had fastened him into the car seat then stood outside her minivan crying. I ran to her saying "Did you play the Halpern?" It was in the car so she pressed play. By the time the door shut his tantrum stopped. It stopped so suddenly that it looked odd to be calm with such a red face. The tantrum happened a week later. After three or four beats he was silent then asked, "Can I have a popsicle?". That day she told me she had hope for the first time. The tantrums in stores, parties, and church had been truly cutting into the sanity of her family. When the fits did return, they were less and less frequent and less intense.

- Another client said she hadn't slept through the night in eight years: "My husband walks in his sleep; every night and I wait for him to go back to bed. My son is two, he's never slept through the night, and has night terrors." She played Halpern on repeat in her room and in her son's, and the next morning before class she told me she'd slept through the night. Her eyes welled up with tears. Then again two months later, when I unexpectedly ran into her so I asked her about sleep. She told me she played the music for only a few more days. They'd all started sleeping, there was no more need.

- Another client, a quiet, reserved who man who hadn't spoken in class when I mentioned Halpern, he said "I've never slept more than five hours a night. As a kid, I was always the first one up. My mom gave up and just told me not to wake anyone else until the sun came up." Until a month ago, I never slept past sunrise. Then my wife took your music class, told me about the music; I put a headphone in one ear and hit the replay. I slept eight hours that night, and I have since.

- A favorite story I love is from a client-in-menopause, she said "I can't sleep, I can't stay asleep, I get up to use the bathroom and can't fall back to sleep." As always, I said "Halpern." She said she'd tried everything and finally listened to a song: "I've never made it to the end, I fall asleep." Which song? everyone wanted to know. It doesn't seem to matter. Over the last 15 years, I've heard from clients that it works and which doesn't matter.

- I used to think the music worked because of the placebo effect until a new mom (chronically exhausted) played it for her infant baby who slept through the night.

- A client who loves her dog told me that she played a song on repeat through the night of the Fourth of July night. Her ordinarily neurotic dog slept soundly, making the phenomenon cross-species. Another client played the music after her dog had surgery and needed pain relief. She said he fell asleep almost as soon as she started this music.

- My dog groomer plays non-predictive (Steven Halpern's compositions) during the entire day. She says all the dogs are peaceful and there is no whining!

Stress increases the frequency of brainwaves to more than 39 per minute, but for the most part waking brainwaves are in a beta state, between 13 and 39 per minute. In a relaxed state, they slow to 8–12 per minute, which is the alpha state. A lower frequency reduces cortisol, improves immunological factors, and increases NK cell activity and lymphokines. Lower cortisol accelerates healing. Any time we have lower stress, our immune system markers improve. We learn better, pay attention better, and think and heal better. Lower stress improves sleep and memory and enhances our pain threshold.

Meditating and listening to slow music entrains our brainwaves, slowing us to the alpha state and improving performance. Listening to music after surgery reduces reported pain by 10% to 30%.[76] Listening to slow music also helps with pain related to arthritis, fibromyalgia, surgery, and chronic conditions. A team of psychiatrists reviewed 768 titles and abstracts on the effects of music on chronic pain and found that music interferes with our pain response and aids in recovery and wellness.[77]

- Music making alters gene expression in people with coronary heart disease (Bittman 2013).
- Musical stimuli activate physiological pathways and can improve body responses (DeNora, T. 2013).
- Group drumming increases NK cell activity and lymphokines and reduces cortisol (Bittman et al. 2001).
- Recreational music-making modulates immunological responses in 65-year-olds (Koyama et al. 2009).
- Recreational music-making improves the immune system in healthy corporate employees (Wachi et al. 2006).

Given the choice of listening to music or thinking about math or reading, we choose music. But even though slow or classical music is good for cognition and focus, it doesn't always improve computation, reasoning, or reading comprehension. When a "listener" chooses unconsciously between paying attention to the music and doing math, their brain will listen to the music if it has a predictable beat (as classical music often does).[78] Listening to non-predictive does not interfere, it can enhance, it can even slow seizures. Non-predictive music enhances attention, increases blood flow which improves attention deficits. When music doesn't follow a repeating pattern, conscious listening fades and allows brain wave frequencies to slow down (which improves cognitive processing.) A non-predictive melody lowers stress and blood pressure so that the brainwaves reach alpha state where the ability to learn, function, and accelerated healing. The time has come to use this magic power for good.

What if kindness, equality, and positive requires music?

Empathy is the human connection that creates a society worth living in. Feeling the plights of others allows us to build relationships, both individually and as a community. The importance of altruistic behaviors for the survival of a community cannot be overstated. In schools, teachers work to build community and compassion between students. Some people lack empathy—including people with neurological conditions like autism, or antisocial personality disorder, for instance—and now brain scans can reveal the neural basis of empathy. Certain parts of the brain show activation when we perceive a person to be like us.

That's not fair, social brutality and civil unrest!

Have you ever watched someone get a gift and felt jealous? The answer may depend on whether you look like them. This study suggests that we don't empathize with people who look different, and this may be setting us up for a dangerous standoff. If people voted for candidates on the basis of discrimination and special benefits, it could lead to them voting against immigrants or affirmative action. Recently NPR surveyed more than 5,000 people and found that black people felt they had been discriminated against and gave examples.[79] Only 17% of the Asians surveyed said they had been discriminated against and gave examples. But 42% of white people believed that whites were discriminated against although they had never personally been a victim, (less than 1% gave an example).

In a ground-breaking study, Tal-Chen Rabinowitch of Washington University measured the reactivity in the frontal cortex when a subject watched someone receiving a gift—first, someone of their own race, and then someone of a different race. In the first case, viewers had a response in the frontal cortex, but in the second case there was less activation. After 3 to 10 sessions of making music together in a mixed-race setting, the scans now showed the brain responded when the person of another race received a gift as when the brain activated watching the gift of the child who belonged to their own race.[80]

> "Music brings people, it allows us to experience the same emotions. People everywhere are the same in heart and in spirit. No matter what language we speak, what color we are the form of our politics or the expression of our love and our faith; music proves we are the same! John Denver

Can music be the revolution?

> "How powerful is your magic flute"
> —Amadeus Mozart

There are times in life, and times in history people can behave in a manner inconsistent with personal beliefs and morals. The Holocaust is perhaps the most dramatic example: once law-abiding citizens engaged in violent acts and contributed to genocide because they were willing to follow orders. Stanley Milgram designed a now-famous study to understand why non-violent people would carry out orders that contradicted their belief systems. In the Obedience Experiment the world of psychology learned people do what they are told (by an authority). Subjects were asked to take part in a learning experiment where another subject (in fact a confederate) had agreed to be electrically shocked for each wrong answer they gave. The experimenters wanted to see if the subjects would be willing to shock another person, even to the point of harm, solely because an authority figure (a "person in a lab coat") told them to continue. People do what they're told, but they also do what they see. Words in song are orders telling the listener what to do, the means by which we listen is the unseen authority.

How the conformist 50s led to the revolt of the late 60s

Social movements in the 1950s began when rock and roll music gained enough of a following that young people were willing to turn against the stringent behavioral expectations of the entire society, conservative conforming archetypes furthered by Hollywood, and reinforced by parents, the community and teachers. The music, the beat, and the powerful emotional effect were in many ways what allowed young people to question every one of the expectations of the 50s. The radical changes to our culture in the 1960s were inspired by changes in music…American music was never the same after.

Elvis Presley's music had such an effect on emotions, as did the Beatles, that adults thought young people had "gone mad". Audiences were inspired to uncharacteristic behavior; so many would jump to their feet, dance wildly, scream out, some cried, groups of people would even run after their car. When the Beatles arrived in the United States, huge crowds met them at the airports and soon after all the screaming, new attire and hairstyles, and new lifegoals including pursuing musical passions instead of traditional careers. And this dramatic effect of music on the youth came when lawmakers were supporting the House Un-American Activities Committee and blacklisting the entertainment industry; politicians claimed, "Rock and roll music is corrupting our youth through movies and music…that that 2-beat pattern is in every number." The claim was music powerful that it must have been "a communist plot to corrupt U.S. youth."[81]

Maybe the most extreme conjunction of music and a revolution happened in the U.S.S.R. While American politicians called rock and roll a communist plot, the Communist Party banned the Beatles and prohibited Soviets from listening to them. Lesley Woodhead, an American spy in Russia at the time, cited Nikita Kruschev as declaring that the electric guitar was "the enemy of the Soviet Union." This one extremely unpopular policy may have single-handedly turned public opinion against the Soviet regime and marked the beginning of the end of the political party.[82]

By the end of the decade, another social revolution had swept the United States. Music played a major role in the civil rights movement. Lawmakers, public leaders, and members of the movement credited music as an inspiration during that violent and bloody time. Support for equal rights and voting for black people in the United States was perhaps best portrayed in the lyrics of popular music: songs like "We Shall Overcome," "Strange Fruit," "Oh Freedom," and "People Get Ready" inspired social and political change and comforted those who worked tirelessly to bring it about.

The Vietnam War grew unpopular in a time when music provided a medium for communicating anger, and calls for the end of involvement are reflected in "Blowing in the Wind," "For What it's Worth," "War (What Is It Good For?)," and "Give Peace a Chance" Protest songs were sometimes the only outlet for artists and citizens who were frustrated and angry about a war they didn't believe in.

The words in a song also influence people's behaviors. "We Are the World" raised 63 million dollars to counter the widespread, life-threatening poverty in Africa. Songs with romantic lyrics lead people in waiting rooms to give their phone numbers to strangers twice as often as other music. And researchers in France tracked tips left for waiters when the music was about charitable giving than controls listening to music with another message. Lyrics bring people together, and creating music together increases empathy, encourages giving, and creates unity for a cause and motivation for change. The Rabinowitz study showed that making music together allowed this effect to happen very quickly. Consider the changes we could inspire!

> "This will be our response to violence: That we will make music more intensely, more beautifully and more devotedly than ever before."
>
> Leonard Bernstein

- Elementary school children learn better after relaxing by listening to music. The APA released the results of twenty studies showing a positive correlation between music and cognitive academics. Slow music reduces stress on test-taking days and creates a positive state. Paul Learning found the use of that playing music during Title I reading instruction in a Brooklyn class resulted in a dramatic rise in scores. The ESEA showed more than 30,000 children in 43 schools, and the ESEA Title I evaluation report on the Wichita Program for Educationally Deprived Children found that gains were made in corrective reading program with music and related arts.
- New Jersey Public Schools used music to improve learning in their ESEA Title I Summer Program. They ran a program with cultural events and vocal and instrumental music for enrichment and additional art, music, P.E., and industrial arts classes. The at-risk children who entered this program had higher math scores. As a result, the California Art Council's Alternatives in Education program has made an average gain of 1.5 times the normal rate in math (.75 years in 6 months).

"The intuitive mind is a sacred gift, while the rational mind is a faithful servant. We have created a society that honors the servant and has forgotten the gift." A Einstein

All learning: listening, writing lyrics, playing an instrument, or singing. Put it into your life, work and classroom…it will change your life. Dos and Don'ts:

Do play music with lyrics that further your purpose. Do write your own lyrics, singing them forces attention to the purpose, and light manipulation. Writing songs set to a familiar tune allow for fast, focused training: beginning-of-the-year song, how to study or tips for test-taking, safety tips for industry or technology, industrial rules, policies or any other boring information an average person would skip over otherwise. Do have others write lyrics; in school for a grade, at work for a competition, at home for fun, bonus points, non-monetary allowance, bragging rights; the sky is the limit.

Don't play music with a fast beat while thinking, reading, writing, calculating, or working in groups. We unconsciously pay attention to music first, which means we have to reread to comprehend things. Research suggests it can add twice the time needed for a task. Some studies show certain rock music lowers the quality of a workout because of its effect on the heart rate. My favorite music reduces strength: the Beatles, Jimi Hendrix, the Rolling Stones, Led Zeppelin, and Janice Joplin.

Do play rock music to increase energy and attention, especially between 1 and 3 p.m., before important events to peak norepinephrine, dopamine and blood flow for alertness!

Do use to transition to a new topic, to help wake up and especially first thing in the morning. The passion for a certain genre of music, whether it's hip-hop, heavy metal, or EDM, provides a magic neural energy for the hardest tasks. Anything you need an individual or group to learn is easier with music.

Don't play any favorite music during a meeting or instruction or test. Play relaxing or non-predictive music. Make sure it's slow or classical music (especially Mozart's K. 448) or something relaxing for ten to thirty minutes before an important class, presentation, meeting to establish a positive state and enhanced cognition.

Do play music while entering and exiting; share the research behind the music.

Do survey your people listening to find their favorite music and find out how soft and non-predictive music affects them personally. Start by playing a song for just five minutes, and then check to see whether it's become unnoticeable or is bothering them. Not everyone responds to sound the same way.

Do require *all* projects to have music. Television shows, commercials and soundtracks and important parts of life have sound and can be scored for a great effect. Use it to encourage face to face interaction, build relationships, or public speaking because this becomes effortless when music is the focus. For school performance, activities and lessons should include a musical component: score the reading, the character, a math formula, vocabulary words, it doesn't matter nor does the song they choose. The important thing is getting the learner to look for the material in music. It's a guaranteed way to catch their attention and create motivation where there isn't any. Picking a song is where they learn the most, because they must understand the concept in order to do so

Do play your favorite music as an invitation to start, build or improve a relationship. Anyone who knows or uses favorite music can integrate things the cares about: use for lessons, use to ask questions, what instrument have you ever wanted to play, who's your favorite artist, what's your favorite song, or movie soundtrack, any information you gather is material for building relationships.

Do pair upbeat music with positive or slow to sad, or scary-sounding music for meaning. Kyoto University researchers found that people who listen to upbeat, happy, or sad music had greater accuracy in giving the meaning of descriptive words used for characters than those who didn't listen to music. What a great way to communicate vocabulary or character! For example, an ominous idea as a photo of Stalin with the "Imperial March," Darth Vader's theme from *Star Wars*. Teachers can quickly create a presentation with a few photos of the dictator, added descriptive information, and hit play. it's a sure way to get the attention of everyone with a brain.

> *Overall,* music seems to involve the brain at almost every level. Even allowing for cultural differences in musical tastes, the researchers found evidence of music's remarkable power to affect neural no matter where they look *in the brain, from primitive regions in, all animals, to more recently evolved regions thought to be distinctively human.*
> — Mark Tramo, neurobiologist, Harvard University

> *Arts education facilitates language development, enhances creativity, boosts reading readiness, helps social development, assists general intellectual achievement, and fosters a positive attitude toward schools.*
> —Hanshumacher

> "One of our greatest assets in this country are the talented boys and girls who devote their early lives to music, to appreciation of music and understanding of it."
> —John F. Kennedy

Do use music to create moods.

- Before everyone leaves for work or for school
- When everyone returns home at the end of a day
- Set the stage during meals to lower stress and support a positive interaction
- Play slow or non-predictive music to relax, lower your heart rate, and improve oxygenation before bed, to
- To energize yourself upon waking up in the morning
- To motivate yourself to do a dreaded task.

For behavior management and to train groups

- To control rambunctiousness (slow, classical and especially non-predictable music)
- Train routine and or give warnings ("When you hear this song. you need to be silent immediately")
- To mark transitions
- for movement activities
- during group work.

For engaging children who are acquiring language (ELA and CLD)

Learning through song is especially effective for children who don't speak English natively. Studies show that they can pick up articulation, word recognition, and sight reading this way. My sister is a professor at Metro State College at University of Denver. She studies language acquisition and has a gift for turning content into lyrics set to familiar and simple songs. For example, she wrote the songs *BICS and CALP* to quickly teach essential information to teachers. Mainstream educators often overlook the specific difficulties faced by second-language learners, but I can use my sister's songs to train everyone. Whether they're interested or not, I hijack their attention and force them to remember content they might not have processed otherwise.

When I'm training clients, I begin by asking a couple of questions about second-language learners:

1. How long before second-language speakers can "visit" using conversational English?
2. How long before second-language speakers can comprehend and use "academic" English?

Their answers vary, and no one is ever confident about the answer. But after singing this song together it is an amazing!!!! She set it to *BINGO*.

BICS and CALP   by Vicki Nilles, PhD
Well in this school we have some kids who speak another language
O that is so great, O that is so great, O that is so great
Let's really celebrate it!
Let's teach them well with what we know about *sheltered instruction*
O this will be fun, O this will be fun, this will be so fun,
We cannot wait to try it! Well ole Jim Cummins has a thought and this is how it goes O,
BICS and BICS and CALP, BICS and BICS and CALP, BICS and BICS and CALP,
And this is how it goes O.
With BICS kids can communicate just using basic English,
O they talk at lunch, O they talk at lunch, O they talk at lunch,
And then they switch to Spanish!

With BICS the kids don't have to wait because they learn it quickly,
Yes in just two years, yes in just two years, yes in just two years,
They really sound terrific!
Now here is where it complicates because they need school language,
CALP is what we want, CALP is what we want, CALP is what we want.
But we will have to wait O.

Oh Just how long will this CALP take as we have tons of content?
This is what we know, this is what we know, this is what we know,
That it takes five to seven!

After everyone sings, I ask the questions again…

- How long before second language speakers can "visit" using conversational English?
- How long before second language speakers can comprehend and use "academic" English?

Year after year of training, *every* time a group sings the lyrics, they have an epiphany of understanding (students acquiring language)! I hear "Oh, I had no idea" and "Wow. It takes that long?" They turn to one another and continue to explain how shocked they are. When a group of people sing lyrics together, it forces attention to the content! It's not me—it's my sister's song and the power of music. Think of how you can push your purpose: parenting, topic, skill, training).

Mission Impossible? If you cannot find how to form a relationship find a song!

I first heard a song that gave me chills while watching a movie in 1986 while sitting in my favorite, Century 21 Theater, with my lifelong friend Brenda. During the life and death scene all I could think about was finding that song—back then, finding music required detective skills and this one wasn't on the soundtrack. It wasn't for twenty years until. I was driving home listening to an NPR fundraiser. I paid $120 that CD ...I had to have that song. The next day I raced to my class to tell them I found it. My smarty-pants high school students asked, "Why didn't you just call NPR and ask the name of the song?" I never thought of that. (If you want to know more about the movie and the song, see the Relationships chapter; it was "Someone to Watch over Me.") Sharing a story, especially involving a song, and playing a chill-inducing song for whatever reason builds connection (students, my clients, my family).

1. "Show and Tell." Select a song that gives "chills" and explain why they selected it; that means you have to share juicy which makes us enticing. Listening to the song and a story increases endogenous opioids, read Essentials chapter. Of all the activities I have used in 20 years of teaching, this is the most effective hook in a relationship. People in a group who had never approached me would come up to me to tell me about other songs and music they liked.

2. To build relationships, or create a meaningful project, pick a song that represents you or a song that relates to something that has happened to you. Explain how a song reflects the importance of __.

3. In the lyrics (of any song), find three of the following: an interesting word, an example of courage, an unfamiliar word, a metaphor, a historical similarity, a reference to science, a reference to geology or geography. Use Disney movies, Classic movie soundtracks, Greatest hits of the 60s or 70s, use songs you know are popular!

4. Listen to non-predictive music for reading and writing and to calm unwanted behavior (at home or in a classroom) or change a mood

or lower stress (in the workplace)—but not for cooperative work, listening to this stops us from talking.

5. Play slow music to mask a noisy room or an unpleasant feeling and to improve physiology and reduce errors in math and science: classical music improves accuracy by 21%.

6. Select a song with lyrics reflecting the content or skill to accelerate learning: vocabulary words, meanings, themes, theses, or spelling.

7. Research music and use for public-speaking presentation or written assignment.

8. Do research on the effects of music. For instance, study the effects of music on plant growth. I like these studies like everyone else, and I can't get enough of the ones that show which songs make plants grow or wither; unfortunately, there isn't much scientific validity to this research, but the sound frequencies of music do stimulate seeds to grow, and studies measuring plant height and number of leaves do seem to show they respond accordingly.

Slow music enhances growth, easy listening music, especially light Indian or Reggae music, stimulates growth. Western rock, traffic sounds, and silence do not. The effects of rap on plant growth--showed grotesquely abnormal cells and significantly different structural development. Even worse, rodents have slower maze-learning times and are more aggressive with each other when they listen to rap and heavy metal. I have not been impressed by the research on these topics, or on the question of the best paint color to improve learning, so at the moment they are just interesting questions in need of high-quality research. I cannot vouch for your plants on music but the neuroscience of your brain on music is compelling!

What to do from here? Choose the music with purpose! Everyone with a brain must play an instrument, sing, or listen to music deliberately. Decide what the effect you are after; making music together for empathy, listening to favorite music or classical or baroque to sustain or change mood, listening to non-predictive for better attention, lower stress, improved sleep. Music allows you to attempt to do what you would if you knew you could not fail!

ENDNOTES

[1] Menegazzi, J. J. et al. (1991). A randomized, controlled trial of the use of music during laceration repair. Annal Emerg Med, pp. 348-50.

[2] Smolen, D. et al. (2002). The effect of self-selected music during colonoscopy on anxiety, heart rate and blood pressure. Appl Nurs Res.

[3] Bernardi et al. (2009). Dynamic interactions between musical, cardiovascular, and cerebral rhythms in humans. Circulation, pp. 3171-3180.

[4] Jia et al. (2016). Music attenuated a decrease in parasympathetic nervous system activity after exercise. PlosOne.

[5] Da Silva et al. (2014). Auditory stimulation with music influences the geometric indices of heart rate variability in men. Int. Arch Med.

[6] Babisch, W, Jarup, L. (2009). Annoyance due to aircraft nose has increased over the years—Results of the HYENA study. Environmental International.

[7] Hughes, N., Fino, J. (2000). The Mozart effect: Distinctive aspects of the music – a clue to brain coding? Clin Electroencephalogr, pp. 94-103.

[8] DeNora, T., Ansdell, G. (2014). What can't music do? Psychology of Well-Being: Theory, Research, and Practice.

[9] Blascovich, J. (1994). Effects of music on cardiovascular reactivity among surgeons. JAMA, 882-884.

[10] Lies, Shelby R., Zhang, Andrew Y. (2015). Prospective randomized study of the effect of music on the efficiency of surgical closures. *Aesthetic Surgery Journal*, pp. 858–863.

[11] Shippert, R. (2005). A study of time-dependent operating room fees and how to save $100,000.00 by using time-saving products. Am J Cosmet Surg, pp. 25-34.

[12] Lee, O. K. A., Chung, Y. F. L., Chan, M. F., Chan, W. M. (2005). Music and its effect on the physiological responses and anxiety levels of patients receiving mechanical ventilation: A pilot study. Journal of Clinical Nursing, 609–620.

[13] Uchiyama, M. (2012).

[14] McCaffrey. (2009).

[15] Ozer et al. (2013). The effect of music on postoperative pain and and physiologic parameters after open heart surgery. Pain Management Nursing.

[16] McCaffrey. (2009).

[17] Bockstael, A. (2018) Presenting and processing information in background noise: A combined speaker-listener perspective. Journal of the Acoustical Society of America.

[18] Copeland, B. L., Franks, B. D. (1991). Effects of types and intensities of background music on treadmill endurance. Journal of Sports Medicine and Physical Fitness, 31(1), 100-103.

[19] Thakur, A., Yardi, S. (2013). Effect of different types of music on exercise performance in [normal] individuals. Indian J Physiol Pharmacol, 448-451.

20   Karageorghis, C. et al. (2017). Interactive effects of music tempi and intensities on grip strength and subjective affect. Scandinavian J of Medicine & Science in Sports.

21   Bigliassi, M. et al. (2016). Cerebral mechanisms underlying the effects of music during a fatiguing isometric ankle-dorsiflexion task. Psychophysiology, pp. 1472-1483.

22   Rauscher, F., Shaw, G., Ky, K. (1993). Music and spatial task performance. Nature, p. 611; Rauscher, F., Shaw, G. (1998). Key components of the Mozart effect. Percept Motor Skills, pp. 835-842.

23   Trimmel et al. (2017). Brain DC potentials evoked by listening to Mozart's sonata K. 448, Albinoni's Adagio, Schubert's Fantasia, and brown noise: Indications of a Mozart effect independent of mood and arousal. Journal of Psychology and Brain Studies.

24   Dolegui, A. S. (2013). The impact of listening to music on cognitive performance. Inquiries Journal/Student Pulse, 5(09).

25   Emery, C. et al. (2003) Short-term effects of exercise and music on cognitive performance among participants in a cardiac rehabilitation program. Heart & Lung: The Journal of Acute and Critical Care, pp. 368-373.

26   Mammarella, N. et al. (2007). Does music enhance cognitive performance in healthy older adults? The Vivaldi effect. Aging Clinical and Experimental Research.

27   Thompson, W. F., Schellenberg, E. G., Husain, G. (2001) Arousal, mood and the Mozart effect. Psych Science, pp. 248-51.

28   Chan, A. et al. (1998). Music training improves verbal memory. Nature, p. 128.

29   Pauwells et al. (2014). Mozart, music, medicine. Medical Principles and Practice, pp. 403-412.

30   Yun et al. (2017). The left middle temporal gyrus in the middle of an impaired social-affective communication network in social anxiety disorder. Journal of Affective Disorders.

31   Herdener et al. (2010). Musical training induces functional plasticity in human hippocampus. J Neurosci, pp. 1377-84.

32   Habibi et al. (2017). Childhood music training induces change in micro and macroscopic brain structure: Results from a longitudinal study. Cereb Cortex.

33   Krista et al. (2009). Music training shapes structural brain development. Journal of Neuroscience, pp. 3019-25.

34   Groussard et al. (2010). When music and long-term memory interact: Effects of musical expertise on functional and structural plasticity in the hippocampus. PlosOne.

35   Tierney A., Kraus, N. (2015). Neural entrainment to the rhythmic structure of music. Journal of Cognitive Neuroscience, pp. 400-408.

36 Cheung et al. (2017). Music training is associated with cortical synchronization reflected in EEG coherence during verbal memory encoding. PlosOne.

37 Gaser, C., Schlaug, G. (2003). Brain structures differ between musicians and non-musicians. J Neurosci.

38 Ozturk et al. (2002). Morphometric comparison of the human corpus callosum in professional musicians and non-musicians by using in vivo magnetic resonance imaging. J Neuroradiol, pp. 29-34.

39 Vaquero et al. (2016). Structural neuroplasticity in expert pianists depends on the age of musical training onset. Neuroimage, pp. 106-119.

40 Cheng et al. (2017). Positive impacts of early auditory training on cortical processing at an older age. Proceedings of the National Academy of Sciences, pp. 6364-6369.

41 Kraus et al. (2017). Music keeps the hearing brain young. Hearing Journal, pp. 44-46.

42 Schellenberg, G. (2004). Music lessons enhance IQ. Psychological Science.

43 · Kreutz et al. (2004). Effects of choir singing on secretory immunoglobulin A, cortisol and emotional state. Journal of Behavioral Medicine.

44 · Riecker, A. et al. (2000). Opposite hemispheric lateralization effects during speaking and singing at motor cortex, insula and cerebellum. Neuroreport.

45 Nyquist, D., Keylie, N. (2017). Aging and the healing power of choral music: A community-responsive evaluation of vintage voices, pp. 99-115.

46 Bartlett, D., Kaufman, D., Smeltekop, R. (1993) The effects of music listening and perceived sensory experiences on the immune system as measured by interleukin-1 and cortisol. *Journal of Music Therapy*, December 1993, pp. 194–209.

47 Maratos, A. (2008). Music therapy for depression. Cochrane Database Syst Review.

48 Gok Ugur, H. et al. (2017). The effect of music therapy on depression and physiological parameters in elderly people living in a Turkish nursing home: A randomized-controlled trial. Aging & Mental Health, pp. 1280-1286.

49 Gold et al. (2009) Dose-response relationship in music therapy for people with serious mental disorders: Systematic review and meta-analysis. Clinical Psychology Review, pp. 193-207.

50 Erkkila et al. (2011). Individual music therapy for depression: randomized control trial. Br. J. Psychiatry.

51 Werner et al. (2017). Effectiveness of group music therapy versus recreational group singing for depressive symptoms of elderly nursing home residents: Pragmatic trial. Aging & Mental Illness, pp. 147-155.

52 Costa et al. (2017). The effect of regular listening to preferred music on pain, depression, and anxiety in older car home residents. Psychology of Music.

53   Chan et al. (2011). Effects of music on depression in older people: A randomized controlled trial. Journal of Clinical Nursing; Chan et al. (2009); Cooke et al. (2009).

54   Hickey, Patel et al. (2020). Memory in time: Neural tracking of low frequency rhythm dynamically modulates memory formation. Neuroimage.

55   Patel, A. (2011). Why would musical training benefit the neural encoding of speech? The OPERA hypothesis. Audit. Cog. Neurosci, p. 42.

56   Chobert, J., Besson, M. (2013) Musical expertise and second language learning. Brain Sci, pp. 923-940; Marie, C. et al. (2010). Influence of musical expertise on segmental and tonal processing. J. Cogn. Neurosci, pp. 2701-2715; Slevc, L., Miyake, A. (2006). Individual differences in second-language proficiency does musical ability matter? Psychol Sci, pp. 675-681.

57   Francois, C., Schon, D. (2011). Musical expertise boosts implicit learning of both musical and linguistic structures. Cereb. Cortex, pp. 2357-2365; Jentschke, S., Koelsch, S. (2009) Musical training modulates the development of syntax processing in children. NeuroImage, pp. 735-744.

58   Stepanov et al. (2018). Children's early bilingualism and musical training influence prosodic discrimination of sentences in an unknown language. Journal of Acoustical Society of America.

59   Kraus, N., White-Schwoch, T. (2017). Feel the vibrations: the hearing-emotion connection. Hearing Journal, pp. 52-53.

60   Tyng, C. et al. (2017). Effects of emotion on learning and memory. Front. Psychol.

61   Kraus, N., Nicol, T. (2017) The power of sound for brain health. Nature Human Behaviour.

62   Spelke, E. (2009).

63   Slater, J., Ashley, R., Tierney, A., Kraus, N. (in press). Got rhythm? Better inhibitory control is linked with more consistent drumming and enhanced neural tracking of the musical beat in adult percussionists and nonpercussionists. Journal of Cognitive Neuroscience.

64   Wood, P. (1990). The comparative academic abilities of students in education and in other areas of a multi-focus university. ERIC; Miller, A., Coen, D. (1994). The case for music in the schools. Phi Delta Kappan, 1994.

65   Moreno, Bialystock. (2011).

66   Spelke, E. (2009).

67   Pietsch, S., Jansen, P. (2011).

68   Mayoral-Chavez, M. (2010) Music offers a simple and elegant way to treat anhedonia, the loss of pleasures in daily activities. The Arts in Psychotherapy Journal.

69   Quarto, T. et al. (2017) Interaction between DRD2 variation and sound environment on mood and emotion-related brain activity. Neuroscience.

70 Maratos, A. (2008). Music therapy for depression. Cochrane Database Syst Review.

71 Hsu, W., Lai, H. (2004). Effects of music on major depression in psychiatric inpatients. Archives of Psychiatric Nursing, pp. 193–199.

72 Chan, M. et al. (2011). Effects of music on depression in older people: A randomised controlled trial. Journal of Clinical Nursing, pp. 776-783.

73 Maratos, A. et al. (2008) Music therapy for depression. The British Journal of Psychiatry.

74 Bygren et al. (1996). Attendance at cultural events, reading books or periodicals, and making music or singing in a choir as determinants for survival: Swedish interview survey of living conditions. British Medical Journal, 21-28.

75 Pauwells et al. (2014). Mozart, music, medicine. Medical Principles and Practice.

76 Good et al. (2001). Relaxation and music reduce postsurgical pain. J Adv Nurs, pp. 208-215.

77 Garza, V. et al. (2017). Music-induced analgesia in chronic pain conditions: A systematic review and meta-analysis. Pain Physician, pp. 597-610.

78 Moreno, R. et al. (2004) A coherence effect in multimedia learning. The case for minimizing irrelevant sounds in the design of multi-media instructional messages. J Educ Psychol, 117-125.

CHAPTER 8

HOLLYWOOD AND VIDEO GAMES: YOU CAN IMPROVE COGNITION, AGING, AND PAIN

I watched movies and television for countless hours when I was a kid. I could cite the actor, the movie and say the lines of favorite movies while I watched Gone with the Wind! The beginning of *any* movie hooked me, and once that epoch movie intro started, I disappeared into the story! I still can! No doubt, by now you have been in awe of Hollywood and the thrill of being in the audience. The flashy and glamorous and blockbuster mesmerizes us with emotional and novel that intrigues, delights, or shocks us. It is the most powerful influence and a major driving factor over our behavior. For better or for worse, this is the gateway to the brain and watching and playing generate the neural highways that culminate in thoughts and behaviors.

Watching a movie and playing a video game stimulates neuroplasticity. Almost instantly, neural networks wire and rewire because of the complex cognitive interaction. That level of intense and engaging Hollywood production is a perfect model designed to get the brain's attention.

The reality of daily life does not compare to that model, and as a result, real life and the mundane responsibilities pale by comparison. Mass mediums have incredible power over attention and invite our brain to engage in their world: movies, television programming, radio, social media and gaming. Our brain is now ratcheted up for highly stimulating and can blunt interest, motivation, learning, and interacting which can lack blockbuster content. Trainers, teachers, parents commiserate about the lack of interest or the inability to get or hold attention. The inability to hold attention and learn could be a core challenge to our society and our future progress. Hollywood knows how to get it and we learn what we see.

Now consider the unthinkable...media as a tool. If you cannot beat them, join them! Movies and video games (and mass media) as the basis for important training enhances cognition. If Hollywood (mass media) engages and motivates, we use it to promote academics, job-training, and social behaviors! Using it may increase motivation for a task and close skills gaps, can help uptake the flow of information to manage *knowledge gaps* and improve innovation and productivity. The most pressing challenges to industry and education center around a lack of research, evidence, and the ability to interact based informed. This use of media can streamline policy and practice for the next level of innovation and problem-solving!

> "More engagement creates a better service, which creates more engagement."
>
> –Tien Tzuo

Using movies and video games to enhance cognition is a radical idea in professional and academic training, but if engages our attention it can help us to master skills, pursue and attain goals and peak performance. What if we now consider them a tool instead of entertainment? For our own good, we must rethink traditional methods and use all resources available to motivate human behavior; continued progress depends on good decision-making to protect our quality of life. For environmental and social viability, we need innovation and intelligence ASAP. The revolutionary change can begin only once we adjust our thinking that it is solely a dangerous and harmful medium and instead utilize them strategically for positive learning, informing and socializing. Learning from watching and playing (mass media) may offer the means to transfer knowledge, evidence, application. There is ample evidence to suggest playing certain video games improve cognition, especially the coveted ability to think critically.[1] Researchers who study the use of certain games have compelling science to use the medium in practice...

- Games activate intense user experiences to a state like flow and enjoyment which also enhances memory, learning and motivation and critical analysis
- Motivation studies show rewards enhance learning outcomes because the reward network signals remember this to the hippocampus![2] The hippocampus creates all memories, and new learning.
- Movies and or video games improve disposition and directly impact mood and can stimulate reflective thinking. Subjects report less pain while watching or playing, as well as lower depression and anxiety symptoms.[3]
- Our brain has the power to motivate itself to do boring tasks; frequent, small rewards improve motivation, increase competence and performance. This is key for motivation.[4]
- Game-based learning is expected to increase from 3.5 billion in 2018 to $17 billion in 2023
- Software design, and video in the workplace is promising in establishing safety behaviors, air filter use, and regular hard surface cleaning.

Can you learn complex material by watching a movie or playing a video game?

We learn what we see crazy fast; mirror neurons, a neural region allows us to get it as if it is happening to you personally. The brain processes visual information effortlessly and much faster than text or auditory information (common to traditional training). Watching stimulates thought, feeling, and behavior and shapes the function and physical structures in the brain. If you are stubborn or say things like "I can't"? Then you are totally wrong…because we never lose the ability to transform our neural reality, and the truth is we can choose to do things that science tell us bring change quickly. Technology forces neurons to accommodate a world of incoming novelty. Multisensory processing involved with media results in extraordinarily complex representations of sensory information and accelerates information processing. The real challenge is to find the courage to use them to train, to facilitate learning, to enhance executive function, and to shape desired and optimal behaviors. In reality, this idea is not forward-thinking, after the attack on Pearl Harbor, our military had to train millions of enlisted men at warp speed, most without any technical background. Films going back to 1941 were successful in training highly sophisticated tasks like flying a plane and medical task involving operating in combat zones…skills with zero room for error. These films were so important for training, Ronald Reagan was denied active duty…he was drafted to acting in the production.

Watching movies and playing video games effects brainwaves, neurochemistry, and functionality.

Hollywood and the gaming industry develop products to entice anyone-with-a-brain to transition from patron to user. What we are watching feels as-if it is happening to us; that means audiences and gamers empathize with the heroes and villains, the wins, and losses! The motivation to play and watch is intrinsic, as we are hardwired to pay attention and respond and remember what we see. This means that consuming the message is effortless because of the engaging watching or playing. This media is so powerful because the neurological reality is explained by the observational learning theory. Watching allowed us to adapt (learn) over thousands of years for survival. Mirror neurons, our highly sophisticated neural function, may explain why we intuitively get what we see when we watch. No effort required.

- Those who watched a movie had significant memory for content 3 hours to 9 months later, despite deliberate distraction to interfere with long-term memory recall remained high.[5]
- Thirty minutes watching an affiliative movie increases progesterone levels but watching a power movie (Bridges of Madison County v. Godfather II) increased testosterone levels. Testosterone drives power, competition and dominance behaviors. Creative writings following each movie was more likely to represent affiliative or power imagery.[6]
- Watching movies trains newlyweds to consider their own behaviors in the relationship, and the study improved marriage success rates by 24%.[7]

- MRIs of the subject watching characters interact in sitcoms featuring empathetic behaviors increased activity in the frontal cortex. Watching a movie with other individuals triggers emotions that cause synchronous brainwaves in an MRI.[8]

Modeling behavior exponentially speeds our learning! Mirror neurons allow us to understand and anticipate the meaning of another immediately, it provides how the audience feels what the characters feel. We respond to the experience we see where the observer's feelings mimic another's state, what they are thinking and emotion *they are feeling*. This is essential for healthy relationships, self-awareness and introspection. During movies, we are engaged as if we are personally experiencing what we watch as those mirror neurons provide lightning-speed processing.

Witnessing any event allows us the visuals, sounds, and experiences that build a frame of reference; that speeds comprehension and simultaneously bonds us with a companion as well as the entire audience. Researchers use MRIs to measure how a movie impacts the brain; imagine this, they found individuals EEGs change in response to watching. The as-if experience impacts hormones. Progesterone increases following a prosocial movie, and testosterone, increases after watching power-themed movies...the audience's brainwaves synchronize. Movies and video games hijack a group and force them to consider the message of the medium. Using a movie or documentary to inform a group on any topic provides an opportunity. It is imperative to counter the information gap and education complacency; we can learn pertinent information from another field of study, another perspective, culture, historical event, and or anything else we need to educate, the sky is the limit....

- The knowledge gap between researchers, evidence and the information needed to inform policy and practice is causing missed opportunities and innovation.[9]
- Researchers propose increasing the flow of evidence from scientists to practitioners is essential for problem-solving.

Learning this way allows people who depend on each other for survival to anticipate behaviors and understand one another and our quality of life.

We get better at relationships the more we communicate. More talking and more listening builds more neural functionality and improves our social skills, even if the feelings and conversation isn't accurate (see the Sex Differences chapter). This is where using dramatic scenes to train comes in. What should I say? Why is that person mad/sad/quiet and so on provides practice which is tantamount to training anyone who is frustrated or lacking social skills.

Teachers and therapists use hit shows to introduce and practice identifying emotions of characters and discussing potential ways to respond in conversation. Especially for people on the autism spectrum, watching others on a show to learn the importance of facial expression, the importance of identifying and label a feeling, and to listen to responses by other characters.

The Big Bang Theory helps special education teachers to train on the social actions and comments. The character Sheldon, a mathematician and physicist is incredibly intelligent but always blows it with his friends. Watching the characters in the scene increases the integration of hemispheres (see Sex Differences chapter) and enhances neural function for better understanding in real life. This means explicit training for social our skills. The workplace, school and every home needs ongoing relationship development and our television shows provide the learning. One of my clients complained about an employee with key knowledge for a project, but that person infuriated the rest of his team because he was rude! We brainstormed shows (movie and television) to watch as an external example of rude comments by the character for training how to get along with others.

Movies and video games take our brain on an experience. That ticket to the theater and that signing into a video game, is engaging because triggers physiological responses; each viewer can experience the compassion, empathy, and other *powerful* emotions. To this day, I watch Top Gun every time it is on my TV and still turn the channel just before Goose dies when they eject! I wasn't the only one moved by that movie; the LA Times in 1987 reported that recruiting offices across the United States had double the inquiries about enlisting. The answer may be in our amygdala, once considered a flight-or-fight structure. Researchers studying fMRIs find it hard to tell the difference in a subject who is looking at a real event and subjects who are viewing images of an event. The pituitary gland responds even when we are only viewing and triggers release of powerful hormones – which I am sure is why I almost jumped out of my chair to run from the theater during the basement scene of *Silence of the Lambs*. Viewing puts the brain into that receptive state where it "absorbs" the suggestions within seconds – a fact that is not lost on researchers for advertising. When our amygdala activates as a result of emotion (fear, rage, disgust, anger, happiness), it increases our chances of storing a memory. Anything emotional increases chances of learning or remembering.

Watching shifts our brainwaves from beta (an active state) to alpha (relaxed and peaceful state) where an increase in creativity and decrease in bad feelings. A shift to alfa happens within 30 seconds of viewing. This allows the frontal lobe and our emotional center and the prefrontal cortex, home of our personality, to reset. These control motor function, memory, language, judgment, impulse control, and social and sexual behavior. While we watch we are consciously aware of our thinking and it is a great place to make goals, consider ideas for relationship conversations, game plan.

Consider what this means for cinema, Hollywood is our possible vehicle to influence, even drive human behavior. "Neurocinematics" is a field of study that seeks to explain what happens in the brain while we are watching a movie. It shows brainwaves entrain and the primary auditory cortex is active, along with the visual cortex, along with the limbic system (depending on how emotional the scene is).[10] Hollywood producers and video game designers know the ingredients necessary for our brain to pay attention, feel emotion, which is why we remember movies without study or rehearsal…the neurological result is a change to our function and structure in our brain and increases the chance we will mimic or be accepting of the message of the medium.

Documentaries and dramatic movies are key to a viable society and even a healthy future.

It's a time for Americans to be informed and aware of pressing world events. In the post-truth era educating as many as possible is essential. Documentaries and nonfiction film mean large audiences can learn information fast. They are a force for social change and to promote action[11]. Watching a documentary or a film about a topic, an historical event, or environmental story should begin all lessons and work-related projects. Movies provide the opportunity for a large or small group to operate from an important base of knowledge as well as set the optimal mood physiologically and that improves our social interaction after viewing.

Documentaries are a powerful means to educate in unprecedented fashion. After more than 100 years of filmmakers telling stories, it's time we use them as the vesicle for social change.[12] Documentaries not only give viewers the insight of the world's expert but the ability to tell a story in a way that can bring positive change to our life and our planet. During viewing, participants brains synchronize EEGs and increase our levels of dopamine. Human beings engage in the story of the movie and remember the content because of the neural engagement.[13]

Protecting our economy and keeping our society safe means we must protect truth and accuracy. Movies, documentaries, and nonfiction supported by science play an important role of helping to educate our society. We are in a time termed the "post-truth era" and it's possible that it's because society is unmotivated to learn or to be an informed member of society. After decades of watching television that desensitizes and disassembles our analytical viewing, evidence suggests for science through movies to be effective it has to be not just competent and trustworthy, but *meaningful* and important.[14] This is an ultimate path to learning again after years of unmotivated people who lack education, experience or specialized education, "humans have indirect means to learn from others that are both faster and considerably less risky."

There are plenty of reasons why playing fast-paced games and watching television have compromised our ability to pay attention for long periods of time. The message producers communicate at lightspeed, and today, seem to only need a few seconds to maintain the attention of the viewers.

In the last few years, *Sesame Street* has changed its format from developing a story in 20 minutes to limiting it to under 5 minutes. A disturbing study on toddlers' attention and watching *SpongeBob SquarePants* found 4-year-olds lost their attention after 2-3 seconds; this suggests watching it depletes their cognitive ability to focus.

Did years of watching and playing leave a large number of Americans unengaged by truth; is it no longer engaging enough to get their attention. False information travels faster and to more people than accurate and true stories, people are more likely to send it to more people on social media. The common traits of people who believe conspiracy theories includes pessimism, feeling powerless, and suffering anxious feelings. Psychologists guess that the belief in the obviously false is a self-protection that gives a feeling of control…the truth is too upsetting. Today the number of people who believe conspiracy theories is at an all-time high. False stories are shared on social media 6 times more than factual stories.[15] Also of concern, the study that people who spend more time using technology are less likely to analyze and use critical thinking skills. The antidote? To counter the loss of these precious skills we need more time reading for enjoyment.

Playing video games, especially action games, improves executive function and attention.

But recent studies show that playing certain games improves the gamers' ability to focus on tasks in the presence of significant distractions. These games require a top-down type of attention and, as a result, increase the ability to select relevant information and to suppress distractibility in both adults and children aged 7 to 17 years.[16] The practice of switching their attention from task to task allows them to improve their task-switching abilities, which improves performance and the cost of switching from one project to another. These gamers are trained by constantly changing environments where they evaluate and reevaluate the task at hand. This behavior requires cognitive flexibility and improves the ability to switch tasks and be more effective. Television does not: It decreases the ability to switch tasks and multi-task effectively.[17] Video games train visual perceptual and enhance problem solving and groupthink is fast and cost-effective.

- Playing serious video games increases attention, cognitive control and working toward rewards with parameters inspires brain plasticity[18]
- Gamers who used spatial reasoning to navigate a video game increased hippocampal neuroplasticity[19]
- Females who play Tetris have more gray matter in the hippocampus[20]

Watching a movie relieves unpleasant emotions and playing the video game improved the depression symptoms and even trained the gamer to get out of a depressive episode. In a New Zealand study, researchers instructed teen subjects who were experiencing depression to play the game SPARX; 44% of those who played recovered vs. 26% of those who did not. The game (Smart, Positive, Active, Realistic, X-factor) is a 3-D fantasy video game that teaches mental behavioral skills for relief from depression.

- Experienced gamers showed increased moral decision-making during the game play[21]
- Playing 60 minutes of Tetris immediately combats PTSD and results in greater hippocampal mass 6 weeks following.[22]
- Females who play Tetris have increased visual processing speed and spatial reasoning skills. [23]
- Action video games require attention, quick information processing and rapid responses. Players have faster reflexes and learn faster, and the skills transfer to other skills.

What is best practice? Use Hollywood and Game Industry to influence, train, improve!

The more we hear it the more likely we are to believe it…familiarity creates our truth. Research consistently shows we are significantly more likely to do what we see, and to be persuaded consciously and unconsciously by the sounds, images, and feelings of that experience. In the face of claims that so many people in our society lack essential skills, it's a better practice to transition from traditional methods (old-style training and school methods that were not as engaging) to the medium that the human brain processes the fastest. Integrating healthy behaviors and prosocial ideals using television and video games is such a promising idea.

Even though it seems counterintuitive, movies and video games can provide fundamental factors for real-world excellence and accelerated learning. Gamers excel at problem-solving, innovative thinking, and working in a group toward a goal.

- The design of video games motivates anyone with a brain and we can begin asap to weave it into curriculum and skills.
- Anytime there is a project (workplace or academics) using available motion pictures allows for a group empathy and bonding[24]
- Movies and video provide engaging information to discuss (talk and listen), work cooperatively (compromise and compete)
- Analyze or rehabilitate a hero or villain and many more interesting and meaningful assessing.
- Television and movie watching and video game playing is a sedentary activity and can be addictive. One additional hour of sitting a day increases chances of depression, anxiety, and other inflammation-related issues.

Playing video games boosts intelligence…experienced gamers learn everything—faster!

The more we play, the more neural challenges we encounter, and the more our neural connections grow, that is functionality. After only 30 minutes a day of playing Super Mario Bros. 64, subjects increased the gray matter in the right hippocampus (the area involved in storing new memories and spatial reasoning). Researchers found an increase in the plasticity of the brain and improved learning times[25] after subjects played video games. Two months of playing for 30 minutes daily, increased in mass in the prefrontal cortex and the cerebellum. The subjects had improved their spatial orientation, memory, strategic planning, and fine motor skills.[26] Adam Gazzaley, neuroscientist at U of California, designed a game for older adults from 60 to 85 years old to train at home because he thought it would improve neural functionality for multitasking, and increase cognitive control. He was right, after playing NeuroRacer at home, they significantly increased their multitasking and cognitive control.[27] The changes in the EEGs showed increased activity in the prefrontal cortex that lasted 6 months after! Their improvement in the digital game improved their eye-hand coordination and visual integration for real world driving.

- Playing video games ends age-related decline in visual search, memory, and spatial reasoning.[28]
- Playing games slows aging in those over 50 who play 2 hours a day. By 10 hours of practice, subjects showed significant improvement. After 5 to 7 weeks, the average subject had delayed 7 years of age-related decline.[29]
- Stroke patients who played video games relearned to plan and execute that plan. Playing the game improved their attention, their cognition, and even improved their motor skills.[30]

> "To learn, we must be enticed to try (students, employees, our children), even if we think we can't or feel afraid; second, we must be willing to put in lots of effort, even if we have little motivation to do so. Finally, we must have some meaningful success after investing so much effort. Movies, television, and video games do just that" J.P. Gee, Linguistics Professor, University of Wisconsin

To upgrade instruction, we need to learn from video games in order to teach essential content and skills in K-12 education. Skills that come from playing serious games (interactive games) generalize to other learning and correlate with increased academic motivation and performance. The misconception that most gamers are unmotivated, desensitized to violence and operate in isolation interferes with our ability to consider the games as useful or practical for real world application. Using games, or movies for training in the workforce, or rehabilitation activities for healthy behaviors can be effective and very motivational. In his book *What Video Games Have to Teach Us About Literacy*, he proposes learning is built into "good" video games. Video games always include video, text, and sound; all of these engage the brain's attention and therefore memory, and Mayer's research showing multimedia increases retention by as much as 80%!

Gamers have experience collaborating to solve a problem and proceed to the next level with time constraints. The takeaway for gamers is the ability to contribute valuable experience in group think and increase innovative creative thinking. Collective intelligence studies overwhelmingly show groups making significantly smarter decisions and displaying 40% more intelligent solutions when in a socially savvy group (read Sex Differences chapter). Games require heavy use of cognitive skills where extraction of information is key under specific constraints. They have *hours* of experience maintaining constant attention, scanning of the environment and ignoring regular distractors.

- Playing requires quick and accurate decision making which necessitates attention and executive function. Longitudinal studies show the result is that gamers increase their cognitive flexibility, have increased working memory, and are faster at processing information.[31] However, since comparing the benefits of each game depends upon the parameters of the study and the requirements of the game means analysis can differ radically.
- More time playing games correlates with increased spatial reasoning, higher executive function.
- Women who play action video games have quicker visual and motor responses than those who do not play.[32]

Games, and even movies, stimulate active learning. Gamers become "real" characters. Research shows that games give a vantage point, a real position with movements that access a virtual world with concrete resources. In this world, players improve competence, master demands, learn real skills, and increase their familiarity with the environment. This is the real experience that will let them learn the skills and content they need.

- Action video games enhance cognitive function and offers therapy and useful real-world application: rehabilitation, academics, and critical thinking, training job-related skills.[33]

- Gamers have quicker responses, more accuracy, and greater neural plasticity with serious games.[34]
- Action gamers who played Call of Duty and reported using spatial strategies show increased gray matter in the hippocampus while those who relied on memorizing directions showed decreased gray matter in hippocampus.[35]
- Playing interactive video games improves motivation and motivational outcomes than traditional learning. Participants who played a game had increased accuracy in critically reflecting on persuasive advertisements.[36] The state of flow (according to M. Csikszentmihalyi's lifelong research) is the intense concentration where thoughts, feelings and senses are focused on a goal and brings feelings of pure joy and satisfaction.
- After 6 weeks of training, the strategic reasoning that players learned transferred to their everyday problem-solving. *Brain Fitness*, *Space Fortress*, and *Rise of Nations* increased white matter, improved connectivity, decreased distraction, and increased working memory.[37]
- Action gaming trains the attention to switch tasks quickly and builds cognitive flexibility.[38]

What if we use a medium that will seduce the brain to engage in learning essential information? If everyone in the 21st-century learns to read (for a purpose), write (for a purpose), to calculate and use math (for a purpose), to collaborate and communicate requires engaging mediums that capture attention. Let's see the end of this thought "young people can't pay attention to anything! They are easily distracted and can't sit still!

> "Today's world is very different from the world Baby Boomers grew up in, is it any wonder that by high school very often both good students and bad students, rich ones and poor ones don't much like school?" --J.P. Gee *What Games Have to Teach About Literacy*

The National Center for Education surveys 12th graders every year: "How meaningful are your studies?" In 1983, 35% said that they found their courses quite or very meaningful. In 2000, 28% found that school was often or always meaningful. Today, the number who find meaning in school has dropped to below 21%. As a defender of education, I want to say this: Students have never found meaning in their schoolwork! Every year the perception of meaningful in education drops! Scores were poor 20 years ago, and they keep getting worse. We can do better!

The human brain only remembers things that it finds meaningful. Without meaning, there is no memory. It is an amazingly simple concept! Research gives us conclusive evidence that we remember emotional information. Emotions trigger chemicals that draw our attention and help our neurons communicate and to store a memory. Emotion drives attention; without it, there is no chance for learning or memory, and it directly affects behavior. Using the model like Hollywood and by video game designers means that we capitalize on highly emotional content and the action that the brain will pay attention to!

Sometimes, different is better than better.

True or False Quiz
1. Sometimes, our classrooms will be void of meaning or relevance! We must teach our students to read and write. T or F
2. Teachers have no choice but to replace the hands-on activities with faster teacher-centered instruction to increase literacy and math scores. T or F
3. Schools may have to remove electives (P.E., Art, Music, and Technology) to make time for additional literacy and math instruction. T or F
4. Some concepts worth teaching just don't have meaning to students. T or F
5. Students who cannot read or write will undoubtedly become illiterate adults who won't make a positive contribution to society. T or F
6. The reason students don't perform in school is because they watch too much television. T or F

1. False. This is a common-sense answer – if there is no meaning, there is no learning. Getting the brain to learn to read and write will be impossible if there is no perception of meaning. Annie Sullivan learned this the hard way. Not until Helen Keller realized why her teacher was spelling out a word in her hand did, she cooperate in the learning process. Until then, Helen's behavior was atrocious!

2. False. Hands-on activities build our intelligence and stimulates our ability to read and write. Playing with our hands and using our fingers allows our brain to integrate information. (While reading, our eyes move right to left, which conditions the optic nerve to track incoming info.) Making things is brain friendly. Centuries ago, we had to make things; it was a part of survival. Perhaps that is why we are motivated to make things. Kelly Lambert, neuroscientist, and researcher at the University of Pennsylvania found evidence that serotonin production increases when we work with our hands. When males are right about something they did (an activity or a project), they write using supporting examples and increase their scores on standardized tests. For girls, making things improve their spatial reasoning and increase their scores in math and science.

3. False. We should never agree to reduce time in electives, as more time in electives correlates with improved performance in all subjects and even post K-12 education. Ironically, instead of cutting time in electives in favor of literacy and math, we should increase time! The effects on motivation are astounding, people consistently report these as their favorite things to do, which should follow us through our lifetime! We core teachers need to build our curriculum and instruction on the backs of our special electives (read Music chapter, Movement chapter).

4. False! If our brain doesn't perceive meaning, no amount of time or effort that we spend teaching will matter – EVER! We are not designed to learn if we don't perceive meaning. Students today are empowered by parents who tell them that they don't have to if they don't want to and have enough leisure time to do it for them. If it doesn't have meaning, they won't learn it anyway.

5. False. Many brilliant engineers, famous writers, TV personalities, TV producers and directors, inventors, and billionaires came from below grade-level illiteracy or dropped out of school! Naturally, education

is a great preparation and ideal. People become literate at different rates, though. Some become proficient readers and writers long after high school.

6. TRUE. Television watching influences behaviors on a regular basis. Stanford University researchers found that one additional hour of watching a day increased the chances that the viewer would have a drink by 9% in the next year and a half. One extra hour of watching MTV increased the chance by 31%. This was true even after controlling against age, sex, and ethnicity.

Additional viewing and gaming do have serious repercussions on health and academic performance!

Television almost never advocates for reading books. Syracuse University found that young people who spend more time watching TV have lower opinions of book reading as an activity. Worse yet, Keleman found that the number of hours of TV viewing is the single best predictor of low grades. It was a better predictor than parents' low educational achievement and insufficient time in school or with family.

The California State Board of Education found that, the more TV a student watches, the worse they do in school...no matter how much homework the student does, how intelligent they are, or how much money their parents earn. Worse yet, children from upper socio-economic households are more negatively affected than those from middle or lower-class ones. Even one hour of TV made things worse and discussing the program afterward didn't seem to offset the effects.

Television viewing reduces educational aspirations. Students who report watching 25 hours weekly had lower educational aspirations and professional goals. The more they watched, the lower the status they reported wanting to pursue. Viewing television within 2 hours of bedtime also increased the level of norepinephrine (from the flickering lights of the television and content), meaning that children and adults have interrupted sleep cycles (read the Essentials chapter.)

We can motivate and educate people in a highly technical world full of multi-tasking, media-craving, and interaction. First, we have to train ourselves that we are less effective when we are constantly doing two things at once! Totally false statements, "I'm a great multi-tasker. I am better with the TV on when I do my homework! I have to do two things at once or I can't concentrate." Second, many controlled studies show subjects need roughly 50% more time to complete a task (both ordinary and complex ones) while multi-tasking. Interruption requires the brain's focus to shift and then refocus, which takes too much time and cognitive effort. A study of drivers interrupted by a cell phone ring took 35% longer to react to the driving event after the sound. Unfortunately, each subject believed their response was faster and be more effective! We are slower to react and slower in responding to a simulated automobile, and while completing homework, and when processing information. Once we understand we cannot attend to the incoming information we can manage the ability to objectify our performance as a result.

How to improve performance means we have to practice! Deliberate efforts to focus the attention improve our ability to do so. Years of research show conclusive results for meditation and mindfulness practice, focusing on our breathing, and games that require attention for recall. (Read the Movement chapter on Navy Seals attention)

We can be trained to pay attention, like gamers who are better at processing incoming information. Gee suggests using video and computer games to keep up with current learning trends. "Our answer is skill and drill our way back to basics with mechanical sampling and multiple-choice testing. Video games allow them to connect with the content and manipulate. They are learning to learn. Video games and computer games have altered how we socialize and in effect learn—kids know it is fun and exciting and stops boredom, that it allows you to do things with friends. Boys say they can compete and they can win. It's a virtual rough and tumble play—without physical contact."

Computer games have allowed 100% of the boys at Chew Magna Elementary to test on grade level! Before using Myst III: Exile, the students had 77% of their 9 to 11-year-olds test at grade level in reading and writing in 2000, but males were at a shocking 67%. In 2004, the number of students at grade level increased to an astounding 93%...with 100% of the boys at grade level. Their teacher, Tim Ryland, brought the computer game and they played as a class. He paused the game regularly to ask questions and ask what they thought would happen where they could write what they would do next. "Go to the right? Go up the staircase? Go down to the beach?" Explain why and use specific examples.

If watching and witnessing and viewing teach us behavior, then games could influence us to behave in life as well. What if a video or computer game influenced us to participate in sports, music, and visual arts, dance, or drama? It turns out, games inspire these activities in real life. Dr. Tod Machover, a composer and game designer at MIT, created *Brain Opera, The Toy Symphony, Hyperinstruments, Hyperscore*. His goal was exactly that, to get more kids to want to play an instrument. His landmark achievement could be the game that he released to get kids to play musical instruments, he designed *Guitar Hero*! Today, the number of students who want guitar lessons has increased by 450%. Video games and computer games have power, playing *Rock Band* and *Dance Dance Revolution* trigger behaviors in real time.

According to a study from Euro RSCG connected and connectivity, today's teens are the most informed, media-aware group in history. They're extremely technology-savvy. They will also choose the computer as their most important tool for socializing with friends, even over email, instant messaging, and cell phones. Today's teens spend more time online than watching TV. Despite the amount of time with TV and computers, however, teens consider interpersonal communication with other people to be the most important thing that they do with their time. For them, connecting this way with other people provides a feeling of community and is still what they consider the most important thing. "A waste of time!" Steve Johnson writes about a different age group who doesn't use it, isn't good at it, and therefore dismisses it. "In the game *Pikmindie*, the character crashes on another planet... The player must problem solve attacks by dangerous creatures, tear down stone walls, build bridges, explore areas of a strange planet in search of the perfect part to the spaceship so he will not perish...all within the allotted time. *Pikmindie* is designed for 6-year-olds." He says that an observing grandfather's comment was..."I guess that is good for hand-eye coordination?!"

> "What we want to see is the child in pursuit of knowledge, and not knowledge in pursuit of the child."
>
> –George Bernard Shaw

We are today quite resistant to using movies to teach. Teachers know that they will be ridiculed for showing a movie as an instructional method. Watching a video is the number-one medium for learning. Today's efficient technology and instant responding puts us in a position where thoughtful reflection is eliminated. There is a tremendous, yet unspoken pressure to respond immediately, which results in impulsive answers and errors in judgment. Why is our media so brain-friendly? We live in a 3-D world and are designed to process it accordingly. Our schooling systems have been largely 2-D since their inception.

> "Books will soon be obsolete in the schools... It's possible to teach every branch of human thought through motion pictures. Our school system will be completely changed in the next 10 years!"
>
> – Thomas Edison, 1913

We can no longer be limited by budget! Watching what we need to learn in a movie, or documentary is efficient because it is brain friendly as well as budget friendly. Real life naturally engages our attention, frontal cortex, visual cortex and more which are key for all learning, so do movies and video games. Located at the lower central back of our brains, these are the primary centers for processing visual stimuli, and 80% of all incoming information is visual. Cambridge University suggested it may be that the visual cortex is our sophisticated learning tool as we potentially process visuals exponentially faster than written text. When we show an image, talk about the image, and then do an activity related to the topic, students' standardized tests increase significantly!

300

"Images aren't a nice touch, they are essential."

– Levy and Lenz

Researchers found that students who learned with visuals scored 36% higher than those who learned without. Richard Mayer showed that students who learn with a text and an image score 42% higher. Sounds are a vital part to all video and computer games, cell phones, and movies. The ability to integrate relevant sounds helps us to be successful in education and the workplace. Video and computer games give us a highly engaging means to educate our students in any discipline. They engage our frontal cortex during play: We make decisions, plan our next move, organize tools, and use rewards toward the best possible ends. All games and movies engage our visual cortex and attention because they utilize sophisticated sounds and music for the best experience. Maneuvering controls or dancing steps interacting with games engages the kinesthetic parietal lobe.

Most important, playing games and watching movies becomes a real emotional experience, and celebrating a victory or loss, reaching a new level, or solving a problem and empathizing with characters in a movie releases very real chemicals that allow us to store memories. The real experiences engage our senses, which means that paying attention, motivation, and engagement in the learning process is natural and effortless. In an fMRI scan, subjects who were shown a dog, a plane coupled with sounds of barking, and an engine roaring remembered only in the highest-level areas involved with perception. When they were asked to recall what they saw and heard, the areas in the temporal lobe (sounds) and the visual cortex fired. Those that involved only the lowest level of sensory processing showed extraordinarily little activation.

What do we learn the fastest? Put the words into the image! Our working memory learns very fast when the image and the text are integrated. For the best instruction, researchers at University of California track how new ideas integrate with existing knowledge faster and have the greatest potential to reach long-term storage and simply placing the words as close to the visual as possible like in a video game with directions or a subtitled movie, speeds processing.[39] Most subjects reported that they

301

did not see the text when it was placed below the visual—common to traditional textbooks.

Educational games outperformed traditional instruction in primary classrooms in important ways. The research showed a strong correlation between the good gamers ability to play the game and their achievement, another important finding was that subject's engagement and motivation was high, regardless of ability.[40] At the end of 12 weeks, students in both groups performed "substantially" higher in tests. The teachers of students learning with games reported the students were more motivated, more likely to pay attention, and noticeably less disruptive. Even skeptics acknowledged the difference.

Researchers at Beth Israel found that surgeons who play video games for three hours a week have 37% fewer mistakes. After playing, they were 27% faster than those who did not play. They improved their motor skills, hand-eye coordination, and reaction time—all the things we love in surgeons. Today, games to train, are affectionately called "Top Gun." For peak performance, the surgeons prepare by increasing blood flow, eye-hand coordination, agility, and accuracy with a game before entering the operating room.

Games bring "stealth learning." The nature and complexity of the games requires players to get help and advice from friends and anonymous contacts who cooperate and work together to solve problems and improve their performance. Learning is the byproduct of playing. The learning is unconscious, like all human learning since humankind began making progress. For gamers, playing is not fantasy; it is real. They are so highly motivated by the fantasy game that it becomes real for them. We can capitalize on this motivation and harness it to influence behavior, teach, train whether its academics, the workplace and especially our personal life.

Good games are games that are popular with consumers. Games made for educational purposes do not follow the same pattern. In educational games, students/players cannot move on until they master the task in a linear fashion. In these games, the player/student does not move to another level by luck or chance or intuition. There is no need or provision for collaboration. It is even prohibited and punished. These games are focused on goals and objectives and knowing or learning the environment is unnecessary. Jennifer Jensen wrote in "Serious Play" that these things remove the motivation for learning. Moving to another level by alternative means such as chance and intuition intrinsically motivates players to continue. They find strengths they did not know they had.

How can we find games that inspire? What is popular? Anything that is easily mastered or education-oriented seems to be unpopular. Years ago, game companies realized that parents would buy games that were marketed as educational. However, kids almost immediately stopped playing them. This is a lesson to already familiar to parents and educators: deliberately teaching a lesson is a downer. Certain video games can facilitate training by creating an atmosphere where motivation is high and learning is a side-effect. By the same measure it is possible our schools have not been inspiring, thinking out of the box, or promoting analysis and creativity. These skills, imperative for our society and our former claim to fame, are now largely missing and undervalued in a quest to increase standardized test scores instead. Ironically, the U.S. has never had high standardized test scores, especially when compared to other countries. The U.S. is known for innovative and creativity. Legislators win campaigns by upsetting parents into voting for them. "Our schools don't compare to other countries!" In their book, *National Similarities and Global Differences* authors expose the myths driving beliefs behind testing as politically motivated propaganda. Sadly, administrators align education policies and leave the rich curriculum aside for test preparation.

What if we challenge out of date beliefs?

When the first phone was introduced at the World's Fair, one man asked, "Why would you ever need to speak to someone who is not in the same room with you?"

- The Earth is flat.
- Talkie films are a fad!

- We will always need typewriters.
- Rock and roll is the work of the devil.

Compare that to our current mindset that games have no place in education...

Steve Johnson author of *Everything Bad is Good for You* says intelligence is increasing but perspectives clash!

- "Books chronically underestimate the senses...unlike the long-standing tradition of game playing—which engages the child in a 3-D world filled with moving images and musical soundscapes, navigated and controlled with complex muscular movements... books are simply a barren string of words on the page."
- "Books are tragically isolating, there is no room for social interaction. While games have for many years engaged the young in complex social relationships with their peers, building and exploring worlds together, books force the child to sequester himself in a quiet space, shut off from interaction with other children."
- "These new libraries that have arisen in recent years to facilitate reading activities are a frightening sight: dozens of young children normally vivacious and socially active, sitting alone in cubicles, reading silently, oblivious to their peers. But perhaps the most dangerous property of these books is the fact they follow a fixed linear path. You can't control their narratives in any fashion—you simply sit back and have the story dictated to you. This risks instilling a general passivity in our children, making them feel as though they're powerless to change their circumstances. Reading is not an active, participatory process; it's a submissive one. The book readers of the younger generations are learning to 'follow the plot' instead of learning to lead."

Games are interesting because they are difficult! Learning is fun when it's intellectually stimulating.

"The game industry is selling products that are complex and hard to master and take a lot of time to master. A game that is too easy gets criticized in reviews. A game should be challenging, fair and deep. If it's not, it won't sell."

– J.P. Gee

Students report being bored in school and naturally tuning out. Games are designed so that players want to learn each new level. Players actively make moves and decisions to attempt to progress, receiving immediate feedback. As they learn more and more, they can apply their knowledge, be rewarded, and become that hero. How could this possibly be a skill that benefits them in life?

The answer is that gamer-like behaviors create ideal employees. Harvard Press featured "Got Game? How the Gamer Generation is Reshaping Business Forever." In this study, employers report that gamers take more risks, react better to disappointments or mistakes, and are open to the possibility that their plans may need to be adjusted! Gamers strive for excellence, compete for promotions, and, most importantly, work better in teams. They have probably learned that they need input from others for success!

Imagine if these were these opinions of school:

"It's fun!"
"I like to feel in control!"
"It releases tension."
"It relieves boredom."
"It develops skills."
"It gives me a sense of mastery!"
...the top answers given by gamers for playing!

ENDNOTES

1   De Jans et al., (2019). Serious games going beyond the Call of Duty: Impact of an advertising literacy mini-game platform on adolescents' motivational outcomes through user experiences and learning outcomes. Cyberpsychology: Journal of Psychosocial Research on Cyberspace.

2   Murayama, K. (2018). The science of motivation: Multidisciplinary approaches advance research on the nature and the effects of motivation. APA American Psychological Agenda.

3   Merry et al. (2012). The effectiveness of SPARX, a computerized self-help intervention for adolescents seeking help for depression: Randomized controlled non-inferiority trial. *BMJ*, 344.

4   Murayama, K. (2018).

5   Furman et al., (2019). They saw a movie: Long term memory from an extended audiovisual narrative. Cold Spring Harbor Lab Press.

6   Schultheiss et al. (2004). Effects of affiliation and power motivation arousal on salivary progesterone and testosterone. Hormones and Behavior.

7   Rogge, R. D., Cobb, R. J., Lawrence, E., Johnson, M. D., & Bradbury, T. N. (2013). Is skills training necessary for the primary prevention of marital distress and dissolution? A 3-year experimental study of three interventions. Journal of Consulting and Clinical Psychology.

8   Nummennma et al. (2011). Emotions promote social interactions by synchronizing brain activity among individuals. PNAS.

9   Dubois et al., (2019). Bridging the research implementation gap requires engagement from practitioners. Conservation Science and Practice.

10 Hasson, U. (2008). Neurocinematics: The neuroscience of film. *Berghahn Journals, 2*(1).

11 Lidskog et al., (2020). Cold science meets hot weather: Environmental threats, emotional messaging, and Storytelling. Media and Communication.

12 Terry M. (2020). Introduction: The Geo-Doc. Palgrave Studies in Media and Environmental Communication. Palgrave Macmillan, London.

13 Lee et al. (2020) What can narratives tell us about the neural basis of human memory. Current Opinion in Behavioral Science.

14 Lidskog et al., (2020).

15 Vosoughi et al., (2018). The spread of true and false news online. MIT Press.

16 Krishnan et al. (2012). Neural strategies for selective attention distinguish fast-action video game players. *Brain Topography.*

17 Cardoso-Leite, P., & Bavelier, D. (2014). Video game play, attention, and learning: How to shape the development of attention and influence learning? *Current Opinion in Neurology.*

18 Nahum, M. Bavelier, D. (2020). Video games as rich environments to foster neuroplasticity. Handbook of Clinical Neurology.

19 West et al., (2017). Impact of video games on plasticity of the hippocampus. Mol Psychiatry.W

20 Haier et al., (2009). MRI assessment of cortical thickness and functional activity changes in adolescent girls following three months of practice on a visual-spatial task. BMC Research Notes.

21 Krcmar, M., Cingel, D., (2016). Moral foundations theory and moral reasoning in video game play: Using real-life morality in a game context. Journal of Broadcasting and Electronic Media.

22 Butler et al (2020). Trauma, treatment and Tetris: video gaming increases hippocampal volume in male patients with combat-related posttraumatic stress disorder. J Psychiatry Neurosci.

23 Gorbet, D., Sergio, L., (2018). Move faster, think later: Women who play action video games have quicker visually-guided responses with later onset visuomotor-related brain activity. Plos One

24 Manninen et al. (2017). Social laughter triggers endogenous opioid release in humans. Journal of Neuroscience.

25 Bavelier et al. (2012). Learning, attention control and action-based games. Current Biology.

26 Kuhn et al. (2013). Playing Super Mario Bros induces structural brain plasticity: gray matter changes resulting from training with a commercial video game. Molecular Psychiatry.

27 Gazzaley et al., (2013). Video game training enhances cognitive control in older adults. Nature

28 Bavelier et al. (2012). Learning, attention control and action-based games. Current Biology.

29 Wollensky et al (2013). A randomized controlled trial of cognitive training using a visual speed of processing intervention in middle Aged and older adults. PLos One.

30 Lee, G. (2013). Effects of training using video games on the muscle strength, muscle tone, and activities of daily living of chronic stroke patients. J. Phys. Ther. Sci.

31 Dale, G., Joessel, A., Bavelier, D., Green, C., (2020). A new look at the cognitive neurology of video game play. Ann. of N.Y. Academy of Sciences.

32 Gorbet, D., Sergio, L., (2018). Move faster, think later: Women who play action video games have quicker visually guided responses with later onset visuomotor-related brain activity. PLos One.

33 Green, S., Bavelier, D. (2015). Action video game training for cognitive enhancement. Current Opinion in Behavioral Science.

34 Swisher, K, Cheema, A, Eastman, R. (2014). Health claim: playing video games improves reflexes. Online: Clickbaitthehealthclaims.com

35 Dale et al., (2020). A new look at the cognitive neuroscience of video game play. Annals of the New York Academy of Sciences.

36 De Jans, S., Hudders, L., Herrewijn, L., Van Geit, K., & Cauberghe, V. (2019). Serious games going beyond the Call of Duty: Impact of an advertising literacy mini-game platform on adolescents' motivational outcomes through user experiences and learning outcomes. Cyberpsychology: Journal of Psychosocial Research on Cyberspace.

37 Stern et al. (2011).

38 Nahum, M. Bavelier, D. (2020). Video games as rich environments to foster neuroplasticity. Handbook of Clinical Neurology.

39 Clark, R., Mayer, R., (2016). E-learning and the science of instruction: Proven guidelines for consumers and designers of multimedia learning, 4th Edition.

40 Bottino et al. (2014). Serious Gaming at School: Reflections on Students' Performance, Engagement and Motivation. International Journal of Game-Based Learning.

CHAPTER 9

HOMEWORK REDUCES INNOVATION AND MENTAL HEALTH AND PUTS SOCIETY AT RISK

"Everybody is a genius, but if you judge a fish by its ability to climb a tree, it will spend its whole life believing its stupid"

–Albert Einstein

What if you were heading for your best self when something invisible tripped you up!?

I can't imagine you are thinking this has anything to do with you. Why would anyone thing homework is relevant to their daily life, you did yours, or not and are finished with school so it's a dead topic. The answer is bigger than we realize, the solution is messier than you'd expect, and it' at the core of our future. Here goes…we have so many complex problems that require solutions that it's time for all hands on deck! The need to reverse global warming, for clean energy, for enviro-friendly recycle, for improved mental health, for innovative solutions to problems that we are desperate for innovative thinkers! Would you stand up against an invisible block to innovation? Homework that requires an individual to use self-discipline to complete an assignment outside of the classroom deters potential great thinkers! Today, our students report the highest levels of stress and cite homework load, parents cite pressures at home and making sure students get work is at the top of the list. One of the top reasons students cite for dropping out of school is homework, one of the reasons students cite for opting out of college is homework, one of the reasons students of color opt out is a host of reasons for the inability to keep up with the homework load. Now is the time to cultivate everyone with a brain to tap our greatest human potential. Revising homework so it doesn't stop our children pursuing education and their ideas.

The only thing I love about homework is it really touches a nerve in everyone who has ever done it. For some of us, no matter how much or little it is supposed to be…it takes forever! Except for me, I loved homework… that alone should have told me I would grow up to be in education! Few teachers embrace it and largely assign it to appease parents and principals who they believe expect it! No matter how you think of homework, the facts just don't support it as a practice that furthers any benefit. Worse yet, there is significant evidence to support the devastating long-term effects of assigning homework as a chief cause of dropout, furthering the socio-economic divide, and the workforce skill gap.

Homework has no conclusive evidence to suggest its existence!

It's the short-term effects of homework that should command every parent's attention. A peaceful and supportive home life is key to lifelong benefit; researchers warn that the greatest threat to a child's performance in school is parents fighting (they don't even have to divorce). Considering the effects of turmoil at home, it's more important than ever after a day at work or at school to plan, with more precision than a vacation, an evening to reconnect. It's often nothing like that …especially during the school year. The pressure at night begins when we sort through what needs to get done before bedtime; whether it involves assignments in backpacks, collecting things to drive to after school activities, getting dinner going, tidying life, or getting my own self situated from my long day…evenings are stressful. But there was a time with less turmoil, like when kids still played outside and someone would call "it's time to come in and do your homework!" As it turns out, the research shows we are better preparing our kids for success and life if we skip the traditional homework assigned and instead forced them outside to play for another hour. In fact, a good deal of evidence suggests homework is counterproductive.

My research into the evidence behind homework began almost immediately when my daughter started Kindergarten and began bringing nightly assignments. I was surprised at how our evenings changed. Nighttime now included managing homework requirements after we were tired, (short-tempered and cranky), in need of bathing, and often involving a late-night scramble to get something someone just remembered they had to have for the next day...often it was me. It was at this time I took on the role of "enforcer" to make homework happen so I could accomplish the rest of the evening requirements. Within weeks of school starting, my daughter rebelled against homework (despite my daily attempts at inspiring her to do it herself), she officially ran away, for 4 minutes, when she was 5 years old. This breakdown *inspired me* to dive into the research on the effectiveness of homework. I had to find out if the big stress to my house night after night was worth the effort.

Ideally, I wanted my child to de-stress and play, and I enforced the opposite by requiring her to sit to complete homework. Worse than that, I would call her in from outside which we now know research tells us improves success; outside time was the most academic after-school activity. Researchers at Harvard are finding 1 to 2 hours outdoors allows for the brain to build attention systems on a neural level. This allows for attention and memory, of course, but also to make good decisions. All of us, especially those with attention deficits, need consistent blood flow to regulate dopamine to fuel their high-level thought processing. Time outside not only allows for learning and memory, but also lowers melatonin, lowers stress, and improves quality sleep. Sunshine is essential for all of us as it stimulates the production of serotonin (one study estimated 10 minutes can increase serotonin by over 800%), more serotonin improves memory, moods and anxiety.

Three years ago, researcher Mollie Galloway found students who spend more time on homework have a greater increase in levels of anxiety, depression, anger and other negative attitudes. As long as teens under stress are more likely to have eating disorders, smoke cigarettes and use drugs and alcohol, keeping a stress-free home is essential.

"Whenever homework crowds out social experience, outdoor recreation, and creative activities, and whenever it usurps time devoted to sleep, it is not meeting the basic needs of children and adolescents."
–P R Wildeman-Education Psychologist 1890.

Does homework provide academic practice or cause the gap in international comparisons?

Important curriculum sent home for learning assumes a good deal of trust. If skills are entrusted to homework, we take a great risk that they may never be learned. A few years ago, American teachers traveled to Japanese Schools to observe practice. The Teacher assigned to their tour responded to one of the questions, "Why do American teachers send important skills home for completion?" She said assigning homework (though Japanese families spend time practicing academics nightly) "meant students may not complete it or worse complete it the wrong way…homework could prevent students from doing well on the test."

I have to admit, I didn't think of this obvious pitfall…though I NEVER sent home anything I thought was important. I was afraid they wouldn't find it interesting and wouldn't do it—I knew I had to convince them it was meaningful. Teachers tell me they assign homework because parents expect it, some demand it. Ironically, in my years of work with Superintendents and Principals, I can't tell you how often I hear "I wish teachers didn't assign homework. Students don't do it, fail classes and then drop out."

Parents have the weight of the world on their shoulders and are usually willing to do anything to provide the academics for their children… even homework.

You'd think students would invest loads of time and energy completing assigned homework. Get serious! Students use all of their self-discipline to make it through a typical day: wake up early, sit quietly in classes for 7 hours (controlling any desire to play, controlling any desire to talk or yell, controlling any desire to eat instead of attending class, controlling their desire to move or run or go outside instead of following daily school rules and expectations). At the end of a day of learning and using self-control, it's possible your child could be as tired as we are after work. And not only that, their sleep cycles are erratic and diets often depleted, so it's not uncommon for the average student to throw together answers to homework that doesn't reflect their best work and certainly doesn't inspire a growth mindset.

Despite the concerns about the benefits of homework and despite the time grading requires, most teachers still assign and spend time. They do what they are told, what is expected, even assign homework, and donate their own time (usually Sundays) grading instead of having a weekend, instead of taking care of themselves, instead of keeping their life in balance. Their time for planning instruction during the school day is already packed, so precious time to work is usually non-existent. Grading homework takes gobs of time and energy that could be used to create engaging projects that further intellectual development…and great projects are what parents really want.

If it meant your child had to miss recess, would you do it?
If it meant your child would lose a letter grade, would you do it?
If it meant your child would graduate, would you do it?
If it meant your child would get into a better college, would you do it?
If it meant your child would get a scholarship, would you do it?

Who completes the homework?

To address these questions the National Science Foundation arranged for Harris Cooper, then at University of Missouri, to research the synthesized body of evidence on the effects of homework on achievement. His work is so influential that today school districts support a 10-minute-per-night-per-grade level prescription as the "evidence-based" guide for the optimal time to spend on homework. His team set out to synthesize the existing research to show whether homework positively impacted academics. For their purposes, homework was defined simply as work completed outside of the classroom. After concluding their investigation into the evidence on homework, Harris Cooper recommended 10 minutes per night per grade

313

level of homework despite the finding that there was no consistent evidence to support homework had an impact on achievement.

How they defined homework:

- Achievement was defined as standardized test scores and class grades
- Grades awarded by teachers who designed the test and assigned homework
- Homework completion researchers collected were assigned by the teacher
- Tests and grades are collectable and reportable

The consistent evidence showed students who completed homework assigned by a teacher who included homework grades in the course grade, had higher grades ... What if the bulk of the longitudinal studies show there is no correlation between homework and achievement?

Cooper's synthesis of more than 100 studies on homework showed little impact on achievement. Each time he reviewed homework evidence (1989 and 2001 and 2006) the finding was no impact or little impact on homework. However, he still recommends assigning homework for 10 minutes per grade, and middle and high school up to 90 minutes to 2 hours. Because his work is the body of research referenced to support homework, it's important to know they reviewed 3 types of research. In the first set of studies that measured achievement, 14 showed homework increased grades and test scores and 6 did not. In the second set of studies, they compared rates of learning between students who completed assignments in-class against homework assignments out-of-class. Those who completed their assignments in-class showed almost twice the results as students who completed the work as homework. His conclusion on the effects of homework compared to completing work in class was "In-class study proved superior!" Cooper himself said it's impossible to know who completes homework.

"Once homework leaves the classroom, it's impossible to know who completes the homework."

Assigning work out of the classroom now depends upon what available at home as help. If there are inequitable resources available at home (someone to monitor homework, someone home to help understand, a family who needs the student to work to help with finances, or other factors out of the teacher's control) a school system that assigns homework is not providing equal access to learning.

What if there is no "evidence" that 10-minutes a night impacts "achievement"? Would we still allow it to shape our home atmosphere? Would you allow your children to give up sleep and live under chronic stress? Our commitment to evidence means the 10-minute rule should be repealed. Cooper's primary work states that he has no reason to believe that homework has any impact on achievement. Worse yet, even though no researchers have studied homework for children younger than 3rd grade; he recommends homework anyway. Many schools support assigning homework to all grades because of his research. According to his findings, the effect on academics is "nearly zero for 3rd through 5th, for middle grades 6-9 was .07 "somewhat higher," and for high school "high" at .25 (Cooper 1989). While a 25% improvement sounds promising, it is a number that represents what happens when a student completes homework assigned for class. His work confirms that students with a teacher who include homework in a class grade will have a higher grade in middle school and even more in high school if they complete homework which is tallied for that grade.

Though he was looking only for the effects of completing homework on achievement (defined as a grade), he recommends homework to cultivate other behaviors his research never addressed. "Homework will grow cognitive capacity, foster independent learning, create responsible character traits, give parents the opportunity to see what is going on at school and express positive attitudes toward achievement." Yet their work included no research on non-academic outcomes of homework like study habits, cheating, participating in community activities or presumably independent learning, responsibility, or positive attitudes about school (Cooper 1989).

Across the nation, school officials work to provide parents an opportunity to see what is going on at school at conferences, back to school night and through direct communication with teachers. They all but beg for parent involvement of this sort. If the parents believe the assigned homework helps to understand the content at school, parents may be looking at the wrong clues! Teachers don't necessarily design homework for parents to understand what is happening in school. The most common reason teachers list for homework is that parents want more homework. As a result, researcher data shows our students from 5-years-old to college aged children do more homework than ever before in history!

Popular books in education defend and suggest the practice as if it is research-based best practice. Robert Marzano, author of *Instructional Strategies That Work,* says the 4th most effective strategy in education is homework and practice. To support his claim, he circles back to refer to Cooper's research, 4th-6th grade shows a 6% increase in achievement (more homework a student completes increases the course grade), and in 7th-9th a 12% increase in achievement (the more homework completed increases grade) and in 10th-12th a 24% increase in achievement (Marzano, 2006). The claim is you will increase your grade if you do the work assigned to get the grade.

Despite the poor evidence, Marzano contradicts his recommendation and warns younger grade levels should have less homework (there is little evidence because there is such a limited scope of studies on homework in Kindergarten, 1st or 2nd or 3rd grade.) In *The Art and Science of Teaching,* Marzano admits there is little evidence to support assigning homework, "In the final analysis, discussions about optimum amounts of homework are still speculative."

> "The Clear Pattern is that homework has little effect"
> –Robert Marzano 2006

Author Douglas Reeves also recommends homework based upon Cooper's finding even though the evidence on homework showed no academic effects. He said "the amount of time is fairly meaningless. It's not time that has a positive effect, it's the proportion of homework completed." (Reeves 2007).

Most districts in the U.S. use Harris Cooper's research as a guideline. Cooper Quotes:

- "All Children in public school are relatively homogenous." Cooper, 1989
- "I am more convinced now that homework is more important than ever." Cooper, 2006
- "In fact, alternative treatments should be devisable that are far superior to homework." Cooper 1989
- "It's just as likely that high achievement causes students to do more homework." Cooper, 1989
- "Many of the studies used poor research designs"
- "...Homework can actually lead to the acquisition of undesirable character traits by promoting cheating." Cooper, 1989
- "The effect of homework on achievement is trivial if it exists at all." Cooper, 1989
- "Homework allows students to express positive attitudes" Cooper 1989
- "Only a few studies look at homework's effect on attitudes toward school and subject matter (with generally negligible results)"
- "Homework is the line of progression is flat in young since it really doesn't matter how much is assigned." Cooper, 1989
- "Educators should assign homework even though it should not be expected to improve test scores." Cooper, 1989
- "Homework *should* help them develop good study habits, foster positive attitudes toward school, and communicate to students the idea that learning takes place at school and at home." Cooper, 1989
- "Today, there is an even stronger association between grades and achievement" Cooper, 2006
- "My recommendations are grounded in research in that none of them contradicts the conclusions of my review." Cooper, 1989

Why care about Harris Cooper's beliefs or his research findings? School administrators care.

Current slogan in education? Rigor. A few years ago, this 4th R showed up as if it belonged in public school mission statements to signal excellence. But well-intentioned schools have missed their mark when they used the word rigor. The meaning of rigorous is NOT positive and does not communicate a desirable goal, it is punitive and even hostile. Alfie Kohn, *The Myth of Homework* points to the definition of rigor.

Webster's: allowing abatement or mitigation; scrupulously accurate; exact; strict; severe; relentless; as a rigorous officer of justice; a rigorous execution of law; a rigorous definition or demonstration. Severe; intense; inclement; as a rigorous winter, violent.

I am a parent, and I talk to parents, and have never heard anyone hope for this for their child! As long as the current trend in education is for "rigor," requiring regular and lengthy nightly homework fits. What I do hear parents ask for is a high standardized test score. Well intentioned parents think test show learning and predict academic success; they don't.

Parent income predicts student's standardized test scores

High income neighborhoods yield above average standardized test scores; zip codes accurately predict standardized test performance. Despite this reality, year after year news reports feature inner city schools with failing grades and test scores that inspire politicians to call for "reform". When schools in poor neighborhoods post low test scores, it's called performance, and the call for reform often means teachers are fired, and sometimes means the school is closed down. Rarely schools in poor neighborhoods attract teachers, for many reasons, and those teachers who are attracted to these neighborhoods and willing to work in difficult situations have a big heart and a desire to make the difference.

Children in the United States are far from homogenous!

The reality is there is a huge range in economic and social privilege. The distribution of wealth has always played a factor in this country and today the number of homeless children is gut-wrenching. According to the study from the National Center on Family Homelessness there are approximately

2.5 million homeless children and half of them are under 6 years old! Resources and access to support are wildly unpredictable and inequitable from one family to the next. Children with educated parents, access to books and reading for enjoyment, and access to enriching activities and who live in a safe home environment have the greatest chance of academic success. Contrary to Harris Cooper's statement, we are not a homogenous society and *never* have been.

Money provides opportunity. Tutors for challenging subjects, training courses to prepare for college-entrance test performance and parents who have the time to supervise a path to education and higher education provide academic success and good test scores. Students with opportunity have the advantage. Students without this opportunity underperform on tests. Students who do not speak the language take the tests, students with special needs, students with intellectual difficulties, all students are required to take our standardized tests regardless of situation. The U.S. mandates all students take and report scores; other countries test the top performing students (in countries with high standardized test scores low performers are not allowed to continue education).

Why are standardized tests resulting in more homework assigned?

Every time the results of an international test where American students underperform in international comparisons, the news reports the discrepancy and Legislators campaign for educational reform. Trouble in schools mobilizes parents and the community toward the polls when there is an identified "crisis." State legislators consistently pass laws to invest in "tests" in attempt to measure growth. As a result, publishing companies' position to make huge profits from a state purchase of a standardized testing system and often a program designed to help test-takers pass the test. For example, Common Core is a curriculum currently popular, aimed at "improving education" as measured by test scores. After years of discussion and lobbying, Pearson Publishing contributed close to 7 million dollars to get Common Core onto legislative policy and is today the sole publishing company for this required test. To prepare for this new test, teachers must now cover even more curriculum on the new standardized test, run out of "time" in class and send essential learning home that would have been taught, practiced, and assessed in the classroom, where research suggests it is more effective!

Assigning homework perpetuates the academic gap and the cycle of poverty!

When teachers assign work outside of the classroom, students who don't have the support to complete assignments cannot learn the important skill and are not likely to catch up. In my classroom I was always tempted to "cover more material" by asking them to complete it as homework, a risky move that potentially leaves students who were behind without access to the learning sent as homework. Students who fall behind are more likely to drop out and spend the rest of their lives missing important economic opportunity.

Homework increases the dropout rates and causes skill gap

Every one of us needs to pay attention to the dropout rate and skill gap as if our life depends upon it. Opportunity is truly the foundation of a safe society and the factor that makes this country great instead of a high crime, high poverty, 3rd world country. Only when the citizens of a country have opportunity to provide a living for themselves and their family do we have the American Dream. The social and economic divide in this country is dependent upon an education. In their book, "Closing the Chapter on Homework", Etta Kralovec, Education Professor at Arizona State University, and John Buell, Political Science Professor at University of Maine, blame the skills gap and dropout rate on the practice of homework for students. This unintended outcome means students without supportive parents cannot learn those skills because once it is outside of the classroom there is no guarantee every student learns. According to "Silent Epidemic" students who dropped out said once they fell behind in coursework, they were no longer able to keep up. Harris Cooper concluded in his research: "homework could accentuate existing social inequities. Children from poorer homes will have more difficulty completing assignments than their middle-class counterparts. Poorer children are more likely to work after school or may not have a quiet, well-lit place to do their assignments. Homework is "not the great equalizer" (Cooper1989).

When learning is assigned outside of a teacher, the racial and economic inequalities cripple opportunities for the next generation. Buell and Kralovec surveyed poor and diverse groups and found radically different relationships to homework. Black and Hispanic students reported on average 6-7 hours of homework a week, while White students reported about 4 hours. Not surprising, students explain the type of help they received and it varied by class! Middle class parents helped their child to figure out the answer and used questions to guide them, whereas, lower socio-economic parents gave the answer. When important lessons are sent to home-life, this country's children are at risk for repeating the cycle of underperforming.

The most compelling question raised by Dr. Buell surprised an audience of educators, "Which one of us believes our kids don't deserve a 40-hour work week?" If 3rd graders are supposed to spend an extra 30 minutes after they arrive home and high school students 2 hours, they are over the 40-hour work week. In high school the time commitment can vary widely but following his guideline adds 7.5 extra hours per week to the 35 hours required during the school day.

Some children spend 2 or more hours each night on schoolwork, some complete their own work, some have access to internet, and our current homework makes for the inequity. For some children after school homework hours are filled caring for siblings or working by necessity. Despite the obvious pitfalls of assigning graded work outside the classroom, a significant portion of GPA comes from homework. Including homework in the course grades means the inequity is high stakes: class rank, awards, honors, selecting a valedictorian, and most important of all college admission and scholarships to college.

"Listen up College Professors and Future Employers…Homework Causes the Skill Gap!"

If more time on homework correlated with an increase in test scores then less time on homework would lower scores… but it does not. Often in

321

countries with high scores, they have the lowest rates of assigned homework. Japan, Czech Republic and Denmark little assigned homework. Greece, Thailand and Iran report high amounts of outside requirements with low test score. In fact, including homework in the course grade is not commonplace like it is in the United States. Jane Bluestein reported other countries have a different relationship with outside coursework altogether. For example, 82% of American teachers include homework scores in the final grade while 14% of Japanese teachers and only 6% of German teachers, according to Moorman & Haller.

Without homework they will not be prepared! Really?

A few years ago, Sara Bennett, author of "The Case Against Homework", addressed a question from the audience in a forum on homework. Clearly annoyed the audience member asked, "Were you prepared for Law School when you got there?" Without hesitation Bennett replied, "NO! I was buried, overwhelmed and upset. However, I wanted to be there and so did what I had to do to be successful." She said she chose to continue her education to law school but pointed out k-12 education is compulsory and we need to prepare them so they want to continue to higher education, where they will learn what they need to know. I hear teachers and parents say homework prepares students for homework. Students with self-discipline turn in assignments; but there is no evidence to suggest homework improves self-discipline. There is reason to believe too much practice is counter productive.

Homework provides much needed practice in a math class...but not so fast!

The U.S. Department of Education published research shown the rule of 5 can save a good deal of time completing homework and limit potential frustrations. Five problems are enough for reinforcement for any student who understands the math question; while more than 5 brings boredom to those who understand and reinforcement for those who do not understand reinforces the inaccuracy (Bennett & Kalish 2006).

But doing homework does not improve the ability to do homework. Alfie Kohn, in his book "The Myth of Homework", said "it's not weight training;

the more we lift weights the bigger our muscles get." Kohn continued, "Why children must be made unhappy years before it is necessary?" It's more than unhappy, our students are leaving learning and dropping out of school at an alarming rate. What if one student quits school because of homework? Our goal is to educate all of them so they may reach their true potential. The 21st century has too many challenges for us to lose any one child who may have the ability to solve a colossal problem.

What the Evidence Does Support?

When Carol Bayer Sager, a grammy award-winning, platinum songwriter received the check for royalties for the first song she wrote, the check was for $34,000.00. That year she was paid $5,200.00 as a teacher. "I wrote that song so quickly and teaching is hard!"

There is one thing we know about teachers…they are not like anyone else in the workforce. They chose their profession without regard for income or interest in climbing a corporate ladder. For this group the passion is for learning, doing things better and making a difference. Every teacher has a college degree, and the majority of them have a graduate degree within 10 years of starting; almost immediately most report putting in more than 50 hours of work per week. Yet in response to teaching, people consistently comment "how lucky you are off in the summers and can be home with your children". If I live that long! Most teachers are shocked at the time and work required for the job and sadly, many teachers confess they put their own children second while they invest time into their students. The exhaustion of teaching means talking themselves through it by holding out for a break on a weekend, a 3-day weekend or holiday.

1. Evidence shows teacher quality is the most dominant variable in student achievement, far greater than any demographic characteristic. What is a great teacher?

The most important quality, next to being born a great teacher, is the ability to connect and empathize with students. Only a great teacher respects students and finds them intriguing. Empathy and connection are the cornerstones of magic. I have found that most great teachers have overcome an adversity and are quite empathetic. Once an instructor has struggled with a learning disability, or academically, or to overcome poverty, or live through a bully, or survive an addiction, lost a relationship or any of life's tragedies they channel that success into becoming a "Great" teacher. The empathy and understanding that comes with it allows for the interaction in a classroom, and inspiration that can and does change people's lives. Maybe because of the adversity and maybe despite the adversity, the experience allows for great teaching. Over and over throughout the years, when a student has no reason to be successful our research tells us there is one teacher that can make that difference... a connection with a person outside the home...most often a relationship they found at school.

A great teacher believes their students are innately valuable and genuinely interesting and chronically intriguing.

To reach greatness as a teacher there must be effective discipline. It is impossible to be great if the classroom is disrespectful. For a teacher to inspire magic, there must be an orderly atmosphere. Though my passion is for children I can't help but think of the dog whisperer, Cesar Milan! The minute he walks into a room with a badly-behaved dog, the dog sits down and acts like a perfect pet. A teacher with effective discipline has the same effect. When I taught high school, I worked with teachers whose discipline skills varied. Some teachers had students who were rude and loud during instruction. I like to think I was among those with good discipline, but there is no question, I worked with a great disciplinarian! I remember one day she had been gone all day at a conference and returned to the school earlier than expected. For whatever reason, she walked past her classroom (still in-session) only to see many students out of their seats wandering and talking, some even had their backs to the substitute teacher who was trying to teach the lesson. She was mortified!

Naturally, she threw the door open and stood in the doorway. Every single student stopped what they were doing, stopped talking, and ran to their desk to sit obediently at the sight of their teacher...the dog whisperer becomes student whisperer!

Only with a teacher who commands respect can a classroom of students reach its full potential. Every classroom has many personalities with people from different places and experiences. If a classroom has healthy discourse then students can be a part of a dynamic classroom. Only now can every student have a positive learning exchange: attempt what they would not otherwise, participate despite fear, realize their own potential. Only now can the class laugh, learn, connect and flourish in learning. One of the most important factors in any learning environment is the interaction between teacher and students...they have to laugh! When I walk into a presentation to an audience with stone faces and no emotion, with arms across their chests (as though they were irritated to be there) I am a complete "dud". Nothing interesting, fun or meaningful comes from my mouth! However, the moment even one person in the audience laughs or nods and smiles...great stuff appears. When they are sullen, tired, resentful, then I am mediocre, even dismal at my job. The group of students makes a teacher great, it's a glorious, interactive, 2-way relationship.

A great teacher has the courage to think out of the box. When I was in school, so many teachers gave boring lectures, assigned nightly homework, used textbooks and tested frequently. I promised myself I would teach in another way. My first year as a teacher finally arrived and I was surrounded by traditional teaching. Before I knew it, I looked just like every other teacher. I didn't have the courage to do it the way I thought I should... shame on me! I wanted to be a teacher so I could engage them and excite them about the topic but I finally arrived and now called writing with chalk a progressive strategy! Great teachers put the students in the driver seat to gain their attention. Finding out their real interests and integrating into curriculum takes courage. Integrating emotion and meaningful events into class every day is essential. It takes courage to not do what has always been done! Allowing student interests to dictate topics and projects means a great teacher has the courage to think out of the box to integrate the essential skills they will need in the future.

Do you like problem-solving, innovation, or generation of new ideas?

Good teaching carefully chooses curriculum that really matters in life. The ability to recognize the guidelines are required by the state but often are archaic, even inconsequential. Education is too important today to waste time on irrelevant content and requires the teacher select content that matters and integrate what students find interesting so all students have a chance to succeed. In addition, the teacher must evaluate whether students are in fact interested and engaged. Too often the reverse is true: teachers droning on about required curriculum despite irrelevance and triviality; no more teachers spending weeks on a topic that plays no role in current society. For example, it's okay to skip the Spanish-American War, it's okay to pick a novel written in the last 20 years instead of a 1930s classic…we are losing their attention. Teachers can no longer fail to realize the class is completely uninterested. Students themselves will contribute what they are interested in learning… this is the most important factor in educating for the 21st century … differentiating learning is too limited without this skill.

For students to reach their full potential, teachers must follow great leader's example by meeting one on one with the other heads of state, to learn the issues, to connect with the reality of their life, to address each where they are. In one survey of 16-year-olds the trend becomes clear, "I don't need a teacher who lectures and carefully compiles all of the notes so I can re-learn it for a test that everyone will take. I need a teacher who can see if I understand the topic and why I need to!"

A great teacher is careful to stay engaged in the learning process themselves by continuing learning. Staying current in their field is a requirement but the benefits far outweighing the cost and time. This allows a teacher to stay in a learning environment to identify with the perspective of the student. Only when I began my graduate classes did I realize homework had the potential to fill all my time, limit my sleep, and compromise the learning itself. I personally sat in class for hours on end and realized I needed my teacher to engage me and stop my body from being numb! I personally learned from a teacher who may or may not be able to recognize my engagement. I personally committed precious time to learn something I may or may not be interested in learning. However, as a graduate student, I am *allowed* to leave class without a pass to use the bathroom, allowed to bring food or drink, to chew gum, and most of all, to choose the class and the teacher...unlike most of our students. A great teacher can empathize with the perspective of students only being a student themselves over their lifetime. This is not a challenge for great teachers either, they crave knowledge and to improve their professional skills to a better version is natural!

Can we predict if a student will graduate from high school?

Yes! Students who build a relationship with teachers graduate. Study after study shows students who have a good relationship with the teacher have academic success. A great teacher with courage to dedicate class time for building a connection is increasing the chances for graduation more than any instructional strategy. Unfortunately, with the current pressure to cover curriculum for the tests, most teachers report building relationships with their students only until 3rd grade!

1. Quality of teacher drives student achievement

   • Improved teacher-student interactions dictate academic performance (Allen et al 2015)
   • During boom time in cities in the U.S. during a time of economic prosperity academic rates grew only slightly, municipalities spend money on capital projects and did not invest in higher wages to attract quality teachers (Marchand et al, 2015)
   • Learning is enhanced in contexts where learners have supportive relationships. They have sense of ownership and control over the learning process and can learn with and from each other in a safe and trusting environment. (McCombs 2004)
   • Student centered learning: Increased occurrence of critical and creative thinking. Basic learning in verbal math and IQ lower dropout rates by 35%, less disruptive behavior by 25% and fewer absences by 25%. (Cornelius-White 2007)
   • Training on social and emotional factors in the classroom improves math performance. Building relationships in the classrooms allow students to be more comfortable in seeking help as well as interact with others (Ottmar et al, 2014)

- Instruction, and the teacher connection to a student, predict achievement, motivation and choice to engage in learning (Keith, 2008)

Why do Parents want what doesn't work? Evaluation v. Assessment

The obvious answer to this question is parents believe a test measures their child's performance. Should the numbers be low…the question is now why didn't the school provide a better education? The fly in the ointment is test scores don't accurately measure how a child is performing and it certainly doesn't accurately measure a good education. Tests don't measure school effectiveness, nor does it indicate our country's strength and worse gives parents and children the idea that they are not on grade level like the others. Forget the fact that these tests have many flaws and don't reflect true learning. The truth is it takes time from in-class projects that inspire creativity. The push toward innovative long-term projects has now become a push for teachers to cover more curriculum, in less time, and pressure to prepare students for the required tests…guaranteed to stop creativity and imagination.

Inspiring our youth toward creative endeavors brings great teachers. Want to know what stops great teaching? A man-made "test". It can't accurately predict life-long success or reflect your child's ability. Human development and achievement is difficult, if not impossible, to measure.

If a parent wants their student to learn to think, create, work with others, work under the pressure of a timeline and expectations…demand real projects. Teachers are passionate about their students and about creating engaging lesson plans! Designing a project kids can't stop working on naturally inspires innovation, problem-solving and experiencing "the fire in their gut." Highly effective schools assess their students understanding when projects and meaningful activities allow teachers and parents to teach the most important skills they will use the rest of their lives. When students are engaged in meaningful coursework assessing learning allows students to excel.

The good news is today parents have the power to demand excellent instructors and protest a school district's policy allowing time on traditional homework, pressure to perform on testing and emphasis given to test scores. More good news is parents across the nation have protested testing by opting out of tests. What the future needs is for our education system to at least begin the switch from traditional homework to meaningful projects.

2. Evidence supports long term success happens when students find a genuine interest

Each state provides "standards" with objectives for every level from kindergarten to 12th grade. The only problem with this is the objectives depend upon the committee members who chose them. The often myopic state standards limit our teaching meaningful topics and with it the ability to engage students with meaningful learning. Naturally teachers want to teach the required objectives, but standards almost always lack insightful content and skills that will really help prepare for the real world.

3. Can you imagine that watching sports increases our ability to learn and improve language?

Cognitive neuroscientist, Sian Beilock found MRIs reveal an increase in activation in the areas associated with planning and controlling action, the same as if they were actually doing the activity. In those involved in a conversation about *hockey*, subjects who had no intention of playing the game boosted understanding for the athletes and also the fans about their sport. When the subjects discussed hockey the same area of the brain responded during speaking and writing about language. Talking about the activity "tapped" into brain networks not normally associated with language. Beilock found this sort of a conversation has "enduring effects on language understanding by changing the neural network that supports comprehension to incorporate areas active in performing sport skills." Integrating personal interests is brain friendly.

- Engaging students in questioning, and discussion is significantly more engaging when students are a part of sharing and discussing relevant topics (Black et. al. 2010)

- Understanding of scientific principles increases significantly when students' interests intersected with freedom to pursue real-life questions more deeply. Motivation to learn increased significantly with authentic questions (Scogen, 2016)
- Any time students are a part of creating curriculum, engagement increases and interaction in the curriculum improves significantly (Rueckert, 2016)
- Student attendance is a key contributor to success (Blackstone and Oldmixon, 2016)
- Performance and engagement for ESL students increases significantly when creating video casts. When students generated curriculum, perceived meaning associated with rotating roles and responsibilities significantly increased motivation and achievement (Santos Green, et.al. 2013)

4. Do you actively inspire your child to read for enjoyment?

If your kid doesn't love reading, we now know why! Over the last 10 years the pressure to increase scores translated into programs that dictated which books children are "allowed" to read. Now pressed to increase scores means more class time to prepare and as a result, teachers report assigning more homework. After 2002, the same time as test pressure increased, Hofferth and Sandberg report significantly fewer children reported reading for enjoyment.

Your child's reading choices are stale, archaic and awful?!

Inspiring reading for enjoyment means exposing students to the wild and unpredictable written world...and that requires teachers and parents to think outside of the traditional assigned book list. We don't have a choice...the research tells us good readers are successful and have long-term success.

How to excite them about reading?

- Get any variety of written text: articles, diaries, books, quotes, novels, cave walls...

- Go to your public library! They allow teachers and parents to check out more than 30 books for weeks at a time.
- Thinking outside the traditional book list allows a teacher to open many important topics instead of limiting our readers to one topic for weeks because we have a class set of one title
- Choosing literature from online sources allows the sky as the limit for interests in text
- Choosing multiple genres of writing allows teachers to broaden the text choices
- Evidence based homework...excite students so they WANT to read and choose their own topic of interest (no more assigning them to read what I assign)

Donalyn Miller, author of "The Book Whisperer: Awakening the Inner Reader in Every Child" says it's time to stop choosing one selection to engage an entire classroom. It is rare to find one text to meet the needs of all learners-especially when any classroom can have 4 or more levels of readers. Choosing to read only one text at a time for all means many interests are ignored...that kills motivation to read. If reading indicates future success, and ability to learn, then we don't have the luxury of alienating students by requiring one book. Inspiring each to read for enjoyment may be the most powerful strategy for the 21st century (not surprising, strong readers do well on standardized tests).

In a time when most of our society is faced toward their cell phone, inspiring reading may seem impossible and at least inconvenient. Miller's idea to pick a theme and find many texts on that topic isn't as hard as it sounds. You won't believe how receptive your child will be if you pick a book to read together, as a family, each night. Start with a section that takes only a few minutes. Then build a few more minutes and a few more chapters each day. To inspire a love of books, spend time nightly reading aloud...(readers of all levels follow along). This allows them the fluency of the reader and improves comprehension, builds vocabulary as well relationships between reader and listener...30 minutes daily is magic for building readers, family bonds, and a love of a written story!

5. Playing an instrument

Children who take music lessons do better on tests than those who take lessons less often or not at all. In high school the results are convincing. Those who play an instrument have a higher score on the SAT and have the highest grades over those who do not. In one of the largest longitudinal studies to date, James Catterall reported out of 25,000 subjects those with music education have the highest scores overall.

Over the decades our fascination with music and its effect on learning inspired Francine Rauscher to study the effect of listening on intelligence and spatial reasoning. After only 2 years of keyboard instruction, children scored higher on standardized arithmetic tests than children in control groups. Groups receiving instruction outperformed controls

Singing increases IQ in 3 months…

Researchers in Canada showed after months of weekly training in piano or voice resulted in a 3-point increase in IQ, while their control group of peers showed none! If we hope to cultivate the future, it's time to sign up for lessons, multiple studies by E. Glenn Schellenberg and his team found for each month of music instruction students increase IQ points by 1/6 which meant after 6 years up to 7.5 points on IQ tests.

Even more encouraging is the British Medical Journal report that attending cultural events, reading and making music or singing in a choir are associated with health and longevity. The 12,675 randomly sampled people between 16 and 74 years old who reported integrating musical events and playing an instrument to have a positive impact on lifelong achievement and wellness.

6. Parental Involvement is the gold standard!

What I really want is for my daughter to do well in school and I thought enforcing homework was my duty. However, there is no consistent evidence to support traditional homework as a method to increase academics. Like me, parents *are eager* to support their children to do well in school.

Ten Things for Involvement…

- Physical activity and nutrition are more important contributing factors to academic success than social status or wealth. Tanden et al 2016

- Play *outside* for 2 hours daily (to the point of sweating, or almost sweating, is best!)

   - John Ratey, Psychiatrist and Researcher at Harvard, says 2 hours allows for the frontal cortex to build dopamine producing "circuits" that fuel all executive function (this allows us to pay attention, behave appropriately, even sit for long periods)

- Resist habits leading to obesity. Children with a BMI over 17 lose a minimum of 2 points off IQ and impairs new learning …especially in math performance and reading skills.

   - University of London in 2012 showed children with more fast food had a lower predicted IQ, while children with more "slow" cooked meals at home were higher.
   - Keita Kamijo (et.al.) found in 2012 that child obesity could cost even up to 28 points on IQ (as compared to non-obese siblings)!
   - Children who eat fast food have lower IQ on average by 2 pts Goldsmiths Univ, London 2012
   - Children who have fast food have slowed developing IQ by min. 2 pts University of Adelaide, 2012

- Walking at a relatively brisk rate for 20 minutes before school (and ideally before a high stakes test or performance)

   - Charles Hillman, researcher at University of Chicago found overweight students to be 8 to 10 points below grade level. A decade of research shows the impacts on learning and how even 20 minutes of walking can counter the cognitive deficit, the effects are immediate.

- Make sure your children eat in the morning and eat lunch. I know this sounds ridiculous but the older they get the easier it is to lose a routine and think they will handle the food (and bedtime routine) like you taught them; mine doesn't. Food increases the neurochemistry that provides energy, motivation and the ability to control bad behavior (especially underachieving or rambunctious, sometimes "naughty" children.)

  - Almost immediately, eating changes chemistry and boosts cognition, improving behavior and moods. The combination of protein, carbohydrates, and fat are perhaps what research tells us to be the most beneficial. The best diet for health, learning, and behavior is one heavy on real, unprocessed food. Loren Cordain, author of the Paleo Diet, found lean protein, vegetables, fruits, seeds and nuts have a profound impact on health, wellness, and cognition.

- Set aside every Monday to begin all goals for the week (a regular reset): eat natural, sleep regularly, exercise daily.

  - Jennifer Miller and J. Jaks conducted an experiment to measure the effect of one day a week instruction on personal choices. Teachers agreed to announce on Mondays the goal to stop drinking soda pop. By the end of the school year, students reported consuming 64% less pop! They really do what is set as a goal...whether they know it or not.

- Every child has a bedtime routine and gets 10-12 hours a night... regardless of age!

  - Over the last 10 years the research has exploded and consistently shows well-rested children have higher academic scores, lower behavioral problems and improved health. Even teenagers (who can't fall asleep until midnight) need a bedtime routine to train their brain that sleep is coming. Sleep increases their human growth factor (implicated in maintaining a healthy body weight, managing belly fat and healthy physical and neural growth).

- The nightly ritual is a place that guarantees the connection that can get lost over the years and busy schedules. A back rub, reading a chapter or section of a book, sharing something about the day, telling a favorite family story, sharing long or short-term goals, a list of what you are thankful for, or playing calming music.

• BAN all electronics 2 hours before bedtime.

- Bright light lowers melatonin levels needed to fall asleep and stay asleep. In addition, neurologists found reading on a phone or electric device increases our norepinephrine, the neurotransmitter that increases energy and attention. Even if your child falls asleep at night, the increase in norepinephrine prevents them from getting into the deepest stages of sleep where memory and learning is solidified.

• Call the teacher…just because! Communication between parent and teacher increase achievement

- When teachers have a good relationship with a parent, student's connection with the teacher improves. Don't expect the teacher to come to you! After elementary school, teachers can have 150 or more students and sometimes a child goes "unnoticed". Help your child's teacher connect to your student by calling attention! Many researchers report positive effects when a parent connects to teachers … academics, behavior and performance at school all improve. Nzinga-Johnson & Baker (2009), Hughes & Kwok (2007) Wyrick & Rudasill (2009) Tan & Goldberg (2009)

• Eat dinner together at least 5 nights of the week…at a dinner table.

- Studies by CASA show more dinners with family correlate with less drug and alcohol use, delinquency, and chance of smoking. In a study by Romero and Ruiz a few years ago, they found children from families with more time together decreased all risky behaviors: smoking, drinking, even hitting or yelling.

- If your family can afford it, don't allow teens to work more than 13 hours a week

  - Any more than 13 hours correlates with more self-reported stress, less hours sleeping, lower participation rates in extra-curricular activities, less time outside...and even, less materialism.

- Assist your child in finding a personal interest in school activities. Mitigate "dull" schoolwork by helping them to find an interesting topic to connect to required curriculum. One way to help find school engaging and motivate from home.

  - All teachers believe their curriculum is engaging and meaningful, I am no exception. However, often students don't let on that they are finding no connection or relevance...your child needs you to help them stay engaged. Taking the time to find out the topics in class is a daunting task if your child is like mine. However, once you do you can now look around your world, your child's interests, current events, family outings to provide a connection so they can see the relevance they may not have noticed before.

- If inspiring your child is impossible for whatever reason, motivation comes in many forms. Film critic David Gilmour, author of "The Film Club" was shocked when his son, a sophomore, came to him to announce he could find no meaning in school and planned to drop out of high school. His father agreed to allow him to drop out...on one condition. If he watched 3 movies with him each week and at the end of the semester, he could drop out. By the end of his senior year, his son still found school boring and his classes to be irrelevant but graduated from high school. Today his son, a college graduate, still laments that high school curriculum was void of relevance.

- Find an extra-curricular activity: in numerous studies it correlates with positive attitudes and improved behavior. For boys after-school activities correlates with higher grades, and for girls extracurricular *sports* correlated with lower rates of sexual activity and teen pregnancy, high self-esteem and good grades.

- Provide more playtime for the entire family…for life!

  - Play provides for crucial development like social skills, language development and spatial-reasoning. In his book, "Play", Stewart Brown, a neurologist who researches innovation cites the phenomenon at Cal Tech Jet Propulsion lab where they found current engineers and scientists to have greater creativity and fewer errors if they played more with their hands as a child! In the last few years, the research supporting the importance of play for academic and social development is staggering. Researcher Jaak Panksepp offers perhaps the most exciting role of play as a potential cure for attention deficits. The researchers at University of Illinois, the team who worked with Charles Hillman, found that 9 months into the study subjects with profound symptoms no longer displayed ADD behaviors after adding only one hour of vigorous movement daily 5 days a week. David Elkind found magic in "The Power of Play" as it enhances physical, social and emotional development (for all ages). Today neurologists are finding more play correlates with higher IQ and creativity. In our culture, playing outside has diminished from years gone by…it's time to return to the "go outside and play" routine.

- Go find your child's genius: other countries consider genius differently than the United States. In other cultures, people reference "the genius in each child." Only in our country do we consider only a handful in a school to be gifted and talented and even fewer to be a genius. Not every child may become an Einstein, but perhaps the greatest thing you can do for your child is help them to find their genius. Our education system has unintentionally required well-intentioned educators to systematically identify what your child cannot do and then compare others. As a result, teachers may miss a gift…that's where parents are priceless!

7. Never give up believing your child is capable of success! While it's easy to read the assessments and test scores and think they mean your child is going to do well or not, the scores are usually dependent upon the ability to read, comprehend and write. Our society now believes without reading and writing upon graduation, our student is doomed!

Gifted famous people… who made it without "traditional" skills.

Many people who cannot read or write or speak or calculate math at the elementary or secondary level can grow into their academic or social ability. Even though their experience in school was poor or even failing, these people may be here to make a GREAT contribution to society! Even more important, their gifts and contribution maybe because of the disability! Read the first name, and guess who it is, I filled in the name at the end of each clip.

"Bill" couldn't read or write and didn't think in words. He could see the big picture but couldn't do step by step processing and therefore, couldn't show his work. His genius didn't show up by graduation but he did go on to win a Nobel Peace Prize as a Cal Tech Biologist for his theories on antibodies. He also invented one of the first protein sequencing machines which launched the human genome revolution. He didn't move one step at a time --he estimated that he moved 16 steps at a time! …Bill Dreyer, PhD, Nobel Peace Prize

"David" couldn't read until 3rd grade and was sent regularly to the principal for reading comic books during school time. While this comic book "offense" is ironic (there is a significant amount of new vocabulary), David Boies, is today chairman of the law firm Boies, Schiller and Flexner, LLP and attended Northwestern and Yale. He successfully argued the Anti-Trust Lawsuit against Microsoft.

- Today a child who does not read until the 3rd grade would be on an Individual Education Plan and have been removed from the classroom for additional help (which often communicates others who stay don't need extra help). Once a student is placed on a plan, they seldom come off. Experts suggest that once a child learns of a cognitive deficit, they underperform in the long term because they don't believe they are capable of the work, they no longer try. Had he gotten the idea he wasn't capable of reading? It could have cost him his genius. ...David Boise, (Attorney who won against Microsoft in trust suit)

"Marilyn" had a stutter in school and felt stupid and was quiet as a result. Only after learning very "breathy" breathing exercises was she able to get through a sentence without difficulty.

...Marilynn Monroe

"Paul" failed 2nd grade and spent most of 3rd grade with the class for children with Downs Syndrome. He remembers one of his favorite things in school was to read aloud! He could follow along and learn interesting things if others read...while he listened. He never showed anyone his handwriting--a policy sure to bring failing grades by today's requirements. At some point in high school his principal suggested to his mother he leave school to pursue something like... carpet installation. His Mother believed he had his own genius and supported him in not only graduating but continuing to college. Here he said he volunteered to do the copying in group projects. His out-of-the-ordinary genius allowed him to found at one time, the largest document copying and business services.

...Paul Orfalea, Kinko's

"Richie" attended school with corporal punishment. Spanked for bad grades and for his uncontrollable behavior, his inability to sit still, and his bad attitude, he didn't do well in school. He couldn't pay attention long enough to remember what the teacher had said and could never seem to write things down. When he did accomplish his work, he said he would often lose it or forget to turn it in. Yet despite the fact he didn't believe he couldn't learn …his genius allowed Richard Branson to become the billionaire owner of Virgin Records and Jet Blue Airways. He is also credited for the use of the e-ticket; he said he had to invent it as he himself constantly lost his ticket and was thrilled to be able to get on a plane without stress.

…Richard Branson

"Charlie" failed remedial English. He said he couldn't write quickly enough to finish a thought, couldn't listen to a lecture or take notes. He couldn't memorize 4 letters in a row and never read a novel or finished a story. These are certainly red flags for educators; today a student without these skills would be on a special program or discouraged from going to higher education. Thankfully, Charlie's genius is the financial institution known as Charles Schwab. He founded the first discount brokerage business and is today a multi-millionaire. Not too many years ago he publicly announced his learning disability in a special forum with hundreds of people. One child in the audience stood to ask a question but stuttered when speaking into a microphone; he came to her side and said "I've found that sometimes you just need to go more slowly." The world found out on that day he had a learning disability.

…Charles Schwab

"George" wasn't very engaged in classes, not surprisingly he would daydream and write his own stories. He liked to work with his hands fixing and racing cars! Not the sort of interests that align with State Standards and traditional curriculum. "I thought of being a car mechanic. I learned the history of automobiles and economics of the industry. I was passionate about this stuff, but in school I was busy memorizing isolated names and facts." His genius was the ability to daydream his ideas and put them into movie theaters, he is now is a multi-millionaire and founder of Lucas Films.

...George Lucas

"Cher" dropped out of high school after years of struggling to keep up in school; reading and writing took so long and were almost impossible. Her dyslexia meant everything reading, writing and school related were exhausting and frustrating. As a result, she learned by listening. Only years later did she realize she had a disability. Perhaps that is why she developed her talents of singing and acting and success in her life.

...Cher

"Temple" threw tantrums when something went wrong or there was a loud noise and would hit someone in reach. She once hit a child in school for kicking dirt on her shoe and was expelled. Peers made fun of her odd behavior, speech and dress, and she had a hard time with all relationships. School was a real challenge as her thinking was concrete, literal and visual, not linguistic or social. "Written words are too abstract for me to remember." But her Mother and Aunt sent her to a ranch while attending high school where she discovered her genius, visually representing in a way to allow her to "think like the animals". Temple Grandin, designer of more than 1/3 of all cattle shuts and is credited for the humane treatment of cattle. She has written many books on animal science as well as her own life detailing what is a true success story for anyone living with autism. She is a professor at Colorado State University, a popular speaker (on the topic of cattle and overcoming limitations) and a millionaire. She uses her genius to speak to audiences and inspire hope for the future geniuses.

...Temple Grandin,
CSU Professor and Author and Public Speaker

"Tom" frustrated his teacher with his constant movement and questioning and scored poor marks in school. His teacher said he had a large forehead and a "scrambled-brain". His Mother took him out of school and reassured him he was perfectly normal. She home-schooled him and allowed his atypical interests to guide their curriculum.

...Thomas Edison

"Jay" had a hard time reading in school because the words jumped around on him. His dyslexia meant he had to focus longer, work harder, and spend more time doing homework than anyone else. His Mother told him constantly that he was capable of what every other kid was capable; he just had to take more time. His life changed when a teacher noticed in the hall how he made others laugh and told him to "write down the things he said" he could use them one day.

...Jay Leno

"Tom" worked hard in school to focus his attention when he was learning. He finished reading a page and had little memory of anything he read. He said had it not been for his Mother's belief in him and insistence that he never give up, he may never have succeeded.

...Tom Cruise

"Keira's" parents refused to allow her to be a part of plays or acting if her grades and schoolwork ever slipped. Words were extremely challenging for her as she was dyslexic and school required more work than her other classmates. She says because of her love of acting she credits her parent's insistence that she work harder at her studies so she would persist in learning, and specifically memorizing.

...Keira Knightly

"Orlando" found school to be difficult as he couldn't read and understand what other kids could. Like all kids he wanted to be like everyone else, his dyslexia meant he was forced to work harder and longer than everyone else. He had many ideas but couldn't get them out and onto paper before they became jumbled up. No question, he said he knew somehow he was smart but felt so stupid every day at school. His Mother tried everything, unsuccessfully, to get him to read a book. One time she agreed buy him a motorcycle for reading 50 books! He never got the motorcycle but got the message that reading and learning were valuable and not negotiable. "Somehow, I mastered reading out loud," and memorizing lines at night and in the morning allowed him to perform on a stage.

...Orlando Bloom

"Agatha" had a terrible time in school. Writing down words and writing down arithmetic were virtually impossible. She taught herself to read at 5 years old. As she grew up and learned more her ability to share her ideas and problem-solve resulted in her being the best-selling writer in history. You can look it up.

...Agatha Christie

"Bruce" would often take 3 minutes to finish a sentence, which of course made people laugh. So, he had to learn to make a stutter funny and build that part of his personality deliberately to save himself. But when he was acting in a play and reading from a script...the stutter stopped!

...Bruce Willis

"Dan" had physical tics and vocal grunts as he was growing up. Naturally, this made school difficult and interacting with children challenging. He was obsessed with some topics and hyper-focused as a result. However, his obsessions, though odd for a child, took him to great topics as an adult (which is when he was identified on the Autism Spectrum). His Tourette's syndrome was diagnosed when he was young, but it was his hyper-focused interest in law enforcement and in Hans Holzer, ghost hunter, inspired him to write "Ghostbusters".

...Dan Akroyd

"Ryan" had such a hard time paying attention in school. He couldn't read well and his attention deficits set him up to be bullied. He said his Mother saved him and homeschooled him for a year. His disabilities did not stop him because of his persistence and his mother's presence. He says, "she's been fighting for me since I was born!"

...Ryan Gosling

"Michael" couldn't pay attention to one thing and often made his teachers and other students crazy. He disrupted others and hated to read and so hated school. His Mother went to every teacher to offer support and always asked what can we do to help that? All the while outside of the classroom she looked for something he could pay attention to. At only 7 years old they got him into a pool where he could be active, which channeled his energy and trained his brain to pay attention so he could learn.

...Michael Phelps

"Whoopi" was heartbroken when kids at school called her dumb. The words moved on the paper for her, so completing schoolwork was impossible. She said if it weren't for her mother who told her all the time, "You are smart, so just ignore them."

...Whoopi Goldberg

"Henry" had a hard time reading as his eyes couldn't see the words on the page. His dyslexia was undiagnosed at a time that his academic behavior came across as lazy and stupid. His parents didn't understand the disability and believed he was stupid. They escaped Nazi Germany to come to the country and make a new life; the thing they valued most, education, was unobtainable to their son. The nickname "Dumb Dog" haunted him until as an adult he realized he was dyslexic. He is a writer, director, producer, and actor but says his most important role to come from his disability is to be a great parent to his children, who have dyslexia. He mentors anyone near him to understand abilities are all around us and finding them is our goal.

...Henry Winkler

Never believe your child is anything but genius. Sometimes a great teacher is not enough to move our children to their best version of themselves. A parent is the most important ingredient for making our children the best version of themselves. A child who struggles in school is begging for their parent or guardian to support them in finding their passion, their gift and the skills to get them where they are going. Never, never, never believe your child isn't gifted. Our job is to find their special talent and show it to them. People who have no business making it in the world, have a parent who never doubts their child's ability to succeed. The key is to be creative, tenacious and consistent...so your child can find it!

"Whenever homework crowds out social experience, outdoor recreation, and creative activities, and whenever it usurps time devoted to sleep, it is not meeting the basic needs of children and adolescents."

...P R Wildeman-Education Psychologist, 1890.

REFERENCES[1]

[1] Bennett, Sara (2006). The Case Against Homework. Crown Publishers: New York.

Buell, John. (2004). Closing the Book on Homework: Freeing Family Time. Temple University Press: Philadelphia.

Galloway, et al., (2013). Nonacademic Effects of Homework in Privileged, High-Performing High Schools. Journal of Experimental Education.

Gomperts, J. (2015). Don't Call Them Dropouts: Understanding the Experiences of Young People Before they Leave School. America's Promise Alliance.

Greenfield, K. My daughter's homework is killing me. The Atlantic: October 2013.

CASA Columbia University (2013). Key Facts for States: Changing addiction changes everything. www.casacolumbia.org

Cooper, Harris. (2007) The Battle Over Homework. Corwin Press.

Elkind, David. (2007). The Power of Play. De Capo Press: Philadelphia.

Kohn, Alfie. (2006) The Homework Myth. De Capo Press: Philadelphia.

Krallovec, Etta and Buell, John. (2001). The End of Homework: How Homework Disrupts Families, Overburdens Children, and Limits Learning. Beacon Press: Boston.

LeTendre, Gerald. (2005) National Differences, Global Similarities: World Culture and the Future of Schooling. Stanford University Press.

Marzano, Robert (2001). Classroom Instruction That Works. ASCD.

Reeves, Douglas. (2001). 101 Questions and Answers about Standards, Assessment, and Accountability. Advance Learning Press.

Reilley, K. (2016). Is homework good for kids: here's what the research says. Time Magazine: August, 2016.

Weir, K. (2016). Is homework a necessary evil? American Psychology Association.

CHAPTER 10

IN THE ZONE AND EQUITY: NEVER FAIL TO PERFORM AT SPORTS OR TESTS AGAIN

By now you have discovered that some things come easy, most take effort, and sometimes being the best does not guarantee a win. The best of the best spends years training, practicing precise and technical execution, working constantly, and anticipating the performance or the game to do it right at showtime. But the truth is, the medal does not go to the best prepared person; on gameday, the win goes to the one with the best mental game. I learned this in a dark moment, with my teammates in the audience. My tennis partner and I were in a tiebreaker against the champion team, both arrogant and pompous, and when I had the easy put-away at game-point, I hit out by two feet. I fell to my knees and vowed never again.

Success or failure is not the outcome of a lucky gamble. The thrill of victory or agony of defeat is far from luck. Winners are not gambling... their performance comes from the winner's neural pathways not doing tailspins in the clutch. It is this pathway that gets tested by NFL coaches hoping the opponent's kicker has a quirky mental game that will interfere at the time of a game-winning field goal. Even great athletes can trip up under pressure, but neuroscientific evidence reveals what triggers this and, thankfully, how to protect ourselves against it. You will not believe what conquering "choke" offers in the non-sport world. You see, preparation for the mind game galvanizes neural pathways and establishes the neural functions underlying intelligence, innovation, and thought (which we use to solve problems we desperately need fixed). For an athlete, training the inner game is training to be a champion, but that peak neural ability also seems to offer the holy grail to becoming the perfect version of yourself.

347

Few of us have the high-stakes performance of a professional kicker, goalie, or golfer, and lifelong training rarely comes down to one single shot, but everyone has a moment when they have to say or do things right. The reason about two minutes of time-out tests a kicker's ability is that all that time to think can allow words of personal concern into the brain, and then a play the athlete could make blindfolded becomes a 50/50 gamble. Thinking reroutes neural communication from an automatic space into our conscious processing, and when that happens, getting it through the uprights is no longer guaranteed. Just the thought "What if I fail?" can tank your performance. Thinking "If I miss, my teammates will lose" or "The fans will hate me" can result in choking. If a personal concern sneaks in, the amygdala responds and interrupts attention to the task. If your attention has ever wandered off your task to thinking of a personal concern…you have only a 50% chance of success. Since no one can avoid a high-stakes moment at some point in life, you must train your mental game.

> "If people perform at their best, doors open. If they perform badly, well, there may not be a second chance!"
> —Sian Beilock, *Choke*

It does not matter that you are not an NFL kicker or a soccer superstar. The ability to perform and concentrate is crucial when life brings the moment. You will need to stay cool as a cucumber so you don't blow an interview, sound like a fool to your boss, or bomb a presentation at work, or test. Training for mental toughness allows you to get it right. An untrained inner-mind game, a "head of glass," will leave you vulnerable, but training to do even a couple things can protect your success. If you are not naturally good under pressure, it might have cost you in ways you didn't notice. But it is not too late to realize your dreams. And one side effect of this training is enhanced cognition and more fluid intelligence: if you can be "iced," you are holding out on your intelligence and innovation and can even sap your courage.

It seems harmless, but the thought "What if I fail?" interrupts your working memory and significantly increases your chances of failure under pressure.[1]

Working memory supports inner speech and thinking during complex cognitive tasks. Any interruption of attention here prevents high-level cognitive processing as effectively as a brick wall. Interrupting attention to a task compromises your intelligence, your memory, and even your ability to drive your car. Research on underperformance in some groups in society offers explanations of the maddening "choke" phenomenon. Stereotype bias exposes the way our own thought processes (worrying about others' beliefs) interfere with our realization of our potential, so that in many cases high performers do the worst. People of groups who are stereotyped (by race, sex, or physical attributes) do not perform at their best when they are prompted to consider those stereotypes. As a result, we have conclusive and detailed evidence of why highly capable individuals fail cognitive tests, behave in out-of-character ways, and inadvertently reinforce societies' beliefs. But we also have the antidote: one extremely effective practice is to think of something you are the best at. The science behind neural connectivity explains the mystery of the "choke" and, mercifully, what stops it.

That attention to the belief and the fear of reaffirming it use the same area of the prefrontal cortex needed for performance (the neurons switch to consciously processing the personal concern). For Black Americans, thoughts about stereotypes trigger underperformance on math exams and verbal reasoning tests and even caused subjects in one experiment to engage in behaviors considered "suspicious" during a legal interview.[2] For women, thoughts of sex bias cause underperformance on math exams, which influences them to avoid studying in technical fields and compromises their fluid intelligence in public settings (the thought of female stereotypes interrupts their working memory).[3] Thoughts of letting others down (the male or female sex, a social group), of not measuring up, or that the failure will reaffirm a bias are devastating. Anyone in the habit of allowing the wrong thought in during a test or performance is not only potentially compromising their own dreams but limiting society's potential for innovation, problem solving, and equity. Underperforming when it matters may stop the best and brightest minds from getting into or keeping powerful positions, costing society brilliant cognitive abilities.[4]

Training against a neural "downshift" can even protect against deliberate attempts to dominate. Take the legal system, for example. While researchers work hard to design experiments to study behaviors and beliefs, a U.S. courtroom is already a petri dish. Female lawyers navigate the beliefs of judges, juries, opposing counsels, and clients. Law professor Lara Bazelon wrote a chilling story in *The Atlantic* of antics meant to remind the judge that women are emotional. More than twenty opposing male attorneys admitted to filing a "no-cry motion" before a trial began to increase their opponents' chances of "choking".[5] This motion brings a contested issue to the judge for a decision, presumably to gain an edge before the trial.

Changes to society's beliefs may take decades but training ahead can counter tactics that may interrupt a person's working memory. The stakes are high in the courtroom because rulings shape democracy (law by precedent changes our society), and a lawyer's ability to access complex information and think quickly may mean life or death for her client.

Thinking instead of a personal trait that you value resets your working memory immediately!

"The imperative to excel under stressful courtroom conditions without abandoning the traits that judges and juries positively associate with being female." Deborah Rhode, Stanford professor, and jurist.

It is improbable you will work to protect your working memory if you do not know an interruption interferes with intelligence, memory, mental rotation, physical ability, and even driving. Decades of compelling evidence shows how beliefs trigger underperformance and how to protect against it. The interruption, or "break" in thoughts, affects everyone! Not only people of stereotyped social groups, allowing thoughts to hijack your attention compromise anyone with a brain.

Starting now you should train yourself, your focus and attention, to use positive words in your self-talk, and to use movements, which have been shown to lower stress and improve performance. Strategic training is non-negotiable for curriculums in school, in the workplace, and at home. There is no need to think you are too overwhelmed to do something. You can only do one thing… "Download" your concerns and fears about the task by writing them down; that is a fast and easy way to prevent a thought that would interrupt you at showtime. It is the most effective way to block a worry and get into the state of effortless excellence athletes call "the zone."

When a skill is automatic, we have a better chance of getting it right when it counts; however, winning comes from a well-disciplined inner game. Training for this mindset depends upon how you answer the question, "Do you want to be lucky, or do you want to be great?" A weak mindset may allow a thought of failure, which will tank your performance, so much so that it surprises researchers. People with the tendency to "consider" problems on math exams, also known as test anxiety, are less likely to go to

351

college. Subjects who are "prone to worry" are more likely to underperform in pressure and over time, and more likely to avoid math-based careers.[6]

Some of us are highly sensitive to factors that arise early, and you won't believe who causes it! Studies trace this tendency studies have traced tendencies toward math anxiety to teachers and parents who have math anxiety or test-taking fears (that means, prone to "icing") and influences the number of students with math anxiety and students with poor math performance[7]. Anxiety is contagious as parents and teachers with math-anxiety *have the most children and students* who underperform.[8] They pass on the belief that they personally cannot succeed at math to their children and their students. Scientists found that such students are less likely to pursue science, technology, math, and engineering professions, which we rely on for innovations and problem solving.[9] Training to perform under pressure is for everyone with a brain.

Worrying while using your brain forces your cognition to juggle your concerns with your task. Complex cognition depends upon working memory, so juggling another thought interferes with ability, whether it is computation, formulating a rebuttal, or kicking a field goal.

Working memory is the ability to use information and process things accordingly, and it is responsible for much of our general intelligence (read the Memory chapter). If you have said the words "I hate math" or "I was never good at math," you have accidentally influenced children to doubt their ability to learn math and increased their chances of underperforming in tests. That is why students whose teachers have math anxiety underperform relative to a mentor without[10] Protecting yourself from a worrying thought means deliberately redirecting your attention to another thought (when it is to a challenging thought, it stops the juggling). Focusing your attention on a challenging thought protects crucial task-relevant working memory and enhances performance.[11]

The second most important thing for training is deciding what challenging thoughts you will focus on during performance pressure. When my thoughts are wandering (between points in a game), I reroute them by saying "Calm yourself down" and exhaling to deliberately take my attention back so I get the next point right.

The next point is especially important for rookies. Their transparent mental toughness shows like a display case. Highly capable athletes who have natural talent and prior successes come and come well-prepared are at an even greater chance of "choking." John Elway, one of the greatest quarterbacks in history, lined up behind the player next to the center "who had the ball." Peyton Manning after many successful years in the NFL, had an excellent season that took his team to the Super Bowl, but after a hiked ball sailed over his head in the first few minutes, spent the rest of the game with a score of 36 - 0 until a last-minute touchdown. Tom Brady, similarly, heading into the end of an undefeated season, lost a game he was expected to win. Even the "greatest" are at risk and must remember their pre-game steps. Federer's play declined rapidly in a tiebreaker after champion point-for-point play in five sets against Djokovic; it was down to the most important points when Federer let up. If I hit out by two feet, it is sickening; I have to look away when it's a champion.

"In these matches and circumstances, mental strength probably plays the most important role. In winning those matches, you need to be able to find that inner strength, mental, physical, emotional, especially when you're down in the finals and when you're playing a top rival" Novak Djokovic on winning the final of the Australian Open 2015

During any high-stakes situation, the amygdala fires, increasing cortisol and norepinephrine, releasing glucose, and consuming oxygen. It responds so whether we are facing a physically threatening situation or an emotional threat! That stress reroutes the neural activity of the prefrontal cortex away from the area essential to mathematical reasoning and other high-level function. During the performance, worry makes us juggle and "shifts us out of" our automatic processing, which compromises our best.

Mitigating the amygdala's response and lowering cortisol protects "showtime" ability. A surge of cortisol creates an increased chance of interrupting our attention, which reduces working memory, especially in women.[12] However, Mother Nature is not equitable, and she bestowed a gift upon males: a surge of cortisol improves men's working memory and performance under pressure.[13] Females must train under cortisol to perform her best under the same cortisol levels. For those with math anxiety, cortisol chokes.

- The more often the amygdala fires, the more neurons it has and the larger its structure, which correlates with greater anxiety. Exhaling calms the autonomic nervous system. After eight weeks, twenty minutes of daily guided meditation also reduced the size of the amygdala and calmed reactivity.[14]
- Even eleven hours of meditation spread over six weeks calms stress, increases ability to pay attention

Vaccinate against the failure to perform; it doesn't cost you a dime.

Writing is also therapeutic. When the brain no longer has to juggle thoughts, the thought does not choke our performance. Writing about an upcoming task increased people's score significantly. For instance, math scores increased by 5%, but writing about the task ahead even protected against an expected 12% drop, for a 17% increase.[15] The control group and those who wrote about a mundane topic did not get this benefit. Putting your thoughts on paper protects your attention because the brain processed the fears immediately before the high stakes, so no unconscious or unwanted thoughts interrupt the neurons' functioning. This allows the brain peak performance, for example frees up working memory to compute math.

> "Take 2 words with you 'No Doubt'. It leads to fear!"
> –Alex Honnold

Control over mind-wandering is even easier if you deliberately choose an engaging thought: thoughts of a positive behavior, or a favorite victory or personal strength of which you are proud.[16] I don't enter a competition without memorizing the powerful plays I intend to execute; it focuses my working memory to a thought deliberately. I now choose to think of serving in a game where I was winning 40-love and then won the final point. Reset that thought to victory, and you reset your brain-generated momentum.

- Imaging qualities about yourself during play: think of a time of a success, a time you were successful or a time of victory. This controls your emotions by resetting physiology.
- Positive movements reduce cortisol: thumbs up, head nod, fist bump. Controlling emotion or physiology.[17]
- A high-five reduced cortisol in 34 college athletes.[18]
- State a positive trait to counter a negative belief. Even a false statement improved subjects math performance— "You have excellent math skills" or "You always excel in test performance."

Getting it out before the high stakes arrive means the amygdala does not need to react to a thought (it has already considered all the concerns of what could go wrong). Now during the performance, the neurochemistry does not switch neurons out of automatic processing into conscious processing. One math teacher had her students write their thoughts about a test immediately before taking it. She could not believe that she found "a minimum of an 11% average increase, in most cases even more." She said that for many of her students, the test was their best performance (though they wrote for only 3 or 4 minutes). Why? They "flushed" their anxieties about the test beforehand, so their brains could do their work automatically.

This is non-negotiable for a championship, a playoff, or must-win!

Here is your warning, never rush the download, and no multi-tasking. Respect the process of writing out (downloading) all your thoughts of concern. If you have one more thought of upset, it can interfere. Keep writing until there is not one more possible concern! Sports and public performance are as much about mental toughness as about physical or cognitive skills. Commitment and dedication to success means training, practice, and determination. To be a great musician, athlete, or performer takes years of practice, so that over time it becomes automatic.

This is the goal. After hours of work and practice building motor and cognitive skills, they become automatic, an established procedural memory. Little conscious thought needed for doing what you have been trained to do, when the performance is effortless and flawless and the performer is at the height of performance and in the zone.

Block negative thoughts and words from hijacking the attention…because that leads to a fail

Block thoughts of "I haven't been playing well" by switching to a focus to inhaling and exhaling *nothing else*. This attention to exhale lowers norepinephrine, lowers blood pressure and protects your performance. Deliberately choosing to reset after a bad shot means training to get amnesia about your last mistake, it is a way to flush it like we do a toilet. It halts thoughts of that last bad play to let you choose to think of an effective thought, like visualization of your best shot. Train yourself to stop words like "I can't believe I missed that last shot" and "What if we miss the next?" It takes discipline to engage in behaviors that improve performance, and stopping intrusive thoughts is hard. A choice to focus on the positive you intend to do will improve your performance and offer "cognitive interference." I put my attention on visualizing placing the ball at the baseline or to forcing myself to move into the net when the ball lands at their baseline.

> "To perform is to make errors!"
> —Colleen Hacker
> (Sport Psychologist, USA Women's Soccer Team)

- Chose the play or calculate the thoughts to memorize before the performance (use your working memory)
- Meditation increases attention and the matter in the insula, the area that responds when you are using self-discipline, and the area that responds during pain.[19]Meditation increases the size of the hippocampus as well, allowing new memories, spatial reasoning)
- Eight weeks of 20-minute sessions increase the functional activity in these areas. One study showed that even two weeks is enough

to enhance attention and improve working memory,[20] which increases general intelligence.

Imagining the great shot increases accuracy when the brain is guided away from unconscious thoughts of doubt, fear, and pride into consciously visualizing victory. Imagining a movement requires cognition and results in the same brain areas being activated as if the movement were actually being performed.[21] That means that imagining an excellent play or hit or performance interferes with a real-time performance deficit and activates the neural pathways as if it were really happening. Mental imagery of the ball sailing through the uprights or to visualize hitting the ball to the back baseline, or playing effortlessly, is increasing chances of returning to an excellent performance.

One of the first fMRIs taken of musicians thinking about playing piano concertos showed brain activation almost identical to that of musicians who were playing.[22] Visual imagery guides us toward a goal, which interferes with words and reinforces neural connections.[23] Sports training has made improvements of up to 45%. Sports psychologists train players to visualize improving their skills and to engage in rhythmic breathing to control their stress responses. After two weeks of mindfulness training for only 10 minutes a day, the brain shows significant improvement in reducing the sympathetic response (cortisol, heart rate, respiration). Do not use more time practicing, but deliberate training in a mind game, to control the pressure.

> "The nomads just don't make mistakes"
> –Alex Honnold, Free Solo

The ability to perform under extreme circumstances makes you a member of an elite group of people we call champions. Developing discipline allows us control for peak performance. When Novak Djokovic tore his shirt then shattered his racket on the court, when he hit a ball unintentionally at a line judge, he did not just lose public opinion, he decreased his likelihood of his best play. Except for John McInroe, very few athletes have ever played at peak performance following outbursts. All athletes should take note and learn how a lack of emotional discipline counters our best performance. That outburst didn't just disqualify him, it provided a public moment to remind everyone that the high road leads to championships. The role of positive gestures and words cannot be overstated, they correlate with increases in win records. It raises the level of grace for all people involved in the game when coaches and players maintain emotional composure. Researchers found the more positive behaviors an athlete displayed the more emotionally stable behaviors correlated with the highest win ratio.[24] These behaviors are at the fingertips of everyone with a brain. Thoughts guided to actions improve performance immediately and that includes thinking under pressure in all aspects of life. As long as positive gestures, words, and movements correlated with increases in win percentage we can bring them with us anytime we need a boost. Champions expect to win, do what it takes to make it happen and the rest of us can too.

The primary driver of change is behavior.

Getting pumped up for the big game increases the testosterone and cortisol levels of athletes in a wide range of sports and improves their physical performance. A warm-up for females is especially important for increasing hormones that enhance competition accuracy. Training to associate the overall "feel" of the increase in hormones allows her to acclimate and protects her from feeling nervous to instead embracing the feeling as the state that increases her accuracy. Practicing playing under pressure improves her performance on game day. The more we win the better it is in the long term. Winning back-to-back competitions increases likelihood of another win, and athletes on a winning streak have higher levels of testosterone. However, an athlete who has lost two in a row does not have the benefits of the testosterone, the high level of cortisol blocks an increase in the accuracy enhancing hormone.[25]

- Most of the research is on men to measure the effects of threat and status-seeking on testosterone levels. Unlike males, the effects of social threat increases testosterone and cortisol in women. This is a similar physiological state during pre-warm-up in subjects who played tennis and volleyball (as it is the same increased levels of testosterone and cortisol). In the competition, female's testosterone remains high, and winners have high testosterone but low cortisol. After a win, her testosterone level is elevated for hours afterward.

- High levels of cortisol stop the behavioral effects of a testosterone increase. For men and women, increased testosterone improves gross and fine motor skills and all perceptual-motor skills, including eye-hand coordination.[26]
- Testosterone is typically associated with dominance, status-seeking, and drive but only correlates with winning for performers with low cortisol.[27]

Cortisol shifts our thinking (doubtful/concern/failure), and increases brain activity in the left hemisphere, where we create words. During a performance, if the brain activity shifts to the language centers it is shifting to an area unqualified for peak performing. The language center engages the prefrontal cortex, which is known for considering negative thoughts of freaky outcomes. Time for thinking tempts the attention, which is exacerbated by an increase in cortisol. Lower cortisol by focusing on the present and it increases chances of winning. A low level of cortisol allows the beneficial effects of testosterone during a performance. This is a sort of goal for our brain, lower our stress so we can carry out life's tasks automatically, using little cognitive effort. Or, as Ian Thorpe put it, "I just let my body do it. It's a lot easier if you let your body do what it's trained for."

Winning creates momentum and that competitive energy increases the chance of another win.

After two successful races, winning athletes were more likely to weather downturns in momentum, and their feelings of self-efficacy decreased less rapidly.[28] Teams who had multiple good matches in a row were significantly more likely to weather a loss and get back to winning; however, a team coming off two losses was more likely to lose again. The psychological state following a loss is more likely to drag play down than a positive state; performance is directly influenced by positive and negative team momentum.[29] Thinking intentionally of a winning streak protects drain to working memory we need for the current competition.

"I can't help what pops into my brain": If I never hear these words again, I'll have succeeded!

That sounds absurd—if you can't help it, then who can? But there's no master genius planting a limiting or unsettling thought for you. It is you; your brain is your remote control. Take back that power! All the preparation in the world is irrelevant if your cortisol peaks and you stammer and blank in the interview and kiss goodbye to your dream job. All the prepping for the game is useless when you make unforced errors. All the rehearsing is useless if the night you are singing or have the dance recital if a spike in cortisol makes you forget the lines you could have said in your sleep. Take back your attention like you would take a remote control and use discipline and design then use the plan for a winning focus.

Professional and an amateur walk onto the green...where they focus attention is the answer!

Years ago, as a teacher, I supervised psychology experiments, and I stumbled onto an article about an experiment by Sian Beilock (at the time she was a graduate student) who set up a situation for putting to figure out why some golfers choke. A former soccer goalie, Beilock says she switched her life path the day game scouts showed up to watch her superstar skills; at half time there were more goals against her than there had been all season. Today, she is a superstar neuroscientist with a vast body of research into peak performance and the factors that make for greatness. The answer is professionals only notice the objective. Both professional and amateur golfers were instructed to putt in high-pressure circumstances, but those who said they were thinking of dropping the ball into the cup had peak performance.[30] Being in front of the cameras and spectators is a setting that can spike our cortisol, amateurs focus interfered with performance in the stressful setting and they recalled feeling pressure. The professionals recalled thinking about the ball dropping but did not recall cameras, spectators, or feelings of pressure.

Never forget, your brain does not focus on more than one thought.

- Attention deliberately to the objective protects you from choking and eclipses a defeating thought

- I force my attention to my objective when speaking to hundreds of people, instead of noticing the stressful setting (many neuroscientists in the audience)
- Change your focus to a great strength or a good shot, or to what you plan to do next.

What will accidentally choke people? Cheering them on. When we watch our team members and cheer for each other during a match, it triggers an untrained mind game to think a limiting thought. Instead, give your teammates a pre-game reminder of training. Never say "You can do it," or "We have to win this to go to finals" or "Go Lions!" because it increases chances of choking. Neuroscience suggests that words meant to be encouraging can cause people to choke.[31] See your favorite shot, flush if you must, see your next play, remember your training! That is the way to show your support.

Seven things to remember

1. Stereotype threats no longer stop anyone from giving a great performance.

   - Concerns about how we will be perceived lead us to doubt our ability, and thoughts about stereotypes directly affect our working memory and cognitive performance. Stereotype bias will lead a group of people to consistently underperform when the belief is held that their social group has a fixed intelligence or ability (Park et al., 2016)
   - Asian females underperformed by 40% on a math ability test when they were told that women do not perform as well as men on tests of spatial reasoning, while Asian women in the control group showed no drop in performance (Cohen, 2011)
   - Black American students and females underperformed because of a self-generated thought of confirming a stereotype of American test-takers on standardized tests impaired their ability to perform well academically[32].

- High-achieving women showed lower intelligence when men who believed females are inferior were present (Edwards et al., 2010).

2. Expectations for the home team and cheering from the sidelines.

As supportive as we are trying to be, team members who mean well and cheering fans reminds performers frontal cortex to consider what's riding on their shoulders and is more likely to prompt conscious thought featuring words during the performance. While their brain is trying to accomplish the task it was prepared for, the prefrontal cortex has been cued of the high stakes event. Males have higher testosterone at home games (females DO NOT) and lower cortisol, which may account for their having more wins at home.[33]

3. A few nights of sleeplessness.

Sleep studies of medical residents show after one month of deprivation, the prefrontal cortex no longer interacts with other areas of the brain to solve problems. That means the brain cannot communicate with itself: the frontal cortex cannot "consult" the experience areas, or the language center to articulate an idea, diagnosis, or innovative thought. Researchers at Cornell University showed that the prefrontal cortex does not work as hard or in sync with the rest of the brain under moderate amounts of fatigue. People with high working memory will downshift very quickly and underperform (due to distractibility, or inability to focus or to hold important information in the mind for processing.) The bad news is that they are at greater risk of underperforming, but the good news is that after they sleep, it vanishes.

4. Allowing the unconscious to become conscious.

Once a skill has been mastered, it is automatic, and the cerebellum is activated during performance (hitting the high note, playing the piano, hitting the strike zone, sinking the putt, solving the equation). A high-functioning working memory (one adept at focus and at processing information) allows us to do calculations in our head, reason through complex problems, process what we hear and formulate responses, but it is susceptible to hijack. Words are a wrench in the machine. Internal dialogue triggered by panic means that questions sneak in like "What if I mess up", "I'll be embarrassed if I lose?" or "Is there is a scout in the crowd?" or "I could lose my scholarship." The thought that the future is riding on the performance triggers the amygdala and causes stress. Remember, your brain pays attention to only one thing at a time; if you notice and switch to a power thought, you are back in control. Attention is instead of your best or favorite shot, visualize it, how does it feel, what's the response from the crowd, (or any situation: test-taking you see yourself answering questions effortlessly, at work presenting ideas without hesitation, at meetings, interacting with the boss, and more.)

5.   Never entertain a thought that others are depending on you.

The prefrontal cortex takes charge, produces words, and stews over who you might let down and your feelings of disappointment. Especially when money is on the line, a surge of cortisol can trigger underperformance. "It is hard to overstate the value we attach to money," according to Sian Beilock, author of *Choke*. In her lab, researchers were surprised at how many subjects underperformed as soon they were told someone was depending on their performance (that it affected a "teammate").[34] "Losing this game will cost my teammates their bonus" or "I'll cost my colleagues a raise," and "My group members will lose a grade" are toxic thoughts.

6.   An excellent working memory can betray you, by stopping peak performance.

The ability to stay focused on a task (a strong working memory) means that what is riding on the performance is never far from conscious thought. When the prefrontal cortex allows a thought like "this test could affect the rest of my life," it compromises the working memory needed for the task. On the other hand, people with a poor working memory choke less often because they forget to worry about the implications of their performance. Having an untrained mind-game allows your attention to switch to consider what a test could mean for a scholarship, college admission, or a raise.

7. A tendency to worry.

The reason worrying is the kiss of death is that the area of the brain needed for worry and self-doubt requires the working memory. Especially with math, anxiety interrupts the work being done by the hippocampus to think a thought of concern. The hippocampus is the area we use, especially males for spatial reasoning and math. Once the amygdala (fight-or-flight) is triggered, math ability is compromised in females (not in males). The stress triggers the limbic system which can compromise a female's performance but norepinephrine improves males' performance.[35] Read the Sex Differences chapter.

Have you ever said any of the following? They all compromises performance, whether in students, children, athletes, or musicians. Have you ever said to someone "Do Your Best"?

- You are capable of doing the work.
- Your future depends on it!
- Others are depending on you (the team, a teacher, the school).
- Do you root for teammates, hoping to give them a home team advantage?
- Do you know the stereotypes about testing gaps for gender or racial groups or people with physical attributes?

How to address the math or test anxiety? Training ahead of the fear seems to have the greatest benefits.[36] The chance to process their thoughts before performing neutralized people's choke factor.[37] But without mental training, self-doubt can take over. This applies to anyone who feels anxious when thinking of things like the following:

- Computing numbers in public (to buy a car or figure a discount, say, or checking a receipt).
- Speaking in public, or to a group at work.
- Thinking about an upcoming performance days or weeks before preparing.

Training strategies allow innovation and creativity by protecting us from "nerves." The future seems to bring more problems for the human intellect to solve. Gifted thinkers are all around us and training all the children and adults in society increases our chances of pursuing math. Math anxiety predicts math test performance and reduces our chances of choosing future math courses and pursuing science, technology, engineering, and math careers.[38] Two months of weekly yoga or meditation sessions significantly reduce general anxiety, depression, and anger for musicians who report high performance anxiety.[39]

- Every one-unit increase in math anxiety equals a 29-point decrease in math scores (Foley et al., 2017).
- The higher the math scores a country has, the lower the average student's math anxiety. The math performance level in Switzerland is 0.34 above the mean, and 0.34 below the mean in levels of anxiety; in Thailand, math performance is −0.81 and anxiety is 0.55 above the mean (OECD, 2013b).
- One unit of difference results in a 73-point score gap in math assessment (Foley et al., 2017).
- In a survey of college students on their reported subjects of greatest weakness, those who were studying to be elementary teachers answered math most frequently and scored the highest in measures of anxiety about learning math (Ashcroft, 2007).
- The NEA surveyed teachers on whether they put moderate or extreme pressure on students to improve their test scores. 72% answered yes. Almost half of teachers have considered changing professions because of the role of standardized testing (Walker, 2017).
- Parents with high math anxiety predicted whether their children would have less math learning and lower achievement. They controlled for economic levels to find that it is not genetics but the way students receive help at home. There was no correlation with language achievement. (Maloney et al., 2015).
- Emotional intelligence and the ability to control and manage emotions result in mental toughness (Nicholls et al., 2015).

- Anticipating math computation causes people with math anxiety to have greater activity in areas of visceral threat detection and the area active during painful experience when compared to subjects who do not have math anxiety (Lyons & Beilock 2012)
- The right amygdala, an area associated with processing negative emotions, is active during high math anxiety in 7- to 9-year-olds doing basic arithmetic (Young et al., 2012).
- First- and second-grade students with high anxiety learn less math over the school year than their peers with high working memory and low math anxiety (Ramirez et al., 2013).

Trigger	How to protect!	Notes
A delay in performance	Allow time for thinking and activating the prefrontal cortex...setting up for underperforming	If you are underperforming, interrupt your poor play with some time for a performance reset
...choose your next play	(kicker waiting to kick a field goal "icing", tennis player waiting to hit a second serve, soccer goalie waiting for the penalty kick, basketball player waiting for a free throw)	• Change your momentum on the sidelines by chewing gum • Drink "an identified performance-enhancing beverage" • Switch out your headband, switch glasses, switch a hat.
Waiting for an upcoming point	Say to yourself "CTSD," "Calm the Self Down." In sports, reflexes allow for a winning shot while a spastic reaction costs the shot, calm counters spastic.	Consciously breathing out lowers stress and focusing on breathing improves performance.[40]
Thinking about the outcome	Focus on breathing in and out for a count of 21.	Mindful training improves high-stakes performance.[41][79]
Getting mad about a bad play or mistake	Say "Flush it" out loud. Imagine and visualize the next shot you plan strategically.	Remind yourself, "CTSD," and exhale for the count of 1-2-3-4.

Before the warm-up and game or performance	10 minutes of meditation or attention to breathing A "high 5" lowers cortisol…that traditional gesture we do to say "well done[42] lowers cortisol [43]	Colzado, L., Kibele, A., 2017
Being upset about missing a play or making an error	Imagine making the perfect play or shot or giving the perfect answer to the next question.	"Flush" the last shot down the toilet.
Having self-doubting thoughts	Stand or sit up straight with your chest puffed out in a "winners' stance." This increases testosterone Improves personal feelings of power and working memory.	Brinol et al., 2009.
Thinking you could lose	Give yourself positive talk and focus on your strengths (i.e., the thing that is my best quality).	Galinsky, Huang, et al., 2011; DenHartigh, 2014.
Pounding heart, shaking hands	Exhale for the count of 10. This lowers norepinephrine and slows breathing and heart rate Use self-talk for a reminder that testosterone increases hormones for motor and eye-hand performance.	Attach your feeling to the feeling of a win (hearts pound and hands shake the same way means more testosterone and increased performance).
Noticing an implied doubt that mimics a stereotype threat A teammate suggests that you are not a great at… Or colleague doubts your talent or ability	Write down what you value most about yourself in a brief paragraph, then seal it in an envelope and give to a teacher, coach, or parent Think of a trait you value most of yourself, or great things people have told you. List two or three or more as you need.	This results in a 40% reduction in racial achievement gaps (Steele, 2011).

Fearing a math test	Write down every fear you have of the upcoming test for ten minutes (it may take less time).	High-anxiety test-takers improved by an average of 15% more than those who did not write. (Ramirez & Beilock, 2008)

Additional Strategies

1. Write down something you value about yourself.

When subjects did this, sealed it in an envelope, and returned it to the proctor, they countered stereotype threats. Geoffrey Cohen, a social psychologist, instructed half of a group of seventh- and eighth-grade students (half Black American and half Caucasian) to write about a trait they valued in themselves. Not only did the minority group's academic performance improve by 40%, the effect lasted for two years.[44] When subjects disclosed their fears of letting down their social group, the act of writing neutralized the stereotype gap. The hippocampus could function and interact with the prefrontal cortex to perform without the amygdala triggering a thought of letting anyone down.

2. Butterflies, or crippling fear is a state that increases chance of success.

The nervous feeling that accompanies a performance is awful. But the same chemicals that give us that awful feeling also give us that great rush when we ride a roller coaster. What if we trained our children and students to redefine that awful feeling into a good rush, so that performers would be excited for upcoming performances.

Our relationship with that feeling dictates our response to it. The suspension bridge experiment, a classic study of the fear response and attraction to the opposite sex showed the powerful effects of fear on other emotions. College males were asked to cross an unstable bridge high above the ground. The bridge caused an adrenaline rush, and researchers looked for the effects of that emotion on the men's level of interest in a female (confederate) on the bridge following the fearful experience. As each subject crossed the bridge, an average-looking female met him halfway to ask a question. Seventy percent of the men contacted the woman for a date; those on a stable bridge did NOT contact the female in follow up). A surge of emotion seems to be susceptible to other interpretations. A fearful rush of adrenaline increased men's attraction to women. The nervous adrenaline that accompanies a public performance is simply reconsidered as a chemical rush that ensures best performance. Reinterpret the jittery feelings "I love the adrenaline before the game" and "The more nervous I feel, the better I perform."

3. Performing after losses or during a slump means you *recall* the glory-days.

Relive, recount, and consciously imagine great wins and successes. Science shows us you can train yourself to see the world you want to see. Researchers instructed non-anxious subjects to find the "happy" face among fifteen ambivalent photos. The subjects reported no memory of a sad or angry face. That is, when they were trained to look for happy faces, they find them; and, more importantly, they did not recall sad or angry ones.

People, especially teenagers, often feel bad, that no one likes them or that everything is going wrong. Training yourself to find the positive is a powerful tool for guiding your performance and the quality of your daily life and moods. In the experiment, the subjects presented with numerous "hapless" photos of faces continued to find happy faces even when the faces were not clearly happy. The before and after surveys showed that the subjects also reported lower stress (saliva tests confirmed less cortisol in their blood stream), which is promising for improving all kinds of performance. If every public performer or athlete trained to find the positive (the excellent performance, the positive feedback, the valuable attributes) and not to perceive the negative or ever allow a performance-compromising thought, it could be the end of the slump. Train your attention to success and limit the negative which prevents choking.

4. Keep a list of excellent performances

    •   Performers journal about successful performances and keep records: "adoring audience," "great reviews," and so forth.

- Athletes track their success statistics.
- Employees record positive feedback from clients and colleagues.
- Teachers keep records of students' positive behaviors.
- Students record all their successes in academics and social interactions for the year.
- Parents keep records of the positive behaviors of their children.
- Children keep records of completing valuable tasks and interacting well with family members.

Records of excellence can include photographs of a win, a promotion, or an excellent grade. Record keeping loads the working memory with successes, fuels positivity, and increases chances of success. It distracts the working memory from worry or fear of failure so that the brain can give its best performance automatically. Focus on your breathing in an unfortunate situation (giving an interview, answering to a boss, interacting with a police officer or a parent, dealing with a teacher, a principal, or a bully); it will serve you well.

5. "Simulate" to training for performing under pressure.

Practice under pressure improves the brain's ability to perform with high amounts of norepinephrine. In one study, researchers found that even practicing under mild stress improved performance.[45] To prepare my IB students for a high-stakes test, I conducted reviews in the testing location for a week before the exam to desensitize them, so they wouldn't be as nervous on test day. Simulation gives you practice ignoring a distraction and hurrying to add as much pressure as possible while performing cognitive or physical tasks. "Pre-game" practice prepares our neurons for game day, just like the way we train muscles. Here are some ideas to think about for spiking "nerves" to simulate game day...

- Everyone is depending on you, and everyone else has done this successfully.
- Everyone else will get a reward if *you* perform well.
- Set up a camera and stream it live for evaluation by a panel.

- Practice under timed conditions, or set up a competition (points, awards).
- Arrange for an audience, or have peers critique a practice performance.
- Deliberately distract performers so that they must ignore you to think of their objective, or the next move.
- Give a monetary incentive—even just play money, or a voucher for services or a special privilege: "If you do well, you get $100, but if you do poorly, you will be charged."

This is a type of exposure-training, a simulator, for peak performance under a bit more stress. It allows practice, which allows the neurons to practice during cortisol more efficiently. We grow more receptors to return to homeostasis faster. The military, NASA, aviation, civil servants, and sports teams have been training this way for decades.

6. Create a performance contract.

A contract allows a performer to systematically develop skills for the purpose of training the head-game. It allows coach and player, manager and employee, teacher and student, or parent and child to commit to practice. The contract is a promise to be aware of mental training, to participate in training, and to measure progress. The contract binds the participants to conscious training for performance under fire and helps make it automatic. We believe what we are told, we believe what we say, we believe what we think. Make sure the contract includes go-to activities (breathing, visualizing, imagining, thinking affirming thoughts), explicitly acknowledges fears related to the performance, includes strategies for calming fear, and addresses obstacles to being coached. If the contract explicitly identifies potential blocks, it allows a vaccination, like "I like to comment on every bad shot I make." The contract may include the following:

- ✓ When I make a bad shot, I will visualize my favorite.
- ✓ When I am angry because I am losing, I will stand tall and walk like I am the most powerful competitor on the field (or salesman, public speaker, test-taker, etc.). I NEVER have a fit.

- ✔ When I think of my future riding on this performance, I will deliberately focus on my breathing into the count of 1-2-3-4, and out 5-6-7-8-9-to the count of 4 to 10.
- ✔ When I hear about the performance gap for my group, I will write down what I value about myself for fifteen minutes.

Include potential complaints that have not yet been made so that the contract can account for these pitfalls. List as many arguments for mental training as possible:

"I have to comment on my mistakes, or I won't improve"
"I have to think about my game, or I won't do well"
"I don't have time for training my mental side; I'm busy practicing
"This is hard"
"This isn't fair"
"What does this have to do with my performance, I just need to do it"
"I can't, I don't have the talent"

To cheer someone on in a performance, tell them things like these:

- Remember your training.
- Focus on your breathing.
- Call your next shot, or visualize the best shot, tell the opponent your shot…you'll still win.

7. The "dominant stance" is a posture that increases testosterone.

Quite literally taking up as much space as possible is a strategy for improving performance. Assuming a dominant posture increases feelings of power and confidence and improves academic and physical performance. People told to make themselves as large as possible selected and perceived more powerful words than people told to slouch and lean into themselves as if to take up less space.[46] People taking up less space are presumed to be in a helpless position, while those who become larger have more confidence and feelings of self-worth. Studies have even been done to show standing and sitting in a dominant "power stance" increases testosterone for a boost to interviews and other performances. A simple strategy to bring to your head-game is this: Anytime you are afraid you are not playing or performing well. stand up and "get big." This is where you get your walk-on. "Peak performance is meditation in motion," as Greg Louganis said.

8. Meditation: 5, 13, or 43 minutes.

Mindful practice, new to Western cultures, is a centuries old activity that develops new neural pathways and increases gray matter in the prefrontal cortex. The training allows us to remain calm even during chaotic pressure, like in high-stakes performances. The more mindful you are of the present, the less likely your mind is to wander to thoughts of the past or the future that could compromise your performance. Training yourself for mental toughness requires this.[47] The ability to pay attention to the present moment and not think of limiting fears allows you to focus on your objective. Training the brain to focus on one idea or thought of your choice gives you the greatest protection from unwanted and limiting thoughts and primes you to do your very best.[48] Athletes who meditate for five minutes or more before a sporting event have the highest rates of success.

ENDNOTES

1   Pennington et al. (2016). Twenty years of stereotype threat research: A review of psychological mediators. *PLOS ONE*. Steele, C. & Aronson, J. (1995). Stereotype threat and the intellectual test performance by African Americans.

2   Adams-Quackenbush et al., (2019). Interview expectancies: Awareness of potential biases influences behaviour in interviewees. *Psychiatry, Psychology and Law*.

3   Schoofs et al., (2013). Working memory is differentially affected by stress in men and women. *Behavioural Brain Research*.

4   Gimmig et al. (2006). Choking under pressure and working memory capacity: When performance pressure reduces fluid intelligence. *Psychonomic Bulletin & Review*.

5   Bazelon, L. (2018, September). May it please the court. *The Atlantic*.

6   Geary et al (2019). Sex differences in mathematics anxiety and attitudes: Concurrent and longitudinal relations to mathematical competence. *Journal of Educational Psychology*.

7   Ashcroft, M. (2019). Mathematics Anxiety: What is Known, and What is Still Missing. Routledge, New York, New York.
     Ashcroft, M., Kraus, J. (2007). Working memory, math performance and math anxiety. Psychonomic Bulletin & Review.

8   Ashcroft, M. (2019). *Mathematics anxiety: What is known, and what is still missing*. New York, NY: Routledge.
     Ashcroft, M., Kraus, J. (2007). Working memory, math performance and math anxiety. *Psychonomic Bulletin & Review*.

9   Choe, K., Jenifer, J., Rozek, C. Berman, M., Beilock, S. (2019). Calculated avoidance: Math anxiety predicts math avoidance in effort-based decision-making. PsyArXiv: Center for Open Science.

10   Ashcroft, M. (2008). Mathematics anxiety and the affective drop in performance.

11   Mrazek et al. (2013). Mindfulness training improves working memory capacity and GRE performance while reducing mind wandering. *Psychological Science*.

12   Mrazek et al. (2011). Threatened to distraction: Mind-wandering as a consequence of stereotype threat. *Journal of Experimental Social Psychology*.

13   Schoofs et al. (2013). Working memory is differentially affected by stress in men and women. *Behavioural Brain Research*.

14   Hölzel et al. (2010). Stress reduction correlates with structural changes in the amygdala. *Social Cognitive and Affective Neuroscience*.

15   Ramirez & Beilock. (2011). Writing about testing worries boosts exam performance in the classroom. *Science*.

16   Pennington et al. (2016). Twenty years of stereotype threat research: A review of psychological mediators. *PLOS ONE*.

[17] Houwer, et al. (2017) Mental toughness in talented youth tennis players: a comparison between on-court observations and a self-reported measure. Journal of Human Kinetics.

[18] Lautenbach et al. (2019). Give me five? Examining the psychophysiological effects of high-5s on athletes. *Applied Psychophysiology and Biofeedback.*

[19] Tang et al. (2015). The neuroscience of mindfulness meditation. *Nature Reviews Neuroscience.*

[20] Mrazek et al. (2013). Mindfulness training improves working memory capacity and GRE performance while reducing mind wandering. *Psychological Science.*

[21] Godde, B., Voelcker-Rehage, C. (2010). More automation and less cognitive control of imagined walking movements in high-versus low-fit older adults. *Frontiers in Aging Neuroscience.*

[22] Blakeslee, S., Blakeslee, M., (2008) The Body Has A Mind of its Own. Random House: New York.

[23] Wali-Menzli et al. (2019). Role of mental representation in enhancing motor learning in gymnastic element. *Science of Gymnastics Journal.*

[24] Houwer R. et al. (2017). Mental toughness in talented youth tennis players: A comparison between on-court observations and a self-reported measure. *Journal of Human Kinetics.*

[25] Henry, A., Sattizahn, J., Norman, G., Beilock, S., Maestripieri D. (2017). Performance during competition and competition outcome in relation to testosterone and cortisol among women.

[26] Wegner et al. (2014). The effect of acute exercise and psychosocial stress on fine motor skills and testosterone concentration in the saliva of high school students. *PLOS ONE.*

[27] Casto, K., Edwards, D. (2016). Testosterone, cortisol, and human competition. *Hormones and Behavior.*

[28] Den Hartigh et al. (2016). A dynamic network model to explain the development of excellent human performance. *Journal of Sport and Exercise Psychology.*

[29] Den Hartigh et al. (2014). How psychological and behavioral team states change during positive and negative momentum. *PLOS ONE.*

[30] Beilock, S., Carr, T. (2001). On the fragility of skilled performance: what governs choking under pressure. *Journal of Experimental Psychology.*

[31] Beilock, S. (2010). *Choke.* Simon & Schuster.

[32] Pennington, et al. (2016). Twenty years of stereotype threat research: A review of psychological mediators. PLOS ONE. Steele, C. & Aronson, J. (1995) Stereotype threat and the intellectual test performance by African Americans.

[33] Casto, K., Edwards, D. (2016). Testosterone, cortisol, and human competition. *Hormones and Behavior.*

[34] Ramirez, G., Beilock, S. (2011). Writing about testing worries boosts exam performance in the classroom. *Science.*

35 Schoofs et al. (2013). Working memory is differentially affected by stress in men and women. *Behavioural Brain Research*.

36 Mahoney, A., Beilock, S. (2012). Who has it, why it develops and how to guard against it.

37 Ramirez, G., Beilock, S. (2011). Writing about testing worries boosts exam performance in the classroom.

38 Whan Choe, K., Beilock, S. et al. (2019). Calculated avoidance: Math anxiety predicts math avoidance in effort-based decision making.

39 Khalsa et al. (2009). Yoga ameliorates performance anxiety and mood disturbance in young professional musicians. *Applied Psychophysiology and Biofeedback*.

40 Turner, M., Jones, M. (2018). Arousal control in sports. *Sports Psychology*.

41 Tang et al. (2015). The neuroscience of mindfulness meditation. *Nature Reviews Neuroscience*.

42 Lautenback et al (2019). Give me five? Examining the psychophysiology of high-fives on athletes. Applied Psychophysiology and Biofeedback.

43 Lautenback et al. (2019). Give me five? Examining the psychophysiology of high-fives on athletes. *Applied Psychophysiology and Biofeedback*.

44 Cohen, G. (2011). Recursive processes in self affirmation: intervening to close the minority achievement gap.

45 Oudegans, R. (2008). Reality based practice under pressure improves handgun shooting performance of police officers.

46 Brenol, P. et al. (2009). Body posture effects on self-evaluation: A self-validation approach.

47 Haymo et al. (2018). Combined effects of breathing and meditating on mental toughness of a tennis player. *International Journal of Physiology, Nutrition and Physical Education*.

48 Colzato, L., Kibele. (2017). How different types of meditation can enhance athletic performance depending upon the specific sport skills.

ABOUT ME

It's important for you to know I am not a writer. I'm a full-time researcher of experiments about the brain and I have been doing for 20 years. I am a public speaker, lecturer and adjunct University Instructor, former high school teacher, business owner and a single-Mom. People pay me to tell them what to do, which makes me a professional "bossy pants". I have researched and designed 18 courses over the years based on what I consider to be the most pressing issues anyone with a brain needs to know. I have placed the most current research and most compelling strategies for how-to-get-to-your-best-life in one place. I don't believe most people have the time to hunt down the underpinnings of the brain and translate it into a meaningful, user-friendly format; so, I did this for you fueled by obsessive passion! I conduct professional development for the most unruly of professionals, offer certificates and professional credit, speak at conferences and have traveled as far as Australia to do it. Finally, after 10 years of my clients, friends and family begging me to just write it down so they don't have to listen to the research I consider "game-changing" here it goes. Should you make some changes and notice something fabulous, please report back to me to let me know.

Printed in the United States
by Baker & Taylor Publisher Services